THE COMPLETE ILLUSTRATED WORLD GUIDE TO
FRESHWATER FISH
& RIVER CREATURES

THE COMPLETE ILLUSTRATED WORLD GUIDE TO
FRESHWATER FISH
& RIVER CREATURES

A natural history and identification guide to the aquatic animal life of ponds, lakes and rivers, with more than 700 detailed illustrations and photographs

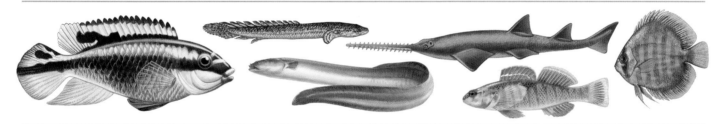

Featuring over 650 fish, reptiles and amphibians, including salmon, chubs, bass, catfish, darters, eels, cichlids, piranhas, tetras, turtles, crocodiles and many more

DANIEL GILPIN • CONSULTANT: DR JENNY SCHMID-ARAYA

HERMES
HOUSE

This edition is published by Hermes House

Hermes House is an imprint of Anness Publishing Ltd
Hermes House, 88–89 Blackfriars Road, London SE1 8HA
tel. 020 7401 2077; fax 020 7633 9499
www.hermeshouse.com; www.annesspublishing.com

If you like the images in this book and would like to investigate
using them for publishing, promotions or advertising, please visit
our website www.practicalpictures.com for more information.

© Anness Publishing Ltd 2009, 2011

ETHICAL TRADING POLICY
Because of our ongoing ecological investment programme, you,
as our customer, can have the pleasure and reassurance of
knowing that a tree is being cultivated on your behalf to
naturally replace the materials used to make the book you are
holding. For further information about this scheme, go to
www.annesspublishing.com/trees

Publisher: Joanna Lorenz
Editorial Director: Helen Sudell
Project Editors: Catherine Stuart, Melanie Hibbert
Editorial Reader: Barbara Toft
Production Controller: Claire Rae
Book and Jacket Design: Nigel Partridge
Artists: Mike Atkinson, Peter Bull, Penny Brown, Vanessa Card,
Felicity Rose Cole, Anthony Duke, Stuart Jackson Carter,
Jonathan Latimer and Denys Ovenden

PUBLISHER'S NOTE
Although the advice and information in this book are believed to
be accurate and true at the time of going to press, neither the
authors nor the publisher can accept any legal responsibility or
liability for any errors or omissions that may be made.

CONTENTS

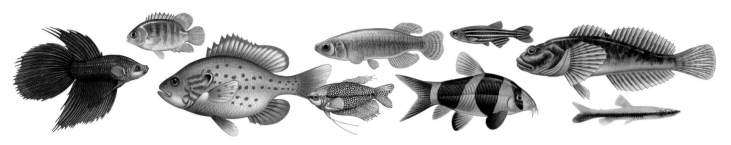

INTRODUCTION

Fish are the most widespread and numerous vertebrates on Earth. Their watery realm covers around two-thirds of our planet. The vast majority of the world's fish live in the sea, the biggest of all natural habitats, but the freshwater world is home to a rather more specialized group.

New species of fish are being discovered and described all the time, both from marine and freshwater habitats. While the majority of fish live in the oceans, there are almost as many species in fresh water. Of the 28,000 known species of fish in the world today, 11,950 are confined to fresh water. Many of these species are unique to the rivers or lakes they live in.

Each body of fresh water is effectively an island, surrounded by land and cut off from other lakes and rivers. Just like islands, many of the creatures they are home to live in that area and nowhere else.

Ocean fish, by contrast, have fewer boundaries. With an average depth of just over three kilometres (two miles), the sea is a habitat in three dimensions, and fish living in it exist throughout the water column. On top of that, every part of the ocean is linked to the rest. Unlike freshwater species, marine fish are not physically separated from one another; a species that occupies a particular niche on

*Below: The foxface catfish (*Goeldiella eques*) has long fleshy 'barbels' which it uses to navigate and help to find food.*

one side of an ocean is very likely to be found in a similar niche on the other side of the ocean.

What this means is that there are very few truly rare fish found in the oceans. Some species are billions in number and have truly vast ranges. Many freshwater fish on the other hand are vulnerable, simply because the ranges they inhabit are so comparatively small.

Variety in abundance

Although all fish have certain features in common, as a group they are incredibly varied. Freshwater fish range from tiny creatures which are barely longer than a human fingernail to giants weighing more than a quarter of a ton. This great diversity reflects their many different lifestyles. The fact that they all live in fresh water can blind us to the true variation in their lives. Some are bottom feeders, others find their food in the water column, while others hunt and forage at the surface. In freshwater habitats there is also a great amount of variation in water quality and flow. For instance, mountain streams run quickly, and are clear and full of oxygen. On the other

*Above: The wels (*Silurus glanis*) is Europe's largest freshwater fish. Like many catfish, it continues growing throughout its life.*

hand, they are often relatively sparse in terms of food. Swamps, by contrast, are full of organic matter, meaning that food is rarely hard to find. However, the water is stagnant, and dissolved oxygen levels are low.

Fish have evolved to live in all of the world's freshwater habitats, from subterranean rivers to the margins of hot springs. Where waters are dark or clouded by sediment many find their way around by touch. Some have even evolved appendages which help them to do this, such as barbels (long, fleshy filaments that look and function like a cat's whiskers). Others rely on different senses – a few have even developed the ability to navigate using electricity.

The role of appearance

As well as in size and dominant senses, freshwater fish vary immensely in colour and shape. Even within species individuals may look quite different, depending on their age and sex. Among fish where the sexes look different the males tend to be more colourful, as it is they who undertake the business of attracting a mate. Often these males develop breeding colours at certain times of the year.

*Above: Pink salmon (*Oncorhynchus gorbuscha) *provide both sport and food for humans. In Japan their flesh is eaten raw: elsewhere it is smoked or cooked.*

Outside the breeding season, when this display is no longer needed, the colours fade so that the males are less obvious to predators.

Colour may be used to attract a mate but it can also help fish to hide. Many species are camouflaged to blend in with their surroundings. Bottom feeders often perfectly match the substrates (or bottom level) where they feed – for example, those living in rocky streams tend to be cryptically patterned in various shades of brown, making them very hard to spot when they are not moving. Fish that feed in clear, open water, such as those found in lakes, are more often silvery to reflect any light that falls on them. This has the effect of helping them to disappear in the blue.

Shape, as well as colour, may be used to help camouflage fish. A few species mimic objects found in their environment, such as fallen leaves. However, shape is more often a reflection of the type of life a fish leads: for example, how it is equipped to feed. Bottom feeders tend to have rather flat, wide bodies, with mouths which are positioned quite low down on the head. Open water feeders, on the other hand, are more streamlined and have their mouths positioned at the front of the head.

Of course, the freshwater world is not inhabited by fish alone. Fish share their environment with amphibians such as toads and frogs, reptiles such as newts, turtles, snakes and crocodilians, and mammals such as manatees and dolphins – not to mention insects, crustaceans and birds. Fish may provide food for these creatures; they may in turn be prey for sharks and lungfish. The co-existence of these different types of creatures has, naturally, influenced the evolutionary process: many creatures have developed specific habits and physical characteristics that reflect their place in the food chain.

Freshwater creatures and us
Our interest in freshwater fish has, historically, been driven by dietary need. Fish are an important source of protein, and some species are farmed intensively throughout the world to meet a consistent demand for food. Freshwater fish are bred for other reasons, too: many people like to keep them as pets. Some people house their fish in garden ponds; others keep them in aquaria, where colourful or predatory species such as cichlids or piranhas – and in some cases reptiles – are often favoured. The aquarium trade is thriving, and it is not difficult to see why: it represents a rather sanitized version of the freshwater world, free of pollutants, and it offers the enthusiast a chance to observe the behaviour of the inhabitants at first hand.

Yet this gives a limited perspective, one based on a careful selection of species. To see freshwater life in all its diversity, one need not necessarily invest in freshwater diving gear. Local streams, ponds, rivers and canals are often teeming with life, and, whether your passion is for spotting fish, reptiles or aquatic birds, being surrounded by nature really brings home the forces at work in the freshwater environment. This book represents some of the world's most successful freshwater families as they appear in their true habitat. Whether your interest lies with the snaking, tropical rivers of central Africa or the Great Lakes of North America, you will see how, just below the calm, cloudy or rocky surface of the many freshwater 'islands', there exists an astonishing array of aquatic life.

*Below: Freshwater fish share their habitats with mammals, such as manatees (*Trichechus manatus latirostris) *and the occasional curious human.*

THE FRESHWATER ENVIRONMENT

The world of fish is more complex than many people imagine. Compared with birds, mammals or other creatures that we are used to seeing around us, few people are able to observe aquatic life to quite the same extent. Yet fish are as interesting and varied as any other group of animals on Earth. There is no doubt that we still have a lot to learn about their lives, but what we know already bears out that they are worthy of our attention.

Fish are the world's most numerous vertebrates, both in terms of species and living beings. To date, some 28,000 different species have been identified and named – more than all of the amphibians, reptiles, birds and mammals in the world put together. A surprisingly large proportion of this enormous group spends its life in fresh water. Being more easily accessible to us than their ocean-going relatives, freshwater fish have been more closely studied and are better understood. Even so, new species continue to be discovered every year.

Although bounded by water, fish have lives that in many ways parallel those of animals that live on land. Like all creatures, they are driven by basic instincts – the need to find food, to avoid predators and to reproduce. These requirements have driven the evolution of a range of body shapes and colours. They have also affected the ways in which senses and behaviour patterns have developed in freshwater fish.

*Above, left to right: Peacock cichlid (*Cichla ocellaris*), freshwater crocodiile (*Crocodylus johnstoni*) and spanner barb (*Barbus lateristriga*).*

*Left: Most fish are either freshwater or marine, but a few species effectively have dual lives. Salmon, such as these sockeyes (*Oncorhynchus nerka*), hatch and live in fresh water as juveniles, but then move downstream and enter the sea when they become adults. The salmon return to fresh water when the time comes to breed, migrating upstream to the exact spots in rivers where they themselves first hatched from eggs.*

WHAT IS A FISH?

This may sound like a strange question, yet many people are unsure exactly how fish are defined. Confusingly, some animals are called fish but are not fish at all – starfish and cuttlefish are just two examples – so it is useful to know what physical features set fish apart from other animals.

Fish are defined by certain physical characteristics. First and foremost, they are vertebrates – animals with backbones. Other vertebrates include mammals, reptiles, amphibians and birds. Fish differ from these animals in having fins rather than legs, and gills which they use to extract oxygen from the water. Some mammals, such as dolphins and whales, look like fish and are often confused with them. However, unlike dolphins and whales, fish can breathe underwater and are not forced to return to the surface

Below: Freshwater tilapia (Oreochromis), caught for food and packed in ice. For many people this is the only way fish are seen.

every so often to fill their lungs with air. (Some fish gulp air to supplement the oxygen obtained from the water through their gills, but none have true lungs.)

Fins and scales

One external feature all fish have in common is fins. These originally evolved for locomotion, to drive fish along and help them control their position in the water. In some species, however, they have since taken on additional roles. Some fish use the supporting spines of their fins for defence, for example. Many more use their fins much like flags for display.

Most fish have seven fins: four paired and three single fins. The paired fins are the pectoral fins, which emerge on either side of the body just behind the head, and the pelvic fins, which emerge from the underside a little farther back. Directly behind the pelvic fins is the single anal fin. Made famous by the film *Jaws*, the dorsal fin is probably the best known fin on a fish. As its name suggests, it emerges from the back. The seventh fin is the

Breathing apparatus
All fish have gills, which they use to remove oxygen from water. Gills are rather like lungs in that they have a very large surface area and many tiny capillaries for absorbing oxygen into the blood.

Below: In beluga and starred sturgeon (Huso huso and Acipenser stellatus), the gill slits, through which oxygen-rich water passes, can be clearly seen.

caudal fin, sometimes known as the tail fin. It is usually split into two lobes, although it may have a rounded or straight rear edge. Generally, fish with crescent-shaped or strongly forked caudal fins tend to be fast swimmers. Those fish with rounded or straight rear fins are slower and normally live in still or very slow-moving waters.

The body plan of bony fish
This is a generalized anatomy of a bony fish. A vast range of body shapes and fin arrangements exist.

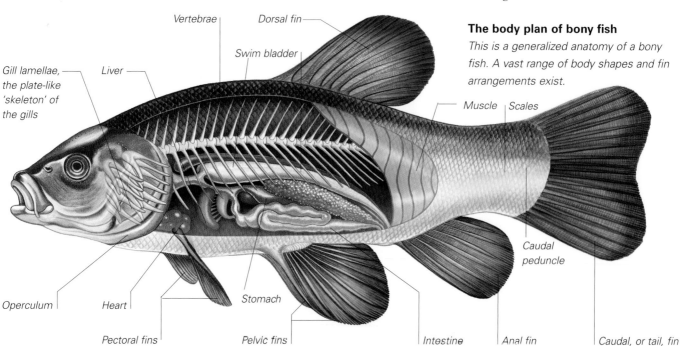

Vertebrae

Dorsal fin

Swim bladder

Gill lamellae, the plate-like 'skeleton' of the gills

Liver

Muscle | Scales

Operculum

Heart

Stomach

Pectoral fins

Pelvic fins

Intestine

Anal fin

Caudal peduncle

Caudal, or tail, fin

Freshwater fish and fin shapes

Above: Leopard sailfin pleco catfish (Glyptoperichthys gibbiceps).

Below: Red melon discus (Symphysodon aequifasciata).

Above: Siamese fighting fish (Betta splendens).

Below: Adult blackear shark catfish (Pangasius larnaudii).

Above: Common chub (Leuciscus cephalus).

Below: Electric eel (Electrophorus electricus).

While seven fins is the norm, it is far from the rule. Some fish have a small eighth fin – called the adipose – between their dorsal fin and caudal fin. Others lack some of the fins or have evolved in such a way that their fins have merged together. Eels are a good example. While they have paired pectoral fins, they lack pelvic fins, and their dorsal, anal and caudal fins have grown together into a single long strip.

The vast majority of fish swim by using their caudal fin. This is swept from side to side, unlike the tail flukes of a dolphin or whale, which move up and down. A few fish, such as rays, move by means of their pelvic fins, but in most fish these are used to help change direction or are sculled to maintain the fish's position in the water. The dorsal fin and anal fin help to keep fish stable and upright as they swim along. These are the fins most often elaborated for display.

All fish have fins and the majority have scales. The scales of sharks and rays (cartilaginous fish) are hard and tooth-like. They jut from the skin giving it a rough texture. Most bony fish have smoother scales, which grow from the outer layer of the skin. These scales have either rounded or comb-shaped rear edges and are only loosely attached. A few fish, such as the armoured catfish, have bony plates (scutes) in place of scales. These offer extra protection from predators.

Internal organs

The bulk of a fish's body is made up of muscle. These slabs of flesh are the fillets we cook and eat. Beneath the muscle the internal organs are not dissimilar from our own. The main difference is the lack of lungs and the presence of a swim bladder. This is an impermeable sac filled with gas, used by fish to control their buoyancy. The amount of gas it holds is increased or reduced, by introducing oxygen from the blood vessels surrounding it, or by absorbing oxygen back into the blood. This feature is unique to bony fish and has been lost by a few bottom-dwelling groups, such as the gobies. Sharks, rays and the jawless lampreys lack this organ completely and sink to the bottom as soon as they stop swimming.

Anatomically speaking, freshwater fish do not differ all that much from their cousins in the sea. Many families have both marine and freshwater representatives. There are even some species that travel between the sea and fresh water. However, fish that are able to do this are rare. Fish have skin which is slightly permeable and in fresh water their bodies are constantly soaking up water, due to the level of dissolved salts in their blood being higher than in their surroundings. To avoid expanding and bursting, freshwater fish have to continually excrete water through their urine and gills – up to ten times their body weight in a single day. Marine fish have the opposite problem. In the sea they lose water from their bodies through their skins to the surroundings, as dissolved salt levels here are higher than in their blood. To survive, marine fish have to continually drink and excrete excess salt.

One peculiarity to some freshwater fish is the presence of the labyrinth organ, which is absent from all marine fish. It is located near the gills and is made up of rosette-shaped plates full of blood vessels. The vessels let fish absorb oxygen from gulped air.

FISH EVOLUTION

Fish are the most ancient vertebrates on Earth, and developed far earlier than land creatures. All other vertebrates – amphibians, reptiles, birds and mammals, including our own species – can trace their ancestry back to fish.

When the first amphibians pulled themselves out of the water onto land, the world's seas and freshwater habitats were already bursting with fish. All three of the major fish groups – jawless, cartilaginous and bony fish – had evolved long before this momentous event happened.

Fish themselves had evolved from more primitive animals known as cephalochordates. These weird-looking creatures represent a link between invertebrates and vertebrates, and are given a subphylum of their own in animal classification. Before the first fish appeared, cephalochordates were the most complex creatures on the planet. They lacked the bones that would later define fish and other vertebrates, but they had many of the other characteristics that we now associate with these creatures.

Below: The fossilized remains of Pterichthyodes, *an armoured placoderm fish which swam in the planet's oceans around 370 million years ago.*

Below: Dunkleosteus *was the largest of all the placoderms – some specimens grew as long as a bus. A fearsome predator, it included other fish in its diet.*

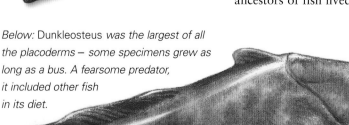

Like vertebrates, the cephalochordates had a spinal cord and V-shaped bundles of muscles along their flanks – features which had never existed in any animals before them. Cephalochordates did not need to move much to find food, but when under attack they were capable of a sudden burst of speed. They used bundled muscles to sweep their flattened tails from side to side which would drive them through the water, like fish today.

A few cephalochordates still exist today. One group, the lancelets, look very similar to the creatures that gave rise to the first ancient fish. Lancelets are filter feeders that survive by sifting plankton from the water, and it is thought that the cephalochordate ancestors of fish lived in a similar way.

*Above: The whale shark (*Rhincodon typus*) is a plankton feeder and the world's largest living fish. Like all sharks it has a skeleton of cartilage rather than bone.*

Well protected

With such a streamlined design, the next stage in fish evolution seems almost a backward step. The first true fish were covered in heavy body armour, which limited their ability to swim much at all. Rather than darting through the water, these creatures were much more plodding and deliberate in the way that they moved. Unlike most modern fish they lacked fins, but they had retained the cephalochordates' flattened, flexible tail, albeit covered with thick, protective scales. When they did lift themselves up from the bottom and swim along slowly, it was by sweeping their tails from side to side as their ancestors had done.

These early armoured fish were the first animals on Earth to have bones. While the cephalochordates had a flexible quill-like structure to protect their spinal cord, these first fish had true vertebrae. Other bony elements in their body structure included a simple skull, which surrounded the brain. To begin with, however, there were still no jaws or teeth. The earliest armoured fish, which lived in the seas around 450 million years ago, were like underwater hoovers, feeding on detritus which they sucked up from the bottom.

Perhaps surprisingly, considering their abundance today, fish were not an instant success. For the first 40 million years after they appeared they remained relatively rare, making up only a small proportion of all the creatures that lived in the world's oceans and freshwater habitats. The restricting factor was almost certainly the fact that they still lacked jaws. This limited their options when it came to feeding – the jawless fish that survive today are all either detritus feeders, scavengers or parasites on other fish.

As the eons passed, the jawless fish did diversify a little in shape but they never grew very large. Few of them reached more than 20cm/8in long. These fish must have been targets for the large invertebrate predators that existed at that time, as they all retained their body armour.

Vertebrates get bite

Around 400 million years ago a new group of fish appeared, the placoderms. Outwardly they looked very similar to the armoured fish that had gone before them but they differed in one important respect – they had jaws. The evolution of jaws gave the opportunity for these fish to expand and diversify. Now they were able to hunt. Although the placoderms only existed for around 40 million years, in that time they came to dominate all of the world's aquatic habitats. A few of them grew into absolute monsters, unlike anything that had been seen on the planet before. Among the last of the placoderms was a particularly famous giant: *Dunkleosteus* (*see opposite page*), a huge predator that grew up to 10m/33ft long. Although its jaws lacked teeth they had fearsome shearing edges, which could slice through the body of almost any prey with ease.

A tale with no end

Evolution is a process that continues today. In the future the world will see new species of fish appear and then become extinct, just as they have in the past.

Many of the fish that are living on Earth today evolved fairly recently – often in response to geographical changes. The cichlids of Africa's Rift Valley lakes, for example, sprang up in the past 12 million years, after the lakes themselves had become cut off from the sea. A few ancestral species, which made their way up the rivers that flowed from the lakes, found them largely uninhabited. These pioneering fish then quickly evolved into new species to fill the many vacant niches, resulting in the great variety of cichlids that live in the lakes today.

*Above: All of the cichlids pictured here are from Lake Tanganyika. This is a young humphead (*Cyphotilapia frontosa*).*

*Below: A male yellowtail slender cichlid (*Cyprichromis leptosoma*). The female is much less colourful.*

*Above: The pearly shelldweller (*Lamprologus meleagris*) lays its eggs in empty snail shells.*

*Below: The convict julie (*Julidochromis regani*) or sardine cichlid is a popular aquarium fish.*

Living in the waters alongside the placoderms were shoals of smaller fish from another group, known as the acanthodians. These creatures looked much more like most of the fish we know today. They had scaly, rather than armoured, bodies and they also had proper fins. These were supported by long spines and could be raised or lowered at will. More importantly, the acanthodians had teeth. Unlike the majority of fish that had gone before them, they swam in open water, rather than spending most of their lives on the bottom. They are the earliest known fish to have possessed the lateral line sensory organ which is able to detect slight disturbances in the surrounding water.

Scientists are divided over the exact position of the acanthodians in the evolutionary scheme of things. Some believe that they were the direct ancestors of the bony fish, which today make up the vast majority of fish species. Others place them in the evolutionary line leading to the cartilaginous fish, which include modern sharks and rays.

Certainly, both bony fish and cartilaginous fish appeared soon after the first acanthodians. While the acanthodians had all died out by the end of the Permian period, 245 million years ago, these other fish lived on. Bony fish were the more successful in terms of numbers, but it was the cartilaginous fish which would become the dominant predators, evolving species that would become the largest fish on Earth, no doubt a factor in their success. Today, of course, they include the sharks and rays – groups that are widespread in the oceans but less common in fresh water.

FISH SENSES

Fish, like all other creatures, rely completely on their senses to survive. Without them they would be unable to detect danger or find food. Certain senses are more important to some fish than others. It all depends on where they live, what they eat and when they are most active.

One sense that all fish possess is the sense of touch. Among freshwater fish, this sense is most developed in species that are nocturnal or live in murky water. The sense of touch is often enhanced by fleshy, whisker-like projections known as barbels. These invariably grow from the head and are usually concentrated around the mouth. Several types of fish bear barbels but they are most common and exaggerated among the catfish. Most of the members of this group are bottom feeders and many are nocturnal, so they use their barbels to locate prey. Catfish have become so successful at this mode of existence that they now dominate the murky bottoms of ponds, lakes and rivers in many parts of the world – having quickly established themselves in most of the places where they have been introduced outside their native range.

The electrical sense
Touch is the sense that we would naturally associate with navigation and locating objects in the dark. Some fish, however, have extra senses which work in tandem with touch, or even replace it. One such sense is the electrical sense found in freshwater rays and in some bony fish. This can be used to detect the muscular activity of other animals,

Below: As its name suggests, the electric eel (Electrophorus electricus) *uses electricity both to sense prey and to stun it.*

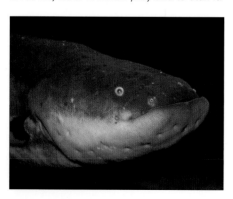

How the lateral line works
The lateral line is used to detect pressure changes in the water. Fish use it to detect the movement of others and to orientate themselves in currents.

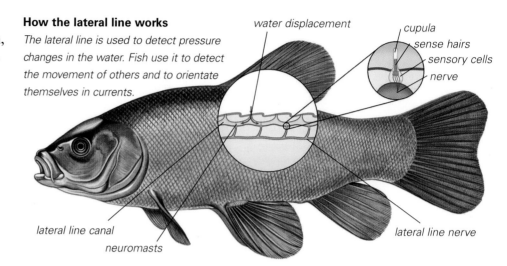

water displacement · cupula · sense hairs · sensory cells · nerve

lateral line canal
neuromasts
lateral line nerve

even when they are buried beneath mud or sand. Freshwater rays use it to find prey hidden in the sediment on the bottom. Other fish with this sense find it just as useful for detecting and avoiding predators in the darkness.

The electrical sense is unique to fish. A few species are able to use it to navigate and detect inanimate objects, as well as living ones. The African knifefish falls into this category. The electric field it emits is weak, but it is constant and surrounds its body. Any objects entering the field distort it and can be detected by the fish. The fish can effectively 'see' objects in the water around it. Its electrical sense gives it a good idea of their shape and size as well as their distance away.

Below: The nocturnal redtailed catfish (Phractocephalus hemioliopterus) *uses its chin barbels to navigate the bottom.*

The lateral line
Other fish have a more basic system for detecting things around them, based on the lateral line. This line is a series of tiny receptors, which usually run from the rear edge of the gill covers to the base of the tail. Each of these receptors contains microscopic hair-like projections, much like those in the human inner ear. These are surrounded by a jelly-like substance and are usually set at the bottom of a short canal or pit in the fish's skin. The lateral line picks up small movements in the water, so it can detect the presence of living things that might be out of view. It cannot detect inert objects, however, nor gauge the distance of moving objects from a fish.

The lateral line plays an important role in helping fish to sense the world around them. It is particularly useful for schooling fish, allowing individual fish to immediately judge and react to the movements of fish adjacent to them. This both helps avoid collisions and enables the synchronized movement displayed by fish shoals.

All fish use the lateral line to detect movements in the water around them. Freshwater fish living in streams, rivers and other areas of flowing water also use it to orientate themselves so that they normally face into the current.

This allows them to hold their position in the water and prevents them from being washed downstream.

A few species use the lateral line to detect prey. Killifish, which feed on insects and other invertebrates that fall into the water, use it to sense the ripples made by prey struggling on the surface. Blind cavefish have large concentrations of the receptors normally found in the lateral line located on their heads. These fish, living in absolute darkness, rely entirely on these mechanical receptors to detect and home in on prey.

Vision

The highly developed mechanical receptor system in blind cavefish is an evolutionary response to their inability to see. The ancestors of most cavefish had perfectly good vision and some species that have only evolved fairly recently still show the remnants of eyes. Vision is an important sense for most freshwater fish, even those that are nocturnal or live in murky waters. In subterranean caves darkness is complete but in freshwater habitats elsewhere there is always some light,

Compensating for blindness

Eyes are useless in the pitch black of caves and most cavefish have lost them completely. In their place these fish have evolved an extreme sensitivity to movements in the water. The fronts of their heads are covered with the sensors normally confined to the lateral lines of fish. Cavefish use these sensors to find prey but cannot use them to navigate. Inanimate objects in their surroundings are sensed by touch.

*Below: Like most cavefish, this species from Oman (*Garra barreimiae barreimiae*) has lost all trace of skin pigmentation.*

*Above: The eyes of most fish, like this leopard sailfin catfish (*Glyptoperichthys gibbiceps*), have circular pupils like our own. The iris is often coloured to blend in with the rest of the head.*

*Below: Striped eel catfish (*Plotosus lineatus*) have barbels but combine their sense of touch with vision to find food.*

even at night. While bottom-living fish may rely on touch or other senses to find food, vision can warn them of danger. A shadow passing overhead is enough to alert most fish.

Vision is most vital for fish that live near the surface or in shallow waters. These species tend to rely on sight more than any other sense. For active predators in particular, the ability to see is indispensable. It is hard to imagine fish such as pike living long without eyes: for these precision hunters, accurate targeting and the ability to follow the movements of prey make the difference between catching it and going hungry. Plant-eating fish also rely on vision to locate food, as do most freshwater species that feed on invertebrates.

Smell and hearing

Being land-living creatures, we tend to think of smell as a sense that only works in air. However, fish can smell just as we can – the only difference is that they smell by detecting organic matter and other particles in water.

*Above: Salmon like these chum salmon (*Oncorhynchus keta*) use their sense of smell to help them find their way back to their home rivers from the sea to build their nests and breed.*

*Below: Goldfish (*Carassius auratus*) are among the few fish known to use hearing to find food.*

Smell is a sense that has been studied relatively little in freshwater fish. However, it is known that some species use it to help them find food. Sharks are famous for their ability to detect minute quantities of blood in the water. Piranhas have a similar ability.

It is also possible that many freshwater fish use smell to help them find their way around. It is known that salmon use it to help them locate their home rivers when returning from the sea to breed. Every river has a unique signature odour which builds up as the water passes over rocks, sand or mud on the bottom. This odour is imprinted in the brains of a young salmon and, when they near the coast as an adult, they sense it and follow it to the mouth of the river in which they hatched.

The significance of hearing in fish is poorly understood, and this sense is not well developed in most fish. A few species, however, can hear quite well – for example, the goldfish, which probably uses hearing to help find food.

FISH BEHAVIOUR

Compared with some creatures, such as mammals, the behaviour of individual fish can appear quite simple. Certainly the imperatives that drive fish are few, and boil down to the need to eat, the need to avoid being eaten and the need to reproduce. Of all these, finding food is the most pressing.

How fish feed

Freshwater fish have evolved to feed on a wide range of organic matter, from detritus and plankton to other fish. Most fish spend a large part of their lives gathering food. Detritus feeders have to rummage through a lot of mud to find enough edible matter to live on. For fish that eat insect larvae and other invertebrates, the most time-consuming part of feeding is finding their small prey. Plankton feeders are surrounded by their food – the tiny animals and algae that live in the water – but gathering and filtering out enough of these to make a meal takes time. Plant-eating fish, like plankton eaters, have little trouble finding food but need to eat quite a lot of it, as plants and algae are relatively low in nutrients. The only fish that spend relatively short periods feeding or finding food are the larger predators. That said, many of these spend long periods lying in wait for prey.

Staying alive

Freshwater fish, like all animals, must eat to live. For most, however, surviving is also a constant battle to avoid becoming meals themselves. One of the most common behavioural responses to the threat of predation is shoaling. By gathering in groups, fish make it harder for predators to pick them off. The majority of shoaling fish belong to species that live in open water, a place where it is virtually impossible to hide. These fish use the bodies of others for cover. A predator following one individual will often see it disappear into the mass and become

Fish that breathe air

A few types of freshwater fish gulp air to supplement their oxygen intake. Most of these species inhabit stagnant pools, swamps or other habitats where the levels of dissolved oxygen are low. Gulping air also has another advantage – it allows some fish to cross land and find new homes. This ability is particularly useful in areas that are subject to drought, where pools often dry up or become overcrowded as they shrink under the heat of the sun.

*Below: By gulping air, the tarpon (*Megalops atlanticus) *is able to live in oxygen-poor water, such as swamps.*

*Above: In the case of guppies (*Poecilia reticulata)*, males (on the left) are smaller but more flamboyant than females.*

*Below: As its name suggests, this whiptail catfish (*Sturisoma festivum) *has long, stout spines at the front of its dorsal and pectoral fins to put off predators.*

*Above: Banded archerfish (*Toxotes jaculatrix) *can 'shoot' prey by propelling beads of water from their mouth.*

*Below: The transvestite cichlid (*Nanochromis transvestitus) *is so-called because the female is more colourful than the male – an unusual feature among fish.*

distracted by the sudden appearance of others. Additionally, many shoaling fish are coloured so that their outlines seem to merge together. This makes it much harder for predators to target individuals. The other advantage of living in shoals is that they act as early warning systems. With so many pairs of eyes gathered together, predators are much more likely to be spotted before they are close enough to attack. For fish, there really is safety in numbers.

Not all fish try to avoid being eaten by shoaling. Many bottom-living fish rely on camouflage to avoid being seen in the first place. This tactic generally works as long as the fish in question keep still. Another common way of staying out of sight is to become nocturnal. Many freshwater fish hide beneath rocks or in underwater crevices by day and only emerge at night to feed. This tactic is particularly effective as a defence against visual predators such as birds. Of course this makes these fish much harder for humans to spot too. As a result, most people are unaware of the wide variety of fish living in their local rivers and streams.

The next generation

The behaviour of fish within species is fairly uncomplicated and predictable, but across the class as a whole it is surprisingly varied. Nowhere is this more true than in the breeding behaviour of freshwater fish. The vast majority of ocean fish scatter their eggs and sperm together in open water and then leave the fertilized eggs to develop and hatch on their own. This type of breeding behaviour is also seen in some freshwater fish, particularly shoaling species that live in lakes and other large areas of open water, but many others put a great deal more effort into the process of reproduction. Many freshwater fish build nests. These vary from simple scrapes in the sand or gravel, such as the redds made by salmon and trout, to far more complex constructions. Three-spined sticklebacks, for instance (*Gasterosteus aculeatus*, p.186) form tube-shaped nests from algae. These are built by the males, which entice females in to lay. Once the eggs have been laid and fertilized, the males guard them until they hatch. They also fan the eggs while they are developing to keep them well-supplied with oxygen.

Other freshwater fish use natural crevices or gaps beneath rocks as nests in which to lay their eggs. Again, the eggs are often guarded and fanned

*Below: The common angelfish (*Pterophyllum scalare*) attaches its eggs to vegetation.*

until hatching. Guarding eggs has the obvious advantage of increasing their chances of hatching, by preventing them from being taken by predators. Nest-building fish that do not guard their eggs tend to cover them up with sediment in an effort to hide them from hungry eyes.

Perhaps the most unusual of all nests are the bubble nests built by some species of freshwater fish. These are formed from bubbles of oral mucus, which float at the surface like rafts. Females lay their eggs, which are buoyant, on the undersides of these rafts; they are then guarded by the male (or occasionally by both parents).

A few freshwater fish have dispensed with nests altogether and instead brood their eggs and their young in their mouths. This behaviour is most common among cichlids. The advantages in terms of protecting developing offspring from predators are obvious, but the disadvantage is that, while brooding, these fish are unable to eat.

Not all freshwater fish lay eggs – a few species, such as the sailfin molly (*Poecilia latipinna*, p.108) give birth to live young. Like mouth brooding, this strategy improves the chances of the young surviving to adulthood. Live young are much larger than eggs, however, so fewer can be produced in a season.

*Above: After returning from the sea, sockeye salmon (*Oncorhynchus nerka*) breed in fresh water.*

Below: A female sockeye salmon uses her fins to excavate her nest, or redd.

Many freshwater fish migrate in order to breed. This is particularly true of species that live in rivers. Breeding migrations tend to be upstream, with eggs being laid nearer the headwaters. As the eggs hatch and the young grow they gradually move down-river, until they are themselves big enough to breed. This behaviour ensures that there is little competition between the adults and younger fish for food, and also that newly spawned fish, or fry, do not end up being cannibalized by larger members of their own kind.

Some freshwater fish spend part of their lives in the sea. Salmon migrate between salt and fresh water, entering rivers and swimming upstream to lay their eggs. Eels make the opposite journey and breed in the oceans.

FRESHWATER FISH CLASSIFICATION

We tend to think of fish as a homogeneous mass, a huge group of animals that share characteristics which separate them from other vertebrates. However, when scientists look at fish, they see them in terms of four very different groups.

Fish comprise four vertebrate classes but each of the other four main vertebrate groups – amphibians, reptiles, birds and mammals – has a class of its own. In other words, scientists consider ray-finned fish and cartilaginous fish to be as different from one another as reptiles are from birds. Three of the four fish classes contain species which live in freshwater habitats. The fourth class, Pteraspidomorphi, contains the hagfish, which are entirely marine and so do not appear on the 'family tree' below.

The vast majority of freshwater fish belong to the class Actinopterygii, as,

indeed, do most marine fish species. Jawless fish species, of the class Chondrichthyes, are about as numerous in fresh water as they are in the sea. Although uncommon, they are quite widespread, occurring throughout most of the world's temperate waterways and bodies of fresh water. Sharks and rays, on the other hand, are almost exclusively marine. The few species found in fresh water tend to be found in the tropics.

Most ray-finned fish belong to the infraclass Teleostei (an infraclass is subordinate to a subclass but superior to an order or a superorder). Better known as the bony fish, this group

contains the bulk of the fish species most of us will encounter in our lives. Teleostei is split into 13 superorders, 8 of which contain freshwater species.

The largest of the superorders is Acanthopterygii, which includes all of the perchlike fish. Although many members are marine, there are also a huge number of freshwater families, including the gouramis, snakeheads, sunfish, archerfish, cichlids, climbing perches and true perches. Superorder Atherinomorpha contains fewer families and is made up mainly of small fish. Most of its members display marked sexual dimorphism, with the males often being very colourful.

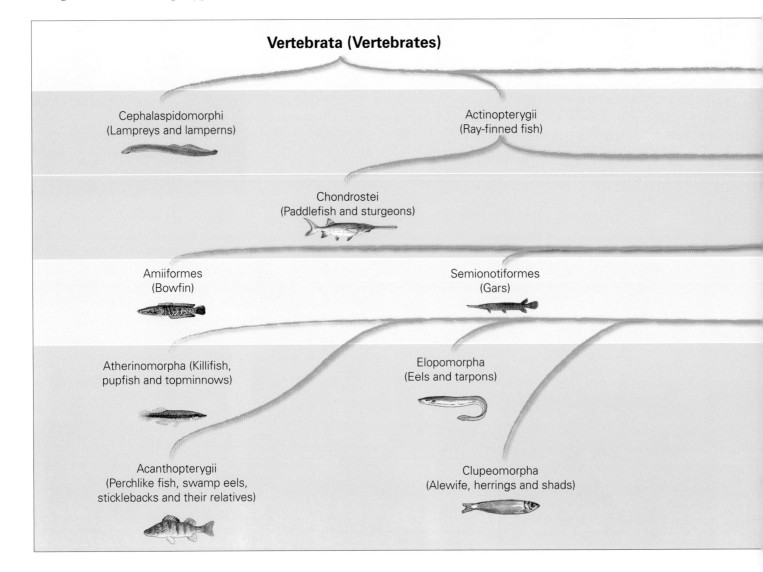

Clupeomorph fish are primarily marine but a few species are found in fresh water. Most of these, however, spend part of their lives in the sea. The same is true of most eels, from the superorder Elopomorpha. The superorder Ostariophysi is widespread, with catfish in particular being found in most of the world's freshwater habitats. The pirate perch, trout perches and cavefish, from the superorder Paracanthopterygii, are confined to North America. Other members of this group, like the anglerfish, are marine.

Bonytongues (Osteoglossomorpha) are considered to be among the more primitive teleosts. They are all found in fresh water, mostly in the tropics, and include some of the largest freshwater fish, such as South America's pirarucu.

The remaining teleost superorder with freshwater representatives, Protacanthopterygii, is the one most

*Above: Common names can be confusing. The pike topminnow (*Belonesox belizanus*) is a member of the superorder Atherinomorpha. True pike are grouped with other Protacanthopterygii.*

familiar to European anglers. This group contains all of the world's trout and salmon, and the predatory pikes.

The family tree shown below demonstrates how freshwater fish are grouped from the level of subphylum downward, with further information on what these groupings actually mean. Within each superorder, there are examples of the major fish families.

*Above: The giant snakehead (*Channa micropeltes*) is a member of the largest superorder, Acanthopterygii.*

*Above: The spotted bonytongue (*Scleropages leichardtii*) belongs to the group Osteoglossomorpha, and is among the most primitive teleosts.*

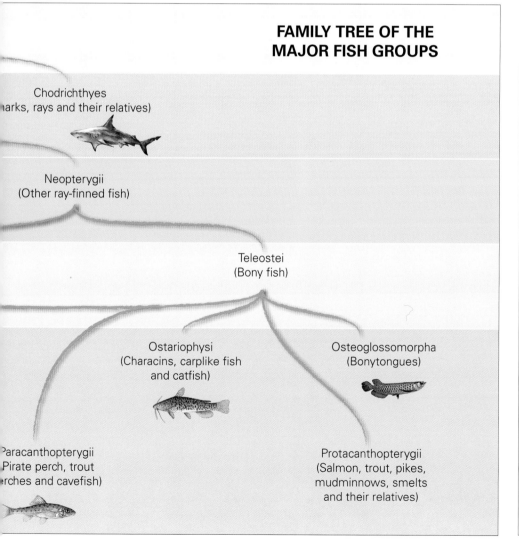

FAMILY TREE OF THE MAJOR FISH GROUPS

Chodrichthyes
(Sharks, rays and their relatives)

Neopterygii
(Other ray-finned fish)

Teleostei
(Bony fish)

Ostariophysi
(Characins, carplike fish and catfish)

Osteoglossomorpha
(Bonytongues)

Paracanthopterygii
(Pirate perch, trout perches and cavefish)

Protacanthopterygii
(Salmon, trout, pikes, mudminnows, smelts and their relatives)

Key

Subphylum The group Vertebrata is one of three subphyla in the phylum Chordata, the other two being Cephalochordata and Urochordata.

Class This is the largest subdivision in the classification of vertebrates. Classes of living vertebrates include mammals, reptiles, amphibians and birds.

Subclass Not all vertebrate classes are split into subclasses but the class Actinopterygii is split into two. Members of the subclass Chondrostei are considered the most primitive ray-finned fish, in that their body structure is closest to that of the group's ancestors.

Infraclass The infraclass Teleostei, which contains all of the world's bony fish, is by far the largest of the three infraclasses of neopterygian (literally 'new fin') fish.

Superorder Teleosts are split into eight different superorders, of which the largest is Acanthopterygii.

JAWLESS AND CARTILAGINOUS FISH

When people think of fish they usually think of teleosts – the bony fish that make up the majority of the the world's fish species. Cartilaginous fish (which include the sharks and rays) are less familiar, but still recognizable. Jawless fish, on the other hand are a mysterious group, unknown to many non-scientists.

Lampreys, lamperns and hagfish are the only jawless fish on Earth today. They are characterized by their long, sinuous bodies, which lack scales and gill covers. The only other fish they might be confused with are eels, but unlike those bony fish, they lack pectoral fins. The disk-shaped mouth is another giveaway, as are the small, circular gill openings on the side of the body just behind the head.

Above: The motoro stingray (Potamotrygon motoro) is one of the most popular freshwater aquarium species.

Above: The eyes of most freshwater rays are raised up, as with this lacticeps stingray (Potramotrygon laticeps).

Ancient lineage

Jawless fish are the most primitive fish alive today. In fact, they are the most primitive of all vertebrate animals. In the past this group contained a great variety of species, including most of the early armoured fish, but its importance waned as jawed fish appeared and began to diversify. Some jawless species, such as the hagfish, are marine, but many spend either part or all of their lives in fresh water. These freshwater jawless fish are the lampreys and lamperns.

Although lampreys and lamperns lack jaws, some species feed on other creatures. Their mouths are like suction cups, circled with numerous pointed teeth which they use to rasp away at skin and flesh. Most of these species are parasitic, and attach themselves to the sides of living fish, gnawing holes in them to drink their blood. This particularly unpleasant lifestyle, combined with their long, slimy, sinuous bodies, has won them few fans among fish enthusiasts. Their appearance alone is enough to make most people's skin crawl. That said, they are eaten in various parts of the world and are considered a delicacy by some – their flesh is said to taste more meaty than that of other fish. Lampreys are a particularly popular food in parts of south-western Europe and during the Middle Ages they were widely eaten across the continent, particularly during times of fasting, when fish was the only permitted meat for eating. King Henry I of England is said to have died in 1135 as a result of eating 'a surfeit of lampreys'.

In most of the places where lampreys are eaten their numbers have dropped significantly in the wild. In other parts of the world, however, they are often considered a pest. In recent decades the Great Lakes of North America have seen lampreys reach plague proportions. Before the last century, these fish were unknown in the Great Lakes; however, the transportation canals, which were built to link the lakes to rivers, provided a means of entry. With no natural predators in this new habitat, lampreys have multiplied unmolested. This has been to the

Using electrical sense

Rays have flattened bodies with their eyes on the top and their mouths on the underside. Since they feed on bottom-dwelling creatures they are unable to use their sight, but have instead developed acute electrical sense that enables them to pick up the slightest muscle activity of their prey – even when this is hidden in the sediment (*below*).

Freshwater rays are able to generate an electric field solely to help them find food. Their marine relatives the torpedo rays (*Torpedo californica*) go one step further. These fish are able to generate extremely powerful electric charges – so powerful that they can stun and even kill other fish in their vicinity.

detriment of the Lakes' commercial fisheries of lake trout and other species which lampreys feed on. Both the US Fish and Wildlife Service and the Canadian Department of Fisheries and Oceans are now involved in programmes to eradicate the invaders, which have met with limited success. Lampreys have not disappeared, but their numbers are at least being held in check.

Perhaps understandably, parasitic lampreys tend to get most of the limited press that is given to freshwater jawless fish. They do not, however, make up the majority of species. Most freshwater lampreys and lamperns are filter feeders which live on detritus sifted out of the mud on the bottoms of the lakes, rivers and streams where they live. Even those species that drink blood as adults tend to be filter feeders when young. A few, such as the brook lamprey, do not feed at all as adults, but survive on the reserves built up as larvae until they breed, after which they die.

*Below: Hagfish (*Eptatretus *species) are evolutionary remnants of the first fish lineages that swam in the ocean 450 million years ago. These jawless creatures lack eyes; instead they have two white patches of light-sensitive cells on their head (visible in this image). Their floppiness and white eye patches give the hagfish a distinctive 'sock-puppet' appearance.*

*Above: Young lemon sharks (*Negaprion brevirostris) *swim among mangroves. This species will sometimes enter rivers.*

Global range

Jawless fish are found only in the world's temperate regions. This is due to the fact that their larvae are intolerant of high water temperatures. Cartilaginous fish, on the other hand, have a worldwide distribution. The vast majority of species inhabit the oceans but a small number sometimes enter fresh water or even spend their lives there.

All cartilaginous fish have jaws and, as the name of their group suggests, a skeleton of cartilage rather than bone. Since jawless fish also have cartilage skeletons, many scientists refer to cartilaginous fish by the Latin name for the class, Chondrichthyes.

Chondrichthyes are split into two subclasses, Holocephali and Elasmobranchii. The subclass Holocephali is entirely marine and contains the chimaeras, sometimes known as ghost sharks, ratfish or rabbitfish, while the subclass Elasmobranchii contains the more familiar sharks and rays, as well as the guitarfish and sawfish families.

Freshwater elasmobranchs are few and are confined mainly to tropical waters. The largest group is made up of the freshwater rays. Like their marine counterparts, these fish have flattened, disc-shaped bodies and long, narrow tails. Most freshwater rays come from South America, although a few species inhabit rivers in Asia.

Freshwater rays are carnivorous and spend their lives on the bottom, feeding on invertebrates and smaller fish. Their ability to detect prey through their electrical sense has made them the dominant river-bottom fish in some parts of their range.

As well as the exclusively freshwater species there are some rays that are found living in both rivers and coastal marine habitats. This is also true of some sawfish and species of sharks. A few rare Asian sharks even spend their whole lives in fresh water.

RAY-FINNED FISH

As we have seen, the enormous class Actinopterygii, commonly known as the ray-finned fish, is split into subgroups comprising paddlefish, sturgeons, bowfin, gars and teleosts. Of these, the teleosts, or bony fish, contain by far the greatest number of species.

Ray-finned fish have colonized every aquatic habitat on the planet and they dominate the freshwater world. While jawless fish are special cases and cartilaginous fish are rare in fresh water, ray-finned fish have diversified into a huge range of forms. They have taken advantage of every available niche in the freshwater environment, from estuaries to the highest mountain streams, and from ephemeral pools to the world's largest lakes. They can even be found underground, in the dark rivers whose waters have carved out some of the deepest cave systems.

Distinguishing feature

As the name suggests, ray-finned fish are defined by the fact that their fins are supported by separate rays. In teleosts these are invariably made of bone, but in some other members of the class they may be made of

Above: South America's rummynose tetra (Hemigrammus rhodostomus) grows up to 4cm/1.6in long and is a popular aquarium fish.

Below: The gar characin (Ctenolucius hujeta) has the long, streamlined body typical of many teleosts.

cartilage. The skeletons of paddlefish, sturgeons, the bowfin and gars are all made mostly of cartilage when these fish are young, but their skeletons develop bony areas as the fish grow older. In evolutionary terms, these fish are more primitive than the teleosts.

As well as being the most numerous, the teleosts are also by far the most widespread ray-finned fish. The more primitive groups have a far more patchy distribution. Paddlefish and sturgeons share a subclass, by virtue of certain features of their skeletons, but they look quite different from one another. Paddlefish are found only in North America and China – indeed, there are only two surviving species. These large and rather bizarre looking fish are filter feeders, swimming through open water and filtering out plankton. Sturgeons, on the other hand, live on the bottom and feed on small fish and invertebrates. They are confined to the waters of North America, Europe and Asia.

The bowfin and gars share their subclass, Neopterygii, with the teleosts in fish classification, but they are significantly different from the teleosts in many respects. The bowfin, which lives in North America, is the last surviving species of a once widespread

Above: The spotted scat (Scatophagus argus), a perchlike fish, occurs in both fresh and salt water, from Kuwait to Vanuatu.

infraclass, called Amiiformes. The extinct Jurassic marine fish Leedsichthys was another member of this group. This giant filter feeder was the largest fish that ever lived, growing to an estimated 22m/72ft long and with a body shape not unlike that of a modern baleen whale. Today's bowfin, by contrast, reaches just 109cm/43in long, but it is a voracious predator, killing and eating everything from crayfish to frogs. The bowfin also hunts other fish. However, compared with the gars it is an amateur. These long-jawed predators have heads that look not unlike those of crocodiles and they hunt fish in a similar way to those reptiles, hanging in the water or moving slowly through it, then grabbing prey suddenly with a quick sideways lunge of the jaws. Gars are found mainly in slow-moving rivers and the still waters of shallow lakes and other, similarly weedy habitats. They belong to the order Semionotiformes, which contains just seven species and is confined to North America, Central America and the Caribbean.

*Below: A piraputanga (*Brycon hilarii*) swims over aquatic vegetation in Brazil. For this fish species, colour and pattern are mainly about species recognition.*

Bony fish

All of the primitive ray-finned fish are found primarily or even exclusively in freshwater habitats. Teleosts, on the other hand, have both freshwater and marine representatives in roughly equal numbers, at least in terms of species. Although they share their subclass, Neopterygii, with the bowfin and the gars, teleosts are classified into their own infraclass, Teleostei, within this subclass. Teleostei is then further subdivided into 13 superorders, 8 of which include freshwater fish.

The variety within these eight superorders is astounding. Freshwater

*Right: The Mekong giant catfish (*Pangasianodon gigas*) is one of the world's largest freshwater fish. Older individuals can weigh more than a quarter of a ton.*

teleosts range from tiddlers to titans. The smallest is the dwarf pygmy goby (*Pandaka pygmaea*), which is found in the streams and lakes of Luzon in the Philippines. It measures just 8.5mm/⅓in in length and weighs 0.005g/0.00018oz. At the other end of the scale are monsters like the Mekong giant catfish (*Pangasianodon gigas*), which can weigh as much as 250kg/550lbs.

As well as size, freshwater teleosts vary a great deal in form. Some, such as the eels, are long and sinuous, others are flattened, arrow-shaped or short and tubby. Each species is perfectly adapted for the life that it leads. While most open-water species are torpedo-shaped for streamlining, other freshwater teleosts are shaped to help with camouflage. There are even species that disguise themselves as sunken twigs or leaves.

Colour is also incredibly diverse amongst teleosts – much more so than it is in other fish. Many species show significant sexual dimorphism, with the males being much more brightly coloured than the females, particularly during the breeding season. As with most birds, when it comes to mating it is the job of the males to impress and the females to choose. Bright colours may also be used to help fish identify others of their own kind in murky or tannin-stained waters, as is the case with the neon and cardinal tetras of South America.

*Above: Most gobies, such as this toothy goby (*Pleurosicya mossambica*), are marine fish, although a few species are also found living in fresh water.*

While freshwater teleosts are incredibly varied, some groups are more common and widespread than others. The most numerous and widely distributed group of all are the perch-like fish, which ichthyologists group together in the order Perciformes. These teleosts make up around 40 per cent of all fish species and so comprise the largest vertebrate order in the animal kingdom. The majority are coastal marine fish but many spend their lives in fresh water. They are found on all of the world's continents apart from Antarctica.

Other teleost orders, however, are more localized. For example, members of the order Characiformes, such as the piranhas, pacus and pencilfish, are confined to neotropical Central and South America, and parts of Africa. But where these fish are found they are both successful and diverse.

AMPHIBIANS

Amphibians have a lot of features in common with fish, particularly as larvae. However, one major difference between the two is in the habitats in which they are found. Amphibians, common in fresh water, are the only group of vertebrates completely absent from the sea.

Amphibians have their own class in the animal kingdom. They are defined by their method of reproduction and also by their skin. To most people the word amphibian conjures up the image of a frog. Frogs are indeed amphibians but there are many other kinds too, including toads, newts and salamanders. There is even a group of legless amphibians, the caecilians, which look like earthworms and spend their lives in soil or leaf litter.

Most amphibians lay eggs that must remain damp in order to develop. The vast majority lay their eggs in water, often in jelly-like strings or clumps. The most familiar example of this to most people would be the frog spawn which appears in local ponds.

Amphibian skin is soft, thin and usually slimy. Many adult amphibians are actually able to breathe through their skin, absorbing oxygen from the water or air around them. Most adult amphibians also have lungs. The aquatic larvae, known as tadpoles, hatch out with gills but then develop lungs as they grow.

Like fish, the majority of amphibians start out life small and grow many times over before they reach adult size. In the process, most undergo a huge change in body shape and form. Frog tadpoles, for instance, grow legs and gradually lose their long, flattened tails. Watching tadpoles grow up is almost like watching evolution in action, as they change from fish-like larvae, with gills, into air-breathing, land-living adults.

Habitat

In fresh water, amphibians often live alongside fish, but they are unable to tolerate brackish or salty habitats. If exposed to salty water they quickly dehydrate, losing fluids through their skin to the water around them.

Most amphibians spend much of their adult life on land and only return to the water to breed. That said, there are exceptions to this general rule. The three largest amphibians, the Chinese giant salamander, the Japanese giant salamander and the hellbender, are completely aquatic. Although all three have legs, they use these to crawl over the bottoms of streams and rivers. Lacking gills as adults, they obtain all of the oxygen they need through their skin.

A few amphibians retain their gills into adult life. As one might expect, these creatures are also completely

Above: Sometimes referred to as 'the walking fish', the axolotl (Ambystoma mexicanum), a salamander, is one of a small number of amphibians that exhibit a state of 'neoteny', meaning that they reach sexual maturity while still in the larval amphibian state. They retain their gills – hence their likeness to fish – as aids to breathing underwater.

aquatic. The best known gilled amphibian is the axolotl – an albino variety of this species with red gills can often be found for sale in pet shops. In nature, this creature is a well camouflaged speckled brown. The axolotl is confined to Mexico but it is one of several gilled salamanders found in North America. Others include the mudpuppy and various species of siren. All of these amphibians tend to be nocturnal, emerging at dusk to search the bottom for prey. Most find the small invertebrates they eat by touch, using the sensitive tips of their toes.

The word amphibian come from the ancient Greek *amphibios*, which literally means 'living a double life'.

Amphibian development

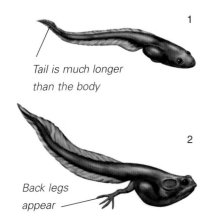

Tail is much longer than the body

1

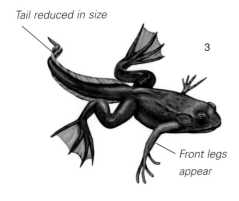

Back legs appear

2

Tail reduced in size

3

Front legs appear

Left: Frog and toad tadpoles hatch out looking almost like fish. As the weeks pass they change. First the back legs appear, then the two front legs. While this is happening the gills disappear and the lungs develop. The tail slowly shrinks also.

*Right: Most frogs, including Wallace's flying frog (*Rhacophorus nigropalmatus*) enjoy highly developed vision.*

*Far right: Toads have drier, wartier skin than frogs, as demonstrated by this south-east Asian species, the giant river toad (*Bufo juxtasper*).*

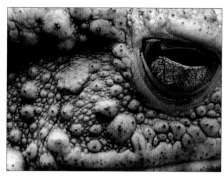

Amphibians live a double life in more ways than one. When young, frogs and toads in particular look like completely different animals from their parents. They feed in a different way too, scraping algae from the leaves and other surfaces of water plants, before moving on later to a diet of flesh. Amphibians are, in fact, unique amongst vertebrates in that all of the 4,000 or so species of their class are carnivorous in their adult form. Amphibians also live a double life in being able to exist both in water and on land. Confusingly, the word 'amphibian' is sometimes used to describe other animals that spend part of their lives in the water, such as otters. While this use is literally accurate – the word amphibian has four different meanings in English – it is unhelpful. In the case of otters, 'amphibious mammals' would be a better description.

*Below: The crocodile salamander (*Tylototriton shanjing*) spends most of its time on land, but it returns to water in order to breed.*

Breeding and development

Most amphibians return to the water to breed. Outside the tropics, this usually happens in spring. Frogs and toads often gather in huge numbers in ponds, lake shallows and other traditional breeding sites, the males croaking or singing to establish dominance and attract females towards them. Spawning occurs over a relatively short period, usually lasting less than a few weeks. Large numbers of eggs tend to be laid by each female. Left to themselves, many will not even hatch and of those that do, few will reach adulthood.

Newts and salamanders also breed in water but the males of these species tend to display to females using visual signals rather than sounds. Often the males develop frills or become more brightly coloured in the breeding season. Eggs are usually laid singly and are often hidden rather than being spawned in clumps.

The tadpoles of most amphibians live in water for several months at least. All frogs, toads, newts and salamanders hatch out with gills. Those that have lungs as adults – and the majority of species do – develop these as they grow. Legs also appear gradually. In frogs and toads the hind legs develop first and the front legs later. Once the legs are fully formed the tail then starts to disappear.

Once they have metamorphosed, most amphibians look like miniature versions of their parents. Relatively few individuals make it this far but even fewer will last the year or more it takes for them to grow old enough to breed.

A few amphibians give their tadpoles a head start, protecting them as eggs until they hatch. The male midwife toad, for example, carries his mate's eggs for weeks, wrapped around his legs. Every so often he dips them in the water to keep them moist. Other species have physical adaptations to protect their spawn. The female marsupial frog from South America, for instance, has a pouch of skin on her back especially to carry her eggs.

*Below: The tadpole (top) and adult (bottom) of the Sabah torrent frog (*Meristogenys orphnocnemis*). As its name suggests, this species lives in fast-flowing water.*

*Below: The mahogany frog (*Rana luctuosa*) lives in the rainforests of South-east Asia. Its tadpoles grow to maturity in rainwater pools.*

REPTILES

More than 300 million years ago, reptiles became the first vertebrate animals to cut their ties to water and make a complete transition to life on the land, leaving the primeval swamps and moving into drier habitats such as deserts.

Unlike slimy-skinned amphibians, which required moist habitats and needed to return to water to breed, reptiles laid their eggs on land and had bodies tough enough to survive even the driest conditions.

Then, long after their ancestors had made the move on to land, some reptiles began to return to the water. These creatures entered lakes and rivers to exploit untapped sources of food. Over time their bodies changed to suit their new, aquatic lifestyles, with some becoming almost as well adapted for swimming as fish are. However, having originally evolved from land animals, aquatic reptiles could not do without air. Although some could dive for quite long periods, they still had to return to the surface every so often to breathe. Unlike amphibians, reptiles relied completely on their lungs for oxygen. Even as youngsters they lacked gills and were unable to breathe through their skin.

Aquatic reptiles were also tied to the land because of the way they produced their young. Just as most amphibians have to return to water to breed, so most aquatic reptiles leave the water to lay their eggs on land (the few exceptions are some sea snakes and other water snakes which give birth to live young).

*Above: The pignosed turtle (*Carettochelys insculpta*) feeds mainly on aquatic plants.*

Since the first aquatic reptiles appeared they have changed a great deal. Giants that rivalled the dinosaurs for size have come and gone. The way aquatic reptiles live has remained the same, however. They may feed and mate in water but they breathe air and must drag themselves out on to land to lay their eggs.

Classification

Reptiles have their own class, Reptilia, in the animal kingdom. Within that class there are four orders: Squamata, which contains the snakes and lizards; Sphenodontida, which contains the lizard-like tuataras of New Zealand; Testudines, which contains the turtles and tortoises; and Crocodylia, which contains the crocodiles, alligators and their relatives. Of these four orders only the crocodilians are all aquatic. Two of the others, Testudines and Squamata, have some aquatic members.

Crocodilians include many of the top predators in freshwater habitats. Many kill land-living animals that come to the water's edge to drink, as well as hunting fish and other aquatic creatures. Crocodiles attack large

Anatomy of a turtle

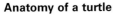

The internal anatomy of a turtle is not hugely dissimilar from our own. Like us, turtles have paired lungs and a convoluted digestive system. Their external anatomy, however, is quite different. The body is protected with a shell and the mouth completely lacks teeth.

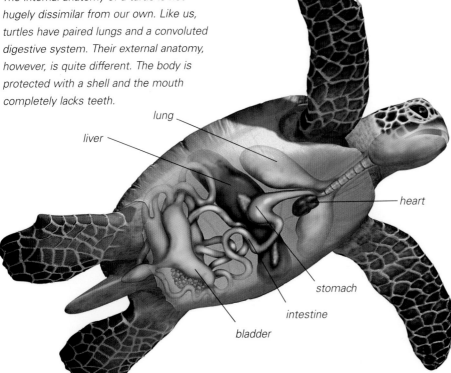

lung

liver

heart

stomach

intestine

bladder

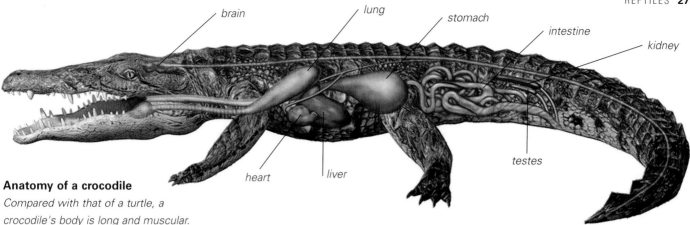

brain | lung | stomach | intestine | kidney | heart | liver | testes

Anatomy of a crocodile
Compared with that of a turtle, a crocodile's body is long and muscular. As a consequence of its shape, its internal organs are much more spread out.

animals with a sudden burst of power. They are strong swimmers and drown their air-breathing prey by rolling over and over with them in the water. Flesh is then grabbed in the jaws and torn off with a violent shake of the head. Fish and other smaller prey are swallowed whole. A few crocodilians specialize in feeding on fish. These species tend to have longer, narrower jaws than their relatives and more numerous, needle-like teeth.

Turtles are much more numerous and widespread than crocodilians. While the latter are restricted to the tropics and subtropics, the former are also found in the world's temperate zones, occurring as far north as Canada. Unlike crocodilians, which are entirely carnivorous, many turtles are omnivores and there are even some with diets dominated by plant matter. That said, many turtles are effective predators of fish and other smaller

*Below: The mangrove snake (*Boiga dendrophila*) is an adept swimmer and often enters the water to swim between trees.*

aquatic creatures. Most hunt by ambush, lying hidden amongst the fallen leaves and mud on the bottom and waiting for prey to swim into reach before attacking.

Freshwater turtles move through the water using their feet, which are usually webbed and are occasionally almost completely paddle-shaped, like those of their marine counterparts. Compared with crocodilians, which use their tails to swim, they move relatively slowly in the water. Their shells, however, mean that they are quite well protected and few creatures prey on them. Some turtles regularly clamber out on to logs or secluded banks to bask in the sun, but other species rarely leave the water.

Snakes and lizards

The vast majority of lizards are entirely terrestrial, but a few species enter rivers and other freshwater habitats to hunt. One of the largest species to do this is the water monitor from southern and South-east Asia. This 1.5m/5ft-long reptile burrows into the banks of rivers and often hunts in the water. It is an excellent swimmer and counts fish and amphibians amongst its prey. It can also hold its breath for up to half an hour when hunting.

Many land snakes are semi-aquatic. In Europe, the grass snake often enters pools to search for frogs and fish. The world's largest snake, the green anaconda, spends most of its time in the water, lying in wait beneath the surface for prey. As well as water birds and mammals, it often hunts and kills caimans, a group of crocodilians unique to South America.

A few Asian snakes have adapted so completely to life in the water that they never leave it. Rather than laying eggs these species give birth to live young which can swim from the moment they enter the world. The largest completely aquatic freshwater snake is the elephant's trunk snake, which is found from India to northern Australia. This fish eater rarely grows more than 2m/6½ft long but its thick, muscular body may be as much as 30cm/12in across.

Reptile skin
The skin of reptiles evolved to be watertight – not to keep water out but to keep it in, enabling reptiles to conquer even the driest habitats on land. Like fish, most reptiles have skin that is covered with scales. The structure of these scales is different from those of fish but their function is the same – to provide their owner with protection. In most reptiles the scales are relatively small but in crocodilians they can be extremely large, particularly on the upper side of the body and along the ridges of the tail. For these creatures, scales really act as body armour, protecting them from the flailing limbs of struggling prey.

*Below: Crocodilians like this American alligator (*Alligator mississippiensis*) have smooth scales on the belly and larger, more knobbly scales on the back.*

AQUATIC MAMMALS

Freshwater mammals fall into two groups: the vast majority are semi-aquatic, spending as much time on land as in water. A few, however, never leave the rivers where they live. These creatures feed, mate, give birth and die in the water.

Mammals are warm-blooded animals that give birth to live young and feed them on milk. The word mammal comes from the group's defining feature, the mammary glands that females have to produce milk for their offspring. The vast majority of mammals also have hair, although some lack this feature – notably dolphins and their larger cousins, the whales. Like most fish, amphibians, reptiles and birds, mammals are vertebrates. They have their own class in the animal kingdom, Mammalia.

There are two groups of freshwater mammals that are completely aquatic – river dolphins and manatees. Like other mammals, these must still breathe air and so periodically return to the surface, but apart from that they are as entirely aquatic as fish.

River dolphins

These little-known creatures in fact exist as several species in fresh water around the globe. There are three species of true river dolphin: the boto or Amazon river dolphin, the Indus

*Below: The American mink (*Mustela vison*) is a skilled hunter both in water and on land. It feeds on eels and other fish.*

Antipodean oddity

Not all freshwater carnivorous mammals are fish eaters. In Australia there is a creature that specializes in hunting freshwater invertebrates, the duck-billed platypus. This is an unusual, primitive mammal which lays eggs rather than giving birth to live young. In common with other mammals, however, it is warm-blooded and

feeds its young on milk. The duck-billed platypus is well adapted to a lifestyle of hunting underwater. Its feet are webbed and paddle-like and its short, smooth fur offers little resistance to the water as it swims. The incredible, soft, fleshy snout for which it is named is extremely sensitive and is used by the platypus to locate its prey on the bottom. As if it is not already strange enough, the duck-billed platypus is also one of the world's few venomous mammals. The rear ankles of the males each bear a hollow horny spur which links to venom glands.

*Left: The duck-billed platypus (*Ornithorhynchus anatinus) *feeds on invertebrates, which it finds on the bottom with its fleshy and sensitive beak.*

---

river dolphin and the Ganges river dolphin. A fourth species, the baiji from China's Yangtze River, was sadly declared extinct in December 2006. Other dolphins enter rivers and some species have populations that spend their whole lives there, as well as populations that are entirely marine. Among these are the tucuxi, which live in the Amazon and Orinoco Rivers of South America, and the Irrawaddy dolphin of South-east Asia. All these species feed almost exclusively on fish.

Like their marine counterparts, they have a highly developed sense of echolocation, emitting clicks and squeaks, then listening for the echoes that bounce back. This enables them to find their prey even in murky waters. Unlike marine dolphins, however, river dolphins tend to live and hunt in pairs or alone, only

*Below: The hippopotamus (*Hippopotamus amphibius) *spends the daylight hours in water and emerges at night to graze on land.*

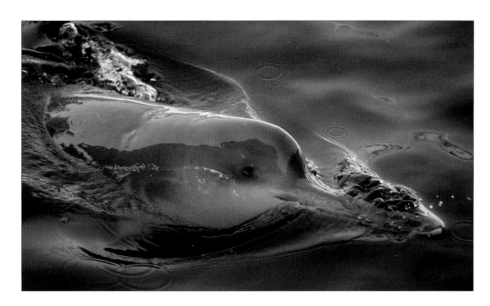

*Above: When this century began, there were four species of exclusively freshwater dolphins. This one, the baiji (*Lipotes vexiliffer*) is now extinct.*

forming larger groups where drought or an abundance of food brings them together.

Manatees

The other entirely aquatic freshwater mammals are the manatees. Manatees and their marine cousin, the dugong, are the last survivors of an ancient mammal group. Their closest living relatives are the land-living elephants and hyraxes. Two species, the West Indian manatee and the West African manatee, also inhabit coastal marine waters. Manatees are large, slow-moving creatures and are wholly vegetarian. At first sight they might appear defenceless but their sheer bulk puts them out of danger from the predatory animals that share their home.

The vast majority of freshwater mammals spend part of their lives on land. These creatures are found on every continent apart from Antarctica. Semi-aquatic freshwater mammals range from tiny shrews and rodents to gigantic animals such as the hippopotamus. There is even a species of freshwater seal, the Baikal seal from Russia. This seal inhabits Lake Baikal, the world's deepest lake and one of the world's biggest in terms of surface area. Today Lake Baikal is more than a thousand miles from the sea, but the presence of the seal shows that it was once linked to ocean waters. All of the world's other seals live in coastal marine habitats.

Otters and mink

Most freshwater mammals are carnivorous and a large number feed on fish. Of these, the otters are perhaps the most well known. Otters are found on five of the Earth's seven continents, being absent only from Australasia and Antarctica. There are 12 species altogether; the most widespread of these is the Eurasian otter, which ranges from Scotland to Siberia and as far south as Java. A close relative of the Eurasian otter, the North American river otter is found through most of the continent after which it is named. Otters tend to be solitary animals, except during the breeding season and when mothers have young. The exception to this rule is the giant otter from South America. This large animal, reaching almost 2m/6½ft long, lives and hunts in family groups, which may include up to nine individuals. Its size and social behaviour have earned it the local nickname of 'lobo del rio' or 'river wolf'. The giant otter occurs in the Orinoco, La Plata and Amazon River systems, but is becoming increasingly rare. Numbers originally declined as a result of hunting for its fur. Although this has now been banned, the giant otter faces new threats from habitat degradation and pollution.

An animal often confused for an otter in North America and Europe is the mink. Mink are more versatile than otters and find a lot of their food on land. However, like otters, they will often dive to catch fish. There are just two species: the European mink, which ranges from France to Russia, and the North American mink, which ranges from Alaska to Mexico. Bred for its fur, the North American mink has escaped and been released from fur farms in Britain and other countries. In most of the places where it has become established in the wild, it is considered a pest.

*Below: Grizzly bears (*Ursus arctos horribilis*) are land animals but they are still effective predators of fish, gathering at prime spots to catch migrating salmon.*

OTHER FRESHWATER ANIMALS

As well as mammals, reptiles and amphibians, freshwater fish share their homes with a wide range of other creatures. The most numerous of these are invertebrates, which usually outnumber the fish in any given area many times over.

Invertebrates are animals without backbones. They include insects, crustaceans and molluscs, as well as many other less well known groups. Some invertebrates spend their whole lives in freshwater habitats, while others live in them as juveniles and then emerge when they turn into adults.

Aquatic insects

Invertebrates form an important link in the food web of almost all habitats. The most familiar freshwater invertebrates are the insects that are seen flying around near the surface. Dragonflies, damselflies, mayflies and many others all bear aquatic nymphs, which are noticed less often, but are much more important in terms of the ecosystems of the habitats themselves. The vast majority of insects with aquatic larvae have relatively short adult lives. Most mayflies, famously, only live for a day as adults – just long enough to mate and lay eggs

*Above: Most mayflies (*Epeorus*) live for just a day as adults. They are hunted by trout and other fish, which jump to catch them.*

before dying. Their larvae, however, live for a full year or more underwater. Dragonfly and damselfly nymphs are also much longer-lived than the adults, with many species spending at least two years in their juvenile form.

Insect larvae are an important source of food for many fish; indeed, some species eat little else. The larvae themselves have varied diets.

*Above: The zebra mussel (*Dreissena polymorpha*) is a filter-feeding freshwater mollusc, sieving tiny particles from the water.*

Mayfly nymphs, for instance, feed on the algae that grows on the bottoms of the streams and rivers where they live. Dragonfly nymphs are carnivores, hunting other insect larvae, tadpoles and even small fish. Other aquatic insect larvae are omnivorous. Caddisfly larvae, for example, feed both on algae and other invertebrates. These larvae are often overlooked because they camouflage themselves so well by building silk cases around their bodies, which they cover with sand, tiny twigs and other detritus.

Most aquatic insect larvae live on the bottoms of streams, rivers, lakes and ponds, but mosquito larvae

Below: Cyclops *are tiny crustaceans which live in most still freshwater habitats as members of the plankton community.*

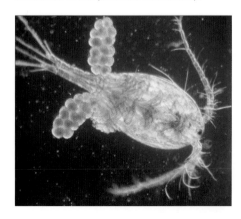

Freshwater birds

Invertebrates are important to fish as food and a few species themselves prey on fish. Birds, however, are far more dangerous to most fish. Many specialize in catching and feeding on fish, from herons and kingfishers to raptors such as the osprey. The threat from water birds is so great that it has driven the evolution of colour and pattern in many fish species. The majority of freshwater fish with protective colouring are only camouflaged on the top half of their bodies – the half that fish-eating birds tend to see.

Kingfishers, herons and raptors strike from above the surface, but some fish-eating birds dive and pursue their prey underwater. Saw-billed ducks such as mergansers hunt in this way, as do grebes and the birds which are known in Europe as divers and in North America as loons.

Of course, not all water birds are a threat to fish. Most ducks, geese and swans feed on plant matter or invertebrates, as do rails such as the moorhen and coot. These birds do, however, affect the lives of fish indirectly. The manure that they drop into the water enriches it with organic material, which is then processed by algae and plants. These in turn feed some fish, as well as aquatic invertebrates which may themselves become fish food.

*Left: A pair of mallard ducks (*Anas platyrhynchos*) upend to reach water plants on the bottom. Like most ducks, their diet is largely vegetarian, although they will eat aquatic invertebrates.*

tend to be found at the surface. They hang suspended from the thin layer that forms on still bodies of water due to surface tension, the breathing tubes of their tails poking through into the air. Mosquito larvae feed on even smaller, free-swimming invertebrates in the water itself. These and tiny algaes make up the freshwater plankton.

Plankton and freshwater worms

Plankton is another source of food widely consumed by freshwater fish, particularly those that live in open water. Common members of the plankton include the almost microscopic crustaceans known as water fleas. Of these, the genera *Daphnia* and *Cyclops* are among the most often present. Other planktonic creatures include the larvae of larger crustaceans such as crayfish, as well as tiny worms and the larvae of molluscs.

Freshwater molluscs are a varied and often overlooked group. Like their marine cousins, most are either slow-moving or live in one spot as adults. Water snails are vegetarian, living on algae and the leaves of aquatic plants. Bivalve molluscs, such as freshwater mussels, sieve the water to obtain their food. Water sucked in

Below: Daphnia *are slightly larger than* Cyclops *(see opposite page) and, like them, can just about be seen with the naked eye.*

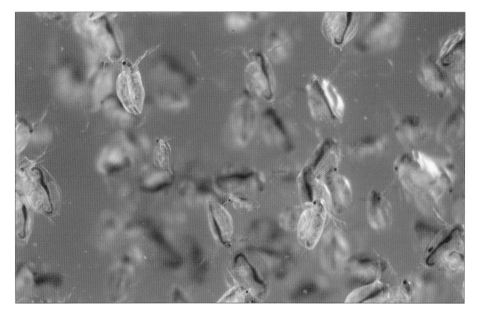

through a tube, known as a siphon, passes over their gills. The gills then both extract oxygen and filter out particles of food. The depleted water is then squirted out of the body through another siphon.

Other freshwater invertebrates include various worms. Among the largest of these are the leeches, aquatic relatives of the earthworms. Leeches are best known for their habit of feeding on blood. In truth, there are only a few species of leech that do this – the vast majority are carnivores that hunt other invertebrates. The medicinal leech is one of the blood-drinking species found throughout Europe, including Britain. It feeds on the blood of large vertebrates, such as deer,

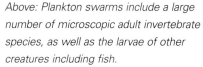

Above: Plankton swarms include a large number of microscopic adult invertebrate species, as well as the larvae of other creatures including fish.

which come down to the water to drink. Unlike some leeches, which are entirely aquatic, the medicinal leech can survive out of water as long as its body remains moist. This species actually lays its eggs out of water, although close enough to it so that the larvae can easily make their way into the water once they have hatched.

Various insects have both aquatic larvae and aquatic adult forms. Among these are the diving beetles, which can grow large enough to kill a small fish. A more unusual predator is the water spider, an arachnid which hunts fish fry, as well as other prey. Like diving beetles, it breathes air and so must return to the surface every so often. To minimize the need for this laborious task, the water spider builds its own 'diving bell' from silk. This impervious sac has an opening at the bottom and is attached to the stem of a water plant. When the spider reaches the surface it traps a bubble of air with the hairs on its body. This air bubble is then carefully taken down to the 'diving bell' and released into it, topping it up. The spider repeats this action a few times until the sac is full, creating a secure underwater retreat from which to assault its prey.

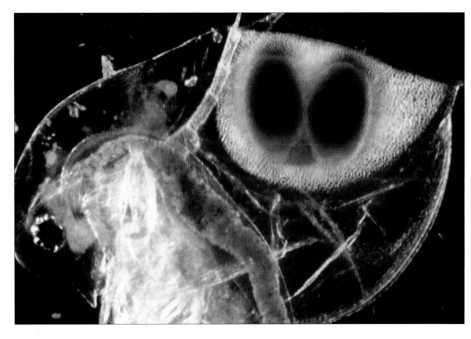

FRESHWATER PURSUITS

For most people, fresh water is never far away. Even in the city there are rivers, or ponds in the park. Rivers and bodies of fresh water have an attraction that draws people to them. Some come to walk on their banks, others to fish or to watch wildlife. Whatever the reason, we seek these places out for pleasure.

Most visits to freshwater habitats involve contact with wildlife, whether that was the intention or not. The creatures that we see most frequently are birds. Air breathers like us, they spend most of their time on the water, on exposed rocks or on the branches overhanging it.

Water birds use fresh water as a place of refuge from predators or as a source of food. Some do both. Birdwatching in these places is often very rewarding. Out on the water, ducks, geese and other waterfowl are easy to observe. They take little notice of people or other creatures on the banks. Just as feeding the ducks at the local duck pond is one of the first contacts with wild creatures that most children have, so a birdwatching trip to the local lake or reservoir is usually

Above: Underwater caves offer some of the most exciting freshwater diving in the world, but the novice should enter them with caution, and under supervision.

one of the first special outings for the young ornithologist. Large and sometimes noisy, birds are easy to spot. Another group of creatures living in and around freshwater habitats that is far more common, but tends to go unnoticed, is the insects. Like water birds, freshwater insects can be seen both on the surface of the water and flying above it. In places where the water is still, creatures such as pond skaters and whirligig beetles can often be seen scooting over the surface. Dragonflies and damselflies hunt above the water, while midges and mayflies often swarm. All of these insects have aquatic larvae which hatch, grow and develop under the water. Most are a source of food for fish.

Angling

The link between insects and fish is perhaps best understood by anglers. Fly fishermen in particular try to catch fish by mimicking the motion of the insects that they normally feed on.

These fishermen aim to catch fish that hunt at the surface using flies. Fishing flies are artificial and often made from feathers or fur, but they are designed to look just like mayflies and other insects in order to attract trout and similar fish. The dancing motion of

Below: Observing the animals and birds, such as this kingfisher (Alcedo athis), which are drawn to the waterside to feed on aquatic life is part of the attraction of the freshwater environment.

The freshwater aquarium

A major threat to wild freshwater fish is their capture for the aquarium trade. However, with commercial breeders now supplying much of the market, this is less of a problem than it once was. The more common species found for sale now tend to come from this source rather than from the wild.

Whatever their source, there is no doubt that freshwater fish in home aquaria provide a great deal of pleasure for many people. As well as being beautiful to look at, they are relatively easy to keep and are said to reduce stress and promote relaxation.

Below: The red-bellied piranha (Pygocentrus nattereri) is a popular home aquarium fish and one, for obvious reasons, often kept on its own.

Above: Arctic char (Salvelinus alpinus) are among the coldwater species regularly caught in icy freshwater habitats.

Above: Small and easy to keep, the pictus catfish (Pimelodus pictus) is commonly sold for the aquarium trade.

the fishing fly on the surface is achieved by careful manipulation of the rod when casting – a skill that takes some time to perfect.

However, most anglers choose to take the slightly easier option of coarse fishing. This involves casting a baited hook into the water and waiting. The bait used varies, and different anglers will have their own preferences for what to attach to the hook. Maggots or meal worms (both types of insect larvae) are popular choices. Their wriggling bodies attract fish in mid-water or near the bottom, wherever the hook ends up hanging. Larger, predatory fish such as pike are usually caught using artificial lures, designed to look like the smaller fish which they prey on. Once a fish has bitten, the skilful part of coarse fishing begins – reeling the fish in without letting it escape or causing the line to break.

In colder parts of the world, ice fishing is popular. Here, anglers use specialized equipment to make openings in the ice, through which they fish for coldwater species such as char, walleye, perch, trout and pike. On longer expeditions, a portable ice 'shanty' or shack may be towed to the lakeside to provide the fisherman with shelter. As with more temperate angling, ice fishers may enter contests – northerly US states such as Minnesota currently host some of the biggest.

At first sight, angling of any persuasion might seem damaging to populations of freshwater fish. More often, the very opposite is true. The fish themselves are hardly ever badly injured by the hooks used to pull them

in and, once unhooked and returned to the water, they quickly recover. The habitats in which these fish live tend to be well looked after – a healthy section of river is likely to be home to a large number of fish, and most anglers are quite protective of the places in which they practise their sport. Private lakes and reservoirs may even be stocked with extra fish to draw anglers in. That said, some species have suffered from angling in the past, particularly large 'trophy' fish, which were rarely put back alive. However, most of these species are now protected by law, in the developed world at least.

Diving in fresh water

Scuba diving is a hobby often associated with marine waters, but freshwater lakes and flooded quarries can make good venues for scuba diving too. Admittedly, one cannot see the

same range of life in fresh water as in the seas, but there are still many reasons for diving in fresh water. Visibility is often much greater: freshwater habitats are not subject to quite the same seasonal swarms, known as 'blooms', of plankton as shallow-water coasts. In addition, divers are not subject to the levels of salt in the water as in marine diving sites, which ultimately takes its toll on hair, skin and clothes.

In some parts of the world, the freshwater landscape is truly spectacular. In Florida, one can venture into underground limestone caves where the water seeps down from the surface through porous rock, later emerging farther downhill as springs and pools. Springs exist in other parts of the world, too, but in those that are naturally heated, local authorities often issue health warnings to divers and swimmers, as parasites carrying disease tend to thrive in them.

At the opposite extreme, some people choose to dive beneath ice, relishing the clarity of the water in this freezing habitat. 'Ice diving', however, is a sport with very obvious hazards, intended only for those who have the experience, skill and specialized scuba equipment to pull it off safely.

Below: Ice diving is a pastime that has become increasingly popular. However, like cave diving it can be dangerous and requires supervision.

HABITATS AND CONSERVATION

Many people perceive freshwater habitats as naturally formed bodies of water, yet humans have also created 'new' homes in the form of canals and reservoirs. Although not built as sanctuaries for freshwater animals, creatures do thrive in them. Sadly, proximity to humanity brings hazards to freshwater life.

The vast majority of towns and cities are built along rivers, which now often pass right through their centres. Back when these urban areas were first founded, hundreds, or even thousands of years ago, rivers were the main means of transporting goods. They were natural highways that cut through the wilderness that separated human settlements.

Today, many rivers have lost much of their traffic. The spread of road and rail networks means we are much less reliant on them than we once were. Nevertheless, those rivers continue to flow and within them there is often a wealth of wildlife living unseen by the people walking along their banks or over the bridges that cross them.

New homes

Other freshwater habitats have been physically built by humans. Networks of canals, for instance, were created by people to carry goods to places rivers did not reach. Today many canals lie unused. Again, like rivers,

Below: Large waterfalls like this are natural barriers to most fish, separating populations and, in some places, even species.

Above: As well as being ugly to look at, the litter and the resulting pollution of this swamp habitat threatens the populations of fish and other creatures that live in it.

these waterways often pass through cities and towns. Some cities, such as Birmingham in England, are filled by them – quiet havens for wild creatures amongst the tarmac, bricks and concrete.

In the developed world, most of us take it for granted that we can turn on a tap and get fresh running water at any hour of the day or night. This water, however, has to be collected and stored before it can be treated and then distributed to people's homes. In many parts of the world, man-made reservoirs are now more common than natural lakes. Fed by rivers, these large bodies of water have become homes for a wide range of fish and other aquatic creatures, as well as water birds and other freshwater life. Some reservoirs are stocked with fish brought in from elsewhere for angling. Although artificial, many of these reservoirs have become important habitats in their own right.

On a much smaller scale, many people have created their own freshwater habitats in the form of garden ponds. Isolated from streams and rivers, these are rarely important homes for native fish but they do provide a lifeline for other forms of

aquatic life. Amphibians such as frogs and newts use them as places to breed, and many insects lay their eggs in them and spend their lives in them as larvae. Garden ponds serve another important function by bringing wildlife closer to people. For many children they are a first introduction to freshwater life.

Wild waters

The majority of freshwater habitats are neither man-made nor found in towns or cities. They are natural parts of the landscape and most have been here much longer than humankind has existed. The paths taken by natural waterways such as rivers and streams may have changed a little over time, but in essence these water courses, and the bodies of fresh water they feed, are permanent features, millions of years old. The major habitat types are lakes, rivers, swamps, ponds and streams, and their capacity to nurture different forms of aquatic life is considered on the pages that follow. Rather like the inhabitants of

Alien invaders

The introduction of non-native fish and other animals to freshwater habitats has often caused problems in the past. New predators have caused devastation, while other species have out-competed native fish for food. In the 1950s the North American bluegill sunfish (*Lepomis macrochirus*) was introduced into Japan and quickly spread. This predator has since wiped out at least one native fish species and badly dented the populations of many others.

Below: The bluegill sunfish arrived in Japan as a gift to the crown prince (now emperor) Akihito.

terrestrial islands, which have evolved to live in rather confined, specialized environments, freshwater species are vulnerable to changes in their habitat. While their homes remain unaltered, they are safe, but in many parts of the world human activity is having a serious impact on freshwater life.

Man-made problems

The most serious threat to freshwater life in most places is pollution. Pollution is the addition of substances to the water which do not naturally

occur there. Sources of pollution include industrial waste, untreated sewage and surface run-off containing pesticides or fertilizers used in farming. Effects on freshwater life depend on the contaminants involved.

Sewage and fertilizers affect water quality by increasing its load of nutrients, such as nitrates and phosphates. While this does not have an immediate impact on fish or other aquatic life it can cause aquatic algae to bloom and clog up waterways. Numbers of bacteria and protozoan organisms also rise. As they do so they use up dissolved oxygen, causing fish and other creatures to slowly suffocate.

Chemical pollutants such as pesticides and contaminants from industrial waste kill more directly. Pesticides sprayed on crops may be washed into rivers by rain, just as fertilizers often are. Industrial waste may be dumped or continually flow into the water. In most developed nations the environmental cost of such pollution is recognized and laws have been enacted to prevent it. Elsewhere in the world, however, such waste continues to be flushed straight into rivers and other water courses, as does sewage.

Acid rain is another serious problem for freshwater habitats in some parts of the world. This is caused by the burning of fossil fuels, particularly the burning of coal in power stations. The chemicals in the smoke produced include nitrogen oxide and sulphur

Above: Even natural habitats may offer limited prospects for aquatic life. Narrow woodland streams in temperate regions, for example, offer fewer feeding opportunities than a slow-moving river rich in algae.

dioxide. When these react with the tiny droplets of water in clouds they form nitric and sulphuric acid, which then falls with the rain. Acid rain has proved a particularly difficult problem to eradicate, mainly because the places where it is produced are rarely badly affected by it. It is other places downwind that suffer. For instance, many of the lakes in Scandinavia are largely devoid of life because of pollution originating in Britain and other parts of western Europe.

While pollution is the greatest threat to freshwater life in most areas, human activity has caused, and continues to cause, other problems. While the building of dams provides us with both power and a reliable source of water, it can also have a serious impact on migratory fish. Species that travel upstream to breed can find their paths blocked and river-dwelling species may have their populations effectively split in two. This may result in a decrease in numbers for both categories of fish.

Left: Dams provide us with electricity and water from the reservoirs they create. However, they act as barriers to river fish, meaning that the range of some species has become much more restricted.

STREAMS

Unlike marine habitats, which are all broadly similar, freshwater habitats vary a great deal. Streams are small waterways that usually feed into rivers. Unlike rivers, they tend to be relatively shallow and narrow. As a result, the fish and other creatures that are found in them are usually small.

Streams can be quite fast-flowing. Fish that live in the open water within them tend to be streamlined and slim-bodied to prevent themselves from being washed away. Bottom dwellers are often horizontally flattened or have flattened bellies to hug the stream bed. Some have suckers or other physical adaptations to help them cling on to submerged rocks or pebbles.

Most streams are largely devoid of plant life. The fast current means that sediment rarely builds up enough for plants to take root. As a result, most fish living in them are carnivorous, feeding mainly on invertebrates (which themselves eat algae and detritus), or filter tiny particles of food from the water. A few fish feed on algae too, which grows on the surface of rocks.

The water in streams is almost always well-oxygenated. Rapid flow and frequent waterfalls mean that air is constantly introduced into the water, allowing large amounts of oxygen to dissolve. Fish and other fully aquatic creatures that live in streams invariably rely on gills or their skin to absorb oxygen. Air breathing is virtually unknown in fish from these habitats.

Above: Rainbow trout (Oncorhynchus mykiss) favour clear-water streams and rivers.

Above: Northern studfish (Fundulus catenatus) live in North American rivers.

Above: Colourful rainbow darters (Etheostoma caeruleum) are often seen 'darting' through rapids.

Above: The riffle sculpin (Cottus gulosus), as its name suggests, favours lively, bubbling streams.

Different conditions

Despite these common features, streams around the world also have key differences. In mountain streams the water is usually soft, at least in the upper reaches. Water flowing quickly over insoluble rocks picks up few minerals. This changes if these streams start to run through moors or heathland. Here, the peaty soil may produce an acid reaction, lowering the pH of the water, while at the same time adding minerals to it.

Streams in tropical forests are usually soft and acidic. Unlike streams that flow beneath open skies, they often carry a significant amount of organic matter in the shape of fallen leaves. Where eddies and pools form, they may start to build up on the bottom. As with mountain streams, water plants in these streams are relatively uncommon – the comparatively rapid flow of water prevents most from getting a root-hold.

Some streams would be rivers if they were in areas of greater rainfall. This is true of many waterways that flow through deserts. Desert streams often differ from typical streams in a number of respects. To start with, they are often slower-flowing, as the land over which they travel is often quite flat. Many of them are also temporary, occurring only after periods of rain and quickly drying up. The exceptions are the desert streams that are fed by springs. A high degree of evaporation sometimes means that these never become rivers. Desert streams are far less rich in life than their counterparts elsewhere. The few fish that do live in them are often highly adapted and able to survive extremes that most other fish could not tolerate. With water often flowing slowly and the heat of the desert sun evaporating much of the little water there is in these streams, oxygen levels can be extremely low and levels of dissolved salts sometimes higher than those in the sea.

Above: The banded leporinus (Leporinus fasciatus) finds its food on rocky stream bottoms.

Above: Spawning bullheads (Cottus gobio) attach their eggs to submerged rocks.

Above: The nase (Chondrostoma nasus) feeds by scraping algae from rocks with its lower lip.

Above: The zebra danio (Brachydanio rerio) may live in paddy fields as well as streams.

TEMPERATE AND DESERT RIVERS

Some rivers rise in mountains; others in bogs or glaciers. At high altitudes, energetic water flow may displace rock; in drier regions, such as deserts, water is lost via evaporation, creating narrow, winding rivers surrounded by scant vegetation. A river varies throughout its course, offering a range of habitats.

Compared with streams, which are generally shallow and flow too quickly for sediment to form, rivers are more sluggish and usually have mud on the bottom. This provides a home for worms and many other invertebrates, and also allows water plants to take root and grow. As a result, the river bottom is often a rich source of food for fish, and many species have evolved that spend most of their lives here. In larger rivers this is the home of sturgeons and catfish. Other river-bottom dwellers include barbels, carp and, in some places, freshwater rays.

In fertile regions, many fish live among the water plants which grow near river banks. Most of the plants here have their leaves above the surface and their stems are usually used for cover rather than food. Species that inhabit these areas are often small, with flattened bodies to help them move easily between the stems. Many have vertical stripes to help to camouflage them from predators in the dappled light.

Above: The bottom-feeding smallmouth buffalo (Ictiobus bubalus) ingests shellfish.

Above: Common stonerollers (Campostoma anomalum) build nests by 'rolling' away pebbles.

Above: The blacktail shiner (Cyprinella venusta) favours rivers with strong current.

Above: The warmouth (Lepomis gulosus) lives in slow-moving rivers with a lot of vegetation.

By contrast, the world's great canyon rivers, such as those of the North American southwest or Namibia in southern Africa, are surrounded by little vegetation. However, the sandy rock they cut through is sometimes deposited as sandbanks and beaches, which support an array of life.

The river channel

Although most river fish live near the banks or the bottom, some inhabit the open channel – the clear water in the middle of a river. These fish tend to be well streamlined and are strong swimmers. Some, such as the silver carp from the River Amur in east Asia, are filter feeders, sifting plankton and other tiny edible particles from the water as they swim along. Others, such as most salmon and trout, are generalists, travelling up and down the water column to take invertebrates, fish fry and other small creatures.

In places where rivers are wide and more shallow, the stones and rubble on the bottom affect the water surface, causing small waves to form. These regions of rivers (and streams), usually upstream, are known as riffles. Where the gradient steepens so that the water flows faster, riffles become rapids.

Riffles and rapids have their own kinds of fish: they tend to be small species that use the rocks as cover from predators and barriers to prevent themselves from being washed away.

Slowing down

Farther downstream, rivers become deeper and more sluggish. These areas are home to some of the world's largest freshwater fish, species such as the Mekong giant catfish and North America's white sturgeon. Winding through largely flat land, the lower reaches of rivers are the sections most likely to break their banks and flood.

*Above: Channel catfish (*Ictalurus punctatus*) occupy the deeper areas of rivers.*

*Above: The river darter (*Percina shumardi*) is one of the easier fish to spot in American rivers.*

*Above: The smooth softshell turtle (*Apalone mutica*) uses its snout to breathe in large rivers.*

*Above: The peacock bass (*Cichla ocellaris*) schools in the rapid water of rocky rivers.*

TROPICAL RIVERS

Rivers vary widely, depending on where they are in the world and the landscapes through which they flow. The world's largest rivers (those which carry the most water) are concentrated in the tropics. The reason for this is simple – it is here that the greatest amount of rain regularly falls.

River habitats are far from uniform. Individual rivers change as they get nearer to the sea, slowing down as the ground levels out and forming great loops known as meanders. They also grow bigger as a multitude of smaller rivers, which we call tributaries, flow into them. Each of these in turn has its own smaller tributary streams. Seen from above, river systems in fact look something like leafless trees, with the main channel forming the trunk, the larger tributaries the branches and their tributary streams the twigs. Together, they gather the rainwater that falls over a vast area and carry it down to the sea. The area drained by this network of channels is known as the river's drainage basin, or sometimes just its basin. The Amazon basin, then, is not just the area drained by the main Amazon river channel but by every single river and stream that flows into it.

Above: The motoro stingray (Potamotrygon motoro) lives on muddy river bottoms.

Above: The South American leaffish (Monocirrhus mimophyllus) hides under leaves on the surface.

Above: Striped for camouflage, the discus (Symphysodon aequifasciatus) is an Amazon fish.

Above: The red-bellied piranha (Pygocentrus nattereri) is one of the world's most feared fish.

The mighty Amazon

The Amazon is by far the largest river in the world. Its enormous basin, which is densely covered with tropical rainforest, occupies much of the northern half of South America. Every day, the river pours as much water into the sea as the Murray river (Australia's longest river) does in a year. In the rainy season, the main channel of the Amazon can be as much as 40km/24.8 miles across at its widest point. Sitting on a boat in the middle, one would see water stretch from one horizon to the other.

For comparison, rivers that drain dry regions are generally smaller than those which flow through tropical rain forest. The Nile, for example, although a similar length to the Amazon, is far narrower. Flowing through the arid countries of Sudan and Egypt, and with a major tributary – the Blue Nile – rising from Lake Tana in Ethiopia, the river discharges an average of 2,830 cubic m/92,824 cubic ft into the Mediterranean sea every second. Although this is a lot of water, it is still 75 times less than that discharged every second by the Amazon.

The type of landscape through which a river flows also affects the water within it. Rivers which flow through tropical rain forest, for instance, tend to have soft, slightly acidic water, which is often stained brown by the tannin released from rotting leaves. They are also warm and, in some places, quite low in oxygen. Tropical fish and other freshwater river creatures evolve to cope with these particular conditions: if the water of breeding tanks or home aquaria is more alkaline, for example, then those fish may suffer.

Above: Red-headed river turtles (Podocnemis erythrocephala) tend to favour calm backwaters.

Above: Paradise fish (Macropodus opercularis) enter paddy fields as well as natural rivers.

Above: The electric catfish (Malapterurus electricus) inhabits rivers in north and west Africa.

Above: The African spotted tilapia (Tilapia mariae) is now farmed throughout the world.

LAKES

Lakes are large bodies of still, fresh water. They are fed by rivers and streams and most, although not all, have rivers flowing from them. In many ways lakes are like freshwater versions of the sea. Like the sea, they have beaches and large areas of open water. Some also plunge to a considerable depth.

Many lake fish live and travel in shoals, particularly those that feed in the water column or near the surface. This offers them some small degree of protection in a habitat that otherwise leaves them exposed.

As we have seen, many open-water lake fish are filter feeders, sifting out meals of plankton as they swim along. Other species spend their lives much closer to the bottom – some in deeper waters and others in the shallows near the shore. In most lakes, plant life is concentrated around the fringes. Where the slope of the shore is not too steep, reed beds and other thickets of plants may grow. The water here is shallow and the gaps between each plant quite small. Fish fry find safety from larger fish here, although they face a different threat from herons and other water birds. A little farther out ambush predators such as the muskellunge use the stems of plants to hide from prey while hunting.

Most larger fish can be found where the water is deeper and aquatic plants are more widely spaced apart. In Europe, these include roach, perch and rudd, and in North America,

Above: Adult flathead catfish (Pylodictis olivaris) tend to live in the still waters of deep lakes.

Above: Trout perch (Percopsis comiscomaycus) spawn over rocks in shallower parts of lakes.

Above: The muskellunge (Esox masquinongy) uses water plants as cover when hunting.

Above: The colourful midas cichlid (Amphilophus citrinellus) is often dominant in its habitat.

bass and buffaloes. These species and other herbivores and invertivores (animals that feed predominantly on invertebrate creatures) are preyed upon by large predatory fish such as gars.

Lakes, like river systems, often have their own particular species or subspecies of fish. The Greek rudd, for instance, is found only in Lakes Yliki and Paralimni in the extreme east of mainland Greece. Often these lake dwellers differ only slightly from other, more common, river fish, betraying their ancestry. Sometimes, however, the differences are so great that it can be hard, or even impossible, to work out from which species lake fish were originally descended.

Freshwater seas

The world's largest lakes are in North America, Siberia and Africa (not including the salty Caspian and Aral Seas, which some authorities define as lakes). The Great Lakes of North America are rich in fish, but have few unique species as a result of their relative proximity by river to the ocean. Lake Baikal in Siberia is the world's deepest lake, although it is only the seventh largest in terms of surface area. Its fauna is relatively sparse, due to its northerly location, and as it does not spawn any rivers, many of its fish exist nowhere else. Africa's Rift Valley lakes, by contrast, are extremely rich in species. Most of the fish that live in them are cichlids and the vast majority of these are endemic to just one of the lakes. The Rift Valley cichlids are a celebrated example of adaptive radiation: the many very different-looking species that now exist evolved from just a few ancestral species. Unfortunately, in recent decades many of these fish have been lost. The cichlids of Lake Victoria in particular have been decimated by Nile perch, an introduced species.

Above: The Arctic charr (Salvelinus alpinus) inhabits the cold lakes of the far northern hemisphere.

Above: The common carp (Cyprinus carpio) is a lake fish very popular with anglers.

Above: The pike (Esox lucius) is a top freshwater predator and favours colder lakes.

Above: Some populations of smelt (Omerus eperlanus) are confined to landlocked lakes.

SWAMPS

Swamps are formed where rivers break their banks and flood flat ground. Swamps in temperate and cold regions tend to be permanent, but in warmer parts of the world they often dry out for part of the year. Wherever they occur, swamp water tends to be low in oxygen.

Swamp water is stagnant and usually filled with rotting vegetation. Without the churning action of waves on the surface, only a limited amount of oxygen enters the water from the air, and much of that is used by the microorganisms that break plant matter down. These conditions are far from ideal for most fish. Indeed, many fish washed into swamps by annual floods are unable to survive for long once the deep water has receded.

However, some fish have evolved adaptations specifically for living in swamps. Many have low metabolic rates to conserve oxygen and highly efficient gills. Some supplement their oxygen intake by gulping air, absorbing it through the wall of the gut or swim bladder. These fish are often obligate air breathers – if denied regular access to air they will drown. A few, such as the European eel, absorb oxygen from the air through their skin. Being able to obtain oxygen from the air gives a species an obvious advantage over other swamp-living fish that cannot.

*Above: Preferring murky water, the taillight shiner (*Notropis maculatus*) is rarely seen.*

*Above: The mud sunfish (*Acantharchus pomotis*) lives in North American cedar swamps.*

*Above: Like related cavefish, the swampfish (*Chologaster cornuta*) has little use for eyes.*

*Above: The South American lungfish (*Lepidosiren paradoxa*) must breathe air to survive.*

It also enables some of them to travel short distances across land to find new pools if the ones they are living in run out of food or become too crowded.

Other residents and visitors

Swamps are home to many other creatures besides fish. Insects are abundant, particularly those requiring stagnant water for their larvae, such as mosquitoes. Amphibians such as frogs are common too. They also require still water for their eggs and many find much of their prey in the water. Unlike most fish, they are happy in water with low dissolved oxygen levels, since they can breathe air. Swamp-dwelling amphibians tend to breed just after heavy rain or floods, when food and dissolved oxygen are most abundant in the water for their young.

Swamps are also a magnet for birds. Some, such as Africa's shoebill, which hunts lungfish, live in swamps all year round. Herons, egrets and other fish-eating water birds are particularly numerous after floods, when swamps are thick with fish washed in from rivers that feed into them.

Other creatures, such as crocodiles and snakes, also profit from a seasonal abundance of fish. Unlike birds, these reptiles are unable to travel far when fish stocks drop. However, they can go for long periods without eating and so can survive until the next floods arrive.

Plants tend to flourish in swamps, particularly in warm regions, and the majority of swamp-dwelling mammals are herbivores. A few, such as Africa's lechwe antelope and South America's capybara, are so well adapted they are rarely found outside swamps. Other mammals are drawn in when greenery becomes scarce in the surrounding areas, particularly in hot, dry parts of the world.

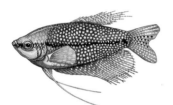

Above: Pearl gourami (Trichogaster leeri) tolerate acidic swamp waters.

Above: The transparency of the x-ray fish (Pristella maxillaris) protects it from swamp predators.

Above: The mudminnow (Umbra karmeri) can tolerate stagnant, dark, silty water.

Above: The American alligator (Alligator mississipiensis) is a famous swamp predator.

DIRECTORY OF FRESHWATER SPECIES

The freshwater world is dominated by rivers. These ribbons of life cut through the landscape and feed lakes, swamps and virtually all other freshwater habitats. Some continents are known as much by their great rivers as by their countries. The names of these waterways alone are enough to evoke the feeling of the regions they flow through, even if those are places we have never been to or seen. Some continents are dominated by just one or a few great rivers. South America, for instance, has the Amazon, while much of Africa is drained by the Niger, Congo and Nile. Other continents, however, have many of these arteries: in North America they include the Mississippi, Colorado and Columbia to name but a few.

Just as rivers are the dominant freshwater habitats, so fish are the dominant vertebrates within them. Fish have evolved a great variety of shapes and forms to take advantage of the diversity that rivers and other freshwater habitats offer. Some fish have become highly streamlined, high-speed hunters, while others have evolved perfect camouflage and spend much of their time almost stationary. Where waters are murky, many fish have become adept at finding their way around using touch and other senses. Physical conditions have dictated the directions in which these creatures have evolved. Although some fish are generalists, many have become so perfectly adapted for living in particular types of freshwater habitats – or even in particular regions within those habitats – that they are rarely found anywhere else.

Above, left to right: Common carp (Cyprinus carpio), bull sharks (Carcharhinus leucas) and African dwarf clawed frogs (Hymenochirus boettgeri).
Left: Zebra danio (Danio rerio) school within a shallow, densely vegetated habitat. The creatures common in this type of freshwater environment are often camouflaged with stripes to blend in with the dappled light and plant roots.

HOW TO USE THE DIRECTORY

The following pages feature some of the world's most interesting and successful freshwater animals. The vast majority of creatures profiled are ray-finned fish from the orders described on pages 22–3, but there are also amphibian, reptile and aquatic mammal species.

This global directory of species is divided into five continental sections, based on the fact that geography greatly impacts the distribution of freshwater life. Each section begins with cartilaginous fish species, then goes on to discuss ray-finned fish in the main, before concluding with amphibians, reptiles and aquatic mammals. Within these broad groups, animals are organized according to scientific convention (such as familial or generic groups), or, as with the selected species from the classes Reptilia and Mammalia, by perceived physical similarities, shared behavioural traits, similar geographical distribution or shared habitats.

It should be noted that common names are not always an indication of family group. For example, catfish, of the order Siluriformes, are one of the most diverse vertebrate orders in the world, consisting of more than 30 recognized families. Within family groups, the relationships between members is hotly contested, and some freshwater biologists advocate using 'superfamilies' as a more accurate means of organization. Extensive groups such as catfish and cichlids (of the family Cichlidae) are found all over the world, so an exhaustive treatment would be impossible in a book of this size. Instead, the directory profiles the more interesting species found on different continents.

This part of the book offers an accessible introduction to the world of freshwater fish and other creatures. Biological terms, where included, are defined with their first mention in the text, or in the glossary at the back of the book. There is also an index of species, listing common and Latin names.

Main headings
The main headings identify the group, or groups, of organisms covered on the following pages. Groupings are based on one or several of a number of factors, including classificatory groups, physical similarities, or shared geography or freshwater habitat.

Introductory text
A few lines of general text introduce the group and describe some of its shared characteristics. Where the treatment of a group is more extensive than usual, such as with cichlids (*below*), the information accumulates over several pages.

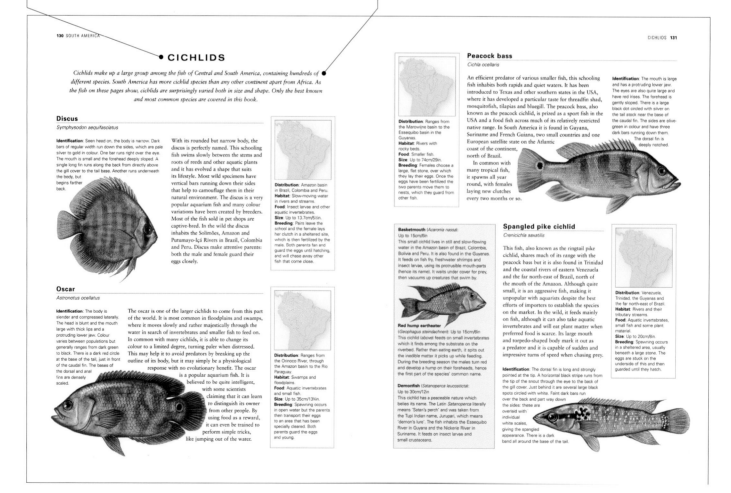

Species name
The common English language name is given first, with the internationally accepted scientific name (pairing generic and species names) underneath. Alternative common names may be noted in the description.

Identification
This text builds a physical profile of the species, including details, such as variations in colour or fin shape, that may not be visible in the illustration.

Description
The main text supplies useful information on the behavioural traits of the animal, such as its predatory or reproductive habits. This behaviour may be noted as typical of its group, or as quite specific to that species.

Distribution map
Based on reported sightings, the maps indicate where, in the broadest sense, the species is likely to occur. Ranges may be quite specific to a certain body of water, or may reflect a wider continental distribution.

Oscar
Astronotus ocellatus

Identification: The body is slender and compressed laterally. The head is blunt and the mouth large with thick lips and a protruding lower jaw. Colour varies between populations but generally ranges from dark green to black. There is a dark red circle at the base of the tail, just in front of the caudal fin. The bases of the dorsal and anal fins are densely scaled.

The oscar is one of the larger cichlids to come from this part of the world. It is most common in floodplains and swamps, where it moves slowly and rather majestically through the water in search of invertebrates and smaller fish to feed on. In common with many cichlids, it is able to change its colour to a limited degree, turning paler when distressed. This may help it to avoid predators by breaking up the outline of its body, but it may simply be a physiological response with no evolutionary benefit. The oscar is a popular aquarium fish. It is believed to be quite intelligent, with some scientists claiming that it can learn to distinguish its owner from other people. By using food as a reward, it can even be trained to perform simple tricks, like jumping out of the water.

Distribution: Ranges from the Orinoco River, through the Amazon basin to the Rio Paraguay.
Habitat: Swamps and floodplains.
Food: Aquatic invertebrates and small fish.
Size: Up to 35cm/13¾in.
Breeding: Spawning occurs in open water but the parents then transport their eggs to an area that has been specially cleared. Both parents guard the eggs and young.

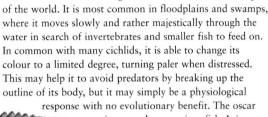

Illustration
All species have been drawn to a uniform size to maximize visual detail. They do not reflect actual size; this information is given in the Factfile data panel accompanying each profile.

Factfile data
This formulaic panel lists the major categories of data often used to identify a species, and gives relevant information where available. An expansion of the treatment of data in this panel appears below.

Typical panel entry
Features species name (common and scientific), maximum size within adult range, and a brief general description of anatomy and behaviour. Directionals are given to clarify which species is illustrated.

Other features of the directory

All descriptions of species are accompanied by a Factfile data panel, which acts as a quick-reference source of diagnostic information. In addition, a tinted panel provides concise profiles of several species related to the main animals described. In a handful of cases, these tinted panels offer fuller information about the ecology of the animal group as a whole.

Food
Identifies the primary food source of the animal.

Size
A species may exhibit quite a range of sizes; this data aims to reflect the maximum end of the adult size range. Where there is a marked discrepancy in the sizes of the male and female of the species, this is stated.

Distribution: Ranges from the Orinoco River, through the Amazon basin to the Rio Paraguay.
Habitat: Swamps and floodplains.
Food: Aquatic invertebrates and small fish.
Size: Up to 35cm/13¾in.
Breeding: Spawning occurs in open water but the parents then transport their eggs to an area that has been specially cleared. Both parents guard the eggs and young.

Distribution
Summarizes the range given in the accompanying map.

Habitat
Gives a broad description of the physical environment favoured by the animal.

Breeding
Summarizes the key aspects of the animal's breeding behaviour, where known.

Basketmouth (*Acaronia nassa*): Up to 15cm/6in
This small cichlid lives in still and slow-flowing water in the Amazon basin of Brazil, Colombia, Bolivia and Peru. It is also found in the Guyanas. It feeds on fish fry, freshwater shrimps and insect larvae, using its protrusible mouth-parts (hence its name). It waits under cover for prey, then vacuums up creatures that swim by.

Red hump eartheater
(*Geophagus steindachneri*): Up to 15cm/6in
This cichlid (*above*) feeds on small invertebrates which it finds among the substrate on the riverbed. Rather than eating earth, it spits out the inedible matter it picks up while feeding. During the breeding season the males turn red and develop a hump on their foreheads, hence the first part of the species' common name.

Demonfish (*Satanoperca leucosticta*): Up to 30cm/12in
This cichlid has a peaceable nature which belies its name. The Latin *Satanoperca* literally means 'Satan's perch' and was taken from the Tupi Indian name, Jurupari, which means 'demon's lure'. The fish inhabits the Essequibo River in Guyana and the Nickerie River in Suriname. It feeds on insect larvae and small crustaceans.

NORTH AMERICA

Stretching from the Arctic Circle to south of the Tropic of Cancer, North America contains a huge variety of freshwater habitats. The fish and other freshwater creatures of this continent have evolved to live in habitats ranging from ice-covered lakes to salty desert springs, from rushing mountain streams to stagnant, steamy swamps.

The astonishingly varied aquatic life of this continent ranges from tiny, short-lived insect-eaters, such as the mosquitofish, to huge predators and primeval monsters, such as the white sturgeon and alligator gar. Some species are found almost across the whole continent, while others are unique to individual rivers or springs. Among their number they include some of the most numerous of all freshwater vertebrates, and also some of the rarest.

North America's fish share their homes with other weird and wonderful animals, creatures such as the hellbender – a giant salamander that breathes through its skin – and its relatives, the mudpuppy, axolotl and various sirens. Some of these animals prey on the fish around them. Others compete with them for food or are themselves preyed upon by larger fish.

*Above, left to right: Alligator gar (*Atractosteus spatula*); mosquito fish (*Gambusia affinis*); hellbender (*Cryptobranchus alleganiensis*).*
Right: Map of North America, showing major freshwater routes and bodies of water.

GREENLAND

Arctic Ocean

Queen Elizabeth Islands

Baffin Bay

Beaufort Sea

Victoria
Island

Baffin
Island

Arctic Circle

MacKenzie R

Great Bear Lake

Selawik Lake

Yukon R

Yukon R

ALASKA

Yukon R

Great Slave Lake

Hudson Bay

Iliamna Lake

Lake Athabasca

Bering Sea

Gulf of
Alaska

CANADA

Smallwood
Reservoir

Fraser R

Saskatchewan R

Lake Manitoba

Lake Winnipeg

Manicouagan
Reservoir

S Saskatchewan R

Lake Nipigon

Columbia R

Missouri R

Lake Superior

Ottawa R

Lake Huron

Lake Ontario

Lake Michigan

Lake Erie

Great Salt
Lake

UNITED STATES

Colorado R

Arkansas R

Ohio R

Red R

Tennessee R

Mississippi R

Atlantic

Ocean

Pacific Ocean

Rio Grande R

Hawaiian Islands

Gulf
of
Mexico

THE BAHAMAS

MEXICO

CUBA

DOMINICAN
REPUBLIC

HAITI

VIRGIN ISLANDS

JAMAICA

PUERTO
RICO

ANTIGUA

DOMINICA

Guadeloupe

Martinique

St. Lucia

Caribbean Sea

Grenada

St. Vincent

KIRIBATI

Trinidad and Tobago

Galapagos Islands

Niue

French Polynesia

LAMPREYS AND STURGEONS

Lampreys and sturgeons include some of the most primitive of all freshwater fish. Lampreys predate even the sharks and rays in evolutionary terms. They have large eyes, one nostril on the top of the head, seven gills on each side and no pectoral fins. Sturgeons are primitive bony fish, with skeletons made partly from cartilage, partly from bone. Their flesh is edible and their roe is used to produce caviar.

American brook lamprey

Lampetra appendix

Lampreys are primitive fish comprising the last living relatives of some of the first fish to appear on Earth. Unlike other fish, they lack jaws and instead have sucker-shaped mouths surrounded by rings of teeth. Many lampreys are predatory or parasitic, clinging to the sides of other fish and using their teeth to slice out divots of flesh. The American brook lamprey, however, is different. Larvae feed by burrowing into sand and silt and filtering tiny organisms, often in slow-water areas of the streams where they live. The adults do not feed at all, and only live long enough to spawn before dying.

Identification: A long, eel-like body with two distinct dorsal fins and a black stripe at the base of them. The oral disc is narrower than the rest of the head. Teeth are blunt rather than sharp and pointed, as they are in predatory or parasitic species.

Distribution: Atlantic river basins south of St Lawrence River, Quebec. Also Great Lakes and Mississippi River basin.
Habitat: Gravel or sandy riffles and runs of clear-water streams.
Food: Protozoans, algae and other microorganisms.
Size: Up to 35cm/13¾in.
Breeding: Gravelly areas. Female lays eggs in saucer-shaped nest, built by the male using his mouth.

White sturgeon

Acipenser transmontanus

One of the biggest freshwater fish in the world – and North America's biggest – the white sturgeon has been known to reach 6.1m/20ft in length, and weigh as much as 630kg/1389lbs (almost three-quarters of a ton). Because of its great size, this fish is hard to miss but it is also very rare. As a top predator, it is naturally less common than many smaller species, but pressure from anglers, combined with the construction of dams in some of the rivers where it lives and spawns, have caused it to decline in parts of its range. River pollution is also thought to have had an impact on the species.

Identification: Unmistakably a member of the sturgeon family (Acipenseridae). Grey or brownish above, with a pale belly. This species is distinguished by having four barbels very close to the snout tip. The barbels are usually closer to the snout tip than they are to the mouth. The snouts of young fish are quite sharp but become more blunt with age.

Distribution: Pacific coast, coastal rivers from Alaska to central California. Introduced into lower Colorado River.
Habitat: Estuaries of large rivers. Colorado River population is landlocked.
Food: Opportunistic – wide range of fish and aquatic invertebrates.
Size: Up to 6.1m/20ft.
Breeding: Adults migrate upstream to breed. Eggs and sperm released into open water during times of peak river flow.

Distribution: Lakes, Atlantic-draining rivers from Hudson Bay through Mississippi drainages to Alabama. Recorded Great Lakes and large lakes in New York State and Vermont.
Habitat: Gravel bottoms of large, clear rivers and lakes.
Food: Smaller fish and aquatic invertebrates.
Size: Up to 2.7m/9ft.
Breeding: Pebbly areas with no mud. No nests – sperm and eggs released into water.

Lake sturgeon

Acipenser fulvescens

This fish resembles the white sturgeon, but is smaller in size and occupies a different habitat range. Like all sturgeons, it has rows of bony plates (scutes) running down its back, belly and the sides of its body. These scutes protect the fish against predators, particularly when they are young, as they make the fish unpalatable. Adult lake sturgeon migrate to the pebbly shores of lakes to breed, where one female may lay as many as 3 million eggs in a single season. Despite being smaller than the white sturgeon, this fish can still reach 1.8m/6ft long and weigh 90kg/198lb on average, and much larger individuals have been recorded over the years.

Identification: The body is olive-brown to grey above and white below. The barbels are farther back than in white sturgeon, lying almost beneath the nostrils. The scutes on the back and sides are the same colour as the skin.

Pacific lamprey (*Lampetra tridentata*): Up to 76cm/30in
As its name suggests, this parasitic lamprey spends most of its life in the Pacific Ocean. However, it also enters the clear coastal rivers and streams of North America's Pacific seaboard to breed. It resembles the American brook lamprey but it has sharper teeth and an oral disc that is wider than the rest of its head. It is the only North American species of lamprey that is known to spawn more than once in its lifetime.

Chestnut lamprey (*Ichthyomyzon castaneus*): Up to 38cm/15in
This freshwater lamprey is most easily recognized by its colour, which also gives it its name, being yellow or tan above and white to light olive-yellow below. Also a parasitic species, it lives in Atlantic-draining rivers and streams, and in lakes along their courses, including the Great Lakes.

Shortnose sturgeon (*Acipenser brevirostrum*): Up to 1.1m/3.6ft
The common name of this species (*above*) highlights its distinguishing feature, the one by which it is most easily separated from its relatives. It inhabits the estuaries and bays of the Atlantic coast from New Brunswick to Florida, travelling up coastal rivers to spawn. It is listed as Vulnerable by the IUCN and is protected by law throughout its range.

Pallid sturgeon

Scaphirhynchus albus

This sturgeon is found in large, silty rivers with swift currents. It was only identified as a separate species in 1905 and is now listed as Endangered by the IUCN. The pallid sturgeon is a larger relative of the similar-looking and more common shovelnose sturgeon (*Scaphirhynchus platorynchus*), which also lives in the Mississippi River basin. It has a flattened, shovel-shaped snout that it uses to stir up the sediment to find its prey. It is one of the largest fish found in this river basin, weighing as much as 36kg/80lb. By contrast, the shovelnose sturgeon rarely exceeds 2.25kg/5lb. Like all sturgeons, it is a long-lived fish, with individuals often exceeding 50 years in age.

Distribution: Main channels of Missouri River and lower Mississippi River.
Habitat: Deep river channels, usually in fast-flowing, turbid water over sand or gravel.
Food: Other fish and aquatic invertebrates.
Size: Up to 1.85m/6ft.
Breeding: Over gravel or other hard surfaces. Eggs take 5–8 days to hatch. Adults may go for as long as 10 years between spawnings, although most breed every year or two.
Status: Endangered.

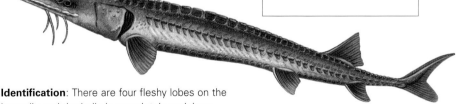

Identification: There are four fleshy lobes on the lower lip and the belly is completely scaleless. The snout is long and flattened. The bases of the outer barbels are usually positioned farther down the snout than those of the inner barbels.

PADDLEFISH, GARS AND BOWFIN

Like the sturgeons, these are among the most primitive of all bony fish. They are all predators, apart from the paddlefish, which is a filter feeder. Gars are easily distinguished from other freshwater species because they have long, slender, cylindrical bodies, long snouts and diamond-shaped interlocking (ganoid) scales. The bowfin is the only surviving member of the ancient family Amiidae.

Paddlefish

Polyodon spathula

This is surely one of the most bizarre-looking of all North America's animals. Its paddle-shaped snout is covered with electro-receptors to help locate swarms of planktonic animals. The fish then feeds by swimming through these swarms with its large mouth wide open, sifting the tiny animals from the water using its gill rakers. Its snout also helps the fish find its way during breeding migrations. The paddlefish is known to be quite long-lived, with some individuals reaching 55 years in the wild. The IUCN now lists the species as Vulnerable.

Identification: An unmistakable long, paddle-shaped snout, which gives this species one of its other common names, 'duck-bill cat'. Dark grey coloration on back and flanks with paler belly. The gill cover has a long, pointed flap on its rear edge. Except for the shape of the head, the body resembles that of a shark.

Distribution: Mississippi River basin, spanning 22 states.
Habitat: Deep, slow-moving water in large rivers. Migrate into areas with sand or gavel bars to breed.
Food: Plankton.
Size: Up to 2.2m/7.2ft.
Breeding: In open water. Several males release sperm while single female releases eggs. Eggs stick to gravel or sand, then develop.
Status: Vulnerable.

Alligator gar

Atractosteus spatula

With its flattened, broad snout and double row of slender teeth in the upper jaw, the alligator gar is well-named. This large fish is a formidable predator, ingesting anything from crustaceans to waterfowl and young alligators, though it feeds mostly on other fish. In common with other gars, the alligator gar is able to gulp air to obtain oxygen when levels in the water become too low. It is one of North America's biggest freshwater fish – the largest ever caught was in the St Francis River in Arkansas, and weighed a massive 159kg/350lb. Its eggs are bright red in colour, and poisonous if eaten.

Identification: Size distinguishes this gar from its relatives. It may also be identified by the relatively short and broad snout. The upper jaw has two rows of fang-like teeth. Young have a light-coloured stripe running along their backs from the tip of the snout to the caudal fin.

Distribution: Gulf coastal plain from Florida to Mexico, Mississippi River basin.
Habitat: Slow-moving large rivers, reservoirs, oxbow lakes and bayous.
Food: Fish, large aquatic invertebrates, aquatic mammals and reptiles, waterfowl, amphibians.
Size: Up to 3m/10ft.
Breeding: Eggs released into water at the same time as males (often several) release sperm. Eggs sink and stick to substrate.

Spotted gar

Lepisosteus oculatus

Somewhat smaller than the alligator gar, the spotted gar is nevertheless a fierce and efficient predator of other fish. Although it may sometimes appear sluggish and lazy, it is capable of extremely rapid movements when it comes to capturing prey, usually with a quick sideways lunge. It prefers slow-moving or still water with an abundance of aquatic plants, which provide its well-camouflaged body with cover and a home for its eggs, which are green and sticky and attach themselves to the leaves of these plants. The spotted gar may often be seen basking at the water's surface on warm days and it can sometimes be heard gulping air.

Identification: Numerous olive-brown to black spots all over the body, head and fins. The snout is quite long with the upper jaw longer than the rest of the head. The upper jaw contains just one row of teeth.

Distribution: Widespread central Texas to west Florida. Mississippi basin, lower Ohio River, Lake Erie, south Lake Michigan drainages.
Habitat: Quiet pools and backwaters, slow-flowing rivers, oxbow lakes, swamps, ditches with vegetation.
Food: Fish and aquatic invertebrates.
Size: Up to 1.1m/3.6ft.
Breeding: Eggs released into shallow, slow-flowing water with rich vegetation.

Florida gar (*Lepisosteus platyrhincus*):
Up to 76cm/30in
This fish is common in the lakes, canals and lowland streams of the state after which it is named. It closely resembles the spotted gar, with black spots over its body and fins, but it has a shorter, broader snout. The Florida gar feeds on aquatic invertebrates and small fish. It often hunts by stealth, floating still near the surface like a stick and waiting for prey to swim into range before suddenly striking.

Shortnose gar (*Lepisosteus platostomus*):
Up to 83cm/32¾in
This species is found in the Mississippi basin and Lake Michigan drainages. It resembles the Florida gar, but lacks spots on the bulk of its body. It often uses submerged logs as a cover from which to launch its sudden, surprise attacks on smaller fish.

Longnose gar (*Lepisosteus osseus*):
Up to 1.8m/6ft
As its name suggests, the longnose gar (*above*) has a longer snout than other species, more than twice as long as the rest of its head. It is sometimes found swimming in small groups with its cousin, the shortnose gar. Large numbers are found in Texas and all along the Mississippi River. In common with other gars, this species has tough, interlocking scales, which protect it from the attentions of most other predators.

Bowfin

Amia calva

The bowfin is the last living member of a very ancient family of fish that was widespread in the Mesozoic era. It gets its name from the long dorsal fin extending along more than half the length of its back. In common with gars and sturgeons, bowfins have a skeleton that is partly cartilage and partly bone. Bowfins are able to obtain oxygen by using their swim bladders and gills. Every few minutes this fish will rise to the surface and breathe. The air passes into the highly vascularized swim bladder which acts as a kind of primitive lung. During spawning, the male bowfin gathers water plants by biting them off at the base, then uses these to prepare a simple nest for the eggs.

Identification: A long, almost cylindrical body. The nostrils are tubular and the pectoral, pelvic and caudal fins are rounded. The back and sides are olive coloured, often with dark mottling.

Distribution: From upper St Lawrence River and Great Lakes down south to Florida and southern Texas. Introduced in small numbers elsewhere.
Habitat: Lakes and large slow-moving rivers with abundant vegetation.
Food: Fish and aquatic invertebrates.
Size: Up to 1.1m/3.6ft.
Breeding: Shallow waters with heavy vegetation. Male builds simple plant nest which may be visited by several females. Male guards nest aggressively.

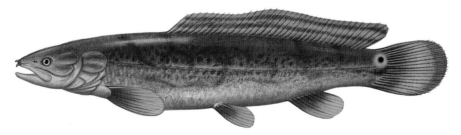

SALMON AND TROUT

Salmon and trout are among the most important of North America's freshwater fish, providing a livelihood for fishermen and food for a wide range of animals. Salmon have a special cultural meaning for many Northern Pacific coastal dwellers – some tribes have a ceremony to honour their annual return – and the grizzly bears drawn to rivers during the salmon migration are one of the world's great wildlife spectacles.

Sockeye salmon

Oncorhynchus nerka

Adult sockeye salmon can be seen crowding the western seaboard's rivers every autumn as they scramble upstream to spawn. Females dig nests in the gravelly riverbed for eggs and sperm, cover them over and then move upstream to dig more. Once they have spawned, the adults die; their rotting bodies add valuable nutrients to the waters where their eggs will later hatch. The rivers where eggs are laid tend to have lakes in their watershed. After hatching, the young make their way down to these lakes, where they spend the first few years of their lives before migrating to the sea. Some develop into adults in these lakes and never leave. They are known as 'kokanee'.

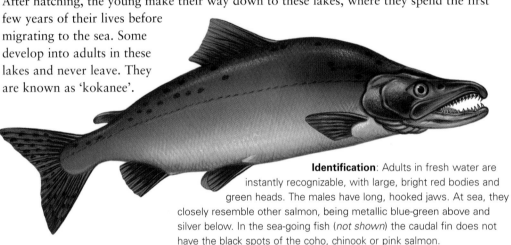

Distribution: Arctic and Pacific rivers; associated lakes from Alaska to the Sacramento River, California. More common in northern part of its range.
Habitat: Lakes and the open ocean.
Food: Plankton sieved from water with gill rakers. Also small invertebrates.
Size: Up to 84cm/33in.
Breeding: Female creates 3–5 nests in riverbed, attended by male.

Identification: Adults in fresh water are instantly recognizable, with large, bright red bodies and green heads. The males have long, hooked jaws. At sea, they closely resemble other salmon, being metallic blue-green above and silver below. In the sea-going fish (*not shown*) the caudal fin does not have the black spots of the coho, chinook or pink salmon.

Coho salmon

Oncorhynchus kisutch

This species occupies a similar range to the sockeye salmon and is superficially similar, apart from its coloration. Like the sockeye, the coho salmon spends most of its adult life in the ocean and returns to rivers along North America's Pacific coast to spawn. At this time, both sexes develop hooked jaws, but these are more noticeable in the males. Their bodies also change colour when they leave the sea. Most fish leave when they are three years old, searching for the rivers where they hatched. A few precocious males, known as 'jacks', will return to spawn when they are just two years old.

Identification: Similar to the chinook, but smaller. Cohos also have whitish gums on the lower jaw and small spots on the upper lobe of the caudal fin. At sea, the body is metallic blue above and silver below (hence the alternative name – silver salmon). When leaving to breed, the body changes to darker shades of green and brown. Breeding males have bright red sides, while those of the females are pinkish.

Distribution: Arctic and Pacific rivers, estuaries from Alaska to Monterey Bay, California.
Habitat: The open ocean, clear rivers and streams.
Food: Plankton, crustaceans and freshwater insects.
Size: Up to 98cm/38½in.
Breeding: Female lays eggs in several nests ('redds') which hatch after 6–7 weeks. Maturing young migrate to the sea.
Status: Not listed by IUCN but declining.

Chinook salmon

Oncorhynchus tshawytscha

This splendid fish, also commonly known as the king salmon, is the biggest North American salmon of all. Adults often exceed 18kg/40lb in weight and individuals as large as 57kg/126lb have been recorded. The name 'chinook' originated among the indigenous Americans of Alaska and Siberia, where it is also found. Unlike most other salmon, chinooks migrate upstream to spawn at various times of the year. Even within a single river there may be as many as four distinct spawning migrations, or runs. Most chinooks remain at sea for between one and six years before returning to spawn and then dying. Some 'jacks' (*see* coho salmon, *opposite*) live for just a few months in salt water before making their way back upstream to breed.

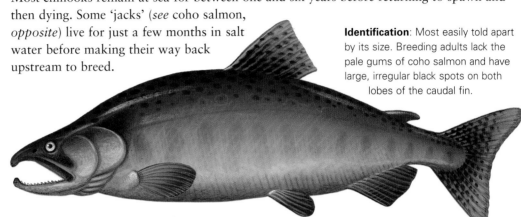

Distribution: Arctic and Pacific drainages from Alaska to California's Ventura River. Introduced to Great Lakes.
Habitat: Rivers and lakes.
Food: Young: aquatic insects, invertebrates; adults: other fish.
Size: Up to 1.47m/4.8ft.
Breeding: Female builds single redd with 4–5 'nesting pockets', then guards eggs until death (up to a month).
Status: Not listed but under threat in many native rivers.

Identification: Most easily told apart by its size. Breeding adults lack the pale gums of coho salmon and have large, irregular black spots on both lobes of the caudal fin.

Pink salmon (*Oncorhynchus gorbuscha*):
Up to 76cm/30in
Both sexes of this salmon have pink sides, which gives the species its name. Large, mostly oval black spots can be found on its back and both lobes of the caudal fin, and its underside is almost white. Breeding males have humped backs and long, hooked jaws. It is native to Pacific rivers and introduced to the Great Lakes. It also occurs in Asian rivers and the western Pacific, as far south as the Sea of Japan.

Chum salmon (*Oncorhynchus keta*):
Up to 1m/3.3ft
Like other Pacific salmon, the chum salmon spends most of its life at sea. Shoals migrate up rivers to spawn from winter to early spring. Unlike other Pacific salmon, breeding males have relatively short hooked jaws and resemble female coho salmon. Chum salmon are sometimes called dog salmon or keta.

Gila trout (*Oncorhynchus gilae*):
Up to 32cm/12½in
This species (*above*) resembles the cutthroat trout, but its 'cutthroat' mark is yellow not red. It is named for the Gila river system in Arizona and New Mexico, its native home. It prefers clear mountain headwaters and lakes and is protected throughout its range as a threatened species.

Cutthroat trout

Oncorhynchus clarki

This species, familiar to anglers across much of the western USA, is native to Pacific rivers but it has also been widely introduced elsewhere. Historically it occurred as 14 distinct subspecies, but these have been blurred as introductions have caused them to mix through interbreeding. In most of its range, the cutthroat trout is migratory, spending almost all of its adult life at sea and swimming upstream only to breed in fresh water. But some populations never leave the rivers in which they were spawned. The species varies widely both in size and coloration. In some places it rarely exceeds 15cm/6in in length, while in others it may reach almost 1m/3.25ft.

Identification: The defining feature is the red 'cutthroat' mark across the neck. Most individuals are heavily spotted.

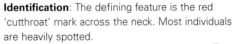

Distribution: Pacific rivers from Alaska to Eel River, California. Also Rocky Mountains. Widely introduced elsewhere.
Habitat: Rivers.
Food: Freshwater insects, other invertebrates and small fish.
Size: Up to 99cm/39in.
Breeding: Adults migrate from the sea into rivers to spawn. Female lays up to 1,700 eggs in shallow nest. Eggs hatch within 7 weeks.

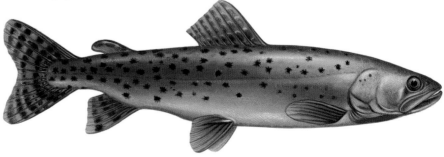

TROUT, DOLLY VARDEN AND GRAYLING

These fish, like their relatives the salmon, are active predators, although they tend to hunt smaller prey. They also include some of North America's most popular game fish but, far from being detrimental to their survival, their popularity with anglers has caused many of these species to spread, as humans have introduced them to new freshwater habitats around the globe.

Rainbow trout

Oncorhynchus mykiss

This popular game and food fish has been introduced into Britain and other parts of the world. In its native North America it is found in lakes, rivers and streams. In some areas of its range it is migratory, spending part of its adult life at sea. The rainbow trout changes colour in salt water. Marine fish are silvery and known as 'steelheads', while interior populations are often called redband trout. Unlike Pacific salmon, most rainbow trout survive spawning and return to lay their eggs year after year. Adults may live as long as 11 years.

Identification: Colour varies hugely. Distinguishing features include a pink to red stripe on the side (except at sea) and radiating rows of black spots on the caudal fin. All individuals have small, irregular spots on the back, and on the dorsal and adipose fins.

Distribution: Universal in North America. Native to eastern Pacific: Alaska to Baja Peninsula, Mexico. **Habitat**: Seas, clear-water rivers, streams and lakes. **Food**: Young: zooplankton; adults: aquatic invertebrates, fish eggs, small fishes (including other trout). **Size**: Up to 1.14m/3.75ft. **Breeding**: Steelheads mature sexually as they migrate upstream. Eggs laid in shallow redds.

Brook trout

Salvelinus fontinalis

Identification: Wavy cream or light green lines on the back and dorsal fin. The caudal fin is only slightly forked and lacks the spots found on many other trout species. The few spots on the fish's side are surrounded by blue halos.

As its name suggests, this fish is an inhabitant of cool, clear, spring-fed streams and pools. Unlike most other trout, which may travel long distances up and down rivers, brook trout are relatively stationary and can often be found near the same spot for most of their lives. Larger fish tend to stick to deep pools, often hiding under cover of large rocks, logs or overhanging banks, and only leaving these spots briefly to feed in shallower waters. This fish is one of the more colourful of the trout species, and breeding males are particularly brightly coloured, turning vivid orange-red along their sides. The brook trout is the state fish of Michigan, where it is commonly found.

Distribution: Native to most of eastern Canada from Newfoundland to Hudson Bay (west side), Great Lakes and Mississippi River basin. Widely introduced North America and elsewhere. **Habitat**: Cool, clear, well-oxygenated small to medium rivers and lakes. **Food**: Aquatic invertebrates, small fish and amphibians. **Size**: Up to 70cm/27½in. **Breeding**: Female digs redd with tail, lays up to 400 eggs. Attendant male fertilizes.

Dolly Varden

Salvelinus malma

The Dolly Varden is a close relative of the more widespread Arctic charr, which occurs throughout Europe, Russia, Alaska and parts of northern Canada. However, the former is distinguishable by having smaller spots on its sides, the largest of which are usually smaller than the pupil of its eye. These spots are thought to have given the fish its unusual name. The story goes that the name was suggested to fishermen in the 1870s by a young lady who thought that the fish's speckled appearance resembled her new patterned dress. The cut of the dress, which was fashionable at the time, was known as the 'Dolly Varden'.

Distribution: Arctic and North-east Pacific rivers from Alaska to Puget Sound, Washington. Also found in eastern Asia.
Habitat: Deep runs and river pools. Some lakes and at sea.
Food: Aquatic invertebrates, fish eggs and small fish.
Size: Up to 63cm/25in.
Breeding: Female digs nest in the gravel, lays several batches of eggs, then covers them. Both sexes die shortly after spawning.

Identification: Similar to the Arctic charr but with smaller spots and fewer gill rakers on the first gill arch (14–21 rather than 23–32). Colour can be variable, ranging from olive green to brown above, with the underside yellow, orange or spotted with red. Sea-going individuals are usually dark blue above and pale below.

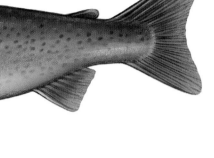

Golden trout (*Oncorhynchus aguabonita*): Up to 71cm/28in
This fish looks similar to the rainbow trout but the adult has ten obvious marks on its side, known as parr marks. These are carried over from its appearance as a young fish (parr). The golden trout is endemic to the upper Kern River basin in California, but it has been introduced to more than 300 mountain lakes and streams in some Rocky Mountain states.

Bull trout (*Salvelinus confluentus*): Up to 91cm/36in
The bull trout is similar to the Dolly Varden but has a slightly flattened and longer head, and eyes positioned higher above the mouth. It is found in deep pools in high, cold rivers and lakes. Like the Dolly Varden it is found in Arctic and Pacific rivers, but unlike its cousin never enters the sea.

Lake trout (*Salvelinus namaycush*): Up to 1.26m/4ft
The lake trout (*above*) is identified by its deeply forked caudal fin. It is native to Alaska, Canada and the Great Lakes, but it has been widely introduced into other parts of the world. It is commonly found in lakes and is restricted to them entirely in the southern part of its North American range. Farther north it is also found in the deeper waters of rivers and streams.

Arctic grayling

Thymallus arcticus

The Arctic grayling is an easily recognized member of the Salmonidae, the family that contains other graylings, salmons, charr and trout. As its name suggests, it is a northerly species that prefers colder waters. Most populations live in lakes or medium-sized to large rivers, but migrate to shallower streams to breed. Here, the males establish territories and attract females by flashing their dorsal fins. The Arctic grayling is quite a long-lived fish compared with other members of its family, often reaching 18 years old. However, it is also unusually sensitive to pollution and has now become extinct in the Great Lakes as a result of it.

Identification: An unmistakably enlarged purple to black dorsal fin, carried by both sexes, and a strongly forked caudal fin. A small mouth with fine teeth on both jaws. The body is dark blue-grey above, with silvery-grey to blue, sometimes pink, sides with scattered black spots.

Distribution: Widespread in Canadian Arctic rivers from Hudson Bay to Alaska and Pacific-draining rivers in Alberta and British Columbia. Widely introduced elsewhere. Also occurs naturally in north-eastern Asia.
Habitat: Cold, clear rivers and lakes.
Food: Aquatic insects, other invertebrates, fish eggs and other fish.
Size: Up to 76cm/30in.
Breeding: No nest – female lays eggs just above riverbed. Tail vibrations during spawning stir up sediment and partially cover eggs.

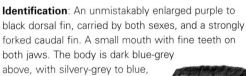

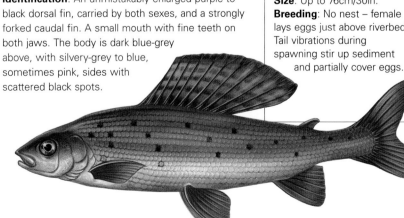

CATFISH AND BULLHEADS

All of the fish on these pages belong to the same genus, Ameiurus. Catfish are named for their long barbels – appendages that look and function very much like a cat's whiskers, amplifying the sense of touch. North American bullheads are actually catfish and are not related to the true bullheads of Europe and Asia, which are more closely related to sculpins.

White catfish

Ameiurus catus

Identification: The common name of this species is misleading. The underside is white or pale yellow, but most of the body is blue-grey to blue-black. The caudal fin is moderately forked and the pectoral spine has relatively large, saw-like teeth on its rear side.

This catfish is native to the south-eastern corner of the USA, from Florida to the Hudson River. A popular game and food fish, it has been widely introduced elsewhere in the country and has also become established in several reservoirs in Puerto Rico. It is a typical member of its family, with long barbels around its head for detecting prey and finding its way around in murky water. It generally reaches around 1.35–2.25kg/3–5lb in weight but can grow much bigger. The largest white catfish ever recorded tipped the scales at 10kg/22lb. Unlike most catfish, which tend to be largely nocturnal, this fish often feeds by day. It is extremely adaptable and will live happily in almost any freshwater habitat into which it is introduced.

Distribution: Native to Florida and eastern seaboard states as far north as New York. Widely introduced elsewhere.
Habitat: Muddy pools, backwaters, lakes and reservoirs. Also found in open channels of some large rivers.
Food: Smaller fish and aquatic invertebrates.
Size: Up to 62cm/24in.
Breeding: Both partners build large nest. Males guard eggs and young while they are still small.

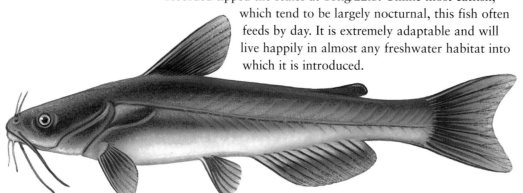

Black bullhead

Ameiurus melas

Despite its common name of bullhead, this species is in fact a close relative of the white catfish. Its native range includes the central plains of the USA, between the Appalachian and Rocky Mountains, although it has been introduced into many other places as well. The black bullhead is also known as the polliwog or the chucklehead cat. It is relatively short-lived, usually dying before it reaches six years old. Adults rarely weigh much more than 1kg/2.2lb, although some have been known to reach 4kg/8.8lb. In many parts of the world, black bullheads are sold as aquarium fish. Although they make interesting pets they are voracious predators and should be kept on their own.

Identification: As with the white catfish, the common name is misleading. The body is usually dark olive, brown or yellow-brown. The chin barbels, however, are dusky or black. The anal fin is relatively short and rounded and the caudal fin is slightly notched.

Distribution: Native to central states of USA. Also introduced to British Columbia, Alberta, Mexico, California, Arizona and Nevada.
Habitat: Muddy pools, oxbow lakes and backwaters.
Food: Plant and animal matter, including carrion.
Size: Up to 62cm/24in.
Breeding: Both partners build a nest in the mud on the bottom and guard eggs until they hatch. Areas with some cover preferred for nesting. Eggs hatch after 4–6 days.

Flat bullhead (*Ameiurus platycephalus*):
Up to 29cm/11½in
This rare fish lives in lakes, ponds, reservoirs and river pools. It has a flat head which, combined with a large blotch at the base of its dorsal fin, helps distinguish it from the similar-looking brown bullhead. Found in Georgia, North and South Carolina and Virginia.

Yellow bullhead (*Ameiurus natalis*):
Up to 47cm/18½in
This species closely resembles the black bullhead but it has yellow rather than dark-coloured barbels. It also has large, saw-like teeth on the back of its pectoral spine. This fish prefers sluggish creeks and rivers and is relatively common. Its native range stretches from New York State to northern Mexico and it has been widely introduced elsewhere.

Brown bullhead (*Ameiurus nebulosus*):
Up to 50cm/19¾in
The mottled sides of this species (*above*) are almost unique – only the flat bullhead has similar patterning. This fish is a nest-builder that guards its tadpole-like young. It is widely distributed throughout eastern North America, occurring from Florida to far north Quebec. It can tolerate pollution better than most other fish and so has remained common throughout most of its range.

Spotted bullhead

Ameiurus serracanthus

Compared with the white catfish and the black bullhead, the spotted bullhead is small. Most adults grow to just 18cm/7in long. Unlike its larger relatives, this species prefers relatively clear, fast-flowing waters, inhabiting rivers and streams with rocky or sandy bottoms. The spotted catfish can be quite beautifully patterned, making it popular with aquarium enthusiasts. In the wild it is rare wherever it is found, although it is not considered vulnerable or endangered. It feeds mainly on freshwater snails, eating far more of these than any other types of prey. This has earned it another common name – the snail cat.

Identification: The light, round spots of this catfish, combined with its small size, make it difficult to confuse with any other species. The fins have black edges and the pectoral spine has 15–20 large saw-like teeth on its rear side.

Distribution: Northern Florida drainages, southern Georgia and south-eastern Alabama.
Habitat: Deep sand or rock-bottomed pools of swift rivers and streams.
Food: Mostly aquatic snails but also other invertebrates.
Size: Up to 28cm/11in.
Breeding: Little known about habits, although breeding is thought to begin early spring.

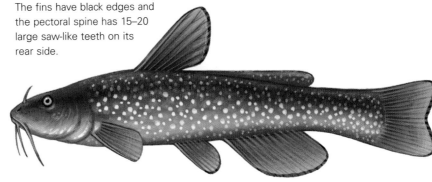

Snail bullhead

Ameiurus brunneus

Distribution: Atlantic slope drainages from the Dan River in Virginia, to the Altamaha River in Georgia. Also found St John's River in Florida.
Habitat: Clear, fast-flowing streams and rivers.
Food: Aquatic invertebrates and some plant matter.
Size: Up to 29cm/11½in.
Breeding: Little known, although small fry appear in streams in mid spring.

Slightly larger than the spotted bullhead but very similar in its general body form, the snail bullhead originates from the far south-eastern USA. Although its range is not vast, it is common almost throughout that area. Like other members of its genus, it does not shoal and is usually found singly, except when breeding. It prefers rocky runs and swift-flowing pools in clear streams and small rivers. Like the spotted bullhead, it is sometimes kept as an aquarium species and feeds mainly on snails. Although it is a relatively abundant fish, it has been little studied and there is still a lot to learn about its general biology and life history.

Identification: A flat head with a blunt, almost square-ended snout when seen in profile. Most of the fish is yellow-green to olive in colour, although the fins have narrow black edges. The anal fin is short and rounded in outline. Some populations, such as the one in the St John's River, are strongly mottled.

CATFISH, BLINDCATS, STONECAT AND MADTOMS

The channel and flathead catfish are two of North America's larger freshwater fish. Like most catfish, they spend most of their time near the bottom. The madtoms are a group of catfish characterized by their squared-off tails, which give them a tadpole-like appearance.

Channel catfish

Ictalurus punctatus

This is one of the larger and longer-lived North American catfish – some have been known to live for over 25 years and weigh more than 14kg/31lb. They prefer cooler, clearer water than many of their relatives, and are often solitary, except when breeding. The female lays up to 70,000 eggs in an excavated nest, which is then guarded fiercely and aerated by the male. The young remain in the nest until they are about a week old. They feed on planktonic animals and insect larvae, graduating to small fish as they grow older. This species is known for its white, tender flesh and is a major food fish in the southern states of the USA. It is also the most widely cultivated warm water fish in that country.

Identification: Most have relatively light-coloured bodies (the exceptions being the smaller young and very largest adults) with scattered dark spots. The anal fin is rounded with 24 to 29 rays and the caudal fin is deeply forked.

Distribution: Native to Great Lakes catchments, St Lawrence, Missouri and Mississippi River catchments. Widely introduced elsewhere. Common throughout USA.
Habitat: Fresh and salt waters. Lakes and deep pools in large rivers.
Food: Aquatic invertebrates, fish, carrion, vegetation.
Size: Up to 1.3m/4.2ft.
Breeding: Monogamous, practises lengthy courtship. Males guard and aerate nest.

Flathead catfish

Pylodictis olivaris

One of North America's larger freshwater species, older individuals may weigh as much as 45kg/100lb. Unlike other catfish, which are scavengers, the flathead feeds only on live fish, which it hunts in the slow-flowing, murky waters where it lives. The species is well named, as it has a much flatter, broader skull than other North American catfish species. It is also known, in various regions of the USA, as the yellow cat, Mississippi cat, mud cat, Opelousa cat, pied cat and shovelhead cat. Young flatheads tend to live among rocks in water with a steady current, but as they grow older they move to more still water and deeper pools. This species is the only member of its genus.

Identification: The wide, flat head distinguishes this from any other catfish. Except in very young fish, the lower jaw projects beyond the upper jaw. The body varies from pale yellow to light brown in colour and has black or brown mottling over most of its surface.

Distribution: Native ranges from lower Great Lakes, through Mississippi drainage basin to northern Mexico. Widely introduced to USA.
Habitat: Lakes, reservoirs and large, slow-flowing rivers. Common in turbid waters with logs or other debris.
Food: Young: plankton, aquatic invertebrates; adults: other fish.
Size: Up to 1.5m/5ft.
Breeding: Up to 100,000 eggs, at warm temperatures. Nests beneath logs, under banks, in underwater caves.

Widemouth blindcat

Satan eurystomus

Distribution: Subterranean rivers and streams around San Antonio, Texas.
Habitat: Water courses in deep cave systems.
Food: Cave-dwelling crayfish and other aquatic invertebrates.
Size: Up to 13.7cm/5¼in.
Breeding: As with almost all aspects of its behaviour, breeding habits are virtually unknown. Thought likely to be a nest-guarder, like most other catfish.

This fish is one of four species of blind catfish that inhabit the underground rivers and streams of North America. The only member of its genus, it was discovered in 1947 inhabiting a well and was given the Latin name Satan, after the Prince of Darkness. As with the other blindcats, it is never seen in daylight and is not a fish most people would ever come across. It lives more than a quarter of a mile underground but is thought to be relatively common in the mysterious, subterranean world it inhabits. All blindcat species lack eyes and pigment in the skin. This fish sometimes goes by the name of the Texas blind catfish. This is misleading as it is one of two species of blind catfish found in that state.

Identification: Lacks eyes and pigment. Superficially similar to the toothless blindcat (*Trogloglanis pattersoni*) with which it shares its home, but distinguished by its well-developed teeth. The similarity in appearance is due to convergent evolution: the widemouth blindcat is actually more closely related to the flathead catfish than to other blindcats.

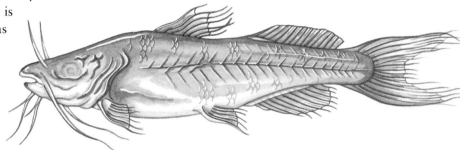

Brown madtom (*Noturus phaeus*):
Up to 15cm/5¾in
This little fish has a stout brown body that is covered with small, slightly darker dots. It lives in tributaries of the Mississippi River in Kentucky, southern Arkansas and central Louisiana, and in the Tennessee River. A typical madtom in many respects, it prefers gravelly riffles and runs near debris. It is common across most of its range.

Speckled madtom (*Noturus leptacanthus*):
Up to 9.5cm/3¾in.
This has a mostly red or yellow-brown body covered with conspicuous, randomly distributed black specks. Its fins are also blotched, with light edges. It lives in small to medium-sized rivers with sandy or rocky bottoms across the south-eastern USA, from South Carolina to Louisiana.

Tadpole madtom (*Noturus gyrinus*):
Up to 13cm/5in
With its large head and chubby body, the tadpole madtom (*above*) looks even more like a tadpole than other members of its genus. It is one of the most widespread, inhabiting lakes, rivers, backwaters and ponds all the way from Quebec and Manitoba, Canada, down to Florida and Texas. Unlike many madtoms, which live among rocks or pebbles, it is often found where the bottom is covered with mud or detritus.

Stonecat

Noturus flavus

The stonecat is one of the most commonly encountered madtoms. It is also the largest member of the group by some distance, being more than twice as long as most other madtoms. The stonecat earned its name by its tendency to hide among stones on the beds of the fast-flowing rivers it inhabits. Like other madtoms, it has poisonous dorsal and pectoral spines, which can give a nasty sting if the fish is handled or accidentally trodden on. The genus name of the madtoms, *Noturus*, means 'back tail' and refers to the fusion of the caudal fin with the adipose fin. In other fish, the adipose fin tends to sit separately on the back, in between the caudal and the dorsal.

Identification: Usually identified by its large size. Other distinguishing features include cream-white spots at the rear of its dorsal fin and on the top corner of its caudal fin. In adults, the lower jaw projects beyond the upper jaw.

Distribution: Most of the USA and southern Canada, east of Rocky Mountains, except far southern US states.
Habitat: Rubble- and boulder-filled beds of fast-flowing streams and rivers. Also found in lakes with gravel bottoms.
Food: Bottom-dwelling aquatic invertebrates.
Size: Up to 31cm/12¼in.
Breeding: Spawns spring and summer. Female lays eggs in a cavity between rocks and the male fertilizes them. Egg mass is guarded by both parents.

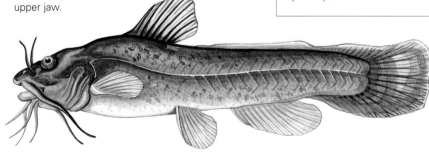

MADTOMS

Although these fish are often overlooked by anglers and thought to be of little interest because of their small size and nocturnal behaviour, they play a crucial role in the ecosystems of rivers and streams, feeding on insect larvae and in turn providing food sources for otters, herons and other creatures. Madtoms are the smallest members of the family Ictaluridae, which includes almost all North American catfish.

Slender madtom

Noturus exilis

Well camouflaged and nocturnal, the slender madtom is rarely seen. By day it spends most of its time hidden beneath rocks and boulders in clear, swift streams, emerging only once darkness has fallen to scour the bottom for caddisfly larvae and other small invertebrates. When the fish is out in the open, it is capable of sudden bursts of speed to evade predators, and is agile and slim enough to slip out of sight in a moment. These madtoms prefer shallow water, less than a foot deep, but often move to deeper pools in the heat of the summer. The slender madtom spawns in late May and June, the females laying their sticky egg masses in sheltered spots beneath rocks. The newly hatched young bunch together for the first few days.

Identification: Similar to other madtoms but generally narrower than most. Thick black borders on the yellowish dorsal, anal and caudal fins. The body is generally yellow-brown to grey-black, with a large, yellow spot on the nape, in front of the dorsal fin.

Distribution: Cumberland, Green and Tennessee River drainages and upper Mississippi basin.
Habitat: Clear, fast-flowing streams and small rivers.
Food: Insect larvae and other aquatic invertebrates. Filamentous algae.
Size: Up to 15cm/5¾in.
Breeding: Female produces egg clusters (150–200 eggs) in a large sticky mass, which sticks to the undersides of rocks.

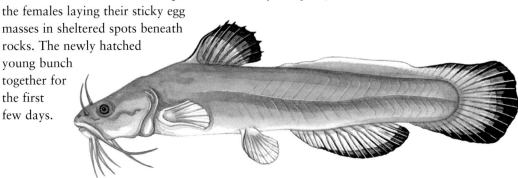

Least madtom

Noturus hildebrandi

Identification: The small size is usually enough to identify this fish. However, it does have distinguishing body features which separate it from the young of other species. The adipose fin (which is fused with the dorsal fin) is white in colour or clear and the short pectoral spine has small teeth on its front edge.

This is one of the smallest madtoms. Only the pygmy madtom (*Noturus stanauli*, not shown), which has a distinctive white snout, is smaller. The least madtom inhabits relatively fast-flowing, lowland rivers and is often found around woody debris, where it finds both cover and food. It is split into two subspecies, *Noturus hildebrandi lautus*, which occurs in the Forked Deer, Obion and Hatchie Rivers in western Kentucky and Tennessee, and *N. h. hildebrandi*, which is found in the Bayou Pierre and Homochitto River in southern Mississippi. A short-lived species, even by the standards of most small fish, adults breed only once – during their second summer – and both sexes die within a few months of spawning.

Distribution: Tributaries of Mississippi River from Homochitto River, southern Mississippi, to North Fork Obion River, south-west Kentucky.
Habitat: Clear lowland streams and small rivers with rocky or sandy bottoms.
Food: Insect larvae and other small aquatic invertebrates.
Size: Up to 7cm/2½in.
Breeding: Beneath rocks in June or July. Female produces up to 38 eggs. Both sexes die a few months after spawning.

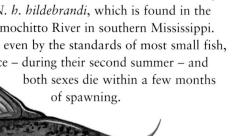

Smoky madtom

Noturus baileyi

Madtoms are small fish that feed on abundant food and, as a result, they tend to be common. The smoky madtom, however, is so rare that it is protected as an endangered species and is listed as Critically Endangered by the IUCN. Its scarcity is due mainly to its very limited range. The entire species inhabits a single creek in the Little Tennessee River system. The population that once lived in a second, nearby creek has recently become extinct. The smoky madtom closely resembles the least madtom and has a similar lifestyle, hunting for insect larvae on the bed of the stream where it lives. Although it is sometimes seen by day, it tends to be nocturnal in its habits.

Identification: This small fish is mostly olive brown on the back and sides, with four yellow saddles across its back, the front saddle usually being very small. The adipose fin has a dark central band.

Distribution: Citico Creek, Little Tennessee River system in Monroe County, Tennessee. Previously occurred also in Abrams Creek, Tennessee.
Habitat: Clear, fast-flowing water over rocks and gravel.
Food: Insect larvae and other small aquatic invertebrates.
Size: Up to 7.5cm/3in.
Breeding: Thought to be similar to that of the least madtom.
Status: Critically Endangered.

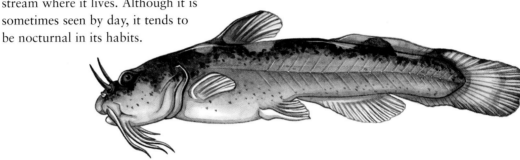

Caddo madtom (*Noturus taylori*):
Up to 7.7cm/3in
This species has a small range – only the Caddo, Ouachita and Little Missouri Rivers of south-west Arizona. It is listed as Vulnerable (IUCN). Its slender body resembles that of the smoky madtom in almost all but colour. The caddo is yellow to dark brown above with four darker brown saddles. Its dorsal fin has a black tip and its caudal fin is more rounded.

Ozark Madtom (*Noturus albater*):
Up to 12cm/4¾in
This little fish has a stout, mottled body and a short head. The feature which separates it from other madtoms is the upper white edge on its caudal fin. It inhabits the upper White and St. Francis River drainages in the Arkansas and Missouri uplands, and prefers clear, fast-flowing water. It is larger than most of its relatives.

Mountain madtom (*Noturus eleutherus*):
Up to 13cm/5in
The mountain madtom (*above*) is found in the rivers of Alabama, Arkansas, Georgia, Missouri, Oklahoma, Pennsylvania and Tennessee. By day, it can be found among woody debris or thick vegetation in or near fast-flowing water over rocks. It feeds mainly on insect larvae, which it hunts for among the rocks at night, returning to the shelter of its favourite patch before dawn.

Checkered madtom

Noturus flavater

Quite unique among madtom species, the clear, striped patterning of the checkered madtom seems almost to have been painted on. Although striking, it is relatively uncommon, so while it might be easy to spot, you are unlikely to see it very often (it was not actually discovered and named until 1969). This species finds the insect larvae and other small creatures it eats among leaves and woody debris, and is usually found in areas associated with these. It is the second largest of all madtoms, after the stonecat, and prefers slightly deeper water than the majority of its relatives. It shares its Arkansas freshwater habitats with the slender madtom and the ozark madtom (*see panel, left*), among other fish.

Distribution: Upper White River system in Arkansas and Missouri.
Habitat: Backwaters and pool banks in clear water.
Food: Insect larvae and other aquatic invertebrates, also small fish.
Size: Up to 18cm/7in.
Breeding: Lays its eggs in nests under rocks. Females lay up to 340 eggs.

Identification: The back is striped with four clear black saddles. A broad black bar stretches across the fleshy base of the caudal fin and a black blotch covers about a third of the surface area of the dorsal fin. The body is relatively large and robust.

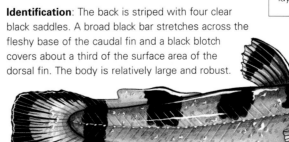

BUFFALOES AND SUCKERS

All of the fish in this section belong to the Catostomidae family. Two distinguishing features, with the exception of the bigmouth buffalo, are the location of the mouth on the underside of the head, and the large, thick lips which all catostomids possess. As a group, they are extremely numerous in North America, making up the majority of the biomass in many of the rivers and streams they live in.

Bigmouth buffalo

Ictiobus cyprinellus

It may be strange for a fish to share its name with a mammal but in this case the comparison is apt. This fish once formed huge shoals in lakes and rivers, but excessive hunting in the 19th and early 20th centuries made it extinct in many places and hugely reduced in others. Today, it is starting to regain popularity as a food fish. It is an unfussy feeder, eating everything from plankton to small fish and plants. This adaptability, and a rapid growth rate, means that it often grows to an impressive size – sometimes as much as 18kg/40lb.

Females may lay up to 750,000 eggs and spawning is very energetic as males jockey to fertilize them.

Identification: A robust, rounded appearance. The head is large and oval-shaped and the mouth sharply oblique and facing forward, a feature unique to this species among buffaloes and suckers. The front of the upper lip is nearly level with the lower edge of the eye.

Distribution: Canada's Red River to Ohio River and south through Mississippi basin to Alabama and Texas.
Habitat: Main channels, pools and backwaters of large rivers. Lakes and marshes.
Food: Plankton, aquatic plants, aquatic insects and other invertebrates, small fish and fish eggs.
Size: Up to 1m/40in.
Breeding: Mass spawnings in shallow open water.

Smallmouth buffalo

Ictiobus bubalus

Identification: A large fish with a relatively small, conical head. The nape, on adults, is strongly keeled (forming a steeply sloping ridge). As its name suggests, the mouth, which is positioned almost horizontally on the bottom edge of the head, is fairly small. The thick upper lip has distinct grooves.

Slightly smaller than the bigmouth buffalo, this is still a sizable fish. Nowadays, it is also much more common, having been spared the attentions of commercial fishermen in the past, although this trend is now changing. Unlike its cousin, which feeds in open water, the smallmouth is a bottom-feeder, stirring up sediments for shellfish and other invertebrates, which it grinds up using bony plates in its throat. Its bottom-feeding habit is reflected in the position of its mouth – like suckers and most buffaloes, it is down-turned and on the underside rather than the front of the snout. Those unfamiliar with the species often confuse it with the common carp. However, this fish can be distinguished by a lack of barbels around the mouth.

Distribution: Lake Michigan drainages. Mississippi River basin from Pennsylvania down to Gulf states, as far east as New Mexico and into Mexico itself. Introduced to Arizona.
Habitat: Main channels, pools and backwaters of rivers large and small. Also lakes and reservoirs.
Food: Shellfish and other river-bottom invertebrates.
Size: Up to 78cm/31in.
Breeding: Spring. Females lay eggs over weeds and mud. Males compete to fertilize.

Quillback

Carpiodes cyprinus

This fish, named for its pointed dorsal fin, is a bottom-feeder and prefers quieter river stretches. It is carp-like both in its shape and its habits, and this is reflected in its Latin name. *Carpiodes* means 'carp-like', while *cyprinus*, its species name, is also the name of the genus which includes the common carp. It has been described as a 'freshwater vacuum cleaner' and it does indeed eat just about anything it can find on the bottom, living or dead. Midge larvae feature high on its menu but other aquatic invertebrates, plant matter and carrion are all eaten too. It makes its way into small, slow-moving streams to breed.

Distribution: Great Lakes and their drainages, the Mississippi basin, Atlantic coast drainages and Gulf Slope drainages as far west as Pearl River, Louisiana.
Habitat: Lakes and slow-flowing rivers.
Food: Aquatic invertebrates, fish eggs, plants and carrion.
Size: Up to 66cm/26in.
Breeding: Over mud and sand in slow-flowing streams. As with other suckers, eggs develop unguarded.

Identification: The dorsal fin has an unusually long first ray. The pectoral fins are white to orange in colour. The quillback could only really be confused with the river carpsucker but, unlike that species, the upper jaw does not extend behind the front of the eye and the lower lip has no nipple at the centre of its front edge.

River carpsucker (*Carpiodes carpio*):
Up to 64cm/25in
This fish closely resembles the quillback, but it has a nipple on its lower lip and a significantly shorter first ray to its dorsal fin. Its upper jaw also extends behind the level of the front of its eye. Like the quillback, it finds food on the bottom of slow-flowing rivers and streams. It occurs commonly throughout the Mississippi River basin and Gulf Slope drainages as far south as Mexico and far west as New Mexico.

Spotted sucker (*Minytrema melanops*):
Up to 50cm/19½in
This fish has a similar body to the redhorses (*see page 72*), but it carries rows of black spots (one on each scale). It ranges from the Great Lakes and the Mississippi River basin to the Colorado River in Texas. It prefers flowing water, but is sometimes found in lakes and reservoirs.

Blue sucker (*Cycleptus elongatus*):
Up to 93cm/36½in
In centuries past, huge shoals of blue suckers (*above*) migrated up and down the Mississippi, providing a seasonal bonanza of food for Native Americans and early pioneers. Today, the fish is listed as Near Threatened by the IUCN. The many dams that have been built across the Mississippi and its tributaries have seriously impeded its migrations and hence its ability to breed.

Razorback sucker

Xyrauchen texanus

With its sharply-keeled nape, the razorback sucker is one of the oddest-looking members of this group. Its other common name is the humpback sucker. Like most other suckers, the razorback finds its food on the bottom, stirring up the sand to expose the invertebrates and other food hidden within. In the past, the species was widely hunted by Native Americans, who considered it an excellent food fish. Today, however, it is rare and is protected throughout its greatly reduced range: it is one of the few large North American fish listed as Endangered by the IUCN. The reasons for its decline nowadays are habitat alteration and predation by non-native fish.

Identification: A distinctive sharp-edged hump on the back. The lower lip is widely separated into two lobes. Adults are dusky brown to olive on the back and yellowish underneath. During the breeding season the belly of the male becomes orange.

Distribution: Once common through south-west USA, now known only in Colorado River upstream of Grand Canyon and large reservoir lakes (Mead, Mohave and Havasu) formed by damming rivers. Attempts being made to reintroduce to some of former range.
Habitat: Rivers with strong currents over sandy bottoms. Also some artificial lakes.
Food: Aquatic invertebrates and algae.
Size: Up to 91cm/36in.
Breeding: Female scatters eggs in open water, males compete to fertilize. Eggs sink to bottom to develop.
Status: Endangered.

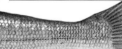

SUCKERS

Suckers are among North America's most common freshwater fish, yet few Americans have ever seen one or even heard of them. Well-camouflaged and lying still or in deep water during the day, they are difficult enough for wild fish-eating birds and mammals to find, let alone humans. Many species look very similar, so the best guide to identification is location, since their ranges mostly tend to be separate.

Flannelmouth sucker

Catostomus latipinnis

This is one of the more common fish of the Colorado River and its tributaries. Even so, it has declined in numbers since the start of the last century due to alterations in its habitat. The Colorado River has been dammed at several points to provide water and power for desert cities such as Phoenix and Las Vegas and now it is only during high-water periods that it flows right to the sea. The flannelmouth once migrated up and down this river to take advantage of seasonal abundances of food, but can no longer do so to the same extent. It overlaps part of its range with the razorback sucker, with which it sometimes hybridizes. This species can reach a weight of 1kg/2¼lb.

Identification: In most populations the caudal peduncle – the area where the tail joins to the rest of the body – is narrow and pencil-shaped. A prominent snout, ventral mouth and well developed lips, the lower lip with large, fleshy lobes. The caudal and dorsal fins are both relatively large. Colour varies from green to blue-grey above, and is paler below.

Distribution: Colorado River basin, from south-western Wyoming to southern Arizona.
Habitat: Rocky pools and runs of the main river channel and its larger tributaries. Less often in creeks and streams.
Food: Insect larvae and other aquatic invertebrates.
Size: Up to 56cm/22in.
Breeding: Thought to spawn in open water, like most of its relatives.

Bridgelip sucker

Catostomus columbianus

Identification: Varies in colour from green to blue-black above and white to yellow below. Males develop an orange band along their sides and extra scales on the rear of their bodies as the breeding season approaches.

A typical member of its family, it is difficult even for experts to distinguish this species. The bridgelip sucker originates from the north-western USA and British Columbia. Its Latin name gives a clue to its stronghold – the Columbia River basin. This fish lacks the indentations at the corners of the mouth that separate the lips in other, closely-related species, hence the name 'bridgelip'. It spawns during late spring, soon after the winter ice that covers many of the smaller rivers has broken up.

Distribution: Columbia River and its tributaries. Also found Fraser River in British Columbia.
Habitat: Lakes and the backwaters and edges of rivers with sandy or muddy beds.
Food: Aquatic invertebrates and algae.
Size: Up to 30cm/12in.
Breeding: Females shed small yellow eggs into open water, where they are fertilized by attendant males.

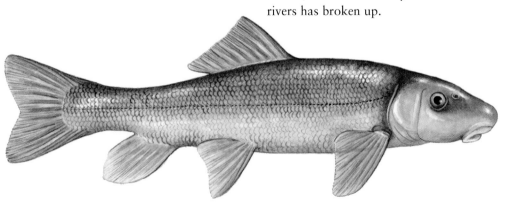

Mountain sucker

Catostomus platyrhynchus

This is one of the most widespread of all suckers, occurring throughout most of western North America, from the Canadian Arctic as far south as the Colorado River. As its name suggests, it is primarily a species of cool mountain streams, being most abundant in the Rockies, although it is sometimes found at lower altitudes. The mountain sucker is unusual because it feeds mainly on algae, scraping it from boulders and smaller rocks. Insect larvae and other aquatic invertebrates are also taken when the opportunity arises but these do not form such an important part of the diet as they do for other suckers. Due partly to the high altitudes at which it lives, this sucker is a late breeder, spawning between June and August.

Distribution: From the Saskatchewan River, Canada, southward on both sides of Rocky Mountains to Colorado River and its tributary streams in California.
Habitat: Clear, swift mountain streams, rivers.
Food: Mostly algae, sometimes small invertebrates.
Size: Up to 25cm/9¾in.
Breeding: Moves upstream to smaller streams to spawn in open water above gravel.

Identification: The body is grey to moss green above, usually with a dark stripe on the side, which turns red in breeding males. The upper and lower lips are separated by deep indentations at the corners of the mouth. The fins are clear to pale red.

Longnose sucker (*Catostomus catostomus*): Up to 64cm/25in
This has an unusually long snout, similar in relative length to that of the razorback sucker, but flatter. It is the most widespread sucker in North America, found throughout most of the northern USA, almost all of Canada and Alaska. A fish of clear, cold deep lakes and their tributary rivers and streams, it also occurs in Siberia.

White sucker (*Catostomus commersoni*): Up to 64cm/25in
This fish is often confused with the similar-looking longnose sucker, with which it shares part of its range. Like the longnose, this species is often found in the headwaters of lakes, though it is more common in small, cold-water streams and rivers. It is most easily told apart from the longnose by the fact that its snout is rounded, rather than flattened towards its tip.

Bluehead sucker (*Catostomus discobolus*): Up to 41cm/16in
With its bluish head, which is quite bright in some individuals, the bluehead (*above*) is one of the more colourful suckers, a group that is generally patterned for camouflage rather than display. It occurs in the Snake and upper Colorado Rivers in shallow, fast-flowing water. The blue of the head becomes darker and more intense in the adults as they age.

Desert sucker

Catostomus clarki

If the mountain sucker is a fish of steep topography and icy waters then the desert sucker is its natural opposite. The rocky rivers this fish inhabits flow through some of the flattest, most scorched landscapes of North America. In common with many other suckers, it stays out of sight during the day to avoid predators. When the sun is up it lurks in the relative safety of deep pools, hidden from most fish-eating birds. It feeds at night, swimming up into the shallow riffles which are the home of most of its insect prey. The desert sucker is found throughout the hot and arid regions of the south-western USA and northern Mexico.

Identification: Varies in colour from silver-tan to dark green above and from silver to yellow below. The upper and lower lips are separated at the corners of the mouth by deep indentations. Caught fish can be told apart from their close relatives by the fact that they have between 27 and 43 gill rakers beneath the gill covers.

Distribution: Common across most of range. Lower Colorado River drainages (downstream of Grand Canyon). Also found in Virgin, Bill Williams and Gila River systems.
Habitat: Small to medium-sized rivers with rocky or sandy bottoms.
Food: Insect larvae and other aquatic invertebrates.
Size: Up to 33cm/13in.
Breeding: Likely to be open-water spawner, in common with most of its relatives.

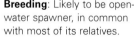

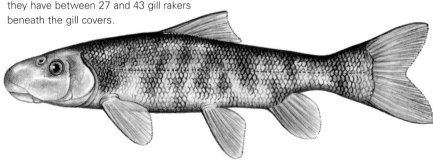

OTHER SUCKERS

The fish shown here are representative of the many medium to large sucker species found across North America. Most of these species differ only slightly in their general morphology and are similar in their habits. The fact that there are separate species at all is usually down to geographical isolation. Hybridization often occurs between them, following introductions.

Largescale sucker

Catostomus macrocheilus

This sucker is native to the Pacific North-west of the USA and British Columbia in Canada, where it lives in large rivers and lakes along their courses. It is also found in some tributary streams. Adults are bottom feeders, feeding on insect larvae and other, larger aquatic invertebrates, as well as algae and, sometimes, water plants. The largescale sucker spawns in spring, leaving its eggs to develop unguarded. Hatched young then stick together in shoals, feeding on planktonic animals in the water column before they become large enough to search on the bottom for bigger prey. Those that survive to adulthood may live for up to 15 years and reach 3.2kg/7lb in weight.

Identification: The scales of this species are indeed large, particularly towards the rear of the body, and are well defined with darker rear edges. The upper half of the body is olive to blue-grey and the underside is white to yellow, often with faint speckling.

Distribution: Columbia River system, the lower Snake River and the Spokane, Pend Oreille and Kootenai River systems.
Habitat: Lakes and slower-moving portions of rivers and streams.
Food: Aquatic invertebrates, algae and water plants.
Size: Up to 61cm/24in.
Breeding: Sandy areas of streams, or sand or gravel banks in lakes. Female lays up to 20,000 adhesive eggs in shallow, open water.

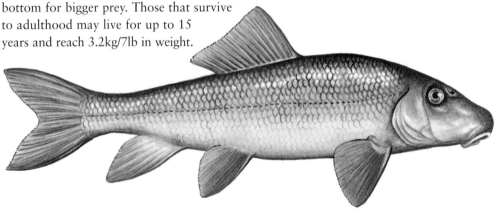

Lost River sucker

Deltistes luxatus

Once common throughout the Lost River in Oregon, this large sucker is now quite rare and has the unfortunate distinction of being listed as Endangered by the IUCN. It is the only living member of its genus. It is a large fish compared with most suckers, but it lives in a similar way to the majority of the members of its family, hoovering up invertebrates, fish eggs and other particles of edible matter from the bottom of rivers. Like the largescale sucker, it is relatively long-lived, sometimes reaching 18 years old.

Identification: The hump on the snout of this fish, combined with its large size, distinguishes it clearly from any other fish that inhabits the same river system. The body is grey to dark olive above and white or yellow below, with the fins similar in colour to the adjacent body.

Distribution: Lost River system (part of upper Klamath River basin), Oregon and California.
Habitat: Lakes, reservoirs and deep pools in rivers.
Food: Aquatic invertebrates, fish eggs and some plant matter.
Size: Up to 86cm/34in.
Breeding: Female scatters eggs into open water, where they are fertilized. Eggs sink to the bottom where they develop unguarded.
Status: Endangered.

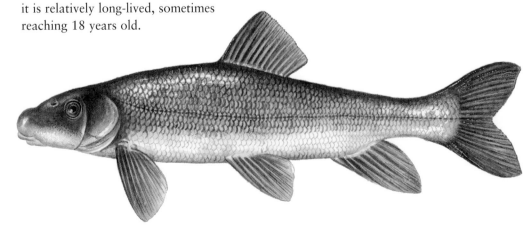

Northern hog sucker

Hypentelium nigricans

This powerfully built fish is a very active forager. It uses its wide, bony head to turn over rocks and pebbles on the riverbed to expose insect larvae and other small creatures. As it rummages around, it holds its position in the water by moving its pectoral fins. Northern hog suckers are often followed by other fish, such as shiners and smallmouth bass, which snap up any morsels the hog suckers miss. This species also feeds on fish eggs and algae, which they scrape from the rocks with their thick lips. During spawning, males stand on their heads to fertilize the eggs, their tails sometimes breaking the surface.

Distribution: Great Lakes, Hudson Bay and Mississippi River basins from New York State, USA, and Ontario, Canada, to Minnesota and south to Louisiana, Arkansas and Alabama.
Habitat: Rocky runs, clear pools of streams and rivers.
Food: Aquatic invertebrates, fish eggs and algae.
Size: Up to 61cm/24in.
Breeding: Females dig shallow riverbed nests. Males compete to fertilize.

Identification: A large, rectangular head, which is wider than the rest of the body. The lips are large and papillose (covered with numerous tiny nipple-like bumps). The eyes are high on the head and between them the head is broadly concave. The upper body is olive in colour with brown saddles.

Sacramento sucker (*Catostomus occidentalis*): Up to 60cm/23½in
This fish closely resembles the Klamath largescale sucker (below) but has a different range, spending most of its adult life in the Mad and Salinas Rivers and Sacramento-San Joaquin drainages of Oregon and California, then moving upstream into smaller tributaries to spawn.

Klamath largescale sucker (*Catostomus snyderi*): Up to 55cm/21¾in
This sucker (*below*) is found only in the Klamath River system of Oregon and California. Although it is quite common here, its limited range means that its global population is relatively small, and it is classified as being Near Threatened by the IUCN. It feeds mainly on bottom-living invertebrates. Although it evolved as a fish of flowing waters it is also common in the Klamath River backwaters.

Tahoe sucker (*Catostomus tahoensis*): Up to 61cm/24in
The tahoe is native to the Lahontan basin in south-eastern Oregon, Nevada and north-eastern California and introduced in the upper Sacramento River. Common throughout its range, it is most abundant in large lakes such as Pyramid Lake and Lake Tahoe, after which it is named. Breeding males develop a bright red stripe along the brassy sides of their bodies.

Creek chubsucker

Erimyzon oblongus

This fish is commonly found in a wide range that encompasses much of the eastern USA. There are two subspecies; the western creek chubsucker, which is found west of the Appalachians, north to the lower Great Lakes basin, and the eastern creek chubsucker, which is found along the Atlantic coastal plain. Like other suckers, they forage for invertebrates on the riverbed, but they also snap up fish fry and other small creatures from open water. This is possible because the mouth is higher up the end of the snout than on most other sucker species. This species swims upstream to spawn in shallow running water.

Identification: Varies in colour from olive to brown above, with five to eight darker blotches running along each side, from behind the gill covers to the tail base. The body is rounded and the small mouth is quite high on the snout. The dorsal fin has a rounded edge and the anal fin is large.

Distribution: There are two populations. 1: Most of eastern USA, from Maine to Georgia and as far west as Texas. 2: Lake Michigan south to Alabama and Texas.
Habitat: Headwaters and clear streams with moderate currents.
Food: Aquatic invertebrates, fish fry and fish eggs.
Size: Up to 36cm/14in.
Breeding: In some locations, males have been seen to build nests. More often eggs are simply scattered and fertilized in open water.

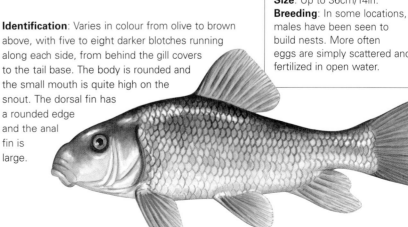

SUCKERS AND REDHORSES

The two suckers here are among the smallest members of the family Catostomidae. Redhorses are also catostomids but they differ from buffaloes and suckers in their coloration. Generally speaking, redhorses have a dark back and silvery sides with a bronze or coppery sheen which, combined with the colour of their caudal fins, gives rise to the 'red' in their name.

Torrent sucker

Thoburnia rhothoeca

This is a handsome little fish with a neat, well-proportioned body and white to pale orange fins. During the spawning season, which lasts for much of the spring, the males look particularly dapper, decked out in full breeding regalia with rusty red stripes running down their sides. The torrent sucker is a fish of small mountain streams. It prefers the faster running sections, swimming effortlessly against the current and holding its position with great agility to feed. Its body design allows it to negotiate this habitat with ease – the head is relatively small and curved to improve streamlining and the swim bladder is greatly reduced, making the fish less buoyant and so less likely to be swept away.

Identification: A small, convex head and a cylindrical body. Two large pale areas at the base of the caudal fin distinguish it from all but the extremely similar-looking rustyside sucker, which lives in the upper Dan River system of North Carolina and Virginia. The upper body ranges from olive-brown to blue-grey.

Distribution: From Roanoke River in northern central Virginia and adjacent West Virginia to upper Potomac River drainage in Virginia and West Virginia.
Habitat: Fast-flowing mountain streams.
Food: Insect larvae and other small aquatic invertebrates.
Size: Up to 18cm/7in.
Breeding: Thought to deposit eggs in sheltered areas or stick them to rocks to prevent them from being washed downstream.

Blackfin sucker

Thoburnia atripinnis

Identification: The small overall size and the large, jet black tip to the dorsal fin distinguishes this from other suckers. The olive-gold body has several narrow black stripes on each side. The caudal fin is small and slightly forked and the underside of the body is shiny white in colour.

This species has a limited range but where it does occur it is relatively common. A small bottom feeder, it lives in a similar way to the torrent sucker, although it inhabits slower flowing water. The blackfin sucker finds its food by rummaging around among the gravel beds of the small rivers where it lives, turning over the pebbles to expose its prey. Like most other suckers it is nocturnal and spends the day hidden in crevices on the riverbed or beneath boulders or overhanging shoreline brush. It spawns in April and deposits its eggs in open water just above the bottom, so that they drop in between the gravel and stones where they are left to develop unguarded.

Distribution: Restricted to upper Barren River system, which forms part of Green River drainages in Kentucky and Tennessee.
Habitat: Streams and small rivers, occurring both in rocky riffles and small pools.
Food: Insect larvae and other small aquatic invertebrates.
Size: Up to 17cm/6¾in.
Breeding: Spawning occurs in open water near riverbed. Eggs are left unguarded and hatch within 2 weeks, if not eaten by other fish.

Greater redhorse

Moxostoma valenciennesi

Growing to over two feet, the greater redhorse is the largest member of its genus and widely distributed across eastern Canada and parts of the USA. Although never common, it is becoming increasingly rare and vanishing altogether from the southerly parts of its range. Its wide distribution, however, means that it is not yet under any serious risk of extinction. It is a bottom feeder, found mainly in large rivers and lakes. Like many catostomids, it moves to shallower waters to spawn, gathering over rocky riffles. The caudal and dorsal fins of both sexes vibrate during spawning and the female often rolls over while releasing her eggs.

Distribution: St Lawrence River, Red River and Mississippi River basins, other rivers from Hudson Bay southward to Kentucky.
Habitat: Lakes and medium to large rivers with sandy or rocky bottoms.
Food: Aquatic invertebrates, small fish, fish eggs, larvae.
Size: Up to 80cm/31½in.
Breeding: Large numbers of eggs over gravelly or pebbly riverbeds. Up to 11 males jockey to fertilize each batch.

Identification: The head is unusually large, making up about a quarter of the entire length of any individual more than 25cm/10in long. The caudal fin is red and the thick lower lip has a V-shaped rear edge. The dorsal fin edge is usually convex, not straight as in some other redhorse species.

River redhorse (*Moxostoma carinatum*): Up to 77cm/30in
This fish looks similar to the greater redhorse but has a much smaller dorsal fin. It inhabits rivers large and small from southern Quebec to central Minnesota and south to Oklahoma and Florida. It is a relatively large fish, weighing up to 4kg/8¾lb and it is a popular target for anglers. Pollution and other factors are reducing numbers in some parts of its range.

Shorthead redhorse (*Moxostoma macrolepidotum*): Up to 75cm/29½in
This small-headed redhorse is unusual among catostomids in being relatively unfussy about where it lives. It is found in lakes, rivers and streams, in both clear and turbid water, overlying beds of sand, gravel or solid rock. It ranges across much of eastern North America from Hudson Bay to Alabama and Oklahoma.

Blacktail redhorse (*Moxostoma poecilurum*): Up to 51cm/20in
This fish (*above*) is found in tributaries of the Mississippi River and other rivers draining into the Gulf of Mexico, from Kentucky and southern Arkansas to Texas and east as far as Florida. It has a longer, more cylindrical body than most other members of its genus and a distinctive black stripe on the lower lobe of its caudal fin.

Copper redhorse

Moxostoma hubbsi

This is one of seven species of Canadian redhorse. It is endemic to a few rivers in the south-western Quebec lowlands and has become rare in recent decades due to changes to its habitat. Urban development and dam construction are the main causes of its decline, but other factors, such as the introduction of non-native species to its rivers, may also have had an impact. It is now listed as Vulnerable by the IUCN and is protected as an endangered species in Canada. It feeds primarily on freshwater shellfish, which it crushes with its flattened teeth before swallowing. Compared with other redhorses it is long-lived, often living to more than 30 years of age.

Identification: The body is stout, deep in profile and gold to coppery, with a reddish sheen and a red caudal fin. The head is short and the back highly arched. The teeth are flattened and molar-like.

Distribution: Stretches of St Lawrence River and Richelieu River in Quebec, Canada.
Habitat: Medium-sized rivers where temperatures rise to 20°C/68°F or higher in summer.
Food: Freshwater molluscs.
Size: Up to 77cm/30in.
Breeding: Spawns from late June to early July, when water temperatures are highest. Spawning grounds are located in fairly slow-moving, deep water, up to 2m/6½ft.
Status: Vulnerable.

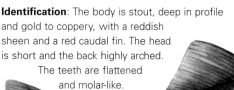

REDHORSES AND JUMPROCKS

The following fish are all very closely related. Jumprocks are redhorses in all but name, belonging to the same genus, Moxostoma. As a group, this genus is quite successful, ranging across most of the North American continent east of the Rockies. All of these fish are bottom-feeders and have mouths with large, thick lips, positioned on the undersides of their snouts.

Silver redhorse

Moxostoma anisurum

Identification: The end of the snout is unusually pale compared with those of other, similar species. The body is stout and the top edge of the dorsal fin straight or slightly convex. Both the dorsal and caudal fins are slate grey in colour. The lower lip is deeply divided with an acutely V-shaped rear edge.

One of the seven redhorse species found in Canada, it also occurs in large areas of the north-eastern USA. Unlike most other redhorses and suckers, it is often found in pools and rivers with muddy bottoms, although it also lives over gravel and rock. The silver redhorse can grow to become quite large: the biggest recorded example caught weighed 10.8kg/24lb. This fact and its wide distribution make it a popular game fish, although catching it is more a matter of luck than knowing where to look, as it is nowhere particularly common. In Canada it goes by several official common names: silver mullet, white-nosed redhorse, white-nosed mullet and white-nosed sucker.

Distribution: Quebec to Alberta and through eastern USA to Arkansas and northern Alabama.
Habitat: Mud, sand or rock-bottomed rivers. Occasionally lakes.
Food: Aquatic invertebrates, fish eggs, plant material.
Size: Up to 71cm/28in.
Breeding: Spawns in April, with adults migrating up into small tributary streams. Eggs are semi-adhesive and scattered at random.

Gray redhorse

Moxostoma congestum

When brought to the surface the gray redhorse is not always as grey as one might imagine. For most of the year, both sexes live up to their name. Breeding males, however, are brassy gold in colour with yellow to light orange fins. Except when caught, this redhorse is very rarely seen. This is because it prefers deeper water than most of its relatives. Like most redhorses it finds its food in the sediment, churning up the mud or sand to expose the invertebrates that make up the bulk of its diet. Although it is locally common, this species has been little studied. Beyond what it eats and how it breeds, little of its biology is known. There is even uncertainty about the total extent of its range.

Identification: Seen from above, the head is broad and U-shaped. The edge of the dorsal fin is straight to slightly concave. The caudal fin is quite large and forked. The upper lobe has a pointed tip, while that of the lower lobe is usually more rounded. Ranges from olive to yellow-grey above with lighter colouration below.

Distribution: Known to occur from Brazos River drainages to Rio Grande River drainages in Texas and New Mexico. Also found in Mexico proper.
Habitat: Bottoms of lakes and deep, often murky pools in rivers.
Food: Aquatic invertebrates and some plant matter.
Size: Up to 65cm/25½in.
Breeding: Eggs are scattered over the bottom of lakes and rivers and left to develop unguarded.

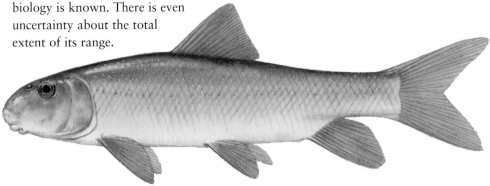

Greater jumprock

Moxostoma lachneri

Despite the fact that the North American continent has been settled for centuries and is now home to the best part of half a billion people, many of its fish have only been fairly recently discovered. The greater jumprock is one such species. Although far from small, it lived unnoticed and unknown to science until 1956, when it was finally officially described. Part of the reason for this long anonymity is its relatively small range. It inhabits the drainage basins of just two rivers in Georgia and Alabama. This jumprock spawns in May and June.

Identification: The body is long and cylindrical. The head is also long, and narrow when seen from above. The snout is blunt. The lower ray of the large caudal fin is white and the lower lobe is rounded. The upper lobe is pointed at the tip.

Distribution: Drainage basins of the Chattahoochee and Apalachicola Rivers in Georgia and Alabama.
Habitat: Small rivers and streams with swift currents, over gravel or rock.
Food: Aquatic invertebrates and fish eggs.
Size: Up to 44cm/17⅛in.
Breeding: Eggs shed into swift, open water over gravel. Males surround gravid females and compete to fetlilize. Eggs left to develop unguarded.

Black redhorse (*Moxostoma duquesnei*): Up to 51cm/20in
This fish is in fact dusky olive above and white or yellow below. It has a long, relatively narrow tail base and a grey caudal fin. It is found throughout the lower Great Lakes and Mississippi River basins from just north of the Canadian border south as far as Georgia and Tennessee. Common in most of its range, it is nevertheless a protected species in Canada.

Black jumprock (*Moxostoma cervinum*): Up to 19cm/7½in
The black jumprock (*above*) is not actually black at all. Its other common name, the blacktip jumprock, is far more accurate, referring to the black tips on its dorsal and caudal fins. It occurs in Atlantic slope drainages from the James River in Virginia southward to the Neuse River in North Carolina. It hides by day beneath rocks in the runs and riffles of streams and small rivers.

Golden redhorse (*Moxostoma erythrurum*): Up to 78cm/30¾in
This species is found in lakes and rivers as far north as Hudson Bay. It spawns May to June in riffles of small rivers which are so shallow that the backs of the spawning fish are often exposed. It can be told apart from the very similar silver redhorse by its dorsal fin, which has 14 rays compared with the silver's 12 or 13.

Striped jumprock

Moxostoma rupiscartes

Growing to just under a foot long, this jumprock is one of the smaller members of its genus. Its size is a reflection of where it lives: the fast-flowing and relatively narrow streams and rivers of hills and mountains. It has dark stripes on its back and sides that are narrower than the pale stripes in between. These characteristics, combined with a wide head, distinguish the species from other similar ones. Like the rest of its genus it is a bottom feeder, finding its prey amongst the gravel and pebbles of the riverbed. It has a relatively small range compared with some other redhorses and jumprocks, but it is common wherever it is found.

Identification: The body is cylindrical and the head, which is flat or slightly convex between the eyes, is wider than it is deep. The edge of the lower lip is virtually straight. In spring, males develop a faint yellow-brown stripe along the side of the body.

Distribution: Occurs from Santee River drainages, North Carolina, to Altamaha River drainages, Georgia. Also found in extreme upper Peedee River drainages in North Carolina, where it may have been introduced.
Habitat: Fast-flowing streams and small to medium-sized rivers and streams with sandy or rocky beds.
Food: Insect larvae and other aquatic invertebrates.
Size: Up to 28cm/11in.
Breeding: Thought likely to be an open-water spawner that does not guard eggs.

GOLDEYE, MOONEYE, SHADS, SMELT AND HERRINGS

All of these fish are shoaling species with silvery sides and compressed bodies. The goldeye and mooneye live only in fresh water but the others, which belong to the herring family Clupeidae, spend part of their lives, or have populations that live, in salt water. Most other clupeids are exclusively marine.

Goldeye

Hiodon alosoides

The goldeye and the mooneye are the only two living species of the family Hiodontidae. The goldeye is caught in large numbers as a food fish in Canada, where it is cured in smoke and sold for high prices as the Winnipeg goldeye. It is a shoaling fish and a voracious predator despite its relatively small size. It tends to feed near the surface in turbid water and catches a wide range of invertebrate prey as well as other fish. In turn, it is preyed upon by larger, more solitary hunters such as northern pike (*Esox lucius*). Goldeyes mature more rapidly in the south than in the north of their range, often reaching adulthood in just three years. Immature fish often undertake large migrations, sometimes travelling 1000km/ 621 miles or more to reach new feeding grounds.

Identification: A deep, laterally compressed silver body. The eyes have bright gold irises, hence the name. The snout is bluntly rounded and the belly sharply keeled. The mouth is small and filled with many small, sharp teeth, which occur on the tongue as well as in the jaws.

Distribution: Mississippi, Missouri, Ohio, Arctic basins. Range extends southwest below Great Lakes to Oklahoma. Ontario, Quebec: James Bay drainages.
Habitat: Deep water in rivers. Also lakes, reservoirs.
Food: Aquatic insects, molluscs and crustaceans, small fish and frogs.
Size: Up to 51cm/20in.
Breeding: Shallow, turbid pools, backwaters. Eggs shed into water column.

American shad

Alosa sapidissima

Identification: A silvery body with one or more dark spots just behind the gill cover. The upper body has a blue-green metallic hue. Adult fish lack jaw teeth and the eye has an obvious eyelid. A row of scales (scutes) form a rough, 'saw-blade' edge along the belly.

The American shad is another important food fish – the literal translation of *sapidissima* is 'most delicious'. In the 19th century it supported a huge part of the fishing industry, with annual catches as high as 23,000 tonnes/22,310 US short tons, but its population has since declined and today's commercial fisheries are relatively small-scale. These are migratory fish that spend much of their adult life at sea. Each spring, when water temperatures reach 12°C/54°F, they gather at river mouths to journey upstream. Spawning occurs in June and July in water temperatures of 13°C–20°C/55°F–68°F, but if the water gets warmer than this, spawning stops. Fish may swim downstream to breed another year, except in the south of the range where they tend to die after spawning.

Distribution: At sea along North America's Atlantic coast, from Newfoundland to Florida. Also introduced to Pacific coast and now range from Alaska to California.
Habitat: Coastal waters and medium to large rivers.
Food: Planktonic animals, small fish and some crustaceans.
Size: Up to 75cm/29½in.
Breeding: Migrates from sea to breed into rivers where it was hatched. Eggs shed into open water, left to develop unguarded.

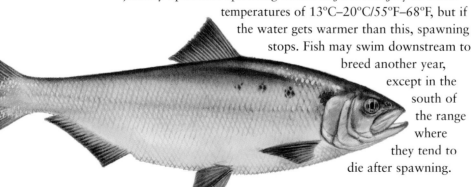

Gizzard shad

Dorosoma cepedianum

Distribution: Middle to eastern regions of the USA and central southern regions of Canada. Also occurs in northern parts of Mexico.
Habitat: Large rivers, lakes and reservoirs. Also found at Chesapeake Bay.
Food: Young: tiny individual animals; adults: plankton.
Size: Up to 52cm/20½in.
Breeding: Open water. Eggs drift to bottom and stick to substrate. Left to develop unguarded. No individual selection of mates.

Although this fish occurs in the brackish and salt water of Chesapeake Bay, it is primarily a freshwater species. It is usually found in large schools in fairly open water, being most common in large rivers, reservoirs and lakes. The adults feed mostly on plankton, swimming along with open mouths and using their gill rakers to filter food from the water. Young gizzard shad eat insect larvae and other tiny animals, which they catch individually. The feeding habits of the adults mean that they are rarely caught by anglers using rod and reel. Unlike American shad, they are not fished commercially. This species spawns in spring in shallower water than its usual home.

Identification: The last ray of the dorsal fin is long and whip-like, and extends out along the back. The body is generally silver, with a large purple-blue spot on the shoulder. Teeth are absent and there are no scales on the nape of the neck. The snout is blunt and there is a deep notch at the centre of the upper jaw.

Mooneye (*Hiodon tergisus*):
Up to 47cm/18¾in
Named for the large round eyes which dominate and seem to stick out from its small head, this fish lives in slow-flowing rivers, lakes and marshes, and is rarely seen, feeding mainly at night on aquatic insects and small fish. Unlike the goldeye, it is not fished commercially. It is found from Saskatchewan, southern Manitoba, Alberta and the James Bay lowlands down to Arkansas and Alabama in the south.

Skipjack herring (*Alosa chrysochloris*):
Up to 53cm/21in
Also known as the skipjack shad, the skipjack herring (*above*) is a common shoaling fish of the western central Atlantic Ocean and the Gulf of Mexico. It is also found in the fresh waters of many large rivers, such as the Mississippi and Ohio. Inland, it is found in fast-flowing water and is renowned for its habit of leaping to escape predators, hence its common name.

Alewife (*Alosa pseudoharengus*):
Up to 25cm/10in
The alewife is a small herring species found in coastal waters from Labrador to South Carolina. Although primarily a marine fish, it has also been introduced into several lakes, including the Great Lakes, where it has become extremely abundant and provides food for many bigger fish.

Rainbow smelt

Osmerus mordax

This fish is native to the coastal waters of the eastern USA, Alaska and Canada. It has also been widely introduced into lakes and reservoirs, where it provides food for large game fish such as walleyes and salmon. The rainbow smelt earns its name from the shimmering appearance of its scales underwater. This disappears if it is removed from the water. Lake-dwelling populations swim up tributary rivers and streams to spawn, laying their eggs by night and returning to the lakes before sunrise. The eggs sink to the bottom and each becomes attached to the gravel by a short stalk which develops from its outer shell membrane.

Distribution: Coastal waters and rivers from Virginia around Canada and Alaska to British Columbia. Also found in parts of north-eastern Asia.
Habitat: Coastal waters, rivers, lakes and reservoirs.
Food: Mainly crustaceans and small fish, but also insect larvae.
Size: Up to 33cm/13in.
Breeding: Eggs shed in open water over gravel. Left to sink to bottom where they develop unguarded.

Identification: A very large mouth, with the upper jaw reaching to the middle of the eye or beyond. The upper jaw contains two large canine teeth, sometimes surrounded by smaller ones. The slender body usually has a conspicuous silver stripe along its side. There is an adipose fin between the dorsal and caudal fins, a feature absent from most of its relatives.

CISCOS AND WHITEFISH

These fish belong to the same family as trout and salmon. As a group, ciscos and whitefish are renowned for being especially difficult to identify, since there can be a huge amount of variation in colour and shape between different individuals of the same species. As with other members of the salmon family, many of the fish on these pages are harvested commercially.

Arctic cisco
Coregonus autumnalis

Identification: The body ranges from blue to dark green, occasionally brown above, and the rest, silvery. The dorsal and caudal fins are dusky, while the fins lower on the body are lighter in colour. The body is robust, but also highly streamlined.

The Arctic cisco lives mostly in brackish coastal waters, spending a large part of its adult life in lagoons and estuaries. In summer, it swims as far as 1000km/621 miles inland to spawn in fast-running stretches of river with gravel beds. After spawning, the fish make their way back to the sea. Although the breeding system of this species has not been studied in detail, the presence of fry suggests that the eggs overwinter and hatch the following spring. The young fish migrate downstream feeding and growing as they reach the river mouth. This species also occurs in some Irish loughs where it is called pollan, and in Russia's Lake Baikal, where it is known as omul.

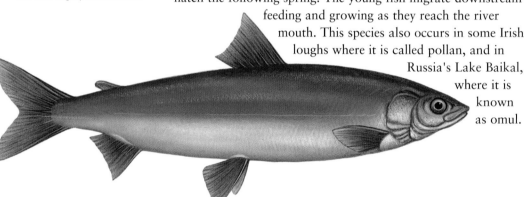

Distribution: From lower Laird River, British Columbia, around Alaska to North-west Territories. Also Irish loughs (Neagh, Erne, Derg and Ree), Lake Baikal, Barents Sea and some coastal Siberian rivers.
Habitat: Coastal lagoons, estuaries and large rivers. Also freshwater lakes.
Food: Planktonic animals, occasionally small fish.
Size: Up to 64cm/25in.
Breeding: Open water. Eggs sink and develop unguarded.

Lake whitefish
Coregonus clupeaformis

A shy and reclusive inhabitant of cool, gloomy waters, the lake whitefish usually swims in large schools at some depth. It is common in the Great Lakes on the border between the USA and Canada. It is rarely found there at depths of less than 70m/213ft and as surface water temperatures rise in summer, it moves into even deeper waters. In many of the lakes where it occurs, the lake whitefish makes up a large part of the commercial catch, and it is generally considered to make excellent eating. A long-lived species, sometimes exceeding 25 years in age, it can grow to weigh more than 9kg/20lb. In the past, this species was overfished, in the Great Lakes particularly, but careful management of fisheries has recently seen numbers recover.

Identification: The skin and scales are dark greenish-brown to dark blue above and silver on the sides and belly. The head is relatively small, as is the mouth. This species usually has 26 or more gill rakers.

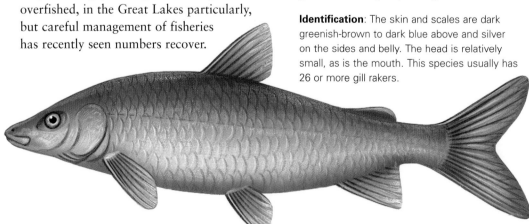

Distribution: Most of Canada and Alaska. Also north-eastern USA, as far south as New England, Great Lakes and central Minnesota.
Habitat: Deep water near or at the bottoms of large lakes. Also found in brackish water in some places.
Food: Aquatic invertebrates, fish eggs and fish fry.
Size: Up to 80cm/31½in.
Breeding: At night near the surface. Eggs and sperm are released within shoal. Fertilized eggs drift to bottom and develop unguarded.

Round whitefish

Prosopium cylindraceum

Distribution: Pacific drainages, British Columbia to Alaska; Arctic drainages east to Hudson Bay; Atlantic drainages, Labrador to Connecticut; inland lakes. Also found Siberian and north Asian rivers.
Habitat: Lakes and clear streams: very occasionally enters brackish water.
Food: Aquatic invertebrates and fish eggs.
Size: Up to 56cm/22in.
Breeding: Eggs laid over gravel, develop unguarded.

This fish is found in many of the same habitats as the lake whitefish and, like the latter, is caught commercially and sold as a food fish. It is a bottom feeder, eating insect larvae (particularly mayfly), freshwater clams, water snails and fish eggs. It especially favours the eggs of lake trout and so often keeps lake trout numbers in check. The round whitefish is slightly smaller than the lake whitefish and tends to be found in shallower waters. It usually occurs at depths of between 15m/49ft and 50m/164ft, so in most deep lakes it will be found on the sloping edges. Spawning takes place over gravel shoals in autumn, in lakes or in tributary streams. Males and females form pairs rather than spawn in the school, and neither parent eats in the days leading up to breeding.

Identification: The body is bronze to brown above with dark-edged scales. The sides and belly are silver to white. The young are silver in colour but have two rows of black spots along their sides and scattered spots on their backs. In some individuals these side and back spots coalesce to form a speckled mass.

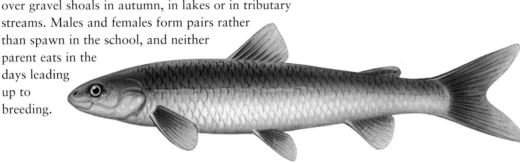

Least cisco (*Coregonus sardinella*): Up to 47cm/18½in
Also known as the sardine cisco, this lives in coastal waters, estuaries, large lakes and rivers from Bristol Bay, Alaska, to Canada's Murchison River, as well as in northern Asia and the Bering Sea. During spawning, the female hovers head-up, almost vertically. She is surrounded by up to five males, which assume the same position and release their milt.

Lake herring (*Coregonus artedi*): Up to 57cm/22½in
This fish (*above*) is also known simply as the cisco or blueback. It is an open water shoaling fish that feeds on free-swimming invertebrates and small fish. It is found through much of Canada and the northern USA, in lakes, as well as rivers and the coastal waters of Hudson Bay. In deep lakes it tends to rise nearer the surface when the water temperature drops.

Bloater (*Coregonus hoyi*): Up to 37cm/14½in
This fish was once found in all of the Great Lakes except Erie, but is now restricted to just three: Superior, Michigan and Huron. It is classified as Vulnerable by the IUCN. Despite the name, it is in fact a rather svelte fish, with a long, laterally compressed body about the same depth as the back of its head. It spends the day on the bottom, moving up to feed at night.

Pygmy whitefish

Prosopium coulteri

As its name suggests, this whitefish is small by the standards of this group and is relatively short-lived, rarely exceeding nine years of age. But it is a fast-growing species and quick to mature: both males and females may be ready to breed by the end of their first year, although it is more common for them to start after two years. In North America this fish occurs in three distinct populations, which have been separated since the end of the last Ice Age. One stretches from the Yukon River drainages in Canada to those of the Columbia River in Washington State, USA. The second occurs in the Wood, Naknek and Chignik River drainages in south-west Alaska. The third is restricted to Lake Superior and its tributaries. The pygmy whitefish is also found in Russia and several other former Soviet countries.

Distribution: Lake Superior and its tributaries, western Canada and Washington State, and south-west Alaska. Also found in much of the former USSR.
Habitat: Lakes and rivers in mountainous areas.
Food: Aquatic invertebrates, particularly crustaceans and insect larvae.
Size: Up to 28cm/11in.
Breeding: At night in early winter, in shallow water over gravel. Eggs left unguarded and hatch in following spring.

Identification: Large eyes, with a diameter about equal to the distance between their edge and the snout end. Each eye is surrounded by a transparent membrane with a distinct notch under the rear edge of the pupil. The head length is slightly greater than the body depth, the snout is bluntly rounded, and the mouth is overhanging, not obviously pointed. The scales are relatively large and number 54 to 70 along the lateral line.

GOLDEN SHINER, HITCH, PEAMOUTH, SQUAWFISH AND HARDHEAD

These fish belong to the carp family, Cyprinidae (known as the minnow family in North America). The golden shiner and hitch are closely related to the Eurasian carps, several of which have been introduced to North America. The squawfish, which include the hardhead, are the largest native cyprinids.

Golden shiner

Notemigonus crysoleucas

Identification: A strongly compressed body which looks slim from above. The lateral line is curved downward towards the belly and the belly itself has a scaleless keel running from the pelvic to anal fin. The mouth, which is on a pointed snout, is small and upturned.

This little fish forms schools in ponds, swamps, overgrown lakes and other other areas of still or slow-moving water. It feeds mainly on planktonic animals, sifting them from the water with its gill rakers. However, it will take small, free-swimming invertebrates individually if the opportunity arises. During the breeding season, males develop a golden sheen to their bodies and fins, the feature that gives this species its common name. Spawning generally takes place over algae or weeds, but occasionally these fish attempt to improve the chances of their eggs hatching by laying them in the nests of bigger, nest-guarding species such as largemouth bass.

Distribution: Much of eastern USA, widely introduced to other parts of the country. Also Canada, from Nova Scotia to Alberta.
Habitat: Weedy lakes, ponds, backwaters, swamps.
Food: Planktonic animals and some insect larvae.
Size: Up to 30cm/12in.
Breeding: Over weeds and occasionally in nests of other fish. Once eggs have been laid and fertilized, they are abandoned.

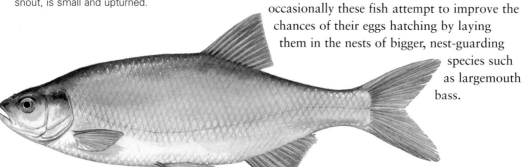

Hitch

Lavinia exilicauda

Identification: The silvery body is strongly compressed laterally. The head is small and the mouth upturned. The anal fin is relatively long and the caudal fin large and deeply forked. As with the golden shiner, the lateral line curves down towards the belly.

The only living species in its genus, the hitch is endemic to central California and was once extremely common. Although its numbers have declined in recent decades it is still fairly abundant in most of the places where it is found. Like the golden shiner, it is a plankton feeder that sometimes also catches individual free-swimming invertebrates. When its main food is scarce it can also eat algae. The hitch is unusually tolerant to both high and low temperatures, and as a result is more widely distributed than any other fish in California's Central Valley. It is also able to cope with significant levels of salt and is found in the Suisun Marsh, the largest saltwater marsh on the west coast of the USA.

Distribution: Confined to inland waters of California: throughout Sacramento-San Joaquin drainage system, in tributaries of the Monterey and San Francisco bays, Clear Lake and the Russian River.
Habitat: Lakes, ponds, backwaters, swamps and sluggish pools in rivers.
Food: Zooplankton, small invertebrates and algae.
Size: Up to 36cm/14in.
Breeding: Over gravel, clay or submerged vegetation. Large, spherical eggs, which hatch after 7 days, unguarded.

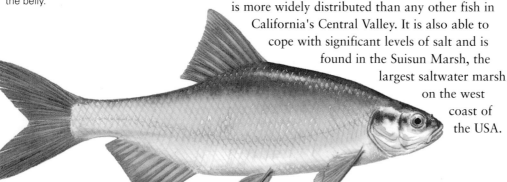

Sacramento squawfish (*Ptychocheilus grandis*):
Up to 1.4m/4.6ft
This species is a voracious hunter. Adults inhabit pools and river runs, while the young are confined to shallow water. This separation of microhabitats is a survival strategy – adults will attack any smaller fish they can, including their own species. It is confined to California: the Sacramento-San Joaquin, Russian, Clear Lake, Pajaro-Salinas and upper Pit River drainages.

Hardhead (*Mylopharodon conocephalus*):
Up to 1m/39½in
The hardhead (*above*) lives alongside the Sacramento squawfish, and closely resembles it, although the hardhead's body is deeper and heavier, and its head is less pointed. It also has more scales along its lateral line. The hardhead is a bottom feeder, not a predator. It is most common in deep river pools.

Northern squawfish (*Ptychocheilus oregonensis*): Up to 63cm/25in
Another solitary active hunter like the Sacramento squawfish, this fish occurs mostly in lakes and ponds. It is found from British Columbia to Alberta in Canada and as far south as Nevada and Oregon in the USA. The largest individuals tend to be found in deep water, with adult males reaching as much as 13kg/29lb.

Peamouth

Mylocheilus caurinus

A schooling fish of lakes and slow-flowing regions of rivers, the peamouth feeds on a wide range of small prey, including aquatic insects and their larvae, molluscs, free-swimming crustaceans and small fish. It is usually found among or near submerged vegetation, although it sometimes ventures into more open water. Spawning occurs close to shore in groups of 50 to 400 fish. After they have hatched, the fry form schools which remain close to the shore, venturing into deeper water after a few weeks. In parts of British Columbia the peamouth is known as the redmouth sucker. It is also known there by the Native Secwépemc people as Tcoktci'tcin, which literally means 'having a bloody mouth'.

Identification: A slender, slightly compressed body and large eyes. Green to dark grey-brown above, and silver-yellow sides with two dark stripes (the lower one ending before the anal fin). Large males have patches of red around their mouths and on their bellies and gill covers.

Distribution: From Nass and Peace River drainages of British Columbia southward to Columbia River drainages in Oregon and Idaho. Also Vancouver Island and some other, smaller islands.
Habitat: Lakes and gentle, meandering rivers with abundant vegetation.
Food: Aquatic invertebrates and small fish.
Size: Up to 36cm/14in.
Breeding: May and June. 1–2 males compete to fertilize. Sticky eggs attach to plants or pebbles and develop unguarded.

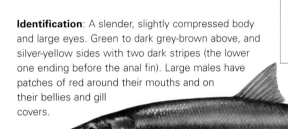

Colorado squawfish

Ptychocheilus lucius

Distribution: Colorado River system above the Glen Canyon Dam.
Habitat: Pools in medium to large rivers.
Food: Fish, amphibians and waterfowl.
Size: Up to 1.8m/5.9ft.
Breeding: The reproductive system of this species has not been closely studied but it is known that it does not guard its eggs.

Identification: The head is very large and may make up as much as a quarter of the total body length. The eyes are small and the large mouth toothless. In colour, this fish tends to be dusky green above, silver on the sides and yellow to white on the belly, although individuals can vary. The scales are comparatively small in size and not particularly visible.

This large fish is also known as the Colorado pike minnow, a name that accurately reflects its general shape. The Colorado squawfish is the biggest predatory fish in the Colorado River system. Like many other fish from that river it is now much rarer because of the damming and draining to provide power and water to the south-west USA's desert cities. Historically, there are examples of this species weighing as much as 36kg/79lb but today individuals weighing 7kg/15lb are rare. This fish once occurred all along the Colorado River down to Mexico but today it is confined to the main channel and large tributaries upstream of Arizona's Glen Canyon Dam. Hopefully, it will eventually be reintroduced into the lower Colorado River.

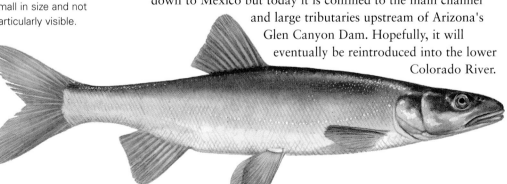

CHUBS

Although they all belong to the carp family, chubs are not easily defined as a group. Generally speaking, they have thickset, rounded bodies, although in some species these narrow considerably towards the tail. As a group, chubs are widespread in North America, with species occurring from the edge of the Arctic Circle all the way down to southern Mexico.

Arroyo chub

Gila orcutti

Identification: The chunky body is silver or grey to olive green in colour and lighter, sometimes white, below. The mouth is small but the eyes are quite large. The base of the tail is deep and relatively thick. Both the individual scales and lateral line are visible although the latter is sometimes quite faint.

The arroyo chub is a small fish – most adults grow little bigger than a European minnow. It is native to a few rivers and streams in California but has been introduced to other waterways in that state and is common in most places where it is found. It has no fixed breeding season but spawns continuously through the year from February until the end of August. During spawning, males follow a ripe female while rubbing their snouts against the area below her pelvic fins. This stimulates her to release the eggs and when these are shed into the water they may be fertilized by more than one male. This chub is omnivorous, but more than three-quarters of its diet (in weight) is made up of algae. Once they have reached two years old, female arroyo chubs tend to grow larger than males.

Distribution: California: Malibu Creek; Santa Clara, Santa Margarita, San Luis Rey River drainages; introduced to most other rivers.
Habitat: Flowing pools and runs in small rivers and streams with sandy or muddy bottoms.
Food: Algae and small aquatic invertebrates.
Size: Up to 12cm/5in, but usually much smaller.
Breeding: Eggs stick to plants, develop unguarded.

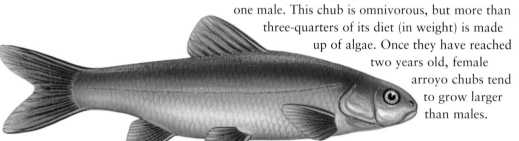

Roundtail chub

Gila robusta

This fish of rocky streams and rivers is split into four subspecies in the USA, *Gila robusta robusta*, *G. r. grahami*, *G. r. jordani* and *G. r. seminuda*. The differences between these are subtle and *G. r. robusta* is by far the most common and widespread. Other subspecies occur in Mexico. The roundtail is an opportunistic omnivore, feeding on everything from algae and water plants to insect larvae and crayfish. It has even been known to eat the eggs of other members of its own species. It spawns from May to July. Young fish survive on the vestiges of their yolk sacs until about ten days after hatching, when they begin to feed.

Identification: The head is somewhat flattened and pointed, although less so than in the humpback chub. The fins are quite large, particularly the caudal fin. In examples where it can be seen, the lateral line curves down towards the belly. In colour this fish is dusky green to bluish-grey above and white or silver below.

Distribution: Found in Nevada, Utah, New Mexico and Arizona in the USA. Also occurs northern parts of Mexico.
Habitat: Rocky streams and rivers. Also found in reservoirs.
Food: Algae, plant matter and aquatic invertebrates.
Size: Up to 43cm/17in.
Breeding: Open water. Eggs drift down, stick to substrate, develop unguarded. They hatch after 4–15 days, depending on water temperature.

Humpback chub

Gila cypha

With its small head, large caudal fin and strongly humped back, this is a distinctive fish that is hard to confuse with any other. It prefers deep, murky waters and is often found around large boulders and steep-sided cliffs. The combination of this and the fact that it is a protected species, listed as Vulnerable by the IUCN, means that it is rarely seen outside aquaria. It is omnivorous, feeding primarily on filamentous algae and insect larvae. It spawns from April to July, when the rivers in which it lives are swollen by flood water from snow-melt upstream. During the breeding season males develop a red tinge to their belly and cheeks.

Identification: The head is small and the back strongly humped. The base of the tail is unusually slender and the caudal fin is large. It is coloured olive-grey above and has silver sides. The belly ranges in colour from silver to white.

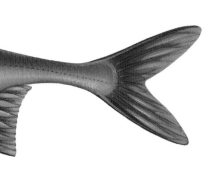

Distribution: Restricted to the Colorado and Green River systems of Wyoming, Colorado, Utah and Arizona.
Habitat: Deep pools, fast-flowing and turbid waters, usually associated with large boulders and steep cliffs.
Food: Algae and aquatic invertebrates.
Size: Up to 38cm/15in.
Breeding: Eggs released into open water. Washed downstream, where they develop unguarded.
Status: Vulnerable.

Blue chub (*Gila coerulea*):
Up to 41cm/16in
This fish is found in the Klamath and Lost River drainages of southern Oregon and the far north of California. It is a dusky olive above with silvery sides. During the breeding season, from May through to August, the males' sides and fins become tinged with orange while their snouts turn bright blue, hence the name.

Silver chub (*Macrhybopsis storeriana*):
Up to 23cm/9in
Previously known as *Platygobio storeriana*, this fish (*above*) has recently been reclassified. This moved it out of the genus it once shared with the flathead chub, which, apart from the silver's rounded head, it resembles in most respects. It occurs in eastern North America, from Manitoba, Canada, south to Texas, in lakes and the pools and backwaters of large rivers.

Leatherside chub (*Gila copei*):
Up to 15cm/6in
This small chub inhabits deep pools in streams and rivers. It ranges from the upper Snake River system in Wyoming and Idaho south to the Sevier River in southern Utah, and has been introduced into the Colorado River drainages. It has small scales with black specks, which gives its skin a leathery appearance. Breeding males develop red bases to their lower fins.

Flathead chub

Platygobio gracilis

This chub is a wide-ranging species, found in a broad band that sweeps down from Canada's Northwest Territories through the centre of North America. Its wide distribution is a reflection of its adaptability; it inhabits both swift and slow-moving stretches of rivers, and is common in turbid and clear waters. It is very active, forming small schools which seem to be almost permanently on the move. These sometimes mingle with schools of other, similar species for protection from predators. Flathead chub are unusual in that a large part of their diet consists of terrestrial and flying insects that fall into the water, although they also eat plant material and aquatic invertebrates. In Canada, water boatmen (*Corixidae* species) feature high on the menu, making up around a third of the chub's diet.

Distribution: East of Rocky Mountains in both Canada and the USA, from the edge of the Arctic Circle south as far as Texas.
Habitat: Rivers and streams.
Food: Insects and other invertebrates. Also plant matter and, occasionally, small fish.
Size: Up to 32cm/12½in.
Breeding: Spawning occurs from June and August. Eggs released directly into the water and develop unguarded.

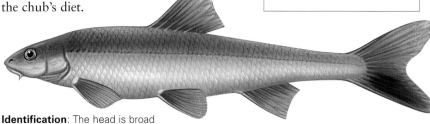

Identification: The head is broad and flat, and tapers to a pointed snout. The dorsal and anal fins are large and have slightly concave rear edges. The body is light dusky brown or olive above and silver on the sides and belly. The lower lobe of the caudal fin is dusky black.

CHUBS AND STONEROLLERS

With the exception of the lake chub, all of the fish on these pages show considerable sexual dimorphism during the breeding season. The males, which tend to be larger than the females, develop bony spines known as tubercles on their heads and undergo changes in colour. The males also change their behaviour, cutting down the amount of time spent feeding and turning their attentions to building nests.

River chub

Nocomis micropogon

The name of this fish indicates its habitat, in which it is very common. It was one of the first fish to be noticed and named by European settlers arriving in North America and it is widely distributed along the east coast. Since it was first named, it has been classified into two separate subspecies. Males of the group *Nocomis micropogon platyrhynchus*, which lives in the New River drainages of North Carolina, Virginia and West Virginia, have bony tubercles that extend right over the top of the head and well behind the eyes. Breeding males of the other subspecies *N. m. micropogon*, have fewer, larger tubercles restricted to the area in front of their eyes.

Identification: The snout is sloping and the eyes small and positioned relatively high on the head. During the breeding season the head of the male, including the snout, is dotted with pointed, bony tubercles. At this time, the male also develops a hump on the top of his head.

Distribution: Great Lakes basin and Atlantic drainages from New York State to Georgia and inland as far as Missouri.
Habitat: Rocky pools and runs of small to medium-sized rivers.
Food: Insect larvae and other aquatic invertebrates. Sometimes small fish and algae.
Size: Up to 32cm/12½in.
Breeding: Male builds nest and protects eggs vigorously.

Hornyhead chub

Nocomis biguttatus

Identification: The young have red caudal fins, while those of the adults are yellow. All the other fins are yellow to orange in colour. Large males have a bright red spot behind each eye, which, in the females, is brassy in colour and less obvious. Body colour is dark olive to brown above and light yellow to white below.

The male of this species, like the river chub, develops bony tubercles that surround its head like armour during the breeding season. The hornyhead chub occurs in small to medium-sized rivers over sand, gravel or boulders. Although it does not need clear waters, it becomes less common if water turbidity increases. Like the river chub, this species builds nests, although it does not guard its eggs or young. The nests are built by the males and are quite complex in structure. Each male excavates a pit about 1m/3.3ft across in the riverbed. He then fills it with gravel, carrying the small pebbles in his mouth until he has built a mound around 20cm/8in high. Finally, he makes troughs in the mound for a female to lay her eggs into, which are then fertilized and covered up. Females will then continue to spawn with other males at different mounds.

Distribution: From New York State to Manitoba and south as far as Kentucky. Rare across much of its range but common in the Ozarks.
Habitat: Small to medium-sized rivers with sand, gravel or rocky beds.
Food: Aquatic invertebrates, algae and some small fish.
Size: Up to 26cm/10¼in.
Breeding: Male builds complex gravel nest in riverbed, but does not guard eggs or young. Females spawn with more than one mate.

Creek chub

Semotilus atromaculatus

This fish, like the hornyhead chub, is an industrious builder. During the breeding season, males excavate pits in the gravel beds of the small rivers and streams they inhabit. Using his mouth, each male piles the gravel he has removed into a ridge just upstream of the pit, which helps to shelter it somewhat from the current. Once finished, he defends his ridge and pit from other males of the species. When a female arrives in his nest, the male encircles her with his body and she releases some of her eggs. The male then fertilizes these and covers them up. Perhaps surprisingly, male creek chub often let fish of other species spawn in their nests. Common shiners, for instance, may seek out these nests and lay their eggs within them.

Distribution: Across most of south-eastern Canada and the east of the USA, but absent from southern Georgia and peninsular Florida.
Habitat: Streams and small rivers with rocky, gravel or sandy beds.
Food: Aquatic invertebrates and small fish.
Size: Up to 30cm/12in.
Breeding: Male digs pit with sheltering ridge in gravel for visiting female. Females may spawn with more than one mate.

Identification: There is a large black spot at the front of the base of the dorsal fin. The mouth is large, stretching from the front of the snout to just beyond the front edge of the eye. Breeding males have between six and twelve large tubercles on their heads.

Bluehead chub (*Nocomis leptocephalus*):
Up to 26cm/10¼in
This resembles the larger river chub, but the breeding males have a more pronounced hump on their heads. Males build nests, which may then be used by other species, such as yellowfin shiners. This fish inhabits streams and small rivers in the east USA, from the Shenandoah River, Virginia, to the Pearl River, Mississippi. It is also found in some of the lower tributaries of the Mississippi River and the upper drainage basin of the New River in Virginia, West Virginia and North Carolina.

Mexican stoneroller (*Campostoma ornatum*):
Up to 16cm/6¼in
This fish (*above*) is similar in appearance to the slightly larger common stoneroller, but breeding males lack bony tubercles on the nape of the neck. It is common and widespread throughout Mexico. It is also found in the Rio Grande system of the Big Bend region of Texas and Arizona's Rucker Canyon and Leslie Creek. Males use their armoured, wedge-shaped snouts to excavate nests on the riverbed.

Lake chub (*Couesius plumbeus*):
Up to 23cm/9in
This fish commonly occurs across Canada, from Nova Scotia and Labrador to British Columbia and central Alaska. It is also found in northerly US states, from New England to Colorado. It eats everything from algae to small fish.

Common stoneroller

Campostoma anomalum

This fish, which is also known as the central stoneroller, lives in streams and small rivers across much of the east and centre of the USA. Its name comes from its breeding behaviour. One or several males build an irregular-shaped nest pit by bulldozing headfirst through the gravel, using their heads to push against and roll away larger pebbles. They also pick up small pebbles in their mouths. Female common stonerollers form small schools a short distance away, then enter this nesting area when ready to spawn. These fish feed mainly on algae and other simple food which they scrape from the rocks. Their lower jaws have hardened edges which act like rasps as they feed.

Identification: Breeding males have orange dorsal and anal fins, each with a black band running through them. They also have bony tubercles on their heads, with some of these forming a small, crescent-shaped row around the inside edge of each nostril. The lower jaw has a hard, gristly ridge protruding in front of the lower lip.

Distribution: Most of the USA east of the Rocky Mountains and as far south as the Rio Grande in Mexico.
Habitat: Streams and small rivers with rocky or gravel bottoms.
Food: Algae and microscopic organisms found in the slime on submerged rocks.
Size: Up to 22cm/8½in.
Breeding: Males build simple nests in gravel. Spawning females head into nesting area one by one to select nest. Eggs are abandoned and left to develop unguarded.

DACE AND FALLFISH

North American dace are small fish that are often brightly coloured, particularly during the breeding season. Although they have no shortage of predators they are common in most of the places where they are found. The fallfish is the largest member of the carp family native to eastern North America and is one of the most frequently seen.

Speckled dace

Rhinichthys osculus

Identification: Extremely variable in appearance across its substantial range and is thought to occur in several subspecies. These have yet to be properly classified and named. Wherever it occurs, however, its skin is well dusted with dark, almost black, specks. The young have a black stripe along their sides which fades as they grow older.

Some fish have common names with obscure origins and limited usefulness while others have completely misleading common names. The speckled dace is not one of these; in fact it could hardly be better named. It looks exactly as one might expect, a pale brown body lightly dusted with darker flecks almost as if it had been sprinkled with pepper. The speckled dace inhabits small rivers and streams where its colouration works to camouflage it almost completely. Holding its position in the water it is almost impossible to see. It is only when it moves suddenly that it catches the eye. This cryptic camouflage is important for its survival since fish this size have many predators, particularly birds such as kingfishers and herons. It obviously works, as the speckled dace is the most common and ubiquitous fish in the whole of the western USA.

Distribution: Pacific drainages, from the Columbia River basin in British Columbia south into Sonora region of Mexico.
Habitat: Small pools and runs of streams and fast-flowing rivers.
Food: Small aquatic invertebrates.
Size: Up to 11cm/4⅓in.
Breeding: Not studied, but thought to scatter its eggs and leave them to develop unguarded.

Rosyside dace

Clinostomus funduloides

Identification: The snout is long and pointed and the mouth large for such a small fish. The body is compressed and the scales are small. In colour, this fish is usually olive above with a dark stripe running along the back and a thin green to gold stripe on each side of the body. The scales on the upper half of the body have dark edges.

The rosyside dace gets its name from the breeding colours of the males, which develop orange to salmon pink sides below the lateral line as winter turns to spring. Another small fish, it is most common in streams and only occurs in the smallest rivers. The rosyside dace is split by biologists into three different subspecies, one of which has yet to be officially described and named. *Clinostomus funduloides funduloides* occurs on the Atlantic slope from the Delaware River basin in Pennsylvania southward to the lower Savannah River basin in Georgia and inland as far as Kentucky. *C. funduloides estor* occurs in the lower Cumberland and Tennessee River basins and the third, but as yet unnamed, subspecies is found only in the Little Tennessee River system.

Distribution: Eastern USA only, where it ranges from Pennsylvania to Georgia and inland to Kentucky and Mississippi.
Habitat: Clear streams and small rivers with rocky or gravel beds.
Food: Small aquatic invertebrates and, occasionally, algae.
Size: Up to 11cm/4⅓in.
Breeding: Spawns in flowing water over gravel. Eggs sink to the bottom and are left to develop unguarded.

Finescale dace

Phoxinus neogaeus

Distribution: Most of Canada from New Brunswick to British Columbia and the Yukon Territory. It is also found in the USA in Wisconsin, Wyoming and New York State.
Habitat: Marshes, ponds, lakes and slow, weed-filled rivers, usually over silt.
Food: Aquatic invertebrates and, occasionally, algae.
Size: Up to 11cm/4⅓in.
Breeding: Eggs are left to develop unguarded.

The finescale dace is a fish of northern bogs, marshes, ponds and sluggish rivers, more common in Canada than the USA. From necessity it is extremely hardy, spending the winter under ice and breeding from April, soon after the thaw has begun. Spawning occurs in large schools, with the bright red and yellow males and more drab females gathering around depressions beneath submerged logs and other vegetation. Spawning pairs dart into these depressions, the female lays her eggs and the male fertilizes them. They then dart back out again, the whole process taking less than a minute. Females grow larger than males and live longer, reaching a maximum of six years. In parts of its range this fish survives largely on a diet of freshwater fingernail clams.

Identification: As the name suggests, the scales are very small. The mouth is large, reaching from the end of the snout to beneath the leading edge of the eye. The body is well speckled with black and there is a dark brown to grey 'cape' which extends along the fish's back and upper side.

Blacknose dace (*Rhinichthys atratulus*):
Up to 10cm/4in
This dace lives in rocky pools and runs throughout eastern Canada and the USA, from Nova Scotia to Manitoba and south as far as Alabama and Georgia. Breeding males develop pads on the upper surfaces of their pectoral fins, but the function of these pads is not known. Despite its name, the fish most notably features black in a spot at the base of its caudal fin and in the stripe that runs down each side of its body.

Pearl dace
(*Margariscus margarita*):
Up to 16cm/6⅓in
The pearl dace (*above*) is common in rivers, ponds and lakes across Canada and the northern USA. In spring, males set up small territories, at distances of at least 1.8m/6ft from one another. They drive any ripe females that stray into their territory to the centre, where they spawn. Males and females also spawn with other partners.

Northern redbelly dace (*Phoxinus eos*):
Up to 8cm/3in
This little fish shares most of its range with the finescale dace and often hybridizes with that species. It has two black stripes along each side of its body. It can be distinguished from the very similar southern redbelly dace (*Phoxinus erythrogaster*) by its shorter, more rounded snout and slightly protruding chin.

Fallfish

Semotilus corporalis

This fish is closely related to the creek chub, with which it shares much of its behaviour as well as many physical characteristics. In spring, the male creates a nest for eggs by removing pebbles with his mouth to create a depression in the riverbed around 1m/3.3ft across. The pebbles are then dumped just upstream of the nest, creating a protective mound. Once the eggs have been laid they are covered up by the male. The name of this fish is quite misleading, as it is not particularly associated with waterfalls. Although it is mainly a fish of rivers it is also found in lakes, inhabiting the shallow water at the margins.

Identification: Notable for its unusually large scales which have dark pigmentation on their inside and outer edges. The body ranges from olive to gold-brown above, with bright silver sides. A dark stripe runs along the top of the back. The snout slightly overhangs the relatively large mouth. Breeding males have bony tubercles on their heads.

Distribution: Eastern North America from James River basin in New Brunswick as far south as Virginia. Also Lake Ontario, Lawrence River and Hudson Bay drainages of Ontario, Quebec and New York State.
Habitat: Pools and runs of gravel- and rubble-bottomed rivers. Also lake margins.
Food: Aquatic invertebrates and small fish.
Size: Up to 51cm/20in.
Breeding: Male builds nest on riverbed. Females lay small batches of eggs many times in the same season. Male covers and guards eggs.

SHINERS

Shiners are the smallest members of the carp family. Although common, shiners tend to be too small to be of any real interest to anglers, and their diminutive size also means that they are relatively difficult for freshwater biologists to study. However, they play an important role as a link in the food chain between aquatic invertebrates and larger, predatory fish.

Common shiner

Luxilus cornutus

Identification: The eyes are large. A dark stripe runs along the midline of the back and one or two more dark stripes run farther down, parallel to the centre stripe when seen from above. In breeding males the normally olive coloured body turns pink, as do the fins.

This shiner, as its name suggests, is a widespread and abundant freshwater fish, found across most of the north-eastern and northern states of the USA, as well as parts of Canada. It inhabits lakes and rivers but is particularly common in the latter, preferring slow riffles, pools and beaver ponds. The common shiner is an opportunistic omnivore. As well as catching a wide range of small prey it eats a large amount of algae and other greenery. In fact, around half of its food intake is made up of plant matter. As the breeding season begins, males develop tubercles on their heads and many start piling up pebbles to build gravel nests. Not all populations do this however – some use the nests of creek chubs or hornyhead chubs as spawning sites instead.

Distribution: Hudson Bay, Great Lakes, Atlantic and Mississippi River basins and south to James River drainages from Virginia to Wyoming.
Habitat: Lakes, small to medium-sized streams with clear, cold waters.
Food: Aquatic invertebrates, small fish, algae and plant matter.
Size: Up to 18cm/7in.
Breeding: Open water over gravel. Eggs develop unguarded.

Bleeding shiner

Luxilus zonatus

If the common shiner is a widespread fish, the bleeding shiner is localized. It is confined almost entirely to the southern half of Missouri, abutting the southernmost reach of the common shiner's range. Although of a restricted geographical range, the bleeding shiner is abundant where it is found. In fact, in many parts of Missouri it is the most common fish. This species lives in clear streams and small to medium-sized rivers, occurring in both rocky runs and deep, flowing pools. It gets its name from the appearance of the adult males, which develop bright, blood red heads and fins during the breeding season. Its limited range means that it has been relatively little studied but it is thought to be a short-lived species, with individuals rarely surviving for more than three years.

Identification: A large black bar around the snout extends along the sides of the body. There is also a narrow black stripe running down the upper half of each side of its body just behind the gill cover. Large individuals have red fins and a red head. In males, these become particularly bright during the breeding season.

Distribution: Restricted to a relatively small area of Ozark-draining tributaries of the Black, Little, St Francis, Missouri and Mississippi Rivers.
Habitat: Clear streams and rivers with rocky or gravel beds.
Food: Aquatic invertebrates, small fish, algae and some plant matter.
Size: Up to 13cm/5in.
Breeding: Thought likely to be a nest builder that leaves its eggs unguarded.

Rough shiner (*Notropis baileyi*):
Up to 9cm/3½in
Native to the states of Alabama and Mississippi, the rough shiner has also been introduced into the Chattahoochee River in Georgia and the Escambia River basin in Florida. It can be identified by its red-brown back and yellow fins. It feeds on just about anything it can find, from algae and plant matter to small invertebrates.

Saffron shiner (*Notropis rubricroceus*):
Up to 8.5cm/3¼in
Despite having a small range that crosses North Carolina, Virginia and Tennessee, the saffron shiner is particularly common in the Great Smoky Mountains National Park. Males become an intense reddish purple during the breeding season. This species occasionally hybridizes with the Tennessee shiner (*Notropis leuciodus*).

Redside shiner (*Richardsonius balteatus*):
Up to 18cm/7in
This shiner (*below*) inhabits drainages on the Pacific side of the Rocky Mountains, ranging through Washington, Oregon and Idaho, southern British Columbia and parts of Alberta, Montana, Wyoming, Colorado, Utah and northern Arizona. It feeds mainly on aquatic invertebrates and small fish, but it will occasionally eat algae.

Rosefin Shiner

Lythrurus ardens

The rosefin shiner lives in fast-moving water in the rocky pools and runs of hill and mountain streams and small rivers. It rarely grows longer than a man's index finger, and feeds on aquatic invertebrates and insects that fall into the water. For a long time, this fish was split into two subspecies but these have now been re-classified as entirely different species. The former subspecies *Lythrurus ardens ardens* is now considered to be the true rosefin shiner. The other, *Lythrurus ardens fasciolaris*, which is more slender and usually has 10 rather than 11 anal fin rays, now has the species name *Lythrurus fasciolaris*. It has yet to acquire a common name.

Identification: Distinguished by a black blotch at the base of its dorsal fin. Breeding males have orange bellies and heads, while their fins are red. A dusky stripe runs along the centre of the back from the top of the head to the base of the tail.

Distribution: *Lythrurus ardens*: Roanoke, York, Chowan, James and New River basins in Virginia and North Carolina. *Lythrurus fasciolaris* (not shown): occupies the rest of what was considered the rosefin's range, from Ohio to Alabama.
Habitat: Clear, fast-flowing streams and small rivers with rocky beds.
Food: Small invertebrates.
Size: Up to 8.5cm/3⅓in.
Breeding: Thought to be a nest builder that leaves its eggs unguarded.

Blacktail shiner

Cyprinella venusta

This is a fish of small to medium-sized rivers, most common in clear pools and runs over sand. In some places, however, it does occur in smaller gravel or rubble bottomed streams and in the west of its range it is often found in turbid water. Wherever it lives it prefers areas of strong current with sparse vegetation. The blacktail shiner spawns from March until early October, with activity peaking between April and the end of the summer. The males form small territories on the riverbed, which they defend from their rivals. Females that enter these territories are enticed to lay their eggs in crevices between any rocks or pebbles that might be lying on the bottom. This shiner is known to make sounds, although the exact function of these vocalizations is unclear.

Identification: The large black spot at the base of the caudal fin is usually enough to tell this fish apart from its relatives. The body is fairly deep and the snout is pointed. The body is dusky olive above with silver sides. From above, a narrow black stripe can be clearly seen running along the back.

Distribution: Much of south-east USA, ranging from Rio Grande basin in Texas to Suwannee River in Georgia and Florida.
Habitat: Small to medium sized rivers, usually over sand.
Food: Aquatic invertebrates and fish fry.
Size: Up to 19cm/7½in.
Breeding: Males defend small territories. Females lay eggs in crevices on the riverbed. Eggs left to develop unguarded.

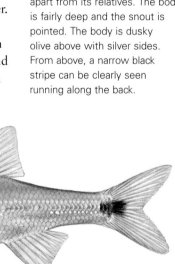

OTHER SHINERS

Shiners are arguably among the most beautiful freshwater fish of North America. They often have gold- or silver-sided bodies that catch the light as they swim, giving them their common name. Most shiners spend the majority of their time in shoals, which offer some degree of protection from the many larger fish that prey on them.

Redlip shiner

Notropis chiliticus

Identification: As its name suggests, this fish has bright red lips, making it look almost as if it is wearing lipstick. The eyes are large and the snout is rounded. Both sexes have a black stripe on the rear half of the side of the body. This ends in a black spot at the base of the caudal fin.

This little fish is related to the saffron shiner and closely resembles it. The redlip shiner's range abuts that of the saffron shiner on its eastern side. Like many of the smaller shiners, it is a shoaling fish that finds its food mainly by sight. It feeds almost entirely on the tiny aquatic invertebrates that abound in the clear streams it inhabits. It matures quickly and often breeds in its first year, during May and June. Rather than disperse their eggs randomly or protect them themselves, these fish seek out the nests of larger members of the carp family, particularly chubs, and lay them there instead. Male redlip shiners are handsome throughout the year but become especially colourful during the breeding season, turning bright red with a green stripe running down their sides.

Distribution: Native to Peedee and Dan River basins of Virginia and North Carolina. Recently introduced into New River through those states.
Habitat: Pools and runs in clear streams with rocky bottoms.
Food: Small aquatic invertebrates.
Size: Up to 7cm/2¾in.
Breeding: Spawn in the nests of larger cyprinids such as chubs, which ultimately guard eggs.

Rainbow shiner

Notropis chrosomus

With his iridescent pink and blue head and alternating body stripes of purple and silver, the male rainbow shiner in full breeding regalia must be considered one of North America's most beautiful fish. From April to July, the male puts all of his energies into this showy outfit, neither building a nest nor making any effort to protect the eggs or young. Instead, rainbow shiners take advantage of the parental diligence of others, seeking out the nests of egg-guarding chubs in which to spawn. The little fish gather around these in shoals of dozens, sometimes hundreds, of individuals, darting in in pairs to shed and fertilize their eggs. Its range is confined to the riffles and pools of small rivers in Georgia, Alabama and Tennessee. While never abundant, it is fairly common in these areas.

Identification: The colours of breeding males are unmistakable. During the rest of the year, the head and body are iridescent pink and blue, with a silver stripe, outlined in black, along the side. The body is compressed and the snout rounded. The eyes are not as large as in most other *Notropis* species.

Distribution: Confined to the Mobile Bay drainages in the Alabama, Black Warrior, Cahaba and Coosa River systems of Georgia, Alabama and Tennessee.
Habitat: Streams and small rivers with gravel or, occasionally, sandy beds.
Food: Small aquatic invertebrates.
Size: Up to 8cm/3in.
Breeding: Couples take it in turns to spawn in the nests of larger cyprinids such as chubs, which ultimately guard eggs.

Mirror shiner (*Notropis spectrunculus*):
Up to 7.5cm/3in
The mirror shiner inhabits rocky pools and runs in mountain streams and small rivers. It occurs mainly in the Blue Ridge habitats of the upper Tennessee River basin, in Tennessee, North Carolina and Georgia. There are also two isolated populations in southern Virginia. It can be distinguished by its orange fins and its eyes, which point slightly upward.

Bluehead shiner
(*Pteronotropis hubbsi*):
Up to 6cm/2¼in
This fish (*above*) is a close relative of the bluenose shiner (*see below*) but lives farther west, most commonly in northern Louisiana and southern Arkansas. Males mature sexually in their first year and develop bright colours, but they become more drab by their second year.

Longnose shiner (*Notropis longirostris*):
Up to 6.5cm/2½in
This small fish has a relatively long, rounded snout and upward pointing eyes like the mirror shiner, suggesting that it catches prey from or near the surface. The slender yellow body is straw yellow to grey above and the lower fins are yellow. It inhabits streams and rivers from western Florida and Georgia through southern Alabama and Mississippi to eastern Louisiana.

Taillight shiner

Notropis maculatus

This is a beautiful small fish that prefers still or slow-moving water with abundant vegetation. It is found across much of the far south-eastern USA. In Florida, it spawns from March to October. Elsewhere spawning occurs only in March, April and May. Because of the often inaccessible nature and turbidity of the swamps and backwaters it inhabits, this fish is rarely seen in the wild, but it is known to be relatively common across most of its range. Young feed on rotifers and other microscopic free-swimming invertebrates, but as they grow their diet alters and they begin to feed more on insect larvae and algae.

Identification: The caudal fin has small black spots on its upper and lower edges and a single large black spot at its base: the areas between these are red. The front of the dorsal fin is covered by a large black blotch. The back and sides of the fish have a cross-hatched pattern. During the breeding season the head and body of the male turns bright red.

Distribution: Atlantic, Gulf and Mississippi drainage basins from North Carolina down to Florida, west to north-east Texas.
Habitat: Backwaters and swamps.
Food: Aquatic invertebrates, insect larvae and algae.
Size: Up to 7.5cm/3in.
Breeding: The breeding system of this fish is not known. Spawning dates are inferred from the abundance of gravid females.

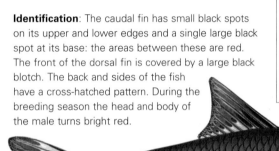

Bluenose shiner

Pteronotropis welaka

With his exaggerated dorsal, pelvic and anal fins, the male bluenose shiner looks quite exotic. Normally these fins are held close to the body but during the breeding season they are brandished like flags to threaten rivals and to entice females to spawn. Perhaps unsurprisingly, this shiner is prized by aquarium enthusiasts and is under threat from over-collecting across parts of its range. In the wild, this shiner forms small schools. These grow larger during the breeding season as the fish concentrate around the nests of sunfish, which they use as places to spawn. Typically the shiners wait for the owner of the nest to become distracted, and then dart in to spawn *en masse* before rushing out again. The whole process takes just a matter of seconds.

Identification: The body is slender and has a thick black stripe which extends down the sides in both sexes. It ends in a spot at the base of the caudal fin. The breeding male has a bright blue nose and enormous dorsal, pelvic and anal fins. Females have the more familiar triangular fins.

Distribution: St John's River drainage, Florida, to Gulf coast drainages in Georgia Mississippi, Alabama and Louisiana.
Habitat: Backwaters and quiet pools of streams and slow rivers, with abundant vegetation.
Food: Small aquatic invertebrates.
Size: Up to 6.5cm/2½in.
Breeding: Breeding shoals spawn in the nests of sunfish, who ultimately guard the eggs.

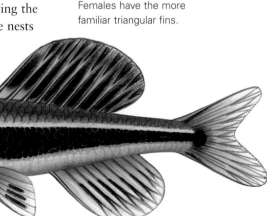

BASSES

Although they are all known as basses, the fish on these pages belong to two different families.
The striped bass, yellow bass and white bass are all members of the family Moronidae, better known
as the temperate basses, which also have representatives in Europe and northern Africa. The other
bass species belong to the Centrarchidae, a family of fish found exclusively in North America.

Striped bass

Morone saxatilis

This is the USA's most important game fish, drawing anglers from all over the country to the lakes and rivers where it is found. It is the largest of the temperate basses, and crucial to the economy of several coastal fishing towns in the southern and eastern states. Although it can spend its whole life in fresh water, it is naturally a fish of bays, estuaries and shallow coastal seas, and only enters rivers to spawn. The striped bass is a large, powerful fish with tasty flesh – the perfect combination for anglers. Individuals can weigh as much as 57kg/125lb and may live up to 30 years, providing they manage to avoid being caught.

Identification: Six to nine dark grey horizontal stripes on each side of the body. The rear of the tongue has one or two patches of teeth. The body is dark olive to blue-grey above and silvery-white on the sides. The pelvic fin and the edge of the anal fin are white on large adults.

Distribution: Atlantic and Gulf slope drainages from St Lawrence River in New Brunswick to Louisiana. Introduced to some Pacific rivers and landlocked lakes.
Habitat: Coastal waters and large rivers.
Food: Young: invertebrates; adults: fish.
Size: Up to 2m/6.6ft.
Breeding: Travels upriver in March. Eggs are semi-buoyant, float downstream in water column then hatch.

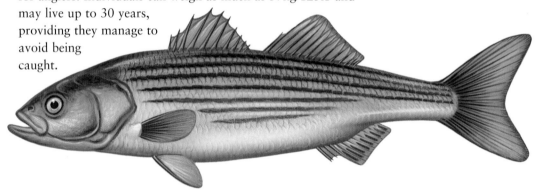

Yellow bass

Morone mississippiensis

Identification: The body is olive-grey above, with silver-yellow sides, displaying five to seven horizontal black stripes. These stripes are offset and broken on the lower half of the fish. The fins are clear to blue-grey in colour. The tongue is devoid of teeth.

If the striped bass is a giant, the yellow bass might be considered something of a dwarf. This fish typically weighs around 0.25kg/½lb and, although it can grow larger, never reaches anything like the size of its sea-going cousin. As a result, it is not actively sought out by anglers, although it is often caught, being fairly common across most of its range. It tends to be found in schools although sometimes it may be seen swimming alone. The yellow bass is an exclusively freshwater fish. A species of slow-moving or still, often turbid, waters, it feeds primarily on insect larvae, worms and crayfish, although larger individuals may capture small fish. Yellow bass sometimes school with the similar-sized white bass (*see opposite page*).

Distribution: Natural range is Lake Michigan and Mississippi River basins. Widely introduced elsewhere.
Habitat: Lakes, ponds and pools in rivers.
Food: Aquatic invertebrates and small fish.
Size: Up to 46cm/18in.
Breeding: Schools enter small streams to spawn over gravel. Eggs are left to develop unguarded.

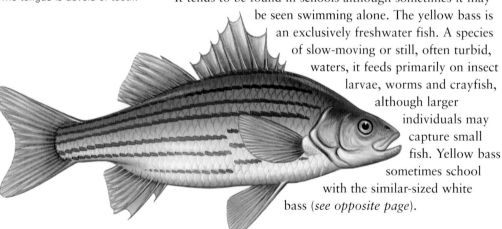

Largemouth bass

Micropterus salmoides

Distribution: Native to eastern half of USA but widely introduced elsewhere. Now common in many parts of the country.
Habitat: Clear ponds, lakes, swamps and pools of rivers with abundant vegetation.
Food: Young: aquatic invertebrates; adults: fish.
Size: Up to 97cm/38in.
Breeding: Male builds nest on bottom in shallow water, guards eggs (typically 3,000) and young.

This fish, also known as the Billy bass, is another favourite with US anglers. In the quiet, clear waters it inhabits it is often the top predator, giving it a certain cachet as a sports fish. It can grow substantially – the largest recorded weighed just over 11.3kg/25lb. It is also long-lived, reaching as much as 23 years in the wild. The male largemouth is a careful parent. As the breeding season begins in spring he builds a crude nest on the bottom and entices a female to lay her eggs in it. If he is successful he fertilizes them, then guards them until they hatch. The tiny fry then school around their father for the first month of their lives.

Identification: As its name suggests, this fish has a very large mouth. There are two dorsal fins, which are almost completely separate from one another. The body is silver to brassy green above, although it often looks brown in the water. A broad black stripe, which is often broken, runs along each side as far as the snout.

Shadow bass

Ambloplites ariommus

The shadow bass and its close relative the rock bass are unusual among freshwater fish in being able to change colour to match their background. This makes them very successful predators but also makes them difficult to spot in the wild. The shadow bass prefers clear, vegetated lake margins and pools in rivers. It spends much of its time sitting still on the bottom, waiting for smaller fish to swim into reach. When they do it reacts with surprising speed, darting out to swallow them up. It can weigh up to 0.8kg/1¾lb but is usually smaller. Common throughout parts of Florida, Georgia, Alabama, Mississippi and Louisiana, there are also isolated populations in Arkansas and southern Missouri.

Identification: A compressed body and relatively large eyes. Its ability to change colour can make identification difficult but most fish have irregular marbling of grey or brown on their sides. There are usually between 15 and 18 rows of scales across the breast, between one pectoral fin and the other.

Distribution: Rivers draining into Gulf of Mexico, from Apalachicola river basin of Georgia to lower Mississippi basin in Louisiana.
Habitat: Vegetated pools of streams and rivers over gravel, sand or mud.
Food: Aquatic invertebrates and small fish.
Size: Up to 22cm/8¾in.
Breeding: Males build nests and guard eggs and young. Nests may sometimes be built close together in colonies.

White bass (*Morone chrysops*):
Up to 45cm/17¾in
This popular game fish feeds at dawn and dusk. Large schools can be seen driving prey to the surface, which leap from the water as they try to escape. The white bass inhabits lakes, ponds and pools in rivers. Its native range covers a broad band stretching from Mexico to southern Canada across the USA east of the Rockies.

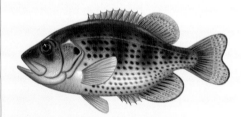

Rock bass (*Ambloplites rupestris*):
Up to 43cm/17in
This fish (*above*) is the largest member of its genus, weighing up to 1.4kg/3lb. It is popular with anglers and is sold commercially as a food fish. It is found in vegetated areas of lakes, rivers and streams across the eastern USA and south-eastern Canada. In parts of Canada it is known as the redeye, redeye bass or goggle eye. Elsewhere it goes by the name rock perch.

Spotted bass (*Micropterus punctulatus*):
Up to 61cm/24in
This fish occupies a similar native range to the largemouth bass, but generally speaking, this is a species of clear rivers, and it is found in areas of stronger current than the largemouth. It can also be told apart from its relative by the rows of small, black spots on its lower side.

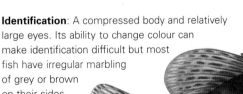

YELLOW PERCH, WALLEYE, FLIER, WARMOUTH, SAUGER AND CRAPPIES

The yellow perch, walleye and sauger are members of the perch family, Percidae. The flier, warmouth and the crappies belong to the panfish group (as do the sunfish) – so called because of their flattened, pan-shaped bodies. Coincidentally, all of them are also popular food fish that tend to be served up fried.

Yellow perch

Perca flavescens

Identification: The body is compressed and fairly deep. The back is green with between six and nine greenish-brown saddles, which extend down over the yellow sides of the body. The first dorsal fin has a black blotch at the rear. The mouth is large and extends to below the middle of the eye.

A species of clear and usually well-vegetated water, the yellow perch is one of the most commonly caught fish anywhere in North America. Its native range is large, stretching from the north-eastern states of the USA across much of Canada and it has been widely introduced elsewhere. As well as good sport it makes good eating and, unlike many of the other fish that share its range, it is active throughout the winter, taking the bait of ice fishermen as commonly as that of other anglers during the summer. The yellow perch is a shoaling fish that hunts invertebrates and fish fry both in open water and on the bottom. In turn, it is preyed on by larger fish, including the northern pike, walleye and various species of bass.

Distribution: Native range is from Georgia to Quebec and east as far as British Columbia. Introduced to most of the rest of the USA.
Habitat: Lakes, ponds and pools in rivers and streams.
Food: Insect larvae and other aquatic invertebrates.
Size: Up to 40cm/16in.
Breeding: A prolific breeder. Spawns spring, over dense vegetation. Eggs are laid in gelatinous strings, left to develop unguarded.

Walleye

Stizostedion vitreum

Also known as the glass-eye, jack salmon, marble-eye, pike perch and white eye, this fish has one of the largest natural distributions of any fish on this continent. It is also the largest of the North American perches, reaching 5kg/11lb. It is an active predator that often travels in schools. In clear waters it searches for prey at dawn and dusk, but where sediment reduces visibility it may hunt through the day. It gets its common name from the reflective layer of pigment over its eyes, which helps it to see prey in low light and turbid water. Like the yellow perch, it remains active during the winter, even when the surface is covered with ice, rather than lying semi-dormant on the bottom as many other species do.

Identification: The very large mouth contains sizeable canine teeth and extends back beyond the middle of the eye, which looks silver and opaque. The rear of the first dorsal fin usually bears a large, black spot. The body is long and slender, the snout pointed and the caudal fin forked.

Distribution: Large natural distribution, from Georgia to edge of Canada's Yukon Territory. Widely introduced elsewhere throughout Canada and the USA.
Habitat: Lakes and medium to large rivers.
Food: Aquatic invertebrates and small fish.
Size: Up to 91cm/36in.
Breeding: Spawns over rocky or gravel banks in April and May. Eggs are left to develop unguarded.

Sauger (*Stizostedion canadense*):
Up to 76cm/30in
This fish is closely related to the similar-looking walleye, but is distinguished by the many small, black crescents on its dorsal fin, between the spines. Its native range is similar to that of the walleye, but it does not occur as far north. It has been introduced widely through the USA as well as southern Canada, where it is harvested commercially.

White crappie
(*Poxomis annularis*):
Up to 53cm/21in
This fish (*above*) occurs across most of the USA east of the Rockies and is widely introduced elsewhere. It is the state fish of Louisiana, where it is known by the common name sac-au-lait. Elsewhere it may be called the white perch. It resembles its close relative the black crappie, but is generally lighter in colour, with six dorsal spines rather than the latter's seven or eight.

Black crappie (*Poxomis nigromaculatus*):
Up to 49cm/19¼in
Widespread across the USA east of the Rockies, this fish has been so widely introduced that its original, native range is difficult to determine. It is a nest builder, like the white crappie, and feeds on aquatic invertebrates and small fish.

Flier

Centrarchus macropterus

Sometimes called the flier bream, this fish is the only living member of its genus. It lives in slow-moving and still waters, which are often acidic and heavily stained with tannins released by rotting vegetation. The flier is common in the forested swamps of the southern US states. It feeds throughout the water column on invertebrates, fish fry and algae and is itself in turn a common prey of larger fish, water birds and turtles. It spawns from February to May. This fish gets its name from its large, wing-like fins. These, together with its hardiness, have made it popular with aquarium enthusiasts.

Identification: A distinctive large black 'teardrop' beneath each of its eyes. An extremely compressed body with rows of black spots running along each side. The mouth is small. The body is usually dusky grey on the back and silver, flecked with bronze and green, on the sides.

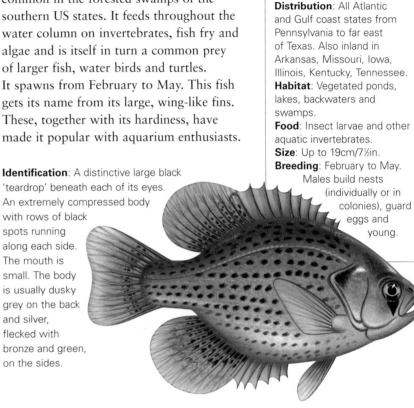

Distribution: All Atlantic and Gulf coast states from Pennsylvania to far east of Texas. Also inland in Arkansas, Missouri, Iowa, Illinois, Kentucky, Tennessee.
Habitat: Vegetated ponds, lakes, backwaters and swamps.
Food: Insect larvae and other aquatic invertebrates.
Size: Up to 19cm/7½in.
Breeding: February to May. Males build nests (individually or in colonies), guard eggs and young.

Warmouth

Lepomis gulosus

Slightly larger than the flier, this is another North American freshwater fish popular with aquarists. In the wild it lives in areas of slow-moving or still water, often with low oxygen levels. It is a nest breeder, the males constructing bowl-shaped nests in the mud, sand or rubble on the bottom, usually siting them near a rock, submerged tree trunk or clump of vegetation. Unlike those of fliers, these nests are almost always well separated from one another. Once the eggs have been laid, the males fan them to make sure that they are oxygenated enough to develop properly (developing eggs in still water slowly use up the dissolved oxygen around them). In some places the warmouth may spawn two or more times every year.

Identification: The mouth is large with the upper jaw reaching to below or beyond the pupil of the eye. The eye is red and has dark red-brown wavy lines radiating from its rear edge. The body is thick and the tongue has a single patch of teeth. The pectoral fin is short and rounded and the ear flap relatively short.

Distribution: Natural range extends through eastern half of USA, and west through Oklahoma and Texas as far as New Mexico. Introduced elsewhere in USA.
Habitat: Swamps, vegetated lakes and ponds, and pools in quiet streams, usually over mud.
Food: Aquatic invertebrates and small fish.
Size: Up to 31cm/12in.
Breeding: Males build individual, well-separated nests, aerate eggs and guard eggs and young.

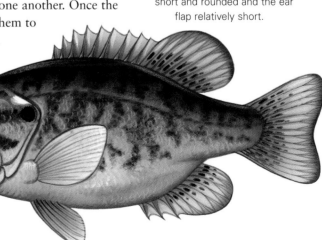

SUNFISH

Freshwater sunfish evolved in North America and are native to this continent alone. Within North America most species have been widely introduced to new regions and habitats by anglers. Some, such as the pumpkinseed, have also been taken abroad and now also live wild in Europe and Africa. Freshwater sunfish are members of the perch family, and are completely unrelated to the ocean sunfish, Mola mola.

Pumpkinseed

Lepomis gibbosus

Identification: The pumpkinseed has a bright red or orange spot on its gill cover. The pectoral fin is long and pointed. The cheeks and gill covers have distinctive wavy blue stripes running over them. The mouth is small with the upper jaw not reaching back as far as the pupil of the eye.

This sunfish is native to the north-eastern states of the USA and the far south-east of Canada, and has been widely introduced elsewhere in North America. It is a fish of clear water with abundant vegetation. Its range overlaps with the rock bass, largemouth bass and bluegill. The male builds nests for breeding, nearly always in shallow water near the shore. Females are enticed to lay in the nest and as soon as one has done so and her eggs have been fertilized the male begins fanning them. He guards them fiercely until hatching and watches over the young fry until they leave the nest after about 11 days. He then refurbishes his nest and prepares to spawn again with the same, or occasionally a different, female.

Distribution: Native to Atlantic drainages from South Carolina to New Brunswick, but widely introduced elsewhere in North America.
Habitat: Vegetated ponds, lakes and pools in rivers.
Food: Aquatic invertebrates and small fish.
Size: Up to 40cm/16in.
Breeding: Male builds nest and guards eggs and young. Pumpkinseeds usually spawn more than once in a single season.

Longear sunfish

Lepomis megalotis

Identification: The body of the adult fish is dark red above and bright orange underneath, with blue spots and marbling. As with the pumpkinseed, there are wavy blue stripes on the cheeks and gill covers. The ear flap is unusually long, and usually bordered by a thin blue line.

This sunfish shares part of its range with the pumpkinseed, but is generally a more southerly species. Like its cousin it is a nest builder with the males guarding both the eggs and young. However, it usually nests in colonies rather than alone. In recent years it has started to become popular with aquarium enthusiasts. As well as being striking to look at, it is widely regarded as being the easiest sunfish to keep. In the wild, it prefers shallow, well-vegetated areas of slow-moving upland streams. It feeds on a wide range of small prey, including fish fry, and occasionally eats algae. There is significant variation in the appearance of this fish across its range and it is thought that there may be as many as six different subspecies, although these have yet to be properly defined and classified.

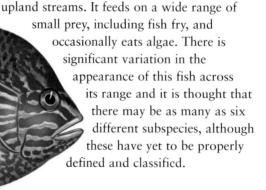

Distribution: Great Lakes to far northeast Mexico; introduced to other regions.
Habitat: Pools of streams and small to medium-sized rivers over rock or sand, usually near to vegetation.
Food: Aquatic invertebrates and small fish.
Size: Up to 24cm/9½in.
Breeding: Males usually nest in colonies and guard both the eggs and young.

Spotted sunfish

Lepomis punctatus

A fish of the south-eastern USA, the spotted sunfish usually inhabits swamps and heavily vegetated ponds, lakes and pools, but is also found in brackish streams near the coast, being more tolerant of salt water than other species of sunfish. It feeds mainly on insect larvae, which it picks from submerged logs and vegetation. This habit has earned it the alternative common name of stumpknocker. Like other sunfish, most of the males build nests, which they defend aggressively from other males. Some, however, act as nest parasites, diving in and attempting to fertilize the eggs of a female as she lays in the nest of another male. Male spotted sunfish make a grunting sound when courting females and trying to induce them to lay.

Identification: This forms two subspecies: *Lepomis punctatus punctatus* has a relatively pale body with many black specks on its head and body. *L. punctatus miniatus* (*below*) has no black specks but does have rows of red and yellow spots on its sides. In both, the pectoral fin is short and rounded.

Distribution: Coastal states, USA, from far south of North Carolina to central Texas. Also Arkansas, Missouri, Iowa, Illinois, Kentucky and Tennessee.
Habitat: Swamps, heavily vegetated ponds and lakes, weedy pools in streams and small to medium-sized rivers.
Food: Insect larvae and other aquatic invertebrates.
Size: Up to 20cm/8in.
Breeding: The nest building male guards eggs and young.

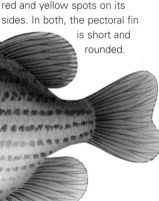

Bluegill (*Lepomis macrochirus*):
Up to 41cm/16in
This fish is native to the eastern USA, south-eastern Canada and north-eastern Mexico, and has been introduced throughout the USA, northern Mexico and parts of Canada. It lives in shallow waters, spawns in colonies and is a prolific breeder. It has a large black spot at the rear of its dorsal fin, a long, pointed pectoral fin and an extremely compressed body.

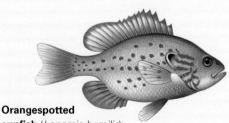

Orangespotted sunfish (*Lepomis humilis*):
Up to 15cm/6in
The native range of this sunfish (*above*) covers most of the central USA. It lives in quiet pools of streams and rivers, often in turbid water. Smaller than most other sunfish, it feeds almost entirely on invertebrate prey. Its silver-green sides are speckled with spots. These are bright orange on the males and red-brown on the females.

Redear sunfish (*Lepomis microlophus*):
Up to 25cm/10in
The redear spawns in deeper water than most other species and so is less often caught or seen. As its name suggests, it has a bright red or orange spot on the back of its ear flap. Native to the south-eastern USA, it has been introduced as far as New Mexico and Michigan.

Green sunfish

Lepomis cyanellus

A real survivor, the green sunfish is able to tolerate much lower levels of oxygen in the water than most other fish and survives in temporary pools during droughts where many other species suffocate and die. It is also quick to breed when conditions change, usually making it the first fish to repopulate such intermittent watercourses. Males construct nests, often colonially, in which females lay their eggs. These nests are usually situated in shallow water near sheltering rocks, logs or clumps of vegetation. Like spotted sunfish, the males often make grunting sounds when courting potential mates. Green sunfish may breed several times in a single year.

Distribution: Central USA; also far south of Ontario and northern Mexico.
Habitat: Lakes, ponds and quiet pools of sluggish streams.
Food: Aquatic invertebrates, small fish and algae.
Size: Up to 31cm/12in.
Breeding: Male builds nest in shallow water (usually in colonies), fans eggs and then guards young.

Identification: The body appears slender but is quite thick. The mouth is large, with the upper jaw extending to beneath the pupil of the eye. There is a large, black spot at the rear of both the second dorsal and the anal fin. These and the caudal fin have orange or yellow edges.

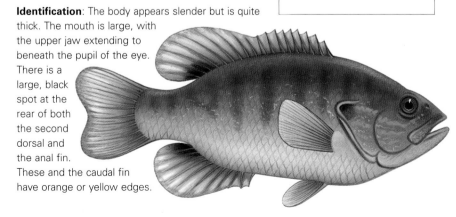

OTHER SUNFISH

Sunfish are predatory fish that feed on smaller prey. They tend to be confined to still or very sluggish water. Although they have been introduced elsewhere, sunfish are found naturally only in US states and parts of Canada that are east of the Rocky Mountains. All display sexual dimorphism and in most species the male is much more colourful than the female.

Mud sunfish

Acantharchus pomotis

Identification: The body is compressed and almost rectangular in shape, and is green or brown in colour. The caudal fin is rounded. Three or four parallel black stripes run across the face and along the body to the base of the tail. The ear flap has a black dot which is edged with orange on large individuals.

Sometimes known as the mud bass, this fish inhabits the small lakes and muddy backwaters along the USA's Atlantic coast. Although it is quite widespread, it is uncommon (in New York State, at the far north of its range, it is classified as threatened). In addition, its coloration and preference for water thick with detritus and often choked with weeds means that it is rarely seen. It feeds almost entirely on insect larvae and small freshwater crustaceans. Although its populations are never abundant, it occurs in acidic water, particularly in cedar swamps and backwaters of rivers that flow beneath pines. The mud sunfish is the only living member of its genus.

Distribution: Freshwater drainages along east coast of USA, from New York State to Florida.
Habitat: Swamps and vegetated backwaters and pools.
Food: Insect larvae and other aquatic invertebrates.
Size: Up to 21cm/8¼in.
Breeding: Spawns in spring. Male builds nest and guards the eggs until they hatch, defending them from other fish until they hatch.

Blackbanded sunfish

Enneacanthus chaetodon

This small sunfish occupies a similar range to the mud sunfish and can often be found living alongside it. However, the blackbanded sunfish is much more common than its larger cousin. In recent years it has become popular as an aquarium fish. Some stock is still taken from the wild but in most places it is now possible to buy captive-bred individuals. This species has a similar breeding pattern to other sunfish. With the onset of spring, the males start to build nests on the bottom, choosing sites protected by water plants or other cover. Females lay their eggs in these nests and are then driven off by the males. The males watch over the eggs until they hatch and then guard the young for a week or so, until they are big enough to leave.

Identification: A dusky yellow-grey body crossed with six black bars. The first of these runs through the eye and the sixth, which may be faint, crosses the stem at the base of the tail. The spine and first membrane of the pelvic fin are pink or red, then black in colour. The first few membranes of the dorsal fin are usually black.

Distribution: Northern Florida and southern Georgia, South Carolina, North Carolina, far south-east of Virginia and areas to the east of Washington DC.
Habitat: Vegetated lakes, ponds and pools in slow-flowing streams and rivers.
Food: Small aquatic invertebrates and fish fry.
Size: Up to 8cm/3in.
Breeding: Male builds nest in spring and defends eggs and young from other fish, including the females.

Bluespotted sunfish

Enneacanthus gloriosus

Distribution: South-eastern Mississippi through whole of Florida and northward up east coast to New York State.
Habitat: Vegetated ponds, lakes and pools of sluggish rivers and streams.
Food: Aquatic invertebrates.
Size: Up to 9.5cm/3¾in.
Breeding: Spawns continuously from early spring to end of summer. Male builds nest and guards both eggs and young from other fish.

This small fish lives in ponds and oxbow lakes with dense vegetation. It feeds on copepods, ostracods and other planktonic invertebrates, as well as small insect larvae, emerging from the cover of weeds to find food at dawn and dusk. It tends to stay hidden during the day. It matures quickly and some fish breed in their first year of life. Within the species, some individuals are much more brightly coloured than others from different areas. The small size and bright colours of this species have led some people to capture and breed it, with a view to establishing it as a fish for the home aquarium. However, its shyness and crepuscular habits mean that it is likely to have only a limited specialist market.

Identification: The body is dusky olive with rows of blue or silver spots along the sides. The caudal fin is rounded. The ear flap has a dark spot which is about two-thirds the size of the pupil of the eye.

Bantam sunfish (*Lepomis symmetricus*):
Up to 9cm/3½in
This sunfish is the smallest member of its genus. It lives for just three years, in oxbow lakes, ponds and swamps, always over mud. It is found in Louisiana, eastern Texas, western Alabama and parts of Mississippi, Tennessee, Iowa, Illinois and Arkansas. Compared with most other sunfish it is relatively drab and chubby. A black spot at the rear of its dorsal fin is perhaps its most distinguishing feature.

Redbreast sunfish (*Lepomis auritus*):
Up to 24cm/9½in
The redbreast (*above*) lives in streams, rivers and lakes, usually over rocks or sand, in all of the east coast states, stretching from New Brunswick to northern Florida. Although its name refers to the colour of its belly, it also has a distinctively long, dark-coloured ear flap.

Dollar sunfish (*Lepomis marginatus*):
Up to 12cm/4¾in
Small, brightly coloured and easy to keep, the dollar sunfish is a popular aquarium fish. It occurs across most of the south-eastern USA, in swamps, sluggish streams and rivers, and pools, usually over sand or mud. It feeds on aquatic invertebrates and fish fry. It is similar to the larger longear sunfish but with a shorter ear flap.

Banded pygmy sunfish

Elassoma zonatum

As its name suggests, this fish is tiny. It is one of the smallest freshwater fish in North America, with adults rarely reaching the length of a man's thumb. However, it is the largest member of its genus, containing five other even smaller fish, all endemic to the south-eastern USA. The smallest of these is the similar-looking Everglades pygmy sunfish (*Elassoma evergladi*) which grows to a maximum length of 3.2cm/1¼in. The prey of the banded pygmy sunfish is also tiny – midge larvae and planktonic crustaceans. It is among the few sunfish that do not build nests or guard their eggs.

Distribution: Central lowlands, Gulf and Atlantic coastal plain from Brazos River in Texas to Roanoke River in North Carolina.
Habitat: Swamps and sluggish streams with abundant vegetation.
Food: Microscopic aquatic invertebrates.
Size: Up to 4.7cm/1¾in.
Breeding: Spawn March and April in open water. Eggs have adhesive coat, are laid over vegetation and stick where they fall. Eggs left to develop unguarded.

Identification: There are one or two large black spots on the back just below the front edge of the dorsal fin. There are between seven and twelve dark green to blue-black bars on each side of the body. The top of the head is devoid of scales. The breeding male turns black with greenish-gold flecks and has alternating black and gold bars on his sides.

PIRATE PERCH, TROUT PERCH, SAND ROLLER AND MUDMINNOWS

The pirate perch belongs to family all its own, Aphredoderidae. The trout perch and sand roller are sole members of another exclusively North American family, Percopsidae. The mudminnows (which include the Alaska blackfish) belong to the Umbridae family, which also has members in Europe and Asia.

Pirate perch

Aphredoderus sayanus

Identification: The head is large, as is the mouth, and the lower jaw juts out in front of the upper jaw. Unusually, the anus is located on the throat. This fish is grey to black above in colour. Large individuals have a purple sheen. There is a black bar at the base of the caudal fin and often a black teardrop just below each eye. The caudal fin is square.

The pirate perch is a secretive fish that stays hidden during the day, burrowing into thick aquatic vegetation or organic debris and avoiding the sunlight. As the day begins to end and the sun sinks below the horizon it emerges to hunt. A solitary predator, it feeds mainly on insect larvae and freshwater crustaceans, although it occasionally catches small fish. It becomes most active and animated in the hours just before dawn, but seeks shelter as the sun rises and goes into hiding again. The pirate perch breeds earlier than most fish, spawning in February and March. For a long time it was thought that this species might be a mouthbrooder, but it is now known that eggs are laid directly into the water and fertilized by the male before drifting down to the bottom.

Distribution: Found Atlantic and Gulf slopes from New York State to Texas. Also Mississippi River basin up through the central USA as far as Great Lakes.
Habitat: Ponds, lakes, swamps, backwaters, quiet pools of streams and rivers.
Food: Aquatic invertebrates, some small fish.
Size: Up to 14cm/5½in.
Breeding: Eggs laid into open water, stick to bottom, and are left to develop unguarded.

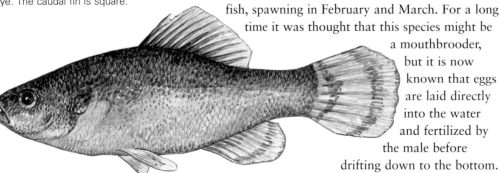

Trout perch

Percopsis omiscomaycus

Identification: The back is yellow to olive and covered with silver flecks. There are rows of seven to twelve dusky spots along the back and sides. The head is large and flattened below. There are large silver-white chambers, known as pearl organs, on the edge of the cheek and on the lower jaw.

This fish is neither trout nor perch but earned its common name because of its passing resemblance to both. It is a fish of lakes and large rivers and tends to be found in the deeper waters of each. Female trout perch grow slightly larger than the males and also live longer, surviving for four years rather than the males' three. Although their lives are quite short, these fish manage to produce a lot of offspring. They breed from the beginning of May through until the end of August and often spawn several times in a year. In lakes, spawning occurs over sandbars or rocks, while in rivers they tend to head into smaller tributary streams to breed. Each female releases her eggs surrounded by two or more males, which release their milt at the same time.

Distribution: North-eastern USA and across most of Canada east of the Rocky Mountains. Also ranges across Alaska.
Habitat: Lakes and deep, flowing pools of rivers and streams, usually over sand.
Food: Aquatic invertebrates and, occasionally, small fish.
Size: Up to 20cm/7¾in.
Breeding: Spawns in open water over sand, gravel or rocks. Eggs sink to the bottom and develop unguarded.

Alaska blackfish
Dallia pectoralis

Distribution: Alaska; ranges also extends west to the Bering Islands and north-eastern Siberia.
Habitat: Swamps and heavily vegetated ponds, lakes, streams, occasionally found in rivers.
Food: Insect larvae, particularly those of mosquitoes and midges.
Size: Up to 33cm/13in.
Breeding: Spawns from May until July. Male builds nest and guards the eggs.

Identification: The body is dark brown to olive in colour with black blotches and mottling on its back and sides. The underside ranges from yellow to white and is covered with black specks. The pelvic fins are tiny, each with just two or three rays. They, like the other fins, are red-brown in colour and are covered with black specks.

Once thought to be herbivorous, this fish is now known to feed almost entirely on midge and mosquito larvae, which abound in the spring and summer in Alaska. It is one of the hardiest freshwater creatures on Earth. As summer ends and ice forms on the surface, it heads for deeper water and goes into a semi-torpid state until spring. Its large gills help it to extract enough oxygen from the water to survive for months in pools which have been sealed off from the air. The native people of Alaska used to rely on these fish for much of their food, catching them in the autumn and leaving them to freeze outside for use over the winter.

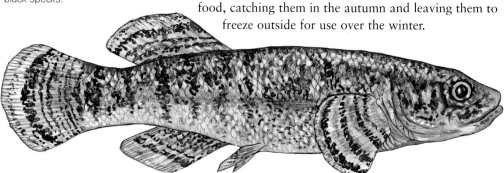

Eastern mudminnow (*Umbra pygmaea*):
Up to 11cm/4½in
This fish closely resembles the central mudminnow but has between 10 and 14 dark brown stripes on its back and sides. It lives in quiet streams, bogs and other wetlands on the Atlantic Plain along the eastern seaboard of the USA, from New York State to Florida. It spawns in April and May, the male making a small nest among the algae.

Sand roller
(*Percopsis transmontana*):
Up to 9.5cm/3¾in
The sand roller (*above*) looks similar to the larger trout perch, to which it is closely related, but it has a more arched back and is darker blue-green above. It is found in the Columbia River system and prefers slow-moving waters over mud or sand. It hunts at night for aquatic invertebrates, and hides by day behind or beneath large rocks.

Olympic mudminnow (*Novumbra hubbsi*):
Up to 8cm/3in
This fish is restricted to the Olympic Peninsula, Washington State and is listed as Near Threatened (IUCN). Like other mudminnows it is found in bogs and other quiet, well-vegetated waters. It has a small pelvic fin, with six or seven rays, and 10 to 15 cream or yellow bars.

Central mudminnow
Umbra limi

Mudminnows are named for their small size and their habit of burrowing into mud when alarmed. They are not actually minnows at all. In fact, they are more closely related to pike. The central mudminnow lives in marshes and well-vegetated ponds, lakes and streams. Its broad range includes areas that freeze over in the winter and others that dry out in the summer. It can survive short periods of drought by burrowing into the mud and waiting for rain to return. It is also well adapted to cope with low oxygen levels in the water, being able to gulp air and absorb oxygen into its blood through the swim bladder.

Identification: The base of the dorsal fin lies in front of that of the anal fin. The caudal fin has a black bar across its base. The body is green to very dark brown above and ranges from yellow to white below. The anal and pelvic fins of the male turn an iridescent blue-green at the start of the breeding season.

Distribution: Great Lakes and Mississippi drainage basins, from Quebec to Manitoba and south as far as Arkansas and Tennessee. Also Hudson River basin and isolated populations in South Dakota and Indiana.
Habitat: Swamps and quiet areas of streams over mud.
Food: Aquatic invertebrates, small fish and algae.
Size: Up to 14cm/5½in.
Breeding: From April onwards, in shallow water. Females lay sticky eggs individually on to water plants. Develop unguarded.

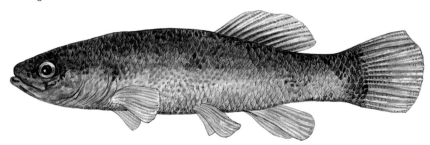

TOPMINNOWS

As their name suggests, these fish spend most of their lives near the surface. This, combined with the fact that they are often brightly coloured, makes them easy to spot and they are among the most frequently sighted fish in the areas they inhabit. Topminnows are found only in North America and on the islands of Bermuda and Cuba.

Plains topminnow

Fundulus sciadicus

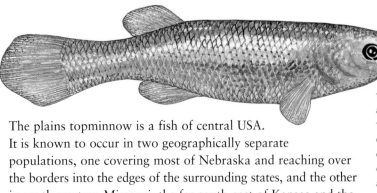

The plains topminnow is a fish of central USA. It is known to occur in two geographically separate populations, one covering most of Nebraska and reaching over the borders into the edges of the surrounding states, and the other in south-western Missouri, the far south-east of Kansas and the north-east of Oklahoma. Numbers are thought to be declining in both of these areas and it is on the endangered list in Kansas. The plains topminnow feeds on mosquito larvae, other aquatic invertebrates and on flying insects that crash into the water's surface. It may also eat algae. It is most common in the clear water around springs and pools, and in the streams that these feed, although it is also found in the backwaters of rivers where the current is slow enough for vegetation to accumulate.

Identification: Blue-green in colour above, with bronze flecks and dark cross-hatching. Just in front of the dorsal fin there is a narrow gold stripe. During the breeding season the male develops a dark orange band on his caudal fin and dark orange edges to his dorsal and anal fins. Both sexes have silver-blue dashes on the side of the head.

Distribution: Nebraska and surrounding states; also south-western Missouri.
Habitat: Springs and the streams and rivers that flow from them, usually around vegetation.
Food: Aquatic invertebrates, particularly insect larvae and, occasionally, flying insects.
Size: Up to 7cm/2¾in.
Breeding: May and June. Eggs deposited onto aquatic plants and algae, left to develop unguarded.

Lined topminnow

Fundulus lineolatus

This pretty little fish is found in the far south-east of the USA. It is particularly common in Florida, where it is often added to garden ponds and other man-made areas of still fresh water to help with mosquito control. Like its relatives, the lined topminnow feeds at the surface and mosquito larvae form a large part of its diet. Males and females look quite different from one another, the males (*below*) having thick, dark coloured bars down their sides, like zebra stripes, while the females have thinner, less obvious horizontal lines. It is found naturally in swamps, in quiet, vegetated pools and the backwaters of slow-flowing streams. Although not especially long-lived, it is relatively easy to keep and has become a popular aquarium fish.

Identification: The male has between 11 and 15 dark green bars on his side, with the thickest of these being the one in, or very near, the middle. The female has between six and eight black horizontal stripes on her side with clear bands of olive green between them. There is a black blotch on the base of the pectoral fin in both sexes.

Distribution: Eastern parts of North and South Carolina, south-eastern quarter of Georgia and through most of Florida.
Habitat: Swamps, weedy ponds and quiet, well-vegetated backwaters of streams.
Food: Mosquito larvae and other aquatic invertebrates.
Size: Up to 8.5cm/3¼in.
Breeding: Eggs scattered into open water over algae or aquatic plants and left to develop unguarded.

Southern starhead topminnow
Fundulus notti

Distribution: Mobile Bay drainages, Alabama, eastward to drainage basin of Lake Pontchartrain, Louisiana.
Habitat: Swamps, backwaters and well-vegetated pools of streams.
Food: Aquatic invertebrates, particularly insect larvae.
Size: Up to 7.5cm/3in.
Breeding: Thought likely to be an egg scatterer that does not guard its eggs or young.

Also known as the bayou minnow, this fish is found in south-western Alabama, southern Mississippi and south-western Louisiana, and is common throughout its range. It prefers swamps, quiet backwaters and overflow pools, where it feeds on insect larvae and small aquatic crustaceans. The southern starhead topminnow shows similar sexual dimorphism to the lined topminnow: the males have barred sides while the females have stripes. Females are also generally darker along the back and have colourless fins. This species is thought to breed in late spring and early summer, the times of year when gravid females have been caught. But the actual process of spawning has not been observed in this species.

Identification The male has between 9 and 15 faint bars on the side, all of nearly uniform width. The first of these bars begins at, or just behind, the base of the pectoral fin. The female has between six and eight thin, horizontal stripes on her sides interspersed with many dark specks and dashes.

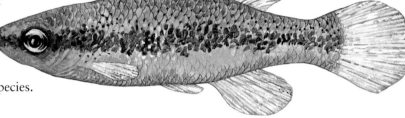

Blackstripe topminnow
Fundulus notatus

This species has the widest distribution of all the topminnows, occurring across much of central USA, from the Great Lakes to the Gulf of Mexico. It is a fish of still or quiet waters, living in swamps, lakes, ponds and backwater pools. It feeds mainly during the day, often foraging in pairs or small groups. It preys on aquatic invertebrates at or near the surface and grabs terrestrial insects that fall into the water, as well as those that creep too near the surface on overhanging vegetation. Like its relatives, this topminnow is short-lived but quick to mature: it often breeds when it is barely 12 months old. Eggs are deposited individually on to water plants, mats of algae or detritus on the bottom. In the north of its range this fish retreats into deeper water in the winter.

Distribution: Drainage basins of Mississippi River, Lake Michigan and Lake Erie; also Gulf Slope drainages from Alabama to eastern Texas.
Habitat: The quiet margins of lakes, ponds, streams and small rivers.
Food: Aquatic invertebrates and flying and terrestrial insects.
Size: Up to 7.5cm/3in.
Breeding: Spawns through most of the spring and summer. Eggs are laid individually and left to develop unguarded.

Golden topminnow (*Fundulus chrysotus*): Up to 7.5cm/3in
This fish lives in the far south-eastern USA. Although primarily a freshwater fish of swamps, ditches and backwaters, it is sometimes found in brackish pools along the coast. It can be distinguished by the golden flecks on its sides. Breeding males develop bright red to red-brown spots on the rear half of their bodies and also on their anal, dorsal and caudal fins.

Blackspotted topminnow (*Fundulus olivaceus*): Up to 9.5cm/3¾in
This handsome fish (*above*) looks similar to the blackstripe but has many small, dark spots on its light tan upper side. It is common in clear waters along the margins of slow-flowing streams and small rivers. Found throughout the Mississippi River basin, it shares much of its range with the blackstripe, but does not occur as far north. It is a popular aquarium species.

Eastern starhead topminnow (*Fundulus escambiae*): Up to 7.5cm/3in
This fish is nearly identical in appearance to the southern starhead topminnow but the females lack the same dark specks and dashes between the stripes. The eastern starhead has a range that abuts that of its close cousin, occurring along the Gulf of Mexico from eastern Alabama into north-western Florida. It also occurs in the same kinds of habitat – either still or very slow-moving water.

Identification: The body is olive-tan in colour above and white to pale yellow below. It has a silver-white spot on the top of its head and a wide blue-black stripe along each side. This stretches around the snout all the way to the base of the caudal fin. The male has larger dorsal and anal fins than the female and is deeper bodied.

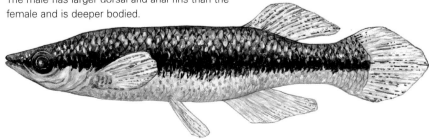

STUDFISH AND KILLIFISH

Four of the species on these pages belong to the same genus as the topminnows. Although they share many physical characteristics, they differ in their behaviour, tending to feed in the water column or nearer the bottom. All of the fish featured here are small and provide food for a great many larger, predatory animals.

Northern studfish

Fundulus catenatus

Despite his small size, the male northern studfish is an unusually aggressive fish. At the start of spring he establishes a territory in shallow water over gravel and for months he defends this vigorously from other males. Spawning occurs in these territories from April until August. Although the male does not tend the eggs, by guarding his territory he does inadvertently protect them from predators. The species has two main populations (*see box*), but smaller communities also exist in south-western Mississippi and in south-western Arkansas. Adult fish are bottom feeders, seeking out insect larvae and water snails. Younger fish hunt near the surface and often leap to grab mayflies and other insects flying above the water. Feeding activity tends to peak in the morning and late in the afternoon. By night, the fish is largely inactive.

Identification: The body is light yellow-brown above with silver blue sides, and rows of small brown or red-brown spots. There is a gold band across the back just in front of the dorsal fin. During the breeding season, the sides of the male turn vivid blue and he develops red spots on his head and fins.

Distribution: Two populations. 1:Tennessee, parts of Kentucky, northern Alabama and northern Mississippi; 2: southern Missouri and northern Arkansas.
Habitat: Streams and small to medium-sized rivers, in margins, pools and backwaters.
Food: Young: flying insects; adults: aquatic invertebrates.
Size: Up to 18cm/7in.
Breeding: Males do not build nests, but defend territories.

Plains killifish

Fundulus zebrinus

Identification: Both sexes have white or yellow bellies and are tan to olive in colour above. The sides are silver-white with between 12 and 26 grey-green bars on each. During the breeding season the male develops bright orange to red coloration on the paired, anal and dorsal fins.

This fish lives in habitats where few other fish can survive. It is very tolerant of both high salt levels and very alkaline water, and has a breeding system that enables it to survive through even the toughest droughts. Once fertilized, the eggs of the plains killifish develop and hatch out in two to six weeks. However, should the pools in which they were laid dry out in that time, they are able to lie dormant for an almost indefinite period. When the rains return and refill the pools, they continue to develop and quickly hatch out. The adults are unfussy feeders, consuming almost anything edible that is small enough to enter their mouths. They spend much of their time buried in sand, on the bottoms of the streams, rivers and pools, with only their mouths and eyes visible. The exact reason for this behaviour is unclear but has probably evolved either to help them avoid predators or to capture prey.

Distribution: Native to Great Plains, down to Gulf of Mexico in south-western Texas. Probably introduced into upper Missouri River basin and Colorado River basin in Utah and Arizona.
Habitat: Headwaters, streams and pools in small to medium-sized rivers.
Food: Aquatic invertebrates, plant matter, algae, detritus.
Size: Up to 10cm/4in.
Breeding: When conditions are favourable. Eggs scattered, left unguarded.

Seminole killifish

Fundulus seminolis

Distribution: Confined to the Florida Panhandle, but is absent from its most southern tip.
Habitat: Open areas of lake margins and pools in quiet streams.
Food: Insect larvae and other aquatic invertebrates.
Size: Up to 16cm/6¼in.
Breeding: Spawning occurs in the months of April and May. The eggs are left to develop unguarded.

Although restricted to Florida, this fish is quite common throughout its range. It occupies lakes and quiet stream pools, feeding mainly on small invertebrates, which it catches in shallow, open areas of water over sand. It tends to swim in mid-water or near the bottom, only rarely nipping up towards the surface to grab a tasty morsel. The young capture even smaller prey, mostly ostracods and other planktonic invertebrates, and tend to form schools around areas of submerged vegetation. The seminole killifish is preyed on by a wide range of bigger fish, particularly the largemouth bass. Fish-eating birds also catch them in large numbers: they are among the top prey of wood storks, especially in coastal areas.

Identification: The body is dark green above and white below, and has metallic green sides covered with broken rows made up of many small black spots. The female has between 15 and 20 often faint dark green bars on each side of her body. During the breeding season the anal fin of the male turns bright pink or red.

Banded killifish (*Fundulus diaphanus*):
Up to 13cm/5in
Compared with many of its relatives, this is a sociable species. Adults spend most of their time in schools in clear, shallow water, which makes them a great favourite of fish-eating birds. Its range covers a broad band from the Atlantic seaboard of the USA, north of South Carolina inland through the Great Lakes region as far west as North and South Dakota. Its name comes from the 10 to 20 green-brown bars along its silver sides.

Rainwater killifish (*Lucania parva*):
Up to 7cm/2¾in
Few fish are more misleadingly named than the rainwater killifish (*above*). It is actually a marine fish found in the coastal waters of the Atlantic Ocean and the Gulf of Mexico, but it enters estuaries, large rivers and coastal wetlands to spawn. This species has been introduced into closed freshwater habitats in Oregon, Utah, Nevada and California, where it seems to thrive.

Pygmy killifish (*Leptolucania ommata*):
Up to 3cm/1⅛in
This dusky green to yellow fish is one of the smallest species in North America. It lives in swamps and heavily vegetated pools from Georgia to Alabama, ranging south to central Florida. It has an almost perfectly round black spot, with a cream halo, at the base of its tail.

Bluefin killifish

Lucania goodei

Outside of its native stronghold of Florida, this attractive little fish is most often seen in home aquaria. It breeds well in captivity and is even more prolific in the wild. It is an opportunistic omnivore, eating a wide range of small invertebrates, as well as algae and some plant matter. It tends to be found in still or slow-moving water with abundant vegetation and is often particularly common around springs. This species is sometimes known by the alternative common name of bluefin topminnow, although this seems highly inappropriate when one considers its behaviour. Unlike true topminnows, it usually swims well below the surface of the water.

Distribution: Almost all of Florida. Also Atlantic seaboards of Georgia and South Carolina.
Habitat: Vegetated lakes and ponds, and pools in streams; often common near springs.
Food: Aquatic invertebrates, algae and plant matter.
Size: Up to 5cm/2in.
Breeding: Spawns spring and summer. Eggs are scattered in open water and develop unguarded.

Identification: The body is fairly slender and compressed, coloured dusky brown to olive above, with a light stripe along its upper side. There is a black spot on the base of the caudal fin and a wide zig-zag black stripe running from here to the tip of the snout. Large males have bright iridescent blue anal and dorsal fins, each with a black band at its base.

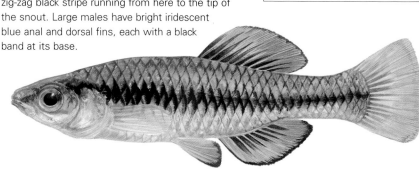

PUPFISH AND SPRINGFISH

Pupfish and springfish are tough little survivors. They have evolved to live in conditions that would kill most other fish and as a consequence most have few, if any, competitors where they live. Pupfish are particularly tolerant of low oxygen levels and can survive in water with concentrations of just 0.13mg per litre, lower than any other fish that breathes by gills alone can tolerate.

Desert pupfish

Cyprinodon macularius

Distribution: Quitobaquito Springs, Arizona; two springs in California; a few irrigation drains and shoreline pools of Salton Sea. Also Mexico.
Habitat: Marshes, lakes, springs and pools in streams, usually over mud.
Food Aquatic invertebrates, algae and detritus.
Size: Up to 7cm/2¾in.
Breeding: Males defend small territories and spawn with females that enter them. Eggs develop unguarded.

Identification: Large males are pale blue in colour and have beautiful lemon yellow to orange caudal fins and bases to their tails. The females and immature males are white below and dark olive above. They have silver sides patterned with dark brown bars or blotches and have smaller dark blotches on their bellies and backs.

In recent decades the desert pupfish has become rare. Historically it was quite abundant, occurring throughout most of southern Arizona and south-east California in the USA, and northern Baja California and Sonora in Mexico. The reason for its decline is primarily habitat loss, caused by the damming and diversion of the Colorado and other major rivers. Although it is an adaptable fish it cannot survive the disappearance of the lakes and waterways in which it once lived. The desert pupfish evolved to survive the extremes of life as a fish in the desert. Individuals can become sexually mature when they are as young as six weeks old, enabling them to breed quickly and take advantage of rare downpours. They can also survive in water with little dissolved oxygen and tolerate levels of salinity three times higher than that found in the sea.

Conchos pupfish

Cyprinodon eximius

Less colourful than the desert pupfish, the conchos pupfish is adapted to live a similar lifestyle and can survive under similarly harsh conditions. Its range is small but within this area it is relatively common. Adults are adaptable feeders, eating virtually whatever is available, from invertebrates to algae, water plants and even detritus. The fry feed almost exclusively on small invertebrates and usually start feeding within a few hours of hatching. As they grow, their diet becomes broader. The year of the conchos pupfish starts in earnest in spring, with the males setting up territories and defending them energetically from their rivals. As with desert pupfish, the juveniles grow quickly and are soon ready to breed themselves. As autumn turns to winter the fish bury themselves in the mud at the bottoms of their pools and become dormant.

Identification: The body is grey-brown above and white below. The sides are silvery and have faint brown blotches, while the upper part of the body has rows of small brown spots. During the breeding season the dorsal fin of the male turns yellow or orange. He also develops dark brown bars along his sides and black dashes and spots on the front half of his body.

Distribution: Extreme south-western Texas and far north-eastern corner of Sierra Madre in Mexico.
Habitat: Backwaters and margins of small to medium-sized rivers.
Food: Aquatic invertebrates, algae and detritus.
Size: Up to 5cm/2in.
Breeding: Males defend small breeding territories. Eggs develop unguarded

Flagfish

Jordanella floridae

Distribution: Throughout Florida Panhandle and as far north as Ochlockonee and St Johns River basins.
Habitat: Vegetated ponds, lakes and slow-moving streams; sometimes enters brackish water.
Food: Algae and aquatic invertebrates.
Size: Up to 6.5cm/2½in.
Breeding: Eggs adhere to algae-covered rocks in nest. Male guards eggs, fans continuously until they hatch.

The common name of this fish is due to its supposed resemblance to the American national flag, with a large blue-black dot and alternating red and thin black lines on the side of its body. A common native of Florida, it has become a popular aquarium fish, in no small part due to its fondness for algae. It also feeds on aquatic worms, crustaceans and insect larvae. The male flagfish is a nest guarder and in fact this is key to the species' survival – the female lays as few as 20 eggs over a period of several days. This is thought to be the lowest number of eggs laid by any fish. As well as chasing off any other fish that comes too close, the male keeps the eggs well supplied with oxygen, fanning them almost continuously with his fins until they hatch.

Identification: A distinctive blue-black spot in the middle of the flank. It also has thin, alternating red or orange and black lines on its sides, interspersed with gold flecks. Females and young males are grey-green above and silvery-white below. Large breeding males are bright orange to red, with darker red wavy lines over much of the body.

Devil's Hole pupfish (*Cyprinodon diabolis*):
Up to 3.4cm/1⅜in
Found only in Nevada's Devil's Hole, this pupfish has a tiny natural population, ranging from about 150 in spring to just over 400 in autumn, after the breeding season. It feeds mainly on algae and it is the decreased growth of this food that causes its winter population drop. It is an endangered species and efforts have been made to breed it in artificial refuges.

Sheepshead minnow (*Cyprinodon variegatus*):
Up to 7.5cm/3in
This fish (*above*) is primarily a saltwater fish, although in Florida it is often found some way inland. It has also been introduced into the Pecos River in Texas, where it is gradually displacing the native Pecos pupfish (*Cyprinodon pecosensis*). It is also known as the sheepshead pupfish, broad killifish or chubby.

Red River pupfish (*Cyprinodon rubrofluviatilis*):
Up to 5.8cm/2⅛in
Like the White River springfish, this is able to tolerate extremely high temperatures – up to 37°C/99°F. The Red River pupfish, however, is also found in much cooler waters, inhabiting shallow pools and runs of streams and small rivers. It occurs in the upper Red and Brazos River drainages on the Texas-Oklahoma border.

White River springfish

Crenichthys baileyi

The White River springfish is an endangered species, listed as Vulnerable by the IUCN. The principal threat to its survival is habitat loss. Many of the warm springs in which it once thrived are on agricultural land and have been polluted, used to feed irrigation systems or interfered with in other ways which have led to them becoming less able to support fish. This fish feeds mainly on filamentous algae, which it grazes from the rocks in warm spring pools and streams. As one might expect, considering its habitat, it is able to survive unusually high temperatures and low levels of dissolved oxygen. In Preston Big Spring it thrives at temperatures of up to 37°C/99°F.

Distribution: Restricted to the White River system of Nevada.
Habitat: Vegetated warm springs and their outflows.
Food: Algae and, occasionally, small aquatic invertebrates.
Size: Up to 9cm/3½in.
Breeding: Spawns in summer. Eggs scattered and left to develop unguarded.
Status: Vulnerable.

Identification: The upper part of the body is dark olive and the underside silver-white. The fins are clear to light olive and often have dusky edges. A black stripe or row of black spots runs along the side of the body and below this there is a second row of black spots, which stretches from the base of the caudal fin to a line directly beneath the base of the dorsal fin.

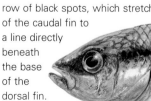

LIVEBEARERS

All of the fish on these pages give birth to live young. Males fertilize the females internally by means of a structure known as the gonopodium, which is formed from modified elements of the anal fin. Livebearers are particularly successful wherever they are introduced, having evolved a system that cuts out the problem of egg predation suffered by most other fish species.

Sailfin molly

Poecilia latipinna

Identification: The huge, sail-like dorsal fin of the male makes it hard to confuse with any other species. This fin has black wavy lines on its lower half, black spots on its upper half and is edged with orange. The head is small and the fleshy base of the tail unusually deep. The sides of the body are olive with iridescent yellow flecks and five rows of dark brown spots.

With its unusual habits, hardy nature and strikingly large dorsal fin, the sailfin molly is a great favourite of aquarists around the world. Over the years several different colour morphs have been bred in captivity and these have increased its popularity as a pet fish. The sailfin molly is native to the southern USA and is particularly common in Florida. It has also been introduced into parts of the western USA and Hawaii. Introductions in California seem to have contributed to the decline of the endangered desert pupfish there. The sailfin molly is an adaptable fish able to survive in a wide range of habitats. It lives in marshes, streams, ponds, estuaries and even roadside ditches. It is also found in coastal marine waters in the Gulf of Mexico.

Distribution: Atlantic and Gulf coasts from far south of North Carolina to northern Mexico. Widely introduced elsewhere.
Habitat: Ponds, lakes, quiet pools and backwaters of streams.
Food: Algae, occasionally aquatic invertebrates.
Size: Up to 15cm/6in.
Breeding: Fertilization is internal, gestation takes 3–4 weeks. Female gives birth to broods of 10–140 live young.

Mosquitofish

Gambusia affinis

Identification: The dorsal and caudal fins each have between one and three rows of black spots. There is a black teardrop below each eye. There are no obvious dark spots or stripes on the sides, as there are in most of the other, closely related *Gambusia* species. The body is yellow-brown to olive-grey above with a dark stripe along the back as far as the dorsal fin.

Named for the insect larvae and pupae that make up the bulk of its diet, the mosquitofish is possibly the most widely distributed freshwater fish in the world. It is native to the southern states of the USA east of the Rockies but has been introduced to tropical and temperate countries around the globe in attempts to suppress populations of *Anopheles* mosquitoes, which transmit malaria. It is also widely kept in home aquaria and is sometimes sold as a live food fish for larger, carnivorous species. The mosquitofish is an extremely hardy species, able to tolerate high salinities, high temperatures and low levels of oxygen. It is quick to mature, sometimes breeding within three months of hatching, and has spread rapidly in most places where it has been introduced. As with all *Gambusia* species, fry are left to fend for themselves immediately after birth.

Distribution: South-eastern USA. Widely introduced in many other parts of the world where malaria remains prevalent.
Habitat: Standing, slow-flowing fresh or brackish water.
Food: Mosquito larvae and other aquatic invertebrates.
Size: Up to 6.5cm/2½in.
Breeding: Fertilization is internal. Between 12 and 100 young born per brood and females may produce up to four broods a year.

Blotched gambusia

Gambusia senilis

The blotched gambusia resembles its cousin the mosquitofish. Ironically, considering the successful international spread of its relative, this fish is listed as being Near Threatened by the IUCN. The reason is not its inability to compete with other fish but rather its limited natural geographic range. This fish is found only in the Rio Conchos River in Mexico. It was once also found in the Devil's River in Texas but is now thought to be extinct in the USA. Like the mosquitofish, the blotched gambusia feeds largely on insect larvae, although it sometimes also eats the eggs and fry of other fish. In the Rio Conchos basin it inhabits springs and quiet, vegetated pools.

Identification: The scales on the sides have dark outlines, which often makes their edges appear like black crescents. The silver coloured sides each have a single black stripe running along them with a short row of black spots below. The black teardrop below the eye is usually large and quite obvious. As with the mosquitofish, a dark stripe runs along the back to the base of the dorsal fin.

Distribution: This fish is almost certainly extinct in the USA and is known to exist in the wild only in Mexico's Rio Conchos River.
Habitat: Springs and vegetated pools of quiet streams.
Food: Insect larvae and sometimes fish eggs and fry.
Size: Up to 5.5cm/2¼in.
Breeding: Females give birth to live young, which are left to fend for themselves.
Status: Near Threatened.

Big Bend gambusia (*Gambusia gaigei*): Up to 5.4cm/2¼in
This fish is listed as Vulnerable (IUCN) and is restricted to a single protected pond in Big Bend National Park in Texas. This population is descended from just three individuals, two males and a female that were moved there in 1956. It was formerly found in two other sites but disappeared after the spring that fed one stopped and the other was contaminated by the introduction of mosquitofish and predatory green sunfish.

Least killifish
(*Heterandria formosa*): Up to 3.6cm/1½in
This live-bearing fish (*above*) is popular with aquarists because it is so easy to keep. Males are tiny, just two-thirds as long as the females and weighing less than half as much. It inhabits heavily vegetated slow-moving or still fresh and brackish water, along the USA's Atlantic and Gulf coasts, from south North Carolina to Louisiana. It is particularly common in Florida.

Pecos gambusia (*Gambusia nobilis*): Up to 4.8cm/2in
This fish is listed as Vulnerable by the IUCN. The springs that once fed many of the streams it inhabited in Texas and New Mexico have dried up. Now several isolated populations remain in spring-fed pools and marshes. Overall numbers of this species are small, but stable.

Gila topminnow

Poeciliopsis occidentalis

Despite its name, this fish is not a true topminnow. It gets its name partly for its appearance but more for its habits, being a small fish that spends most of its time at the surface. It is listed as Near Threatened by the IUCN. The main threat to its survival, in the USA at least, is competition with the mosquitofish, which has been introduced into much of its range. This species is split into two distinct subspecies. The true gila topminnow, *Poeciliopsis occidentalis occidentalis*, has a short snout and a dark stripe extending along its side as far as the gill cover. The other subspecies, *P. occidentalis sonoriensis*, sometimes called the Yaqui topminnow, has a longer snout and a shorter stripe, which reaches only to the point above the pelvic fin.

Identification: Small black spot at the base of the dorsal fin and a dusky to dark stripe running along each side. The gonopodium of the male is very long – more than a third of the entire body length. The body is light olive-tan above and white or yellow below. Large males are black with orange at the base of the gonopodium.

Distribution: Gila River system of Arizona and New Mexico, and Mexico's Rio Yaqui basin.
Habitat: Vegetated springs, pools and margins of streams, small to medium-sized rivers.
Food: Aquatic invertebrates and algae.
Size: Up to 6cm/2¼in.
Breeding: Fertilization is internal; birth takes place a few weeks later.
Status: Near Threatened.

TETRA, SILVERSIDES, SWAMPFISH AND CAVEFISH

The Mexican tetra is the only member of its family in North America. The two silversides featured here are exceptional in being freshwater fish – the majority of silversides are marine fish. The swampfish and various cavefish find their food by touch and have large sensory papillae scattered all over their bodies.

Mexican tetra

Astyanax mexicanus

Identification: This fish has silver sides with two or three dusky black spots above the pectoral fin. The body is deep and compressed, and the snout blunt. There is a small adipose fin on the back between the dorsal and caudal fin. Inside the mouth there are large, sharp teeth on both the upper and lower jaws. The fins of large individuals are yellow, with red on the front of the anal and near the back of the caudal fins.

The Mexican tetra is a schooling fish that can sometimes be seen gathered in groups that number in the thousands. Life within these schools is very rarely harmonious, in fact there is often a great deal of aggression between individuals. Aggressive behaviour ranges from fin spreading – the first sign of unease – to circling and, finally, tail beating, ramming and biting. Bites can be fairly serious and usually result in at least the loss of a few scales. Most Mexican tetras are colourful little fish, but in the Sierra de el Abra a cave-dwelling race has evolved. Although considered to be the same species, these cave-dwelling, or hypogean, Mexican tetras have reduced eyes and very little body pigmentation. For obvious reasons they are commonly known as blind Mexican tetras.

Distribution: Native to far south of Texas and south-eastern New Mexico in the USA, also found across much of eastern and central Mexico proper.
Habitat: Springs and pools of streams and rivers, usually over sand or rock, also caves.
Food: Aquatic invertebrates, small fish, algae and plant matter.
Size: Up to 12cm/4¾in.
Breeding: Open water. Eggs develop unguarded.

Brook silverside

Labidesthes sicculus

The name of this fish is slightly misleading as most of its body is actually transparent. It is a small, schooling predator of copepods, water fleas and other small aquatic invertebrates, although it will also eat algae when its preferred food is scarce or unavailable. When midges, mayflies or other flying insects are abundant it turns its attentions to them and can often be seen jumping at the surface to catch them, especially on moonlit nights. The brook silverside's transparent body is a defence against predators but nevertheless it is still preyed upon by many larger fish, including the bowfin, green sunfish, yellow perch and largemouth bass. The brook silverside is a short-lived fish, rarely living for longer than two years. It spawns once in its life, then dies.

Identification: The body is largely transparent, but the spinal column and most of the internal organs are silvery. The snout is long and beak-like and the eyes are large. There are two dorsal fins, which are widely separated: the first of these is small and has spines. The front edge of the first dorsal fin is directly above that of the anal fin.

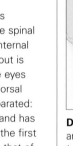

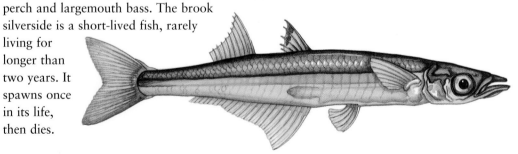

Distribution: St Lawrence and Great Lakes basins (except that of Lake Superior). Also Mississippi River basin and Atlantic and Gulf coast drainages from South Carolina to Texas. Also introduced elsewhere.
Habitat: Lakes, ponds and quiet pools in rivers, near or at the surface.
Food: Aquatic invertebrates, flying insects and algae.
Size: Up to 13cm/5in.
Breeding: Open water. Eggs develop unguarded.

Swampfish
Chologaster cornuta

Distribution: Atlantic Plain from eastern Georgia, through eastern halves of South and North Carolina to south-eastern Virginia.
Habitat: Vegetation and debris at the bottom of swamps, quiet pools and backwaters of streams.
Food: Tiny bottom-living invertebrates.
Size: Up to 7cm/2¾in.
Breeding: Eggs are brooded in the mother's gill chambers. No parental care after hatching.

The swampfish belongs to the same family as the spring, northern and southern cavefish, *Amblyopsidae*. Although it has eyes, these are severely reduced, being of little use in the murky waters it inhabits. It uses them mainly to detect shadows passing overhead – a sign of danger. The small creatures it feeds on are caught at night and found by touch rather than vision. The swampfish has an unusual breeding method. Pairs form in April and the male sheds his sperm over the eggs soon after they are laid. The female then takes the fertilized eggs in her mouth and forces them into her gill chambers. Here they incubate safe from predators, swimming out of their mother's mouth once they have hatched. Because of their habitat, swampfish are rarely seen in the wild but they are often kept in home aquaria.

Identification: The eyes are small and there are no pelvic fins. The body is dark brown above and yellow to white below, with a sharp division between the two. There are three narrow, black, horizontal stripes on each side of the body. The lowest of these, on the lighter half of the body, is wide at the front and narrow at the rear.

Inland silverside (*Menidia beryllina*):
Up to 15cm/6in
The inland silverside closely resembles its cousin, the brook silverside, but the base of its first dorsal fin begins in front of the base of its anal fin. Its name is confusing as it is actually a marine fish that enters rivers, spawning over beds of aquatic vegetation. The inland silverside occurs in rivers and streams around the North American Atlantic coast, from Maine to Mexico.

Southern cavefish (*Typhlichthys subterraneus*):
Up to 8.5cm/3½in
This little fish (*above*) inhabits caves in central Tennessee, Kentucky, northern Alabama, north-eastern Georgia and far south Indiana, as well as Missouri and north Arkansas. It shares the gill-brooding habits of the rest of its family. It feeds on invertebrates that share its habitat, most of which have also lost their eyes and pigmentation through millennia of evolution.

Northern cavefish (*Amblyopsis spelaea*):
Up to 11cm/4¼in
This looks very like the southern cavefish, but it is slightly deeper-bodied and has a tiny pelvic fin. Although it lacks true eyes, it has vestigial eyes beneath the skin on its head which are able to distinguish between light and dark. It lives in caves in south Indiana and north Kentucky and is listed as Vulnerable (IUCN).

Spring cavefish
Forbesichthys agassizi

Although it is called a cavefish, this species seems reluctant to make the move to a completely troglodytic existence. The spring cavefish does indeed spend its life in caves in parts of its range but in others it emerges from them at night via springs to search for food beneath the light of the stars and the moon. A few of these part-time cavers even remain at the surface by day, hiding out under rocks, submerged logs or leaf litter. Nowhere is it found at any great depth in the cave systems it inhabits. It has a similar breeding system to its cousin the swampfish (*above*). Females produce about 100 eggs per spawning, then suck the fertilized eggs up in their mouths and hold them in their gill chambers until they hatch.

Distribution: Cave systems in central Tennessee, western Kentucky, southern Illinois and the far east of Missouri.
Habitat: Springs and underground waterways.
Food: Worms and other small aquatic invertebrates.
Size: Up to 8.5cm/3¼in.
Breeding: Eggs are brooded in the mother's gill chambers. No parental care after hatching.

Identification: The body is extremely long and slender, rather like that of a salamander. The eyes are small and there are no pelvic fins. The body is dark brown above and white to yellow-brown below. The caudal fin is dusky black with a solid black bar at its base. The pink gills are visible through the skin.

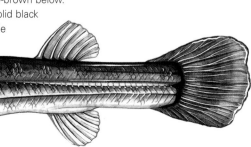

DARTERS

In total there are 113 members of the genus Etheostoma, *commonly known as darters, and all of them are found only in North America. Most of these differ so subtly in appearance that they can only be told apart by experts, and then often only by looking at their skeletons and internal organs. Although some darters are widespread, most inhabit restricted ranges and some are endangered.*

River darter

Percina shumardi

Identification: Predominantly dusky olive in colour, with between 8 and 15 black bars running down each of its sides. The first dorsal fin has a small black spot at the front and a large black spot near the back. There is a black teardrop below each eye and a small black spot at the base of the caudal fin. The snout is fairly blunt.

The Latin name of this fish was given in 1859 after the man who discovered it. Dr. G.C. Shumard was a surgeon travelling with the US Pacific Railroad Survey. At the time, it was common practice for the surgeon on an expedition to double up as the resident naturalist and Shumard spent much of his time documenting the many new plants and creatures he saw. The river darter could not have been easy to spot. With its dappled olive and black body it is well camouflaged against the rocks and gravel of rivers. It spends much of its time on the bottom, propped up by its pectoral fins, or hiding behind rocks. It is only when it moves that it really becomes visible and when it does, it does so quickly, as its name suggests.

Distribution: Hudson Bay, Mississippi River and southern Great Lakes drainages. Also found in drainage basin of San Antonio Bay.
Habitat: Rocky riffles of rivers.
Food: Insect larvae and other aquatic invertebrates.
Size: Up to 7.8cm/3in.
Breeding: Spawning begins in January in Texas but later farther north. Eggs scattered and develop unguarded.

Logperch

Percina caprodes

Identification: Yellow-brown in colour above and lighter below. There are many alternating long and short bars on the side, which extend over the back to join those on the other side of the body. The bars are fairly uniform in width. There are no scales on the top of the head. The snout is upturned and there is a dusky teardrop beneath each eye.

The Latin name of this fish describes it quite well. *Percina* means 'little perch' and *caprodes* means 'pig-like', a reference to the snout. The common name is a bit more mysterious. It may refer to the fish's overall shape or to its tendency to shelter next to large submerged objects. The logperch, like other darters, feeds on the bottom, eating mainly caddisfly, stonefly and other insect larvae. It finds these by using its snout to flip over small stones. Any creature this exposes is snapped up quickly before it has time to escape. The logperch congregates to spawn over gravel runs. Gravid females are often accompanied by several males, who each release their sperm as the female releases her eggs. Many of these eggs are then eaten by the other, smaller males which fail to get close enough to breed.

Distribution: Most of eastern USA and south-eastern Canada. Absent from most of the Atlantic Plain.
Habitat: Lakes, rivers and streams; most common over gravel and sand.
Food: Insect larvae and other aquatic invertebrates.
Size: Up to 18cm/7in.
Breeding: Spawning occurs late spring and early summer in open water over gravel. Males compete to fertilize eggs. Eggs develop unguarded.

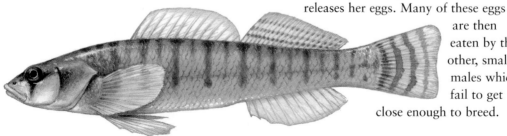

Greenside darter

Etheostoma blennioides

The greenside darter feeds on insect larvae on the beds of rivers and streams. A visual predator, it feeds by day and spends the hours of darkness in hiding, using large rocks or logs as shelter from nocturnal predators. Like other darters, it lacks a swim bladder and this helps it to maintain its position on the bottom. If it spots a predator by day it tends to freeze, relying on its coloration to help it blend into the background. It only swims away if the offending creature comes too close; otherwise it stays stock still until the danger has passed. This fish is most common in areas where the rocks on the bottom are covered with filamentous green algae. Although this algae is not fed on by the fish themselves it shelters most of the invertebrates they eat.

Identification: The body is yellow-green in colour with six or seven square, dark green saddles. There are between five and eight green bars on each side, sometimes forming W or U shapes. The skin of the snout is fused to that of the rear edge of the upper lip. The dorsal fins of the male are green, while those of the female are dusky or clear. The bases of these fins are red in both sexes.

Distribution: Eastern and central USA but virtually absent from the Atlantic Plain.
Habitat: The shores of large lakes and rocky riffles in streams and small to medium-sized rivers.
Food: Insect larvae and other aquatic invertebrates.
Size: Up to 17cm/6¾in.
Breeding: Males defend small territories among algae covered rocks and gravel. Eggs develop unguarded.

Johnny darter (*Etheostoma nigrum*): Up to 7cm/2¾in
This darter has a large natural range, stretching from Alabama to Saskatchewan, Canada. It has also been widely introduced outside its native range. The johnny darter has black X and W shapes on its sides and just a single anal fin spine. It prefers clear waters but is unusually tolerant of pollution and other disturbances to its habitat.

Blackside snubnose darter (*Etheostoma duryi*): Up to 7cm/2¾in
This fish (*above*) is unusually colourful for a darter. Males in particular seem almost to glow, especially when breeding starts in April. The blackside snubnose is common in rocky pools and riffles in the small rivers and streams of Tennessee, Georgia and Alabama. Like other darters, it feeds mainly on aquatic insect larvae.

Naked sand darter (*Etheostoma beani*): Up to 7cm/2¾in
This darter has a relatively small range, covering Mississippi, eastern Louisiana, western Alabama and western Tennessee. As its name suggests, it prefers sandy runs in streams and small rivers. It is devoid of markings on its back and sides, and has no scales, except along its lateral line (hence the 'naked'). It does, however, have a prominent black band at the centre of each of its two dorsal fins, which helps to distinguish it.

Variegate darter

Etheostoma variatum

This fish lives in large streams and small rivers. It winters in deep pools, but moves to faster-flowing, shallower water to breed. Males establish small territories which they defend from other males. When a female has selected a territory she seeks out a sandy area, usually within the lee of a large rock, and is followed by the male. She then burrows her head and the front of her body into the sand and is clasped by the male between his pelvic fins. The female then vibrates for up to 30 seconds as she releases her eggs, while the male sheds his sperm over them. The female then leaves but later spawns again, sometimes with the same mate, sometimes with a different one.

Identification: This fish has large eyes and four large brown saddles, which stretch down and forwards on the sides. The first dorsal fin has a brown base, red edge and blue band in the middle. The side of the body has green and orange bars. During the breeding season the male turns deep blue and his belly turns orange or red. He also develops orange spots on his sides and fins.

Distribution: Ohio River basin and Kanawha River system below Kanawha Falls.
Habitat: Swift riffles in small to medium-sized rivers, over gravel.
Food: Midge and other insect larvae, other aquatic invertebrates.
Size: Up to 11cm/4⅓in.
Breeding: Male defends territory but does not guard fertilized eggs or young.

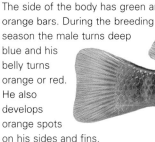

OTHER DARTERS

This group of fish is well-named. Darters are slender, fast-moving fish that zip up and down the streams and rivers in which they live. Most are well camouflaged and are difficult to see when they are still. Because they move suddenly and at speed, they are very difficult for herons and other fish-eating birds to catch. For this reason they are often numerous.

Greenthroat darter

Etheostoma lepidum

Identification: The body is olive above with dark saddles, and ranges from white to orange below. The male has long green bars down each side, interspersed with dark orange specks or spots. The female has short dark brown bars separated by bars of yellow. The first dorsal fin has a blue-green edge and the second is green with red spots. Both sexes have a thin black teardrop below the eye.

The greenthroat darter is confined to Texas and New Mexico, where it inhabits headwaters, streams and small rivers, particularly those running over gravel or rubble and fed by springs. Often it is found in areas with dense aquatic vegetation. It occurs in two distinct populations. The larger of these is on the Edwards Plateau in Texas, where this fish is relatively common. In the Pecos River system of New Mexico, the other place where it is found, the greenthroat darter has now become rare. In Texas it shares its range with the slightly larger orangethroat darter (*Etheostoma spectabile*) but as that species prefers clearer runs with less plant growth, the two rarely compete for prey.

Distribution: Guadalupe, Nueces and Colorado River basins in Texas; Pecos River basin in New Mexico.
Habitat: Gravel and rubble riffles in headwaters, streams and small rivers.
Food: Insect larvae and other small aquatic invertebrates.
Size: Up to 6.5cm/2½in.
Breeding: The breeding system of this species has not been studied but is thought likely to be similar to those of other darters.

Rainbow darter

Etheostoma caeruleum

Identification: The body is quite deep for a darter. It is coloured light brown above with six to ten darker saddles over the back, and dark bars on the sides. The underside is yellow, green or red. The anal, dorsal and caudal fins are all red and have blue edges. Large males have blue pectoral fins, red pelvic fins, blue cheeks and, in some populations, red spots on the side of the body.

This handsome little fish is one of the most common of all the darter species and is one of the most widespread, occurring throughout much of the eastern USA. It inhabits fast-flowing streams and small rivers. Typically the adults occupy slightly deeper water than do the young. As with other darters this fish feeds mainly on insect larvae, showing a distinct preference for caddisfly larvae. These juvenile insects build protective and camouflaging cases around their bodies using sand and detritus, but these do nothing to protect them from the attentions of the active and sharp-eyed rainbow darter. This fish really earns its name during the breeding season, when the males become particularly brightly coloured.

Distribution: Mississippi River and Great Lakes basins from southern Ontario south to Alabama and Arkansas.
Habitat: Riffles over gravel and rubble in fast-flowing streams and small to medium-sized rivers.
Food: Insect larvae and other aquatic invertebrates.
Size: Up to 7.5cm/3in.
Breeding: Males defend territories and mate individually with females, half buried in sand. Eggs left to develop unguarded.

Ashy darter
Etheostoma cinereum

Distribution: Most of Tennessee, parts of Georgia, Kentucky, Alabama, Virginia.
Habitat: Small to medium-sized rivers.
Food: Insect larvae and other aquatic invertebrates.
Size: Up to 12cm/4¾in.
Breeding: From February until April. Eggs develop unguarded.
Status: Vulnerable.

The ashy darter is a typical member of this genus, handsome but not especially brightly coloured, and rare. In common with many other darters, it is listed as Vulnerable by the IUCN. It is confined to the Cumberland and Tennessee River drainage basins, being found in many of the smaller tributaries, usually around vegetation. Although its spread is fairly continuous within its relatively small range it is never common in any of the localities where it is found. The ashy darter feeds by day, searching the river bottom for insect larvae and worms. It breeds in spring, with males defending small territories from their rivals, and females choosing where to lay eggs.

Identification: The upper part of the body has longitudinal rows of small brown spots and there is a row of small black rectangles along each side. Breeding males have red dorsal and pectoral fins and a greatly enlarged second dorsal fin. They also have blue pelvic and anal fins. The first dorsal fin on all adults has a dark orange edge and is covered with wavy red lines.

Orangebelly darter (*Etheostoma radiosum*):
Up to 8.5cm/3¼in
The orangebelly darter is found in the Red and Ouachita River basins of south-western Arkansas and south-eastern Oklahoma. It can be distinguished by the dark bars along its side, each split into upper and lower halves by a yellow stripe that runs along the lateral line on the fish's side. It inhabits rocky and gravel runs and is abundant throughout its small range.

Lollypop darter (*Etheostoma neopterum*):
Up to 9cm/3½in
This fish (*above*) gets its name from the male's dorsal fin rays, which, during the breeding season, end in round yellow knobs. This darter is also unusual in that the male guards the eggs. It inhabits a small range in western Tennessee and western Kentucky. It is also found in the Bayou de Chien, which extends over the Tennessee border into Mississippi.

Least darter (*Etheostoma microperca*):
Up to 4.5cm/1¾in
This fish is found in two separate populations. One extends down and outwards from the southern edges of the Great Lakes, the other stretches from south-western Missouri into Oklahoma. Despite its name, the least darter is actually only the second smallest darter. The smallest, by a tiny margin, is the fountain darter.

Blueside darter
Etheostoma jessiae

In the months from March to May, male blueside darters brighten up the streams and rivers where they live, sitting like little jewels on the bottom just waiting to be discovered. Each little fish defends his patch vigorously from other males, driving off smaller would-be usurpers and making sure that his neighbours know where their territories end and his begins. The blueside darter is common across most of its range, which includes the majority of the Tennessee River basin. Like other darters, it is a fish of clear water, inhabiting rocky pools and riffles of fast-flowing streams and small rivers. It often feeds amongst large pebbles.

Distribution: Middle and upper Tennessee River basin, covering parts of Alabama, Georgia, North Carolina, Virginia and Tennessee.
Habitat: Rocky pools and riffles of clear, swift streams and small rivers.
Food: Insects larvae and other aquatic invertebrates.
Size: Up to 7cm/2¾in.
Breeding: Male sets up and defends a small territory in clean shoals of sand or gravel. Eggs left to develop unguarded.

Identification: The body is light brown above and white to yellow below. Young and female fish have between seven and eleven dark brown squares on their sides. The male has a similar number of deep blue bars on his body and fins. During the breeding season the head of the male turns blue. The snout of both sexes is pointed and the eyes are quite large.

MUSKELLUNGE, PICKERELS, DRUM, EEL AND STICKLEBACKS

These fish display a great variety of body shapes and sizes, reflecting their habits. The predatory muskellunge is streamlined and muscular, while the American eel is sinuous and able to seek prey in gaps too small for other large fish to probe. The freshwater drum, with its flat underside, is a bottom-feeder.

Muskellunge

Esox masquinongy

Identification: The back and sides are light yellowy-green and are patterned with dark spots, patches or bars. The cheeks and gill covers are only partly scaled. The underside is cream to white with small blotches which vary in colour from brown to grey. With very large individuals the body may appear greyish above, rather than green.

Compared with most freshwater fish, the muskellunge is a giant. Large individuals can weigh more than 30kg/66lb. Despite its size, it is an ambush predator, lying in wait behind logs or under the cover of aquatic plants to launch itself at any smaller fish that comes into reach. In most places it is a solitary hunter but where prey is plentiful it has been known to form schools. It is the largest member of the pike family and a close relative of the northern pike (*Esox lucius*), with which it shares much of its range. The northern pike is actually more common and widespread in North America, being found across most of Canada, as well as much of northern Asia and Europe, where it is known simply as the pike.

Distribution: Native to Great Lakes, Hudson Bay, St Lawrence and Mississippi River basins, but introduced along much of rest of the Atlantic seaboard and elsewhere inland.
Habitat: Clear vegetated lakes and pools of rivers.
Food: Fish, water birds and small mammals.
Size: Up to 1.8m/6ft.
Breeding: Strings of eggs are laid and attach to underwater vegetation. They are left to develop unguarded.

American eel

Anguilla rostrata

Identification: The snake-like body is hard to mistake for any other freshwater fish. The nearest equivalents to it in terms of appearance are the lampreys but unlike these it has pectoral fins and a terminal mouth rather than one on the underside shaped like a sucker. The American eel also has a long dorsal fin, which runs into and is continuous with the caudal and anal fins.

The American eel is one of the natural world's great travellers. Like its close relative, the European eel (*Anguilla anguilla*), it swims all the way to the Sargasso Sea just south of Bermuda to breed. The young eels, known as elvers, then travel all the way back to North America's Atlantic coast and enter rivers, swimming up them to settle and grow in fresh water. The females swim much farther upstream than the males, and tend to make their homes in freshwater habitats nearer the coast. As a species, the American eel probably has a greater natural range than any other North American freshwater fish. As well as being found throughout the east of the USA and the far east of Canada, it is also found in Greenland, eastern Mexico, and Central and South America as far as Brazil.

Distribution: Eastern USA, eastern Mexico, far east Canada. Also Greenland, Central and South America.
Habitat: Rivers and streams.
Food: Aquatic invertebrates, fish and amphibians.
Size: Up to 1.5m/5ft.
Breeding Migrates to Sargasso Sea to breed. Spawning thought to occur in deep water.

Freshwater drum

Aplodinotus grunniens

Distribution: Most areas east of the Rocky Mountains and west of the Atlantic Plain, from Quebec in Canada as far south as Guatemala.
Habitat: Lake and river bottoms.
Food: Aquatic invertebrates and small fish.
Size: Up to 89cm/35in.
Breeding: Eggs scattered in large numbers in open water. Float to the surface where they are left to develop unguarded.

This fish is the only freshwater member of its family in the world. Drums are so called because of the low-pitched grunting sounds they make. When heard underwater these sound not unlike the percussion section of a band. The male of this species becomes particularly vocal during spawning, which occurs near the water's surface. Sometimes pairs spawn alone but on other occasions whole schools spawn at once. The eggs are unusual in that, rather than sinking to the bottom, they float to the surface. With each female laying in excess of 40,000 eggs this can leave large areas of water thick with these rafts. This fish is popular with anglers and is said to have very tasty flesh. When pulled from the water it often makes a loud croaking noise like a bullfrog.

Identification: The body is silvery on the back and sides and white below. It is strongly arched and the fins are dusky, apart from the pelvic fins, which are white. The outer pelvic ray forms a long filament, which extends out from the rest of the fin. There are two dorsal fins, the second longer than the first. The caudal fin is usually pointed, with the lower edge longer than the upper.

Chain pickerel (*Esox niger*):
Up to 99cm/39in
This relative of the muskellunge is named for the interlocking pattern of dark bands on its sides, resembling a chain-link fence. The chain pickerel is an ambush predator of smaller fish, found in swamps and vegetated lakes and pools of large rivers. It is native to the waterways of the Atlantic and Gulf slopes of the USA but has been introduced as far west as Colorado.

Fourspine stickleback (*Apeltes quadracus*):
Up to 6.5cm/2½in
This little fish (*above*) is found in salt and brackish waters as well as freshwater habitats. It occurs along the Atlantic seaboard of the USA and Canada, ranging from North Carolina as far as Newfoundland. Regarded head on, it looks almost triangular, with a flat belly and sharp, sloping back. This characteristic distinguishes it from other sticklebacks.

Grass pickerel (*Esox americanus*):
Up to 38cm/15in
This species is the dwarf of the pike family in North America. It is a common native to most of the eastern USA and has been widely introduced elsewhere in the USA. Like its cousins, it is an ambush predator of other fish. Apart from when making a swift attack, most of its time is spent almost motionless in the water.

Brook stickleback

Culaea inconstans

This is a small fish of ponds, lakes, rivers and streams. Its name is a reference to its spines – 'stickle' is an Old English word meaning thorn. The male brook stickleback is a nest builder who fiercely guards his territory from other males. Territories are set up in shallow water and the nests built from algae and bits of aquatic plants. Each finished article is about the shape and size of a golf ball and has a single opening in the side. Females arrive in the area not long after building has finished. As soon as a female enters a male's territory he rushes out to guide her to his nest, sometimes physically pushing her towards it. If suitably impressed she enters the nest and lays her eggs. The male then swims in behind her and fertilizes them before chasing her away.

Identification: The body is deep and strongly compressed for a stickleback, with four to six dorsal spines. It is coloured olive with flecks of pale green above and silvery-white to light green below. Breeding males turn very dark green or even black. Sometimes they also develop red patches on the pelvic fin.

Distribution: Most of Canada east of the Rockies, except much of the Northern Territories and northern Quebec. Also far north-eastern USA.
Habitat: Vegetated areas of ponds, lakes and slow-flowing rivers and streams, usually over mud.
Food: Aquatic invertebrates, fish eggs and, occasionally, algae.
Size: Up to 8.5cm/3½in.
Breeding: Male builds a nest and defends eggs and young until they are big enough to leave his territory.

SCULPINS

Most of the world's sculpins live in marine habitats but a few have evolved to spend their lives in fresh water. Freshwater sculpins are confined to North America, northern Asia and Europe. Sculpins are among the most difficult of North American fish to tell apart. All have similarly shaped bodies and they vary only very subtly in coloration.

Mottled sculpin

Cottus bairdi

Identification: The body is robust and the head quite large. The two dorsal fins are joined together at the base. There are two or three black or dark brown bars on each side beneath the second dorsal fin. In colour this fish is brown above with darker brown or black mottling on its back and sides. The first dorsal fin has large black spots at the front and the rear.

This is a beautifully camouflaged fish. Lying still on the bottom of a river or stream, it blends in so perfectly that it can be impossible to see, even when you are looking straight at it. As if this camouflage was not enough, the mottled sculpin commonly hides beneath large rocks and may only be seen when disturbed after one of these has been turned over. These fish breed in spring, which can mean anytime from March to June. Adult males set up their breeding sites in cavities beneath large rocks and wait for females to approach. When a female does come into range the male swims out to meet her, shaking his head and opening his gill covers as a display to entice her in.

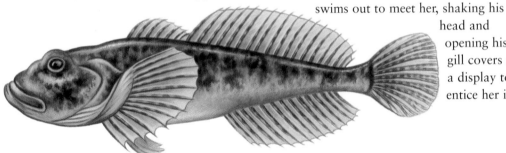

Distribution: Widespread, occurring in two distinct populations separated by Great Plains.
Habitat: Streams and small rivers over gravel or rubble; also the rocky shores of some lakes.
Food: Aquatic invertebrates, fish eggs and small fish.
Size: Up to 15cm/6in.
Breeding: Males defend nest cavities beneath rocks. They fan and guard the eggs until they hatch.

Marbled sculpin

Cottus klamathensis

Identification: The body is fairly deep for a sculpin. The first dorsal fin has a black spot near its rear edge and is joined at the base to the second dorsal fin. The back and sides are pale brown with black mottling and the underside is white or yellow. The fin rays have a marbled pattern of light and dark spots, hence the common name of this fish.

This sculpin lives in the border region between California and Oregon. It inhabits mainly soft-bottomed streams with abundant vegetation, but only in places where there are boulders, cobbles or other large rocks. Like the mottled sculpin, it is beautifully camouflaged, but its coloration is designed to help it blend in with sand and gravel rather than rocks. It feeds on insect larvae and rarely swims more than a few centimetres above the bottom. Breeding occurs during February and March. The males defend burrows beneath cobbles and display to entice females to lay eggs inside them. Females lay their eggs in a small mass which sticks to the underside of the rock. The largest males are the most successful, sometimes attracting several different females to lay in their nest burrows.

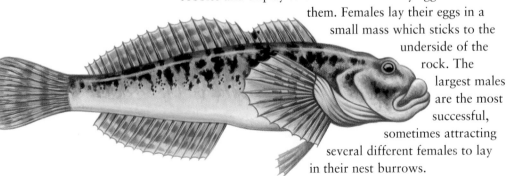

Distribution: Klamath River drainages and parts of Pit River system in Oregon and California.
Habitat: Soft-bottomed runs of clear streams and small rivers.
Food: Aquatic invertebrates and, occasionally, fish eggs.
Size: Up to 9cm/3½in.
Breeding: Males defend nesting burrows. They fan and guard the eggs until they hatch. Several different females may lay eggs in the same nest burrow.

Riffle sculpin

Cottus gulosus

Distribution: Pacific slope drainages from lower Columbia River basin in Washington to California's Morro Bay. Absent from northern California and southern Oregon.
Habitat: Riffles and runs of headwaters, streams and rivers over sand or gravel.
Food: Insect larvae and other aquatic invertebrates.
Size: Up to 11cm/4¼in.
Breeding: Eggs are laid on the undersides of rocks and in cavities in rotting logs.

Another west coast sculpin, this species forms two large and separate populations, one in California and the other in Oregon and the far south-west of Washington State. As its name suggests, it inhabits riffles and runs in headwaters, streams and rivers, usually over sand or gravel. It spawns from February until May, with females depositing their eggs in small clusters in blind pockets of rotting logs and on the underside of rocks. It is not known whether these are guarded by the males. Once they have hatched, the tiny fry spend the first few days living off the remains of their yolk sacs after which they must feed by themselves. To begin with they feed on amphipods and other tiny crustaceans but move on to a diet of mayfly, midge and other insect larvae as they grow.

Identification: A large mouth, which is wider than any part of the body behind the pectoral fins. The fleshy base of the tail is deep and flattened vertically. There is an area just behind the base of the pectoral fin that is covered with prickles, but these do not occur anywhere else on the body. Five or six small black saddles cross the back.

Spoonhead sculpin (*Cottus ricei*):
Up to 13cm/5in
Found in the Great Lakes and across most of Canada east of the Rockies, this species is also known as the spoonhead muddler and Nelson's or Rice's sculpin. It lives on the bottom of clear lakes and large rivers as well as smaller streams. It may be identified by its very wide, flat head and the many prickles covering the top and sides of its body.

Coastrange sculpin (*Cottus aleuticus*):
Up to 17cm/6¾in
An aptly named sculpin, this fish (*above*) inhabits the rocky shores of lakes, riffles in large rivers and estuaries along sections of the Pacific coast from California to Alaska. Nowhere is it found much more than 100km/62 miles inland. It can be most easily identified by its long pelvic fin, which reaches as far back as the anus.

Torrent sculpin (*Cottus rhotheus*):
Up to 15cm/6in
The torrent sculpin lives in the Pacific drainages of Washington State, northern Oregon, western Idaho and south-eastern British Columbia. Despite the name, it is not restricted to torrents but is found near rocky lake shores, as well as in the riffles of rivers. It is a solitary hunter. It has a large head and a wide mouth that enables it to catch and swallow surprisingly large prey, including other fish.

Banded sculpin

Cottus carolinae

This fish is found in gravel- or rubble-bottomed streams of all sizes. Like other freshwater sculpins it is common in streams yet it is usually found alone. Even the fry live and hunt individually rather than form schools. This fish stalks and ambushes its prey, moving slowly into range then darting suddenly to grab it from the water column or pluck it from the rocks. As well as insect larvae, it may also capture salamanders, small fish and crayfish. Like other sculpins it is cannibalistic and may feed on smaller members of its own kind. It hides under rocks by day, emerging to hunt at night.

Identification: The body is red-brown, olive or tan above with four or five dark brown saddles. The last three of these reach down the sides of the body to form clear and well-defined bars. The chin is mottled and the two dorsal fins completely separate. Both dorsal fins are plain and devoid of large spots. Most individuals have bodies that are completely free of prickles.

Distribution: Streams in Mississippi River basin and the Mobile Bay drainages, from eastern Oklahoma to Virginia.
Habitat: Springs, streams and small rivers over gravel or rubble.
Food: Aquatic invertebrates, fish eggs and small vertebrates.
Size: Up to 18cm/7in.
Breeding: Spawns in early spring. Eggs are scattered over gravel and develop unguarded.

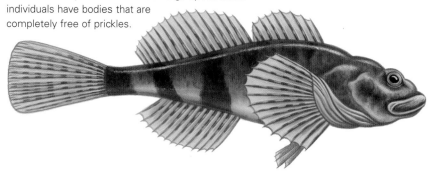

AQUATIC SALAMANDERS

North America is home to several aquatic salamander species. Although these creatures are amphibians, they look and behave much like fish. As adults, aquatic salamanders breathe using gills, a feature that sets them apart from most other amphibians, which have lungs. They include small fish among their prey, but are in turn sometimes preyed upon by larger fish species.

Hellbender

Cryptobranchus alleganiensis

With an average weight of 1.5–2.5kg/ 3–5lb, the hellbender is the world's third heaviest living amphibian: only the Chinese and Japanese giant salamanders weigh more. Unlike most other amphibians it is completely aquatic, spending its entire life in one particular river or stream. The hellbender is a solitary, carnivorous creature. It spends the day hidden beneath large rocks and emerges at night to seek out crayfish and other prey. Although it can swim, it prefers to walk along the bottom, using its sturdy legs. Prey, when encountered, is sucked into the mouth from the surrounding water. Except during the breeding season, hellbenders are extremely intolerant of others of their own kind and fights between evenly matched individuals are often violent. The hellbender is the only member of its genus.

Identification: Usually identified by its size and flattened body. The eyes are extremely small and the loose skin highly folded (to extract oxygen from the water). Adults have four toes on the front feet and five on the rear. The young have external gills.

Distribution: Eastern USA, from New York State east to Missouri and Arkansas.
Habitat: Clear, fast-flowing streams and rivers, usually with rocky bottoms.
Food: Crayfish and worms. Occasionally small fish and smaller members of its own species.
Size: Up to 72.5cm/28½in.
Breeding: Males excavate nests beneath flat rocks and defend eggs, which are laid in strings, until they hatch.

Mudpuppy

Necturus maculosus

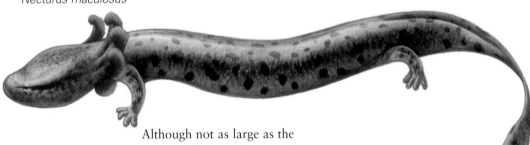

Although not as large as the hellbender, the mudpuppy is still a sizeable animal. The ranges of these two aquatic salamanders overlap. Unlike the hellbender, the mudpuppy never loses its external gills, but keeps them throughout its adult life. Generally speaking, mudpuppies prefer shallow water with plenty of places to hide, although they have been recorded in lakes at depths of up to 27.5m/90ft. In clear water they are almost exclusively nocturnal but where the water is muddy or choked with weeds they may sometimes be active by day. They mate in autumn or winter and the females lay their eggs the following spring, attaching them to the undersides of large rocks. Unusually for amphibians, fertilization is internal.

Identification: Both adults and young have large, maroon coloured external gills. Those that live in cold water (which contains more oxygen) have shorter gills than those from warmer waters in the southern parts of the range. The tail is flattened, with fins on the upper and lower edges for swimming. There are four toes on each of the limbs, front and rear.

Distribution: Southern Quebec to south-east Manitoba, and south to Missouri and Georgia.
Habitat: Lakes, ponds, rivers and streams.
Food: Aquatic invertebrates and small fish.
Size: Up to 33cm/13in.
Breeding: Females lay between 50 and 100 eggs in spring. The mothers stay with their eggs and guard them until they hatch. This may take from 4 to 8 weeks.

Distribution: South-eastern USA, from Washington DC to Florida and southern Alabama.
Habitat: Shallow and well-vegetated ponds, lakes, streams and ditches.
Food: Aquatic invertebrates, small fish, aquatic plants and eggs.
Size: Up to 97cm/38in.
Breeding: Eggs are laid in February or March and hatch two months later. Hatchlings are around 15mm long.

Greater siren

Siren lacertina

With its long, winding body, the greater siren looks more like an eel than a salamander. Its preference for ditches, ponds and other slow-moving or still fresh water mean that it is often mistaken for that fish. The greater siren is nocturnal, spending the day hidden in thick aquatic vegetation or beneath logs or rocks. As night falls it emerges to search for its prey, which includes most aquatic invertebrates and small fish. When it finds them, it also eats the eggs of fish and amphibians. If other food is short it will even eat the leaves of aquatic plants. The greater siren prefers shallow waters and by necessity has adapted to cope with drought. If the pool or stream in which it lives starts to dry out it buries itself in the mud and remains there until rain refills its home.

Identification: Tiny front limbs, with four toes, and no hind limbs at all. The external gills are so large that they may obscure the front limbs completely. Adults are usually olive or grey in colour, with dark spots on the back, sides and head. The sides also have many faint greenish-yellow blotches. The tail is flattened and has a rounded tip.

Lesser siren (*Siren intermedia*):
Up to 68cm/ 26¾in
Even experts find it hard to tell the greater and lesser siren apart. Apart from size, the main difference is the number of ribs. These form visible grooves in the skin. The greater usually has more than 36 of these grooves, while the lesser has 35 or fewer. The lesser siren is found in the southern US states, ranging from Virginia to Texas, and in north-eastern Mexico.

Two-toed amphiuma
(*Amphiuma means*):
Up to 1.1m/3.8ft
This amphibian (*above*) looks almost exactly like an eel (and is sometimes called the Congo or lamper eel). Only the four tiny legs and lack of dorsal, anal or caudal fins give it away. It is a large animal and feeds on a wide range of animals, killing smaller prey with its jaws and subduing larger creatures with constriction. It lives in swamps, ponds and ditches in the southern US states, from Florida and Georgia west to Louisiana.

Dwarf waterdog (*Necturus punctatus*):
Up to 16cm/6½in
This is the smallest North American aquatic salamander, found in still or slow-moving water, in North Carolina, South Carolina, Virginia and Georgia. It feeds on worms, insect larvae and other aquatic invertebrates. It has a dark coloured back and sides but a very pale belly. It has four toes on each foot and large external gills, which it keeps throughout its adult life.

Axolotl

Ambystoma mexicanum

This amphibian is often kept as a pet, usually in the albino form. Wild axolotls are darker in colour. Historically, the axolotl lived in two large, high altitude freshwater lakes, not far from Mexico City. One of these lakes, Lake Chaco, has now been completely drained for drinking water and the other, Lake Xochimilco, is now little more than a scattering of swamps and canals. The IUCN lists the axolotl as Critically Endangered. While it may well be threatened with extinction in the wild, the future of the species seems secure since so many individuals are kept in captivity. The name axolotl is Aztec in origin and is a derivative form of Xolotl. Xolotl was the Aztec god of the dead and the resurrected, and brother to the better-known Quetzalcoatl.

Distribution: Only found in Valley of Mexico, near Mexico City.
Habitat: High altitude lakes.
Food: Aquatic invertebrates and small fish.
Size: Up to 30cm/12in.
Breeding: March until June. Females lay between 100 and 300 eggs which are attached singly to water plants or rocks.
Status: Critically Endangered.

Identification: The external gills are large and feathery. The tail is flattened and has large fins on the upper and lower edges for swimming. Axolotls are relatively bulky compared with most other aquatic salamanders. The wild form is brown or grey with darker spots scattered all over the body.

REPTILES

Several reptiles live alongside North America's freshwater fish. Some of these reptiles prey on them while others compete with them for food. The most commonly seen freshwater reptiles are turtles, most of which eat fish when the opportunity arises. In fact, because of their habit of basking out of the water to warm up their bodies, reptiles are often much easier to spot than fish.

Painted turtle

Chrysemys picta

The painted turtle is the most common and widely distributed turtle in North America, occurring in lakes, ponds, rivers and swamps from southern Canada to northern Mexico. It prefers quiet and relatively shallow waters over thick mud. Young turtles are carnivorous but as they grow older they eat more and more plant material. Painted turtles spend a lot of time basking in the sun and seem to favour particular sites. Sometimes as many as 50 may be seen crowded on to a single log. In most parts of their range they bask from sunrise until around nine or ten in the morning, then begin foraging. They rest during the middle of the day and then often forage again from late afternoon until the early evening. In winter, these turtles become inactive, burying themselves in the mud at the bottom and absorbing oxygen through their skin.

Identification: One of North America's smaller turtles. The carapace is smooth and flattened, and ranges from green to black in colour. Some populations have red markings on the carapace. The skin ranges from black to olive and has red and yellow stripes on the legs, tail and neck. The head has yellow stripes only. Both sexes have visible tails.

Distribution: Occurs right across North America, from the Atlantic to the Pacific coast.
Habitat: Shallow, slow-moving or still fresh water.
Food: Aquatic invertebrates, fish, plant matter and carrion.
Size: Carapace up to 25cm/10in long.
Breeding: From May until July. Female digs nest in soil at the water's edge, lays eggs, then covers them up and leaves them to develop unguarded.

Common musk turtle

Sternotherus odoratus

This is another common North American turtle, although it is restricted to the eastern half of the continent. The common musk turtle inhabits shallow, quiet areas of lakes, ponds and rivers. It forages for food on the bottom and is unusual in that it uses its legs to walk along on the bottom rather than swimming. Like the painted turtle it is an omnivore, feeding on a wide range of water plants and eating whatever animals it can catch. It also feeds on carrion. This turtle is perhaps best known for its unusual and unpleasant defence system. If it finds itself under attack it releases a foul-smelling liquid from its musk glands. This habit has earned it another common name, the stinkpot turtle. The males in particular are very aggressive and will not hesitate to bite.

Identification: The carapace is highly domed and has a distinct keel running along its length. It is black or brown in colour. The skin ranges from dark olive to black. Two yellow lines run along the side of the head, one from the top of the eye and the other from the edge of the mouth, joining up at the base of the neck.

Distribution: Southern Ontario and Quebec, Canada, southward to Florida and Texas.
Habitat: Shallow still or slow-moving fresh water.
Food: Aquatic invertebrates, small fish, plant matter and carrion.
Size: Carapace up to 13cm/5in long.
Breeding: Females dig nests at the water's edge, sometimes communally. The eggs develop unguarded, and hatch after 75–80 days

Alligator snapping turtle

Macroclemys temminckii

Distribution: Watershed of Mississippi River, also found Missouri River basin. Isolated populations north to Ontario.
Habitat: Swamps, lakes and slow-moving streams.
Food: Fish and other aquatic vertebrates.
Size: Carapace up to 80cm/31½in long.
Breeding: Nests dug end spring–early summer at least 40m/131ft from water's edge. Eggs develop unguarded.
Status: Vulnerable.

This formidable creature is the heaviest freshwater turtle in the world. The biggest verified individual on record weighed 107kg/236lb – more than a fully grown man. As its name suggests, the alligator snapping turtle is a predator with a fearsome bite. It feeds mainly on fish, which it attracts into range with its pink, worm-like tongue. It wriggles this lure while lying completely still on the bottom, its irregular, brown carapace merging in with the logs and plant debris in swamps and bayous. The head and jaws of this reptile are so massive and powerful that it has even been known to kill and eat other turtles, crushing their shells to get at the meat inside. The alligator snapping turtle has been widely hunted by humans in the past. It is now listed as Vulnerable by the IUCN and is protected by law.

Identification: The head is huge and the powerful jaws strongly hooked. The tongue is pink and worm-like. The tail is long and the carapace is thick, with three ridges of large, pointed scales. In the wild, these turtles are often covered with algae, which enhances their camouflage and reflects their largely sedentary habits.

Cooter (*Pseudemys floridana*): Carapace up to 38cm/15in long
This turtle is common in Virginia and Florida – the entire extent of its natural wild range. It prefers slow-moving waters over mud and, being mainly herbivorous, is only found where there is abundant vegetation.

Common snapping turtle (*Chelydra serpentina*): Carapace up to 50cm/19¾in long
Smaller and less infamous than the alligator snapping turtle, this species is still a formidable predator. It is an ambush hunter that sometimes buries itself in the mud to hide from prey. It is found from Alberta to Nova Scotia, Canada, down through the USA to the Gulf of Mexico and central Texas.

Smooth softshell turtle (*Apalone mutica*): Carapace up to 35cm/13¾in long
With its leathery, pancake-like carapace and visible backbone and ribs, this turtle (*above*) looks quite unlike its hard-shelled relatives. It feeds on aquatic invertebrates, fish and other small vertebrates, and uses its long tubular nose like a snorkel to breathe – a habit which helps keep it safe from herons and storks. It occurs in large streams and rivers, as well as lakes and swamps from Ohio, Minnesota and North Dakota to Florida and the southern states, as far as Texas and New Mexico.

Alligator

Alligator mississippiensis

This is the largest reptile in North America and the top predator in the lakes and waterways where it is found. Its enormous jaws are filled with pointed teeth that, when the jaws are closed, become virtually invisible, each slotting into a socket in the opposite jaw. The only wild crocodilian in the USA, it hunts a wide range of vertebrate prey, from turtles to birds, and takes large numbers of fish. Younger alligators are themselves often killed and eaten by larger adults. During the breeding season in April and May, males hold territories and bellow to attract females into them to mate. The largest males may mate with several females. A few weeks after mating, the females build nest mounds with a depression on top, into which they lay their eggs, which they then cover over. Alligators are active from spring until autumn. As winter approaches, they enter shallow dens, in which they hibernate.

Distribution: South-eastern USA, from North Carolina as far west as Texas.
Habitat: Swamps, lakes and rivers.
Food: Fish, turtles, birds and other vertebrates.
Size: Up to 5m/16½ft.
Breeding: Female builds nest mound with torn vegetation, up to 1m/3¼ft high and twice as wide. Guards eggs until they hatch, carries young to the water in her mouth.

Identification: Seen from above, the snout is broad and rounded. The body is covered with tough scales. The tail is long and muscular, and is used to propel the animal through the water.

SOUTH AMERICA

South America contains the largest river on Earth, the Amazon. This vast waterway carries water from 40 per cent of the land on the continent and contains a fifth of all the liquid fresh water on Earth. Such figures reveal the significance of this river to the evolution of the continent's freshwater fish. Together with its tributaries it is home to a huge number of species, many of which have yet to be properly named or described by scientists.

Although it is the largest, the Amazon is far from the only river on the South American continent. To its north lies the Orinoco and farther south are a great many smaller waterways. Some of these rivers share species that are found in the Amazon but most also have unique fish and other freshwater creatures not found elsewhere.

While South America is rich in rivers it has few large permanent lakes compared with the other continents. That said, there are areas of the Amazon river that are so wide and slow-moving that in many ways their waters resemble those of lakes.

As well as South American fish, this chapter includes species from Central America south of Mexico. As one might expect, many of these fish have more in common with the fish of North America than those of South America.

*Above, left to right: Bigtooth river stingray (*Potamotrygon henlei*); red pacu (*Piaractus brachypomus*); twist-necked turtle (*Platemys platycephala*).*
Right: Map of South America, showing major routes and bodies of fresh water.

BELIZE
GUATEMALA
HONDURAS
EL SALVADOR
NICARAGUA
Lago de Nicaragua
COSTA RICA
PANAMA

Caribbean Sea

ATLANTIC
OCEAN

Trinidad and Tobago

VENEZUELA
Orinoco R
Meta R
W. J. van
Blommestein
Meer
GUYANA
SURINAME
FRENCH
GUIANA

Galapagos Islands

COLOMBIA
Magdalena R

ECUADOR

Negro R

Amazon R

Amazon R

Madeira R

São Manuel R

Xingu R

PERU

BRAZIL

Guaporé-Itenez R

Lago de Titicaca

BOLIVIA

Grande R

Paraguay R

Lago de Poopó

Pilcomayo R

PACIFIC

CHILE

PARAGUAY

Parana R

OCEAN

Parana R

Lagoa dos Patos

*Lago Artificial
Rincón del Bonete*

Parana R

URUGUAY

Lagoa Mirim

ARGENTINA

ATLANTIC

OCEAN

Falkland Islands

South Georgia

C a p e   H o r n

SHARK, RAYS, SAWFISH AND ELECTRIC EEL

We tend to think of sharks and rays as marine fish but some species are equally at home in fresh waters. A few even spend their whole lives in rivers and lakes. Sharks, rays and sawfish belong to the class Chondrichthyes, as fish with skeletons made from cartilage. The electric eel has a skeleton made of bone.

Bull shark

Carcharhinus leucas

This is one of the few large shark species to enter fresh water. Adults are big enough to overpower a human, and several people have been killed by this shark species over the years. It is an apex predator that kills and eats a wide variety of prey, although its diet is mostly fish. In fresh water it spends much of its time swimming slowly near the bottom but it is capable of sudden bursts of speed when chasing prey. In tropical South and Central America it occurs in most large rivers and has been recorded 3,700 km up the Amazon in Peru. It also lives in Lake Nicaragua, where it is known as the Nicaragua shark.

Identification: Dark grey above fading to white underneath. The body is extremely robust and the snout blunt and rounded. There are two dorsal fins: the first is large and triangular with a slightly curved leading edge; the second is much smaller and located near the tail. The upper blade of the caudal fin is much longer than the lower.

Distribution: Subtropical and tropical coastal waters and adjoining rivers worldwide.
Habitat: Coastal waters, estuaries, large rivers and lakes.
Food: Fish and other large vertebrates.
Size: Up to 3.5m/11½ft.
Breeding: The female gives birth to 1–13 live young, which are able to fend for themselves immediately. The species has been known to breed in fresh water.

Motoro stingray

Potamotrygon motoro

Identification: An almost circular body when seen from above. Large eyes and a short tail for a stingray – less than twice the body disc's width. The body is tan to dark brown, and the upper part is covered with large, round spots. The spots can vary from white to orange, both between and within populations.

This fish, also known as the ocellated or orange spot stingray, is one of the more common freshwater rays of South America. It is often very beautifully patterned, so it has become popular with specialist aquarists and is often found in zoos. The motoro stingray lives in shallow water and spends much of its time buried in soft mud or sand on the river bottom. As with most other rays, its eyes are positioned high on its head to enable it to see even when the rest of its body is completely covered up. Just beneath the eyes are the spiracles, specialized holes into which water is drawn to pass over the gills. The gill slits are on the underside of the body. The sting of this ray is a serrated spine (occasionally two spines) on the upper side of the tail. This is used as a defensive weapon but only when the stingray is severely provoked.

Distribution: The Orinoco, Amazon, Uruguay and Paraná-Paraguay River basins.
Habitat: Shallow areas of large rivers.
Food: Bottom-dwelling invertebrates and small fish.
Size: Up to 99cm/3ft across.
Breeding: Fertilization is internal. The female gives birth to 1–12 young. These begin hunting for food a few days after birth.

Large-tooth sawfish

Pristis perotteti

This massive fish is now, sadly, much rarer than it was in the past. Indeed, it is listed as Critically Endangered by the IUCN. The reason for its decline has been over-fishing, both as meat and as a trophy fish sought after by sport fishermen. There was once a large population in Lake Nicaragua but this has now been almost completely wiped out. Around the coasts and within the large rivers of Central and South America the species still clings to survival but in other parts of its former geographical range, such as the Mediterranean Sea, it has disappeared. The large-tooth sawfish uses its distinctive snout to stir up the bottom and expose hidden fish and invertebrates. It may also swipe it through shoals of prey fish to kill them.

Identification: This fish species can not be confused with any other because of its long, flat snout edged with pointed teeth. The only similar fish that shares parts of its geographical range is the small-tooth sawfish (*P. pectinata*). As its name suggests, this species has smaller teeth, but it also has more of them: 23–34 down each side of its snout rather than the 14–21 seen on the large-tooth sawfish.

Distribution: Warm coastal waters on both sides of the Atlantic and Pacific Oceans. (South American distribution shown above.)
Habitat: Shallow coastal waters, estuaries, large rivers and lakes.
Food: Fish and large, bottom-dwelling invertebrates.
Size: Up to 6.5m/21¼ft.
Breeding: Fertilization is internal. Between 1 and 13 live young are born after 5 months.
Status: Critically Endangered.

Bigtooth river stingray (*Potamotrygon henlei*): Up to 61cm/24in across
This striking fish (*above*) has a relatively restricted range compared with other South American rays, being found only in the Tocantins and Araguaia Rivers of the Tocantins River catchment in Brazil. Its beautiful patterning makes it popular with aquarists and there is concern that the capture of wild specimens to feed this trade may put the species at risk.

Discus ray (*Paratrygon aiereba*): Up to 1.8m/6ft across
This ray lives in the Amazon and Orinoco River basins in Bolivia, Peru, Brazil and Venezuela. Apart from a concave indentation at the front, its body is almost completely circular. It has a thin, whip-like tail. It is a large fish, with some individuals weighing as much as 53kg/116lb. It feeds on a wide variety of invertebrates and fish, which it finds on the bottom.

Smoothback river stingray (*Potamotrygon orbignyi*): Up to 35cm/13¾in across
This small and hardy fish is popular among aquarists. It lives in the Orinoco and Amazon River basins, most commonly in stream-fed swamps and floodplain lakes. It feeds mainly on invertebrates. Like all stingrays, it has a venomous spine on its tail to use for defence.

Electric eel

Electrophorus electricus

After the red-bellied piranha, the electric eel is probably South America's most famous fish. Tales of its ability to generate electrical shocks powerful enough to knock a man off his feet are true. Using special muscles which run down the posterior of its body, it can generate shocks of up to 550 volts. However, it usually reserves these shocks for stunning and killing smaller prey fish. This eel is not a true eel at all. It has its own family and is most closely related to the knifefish (*see* p.129). Like them, it has an elongated anal fin used for locomotion. It is an obligate air breather and surfaces frequently to gulp air. Up to 80 per cent of its oxygen may be obtained in this way.

Identification: The body is long, thick and cylindrical and the head slightly flattened. There are no caudal, dorsal or pelvic fins. The skin is thick and slimy and ranges from grey to dark brown, with very few scales. It is usually more yellowy beneath the chin and the underside of the front end of the body. The large mouth is filled with conical teeth.

Distribution: Ranges through north-eastern South America.
Habitat: Calm, turbid waters of streams and rivers: also found in swamps.
Food: Fish, invertebrates and small mammals.
Size: Up to 2.5m/8¼ft.
Breeding: The male builds a nest of foamy saliva, which he guards. He also guards the larvae until they reach about 10cm/3in long.

PIRARUCU, AROWANAS, LUNGFISH, LEAFFISH AND KNIFEFISH

The pirarucu and arowana are distantly related, both being osteoglossomorph or bony-tongued fish. They are able to gulp air to obtain oxygen, thanks to a modified swim bladder. The unrelated South American lungfish has taken this ability to the extreme, replacing its gills with primitive lungs.

Pirarucu

Arapaima gigas

The pirarucu is one of the world's biggest freshwater fish. Old individuals can weigh more than 200kg/440lb, although today fish of this size are rare as they are widely caught for food across most of their range. Finding pirarucu is not difficult as they are obligate air breathers and must break the surface every 15 to 20 minutes to take a gulp of air in order to survive. When they do so, they make a sound between a grunt and a cough. Air is swallowed and forced into the swim bladder, which acts as a primitive lung. Considering its size, the pirarucu is the top predator in most of the areas it inhabits, feeding on other fish, and sometimes even birds and small mammals.

Identification: Its large size is usually enough to identify this fish. However, several features distinguish small individuals from other species. Compared with the rest of the body, the head seems undersized, being somewhat flattened. The body is grey or green with orange speckling towards the rear. A long fin runs along the final third of the back, mirrored by another running along the underside.

Distribution: Found only in the Amazon River basin.
Habitat: Rivers and floodplain lakes.
Food: Fish, water birds and small mammals.
Size: Up to 4.5m/14¾ft.
Breeding: Occurs February to April when water levels are lowest. Nests are built on the bottom in sandy areas. Both parents guard the eggs until they hatch.

Arowana

Osteoglossum bicirrhosum

Identification: A silver body, covered with unusually opalescent large scales (up to 6cm/2½in).The long dorsal and anal fins are almost fused with the caudal fin, which is relatively small and rounded. The mouth is large and points upwards and the eyes are located near the top of the head. Two barbels protrude from the tip of the lower jaw.

This large and rather beautiful fish is a common inhabitant of the Amazon and Orinoco River catchments. It is sometimes described as an omnivore but it has never actually been seen feeding on plant material. The leafy contents of its guts are, in all likelihood, accidentally ingested as a side-effect of its unusual hunting behaviour. The arowana catches much of its food above the surface, leaping from the water to grab insects and even small birds from the overhanging branches and twigs. This peculiar habit has earned it another common name, the water monkey. The arowana is prized by fishermen for its flesh, which has a significantly higher protein content than that of most other Amazonian fish. It is also collected alive for aquarium specialists.

Distribution: Amazon and Orinoco basins; the Rupununi and Essequibo systems of the Guyanas.
Habitat: Rivers, floodplain lakes and swamps.
Food: Insects, small vertebrates, and occasionally, birds.
Size: Up to 1.2m/3.9ft.
Breeding: After the eggs have been fertilized, the male takes them into his mouth to develop. The young also shelter in the mouth of the male.

South American lungfish

Lepidosiren paradoxa

Distribution: Amazon, Paraguay and lower Paraná River catchments.
Habitat: Rainwater pools, swamps and other areas of still, shallow water.
Food: Aquatic invertebrates and algae.
Size: Up to 1.25m/4.1ft.
Breeding: Adults build nests and the male guards young. During breeding season the male develops external gill-like structures which he uses to add oxygen to the water around the nest.

This is the only lungfish found anywhere in the Americas. Although it occupies the same scientific order as the African and Australian lungfish species, it has its own family. It is not only able to breathe air, it has to do so in order to survive. Juveniles have feathery external gills that resemble amphibian larvae, but these gradually disappear as the fish grow larger. The young first start gulping air when they reach about seven weeks old. This lungfish prefers stagnant water where there is no current. If the habitat dries up, it can burrow into the mud and seal the entrance to retain moisture. The fish then goes into a period of aestivation, slowing its heartbeat and metabolism to save energy until the next rain arrives.

Identification: The body is long and slender, rather like that of a salamander but covered with scales. There are no fins, but there are two thin, thread-like structures where the pectoral fins would ordinarily be and two rather sturdier but similar looking structures in the position of pelvic fins. The eyes are small and the mouth resembles that of a frog.

Black arowana (*Osteoglossum ferreirai*):
Up to 1.2m/3.9ft
This fish closely resembles the arowana. Despite its name, its body is silver, although it has black markings around the head and tail. In the wild it is restricted to the Rio Branca, a tributary of the Rio Negro that flows into the Amazon River. Like its cousin, it is a popular aquarium fish but has a strong tendency to jump and so should be kept in a tank with a lid.

Black ghost knifefish
(*Apteronotus albifrons*):
Up to 48cm/19in
This fish (*above*) lives in fast rivers and streams over sandy beds. It closely resembles the banded knifefish, but has a much more striking 'outfit', which has made it popular with aquarists. It is a nocturnal hunter, feeding almost entirely on insect larvae and other tiny prey. In the wild, the black ghost knifefish is found from Venezuela to Paraguay and as far west as Peru.

Banded knifefish (*Gymnotus carapo*):
Up to 61cm/24in
This fish is widespread in both Central and South America, from Mexico to Paraguay. It is also found in Trinidad. It lives in still or slow-moving waters and is mainly nocturnal, feeding on small fish and invertebrates. As it swims it produces a weak electrical current. The muscle activity of other creatures interferes with this current and the knifefish is thought to make use of this to detect its prey.

South American leaffish

Monocirrhus mimophyllus

This fish could not be more appropriately named, looking exactly like a fallen leaf. The disguise keeps it safe from almost all the normal predators of fish, particularly birds such as kingfishers and herons. The South American leaffish is so well disguised, in fact, that it was only discovered by scientists in 1920, despite being relatively common across its range. It was, however, already well known to the native Marabitanas people of the region of Brazil where it was found. Unsurprisingly, they had come up with the same name for it – pirá-cóa, which translates literally as 'leaf-fish'. As if its cryptic shape was not enough, this fish drifts slowly through the water just as a fallen leaf would. It is also able to change colour and perfectly match the real fallen leaves in the water around it.

Distribution: Amazon River basin in Venezuela, Colombia, Peru, Bolivia and Brazil.
Habitat: Shallow areas of still or slow-moving water beneath dense vegetation.
Food: Fish fry and aquatic invertebrates.
Size: Up to 10cm/4in.
Breeding: The female lays around 300 tiny eggs, which are attached to the underside of a leaf. The male parent guards and fans them until they hatch.

Identification: This fish is almost impossible to pick out in the wild, as its camouflage is so perfect. The snout is pointed and the fins are normally held close against the body to avoid disrupting its leaf-like shape. The fish swims with its head pointing downward. It sucks in small prey by suddenly opening its large mouth.

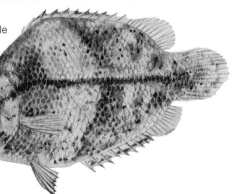

CICHLIDS

Cichlids make up a large group among the fish of Central and South America, containing hundreds of different species. South America has more cichlid species than any other continent apart from Africa. As the fish on these pages show, cichlids are surprisingly varied both in size and shape. Only the best known and most common species are covered in this book.

Discus

Symphysodon aequifasciatus

Identification: Seen head on, the body is narrow. Dark bars of regular width run down the sides, which are pale silver to gold in colour. One bar runs right over the eye. The mouth is small and the forehead deeply sloped. A single long fin runs along the back from directly above the gill cover to the tail base. Another runs underneath the body, but begins farther back.

With its rounded but narrow body, the discus is perfectly named. This schooling fish swims slowly between the stems and roots of reeds and other aquatic plants and it has evolved a shape that suits its lifestyle. Most wild specimens have vertical bars running down their sides that help to camouflage them in their natural environment. The discus is a very popular aquarium fish and many colour variations have been created by breeders. Most of the fish sold in pet shops are captive-bred. In the wild the discus inhabits the Solimões, Amazon and Putumayo-Içá Rivers in Brazil, Colombia and Peru. Discus make attentive parents: both the male and female guard their eggs closely.

Distribution: Amazon basin in Brazil, Colombia and Peru.
Habitat: Slow-moving water in rivers and streams.
Food: Insect larvae and other aquatic invertebrates.
Size: Up to 13.7cm/5½in.
Breeding: Pairs leave the school and the female finds a sheltered site in which to lay her clutch, which is then fertilized by the male. Both parents fan and guard the eggs until hatching, and will chase away other fish that come close.

Oscar

Astronotus ocellatus

Identification: The body is slender and compressed laterally. The head is blunt and the mouth large with thick lips and a protruding lower jaw. Colour varies between populations but generally ranges from dark green to black. There is a dark red circle at the base of the tail, just in front of the caudal fin. The bases of the dorsal and anal fins are densely scaled.

The oscar is one of the larger cichlids to come from this part of the world. It is most common in floodplains and swamps, where it moves slowly and rather majestically through the water in search of invertebrates and smaller fish to feed on. In common with many cichlids, it is able to change its colour to a limited degree, turning paler when distressed. This may help it to avoid predators by breaking up the outline of its body, but it may simply be a physiological response with no evolutionary benefit. The oscar is a popular aquarium fish. It is believed to be quite intelligent, with some scientists claiming that it can learn to distinguish its owner from other people. By using food as a reward, it can even be trained to perform simple tricks, like jumping out of the water.

Distribution: Ranges from the Orinoco River, through the Amazon basin to the Rio Paraguay.
Habitat: Swamps and floodplains.
Food: Aquatic invertebrates and small fish.
Size: Up to 35cm/13¾in.
Breeding: Spawning occurs in open water but the parents then transport their eggs to an area that has been specially cleared. Both parents guard the eggs and young.

Peacock bass

Cichla ocellaris

An efficient predator of various smaller fish, this schooling fish inhabits both rapids and quiet waters. It has been introduced to Texas and other southern states in the USA, where it has developed a particular taste for threadfin shad, mosquitofish, tilapias and bluegill. The peacock bass, also known as the peacock cichlid, is prized as a sport fish in the USA and a food fish across much of its relatively restricted native range. In South America it is found in Guyana, Suriname and French Guiana, two small countries and one European satellite state on the Atlantic coast of the continent, north of Brazil.

In common with many tropical fish, it spawns all year round, with females laying new clutches every two months or so.

Distribution: Ranges from the Marowijne basin to the Essequibo basin in the Guyanas.
Habitat: Rivers with rocky beds.
Food: Smaller fish.
Size: Up to 74cm/29in.
Breeding: Females choose a large, flat stone, over which they lay their eggs. Once the eggs have been fertilized the two parents move them to nests, which they guard from other fish.

Identification: The mouth is large and has a protruding lower jaw. The eyes are also quite large and have red irises. The forehead is gently sloped. There is a large black dot circled with silver on the tail stock and the base of the caudal fin. The sides are olive-green in colour and have three dark bars running down them. The dorsal fin is deeply notched.

Basketmouth (*Acaronia nassa*):
Up to 15cm/6in
This small cichlid lives in still and slow-flowing water in the Amazon basin of Brazil, Colombia, Bolivia and Peru. It is also found in the Guyanas. It feeds on fish fry, freshwater shrimps and insect larvae, using its protrusible mouth-parts (hence its name). It waits under cover for prey, then vacuums up creatures that swim by.

Red hump eartheater
(*Geophagus steindachneri*): Up to 15cm/6in
This cichlid (*above*) feeds on small invertebrates which it finds among the substrate on the riverbed. Rather than eating earth, it spits out the inedible matter it picks up while feeding. During the breeding season the males turn red and develop a hump on their foreheads, hence the first part of the species' common name.

Demonfish (*Satanoperca leucosticta*):
Up to 30cm/12in
This cichlid has a peaceable nature which belies its name. The Latin *Satanoperca* literally means 'Satan's perch' and was taken from the Tupi Indian name, Jurupari, which means 'demon's lure'. The fish inhabits the Essequibo River in Guyana and the Nickerie River in Suriname. It feeds on insect larvae and small crustaceans.

Spangled pike cichlid

Crenicichla saxatilis

This fish, also known as the ringtail pike cichlid, shares much of its range with the peacock bass but it is also found in Trinidad and the coastal rivers of eastern Venezuela and the far north-east of Brazil, north of the mouth of the Amazon. Although quite small, it is an aggressive fish, making it unpopular with aquarists despite the best efforts of importers to establish the species on the market. In the wild, it feeds mainly on fish, although it will also take aquatic invertebrates and will eat plant matter when preferred food is scarce. Its large mouth and torpedo-shaped body mark it out as a predator and it is capable of sudden and impressive turns of speed when chasing prey.

Identification: The dorsal fin is long and strongly pointed at the tip. A horizontal black stripe runs from the tip of the snout through the eye to the back of the gill cover. Just behind it are several large black spots circled with white. Faint dark bars run over the back and part way down the sides: these are overlaid with individual white scales, giving the spangled appearance. There is a dark band all around the base of the tail.

Distribution: Venezuela, Trinidad, the Guyanas and the far north-east of Brazil.
Habitat: Rivers and their tributary streams.
Food: Aquatic invertebrates, small fish and some plant material.
Size: Up to 20cm/8in.
Breeding: Spawning occurs in a sheltered area, usually beneath a large stone. The eggs are stuck on the underside of this and then guarded until they hatch.

OTHER CICHLIDS

Members of this group have evolved to fill most of the niches available to fish in freshwater habitats, from top predators of lakes and rivers to small invertebrate feeders found in swamps and other well vegetated areas of standing water. As a group, cichlids are notable for their pair bonding and the high level of care they show to their eggs and young.

Midas cichlid

Amphilophus citrinellus

Identification: Most wild fish are grey with six dusky or black bars on their sides, a large black blotch in the middle of each side and a smaller blotch at the base of the tail. The less common 'gold' individuals (*below*) are bright orange or red. During the breeding season both sexes develop humps on the forehead (larger on males).

This cichlid is named after the legendary King Midas. While this fish does not turn everything it touches to gold, some individuals do themselves turn gold as they grow older. Juveniles are cryptically coloured to help them avoid larger, predatory fish, and the majority of the adults are also fairly unspectacular. A minority, however, transform into some of the boldest and brightest of any cichlids. In the wild, these vividly coloured fish tend to be dominant over their duller relatives. However, they are also more vulnerable to predation.

This fish is native to Nicaragua and Costa Rica and has also been introduced into parts of Florida in the USA, much to the detriment of some of the native fish species.

Distribution: Atlantic slope and inland rivers of Nicaragua and Costa Rica.
Habitat: Lakes and, less commonly, rivers and streams.
Food: Aquatic invertebrates, fish fry and some plant material.
Size: Up to 24cm/9½in.
Breeding: Nests in caves or crevices between rocks. The eggs are stuck to vertical surfaces and guarded until they hatch.

Mayan cichlid

Cichlasoma urophthalmus

Identification: Both the first dorsal and the anal fin are spiny. The body is olive-brown, with five to seven wide, dark green bars on each side. There is a dark spot with a halo of silver at the base of the tail. It is this feature that gives the fish its scientific species name, urophthalmus (ur from the Greek 'oura', meaning tail, and 'ophthalmos' for eye).

This cichlid is unusual in that it prefers brackish waters and sometimes enters the sea. It is common in mangrove swamps and estuaries, but it is also found in fresh water further upstream. The Mayan cichlid is native to Atlantic-draining waterways from Mexico to Nicaragua. In the 1980s it was introduced into Florida Bay and it has since become established in the Everglades. It feeds on smaller fish and aquatic invertebrates, including molluscs and other crustaceans, which it crunches up with the tooth pads at the back of its mouth. A popular game and aquarium fish, it is sometimes also called the Mexican mojarra, orange tiger or false red terror. It is one of the most aggressive cichlids.

Distribution: Atlantic-draining rivers of Central America, from Mexico to Nicaragua.
Habitat: Rivers, estuaries, mangrove swamps and coastal waters.
Food: Fish and aquatic invertebrates.
Size: Up to 40cm/15¾in.
Breeding: The breeding system of this species has not been closely studied, either in the wild or in captivity. However, it is known to guard its eggs from other fish.

Wolf cichlid

Parachromis dovii

The wolf cichlid is a large and formidable predator that hunts the young of other cichlids and similar-sized fish. It lives in lakes and large rivers from Honduras to Costa Rica and is relatively uncommon, not because it is hunted but because of its position near the top of the food chain. It is a popular game fish and is said to make very good eating. Large males may weigh up to 6.8kg/15lb. Females are smaller, typically around two-thirds the length of the males. Wolf cichlid courtship can appear quite aggressive, although neither partner is actually harmed. Courting behaviour includes head quivering, gill flaring and the locking together of jaws. This species is also known as the rainbow bass or Dow's cichlid.

Distribution: Found throughout most of Honduras, Nicaragua and Costa Rica.
Habitat: Large rivers and lakes.
Food: Fish and some aquatic invertebrates.
Size: Up to 72cm/28in.
Breeding: The female lays up to 1500 eggs which are guarded by both parents until they hatch. The male also guards the young for the first few weeks after hatching.

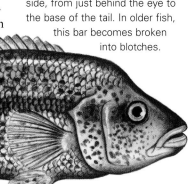

Identification: The body is greenish white with a purple sheen and covered with black speckles. There are green speckles across most of the face. The mouth is large and the eyes set quite far back on the head. A thick black bar runs along the side, from just behind the eye to the base of the tail. In older fish, this bar becomes broken into blotches.

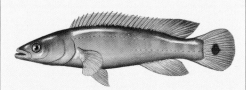

Atabo red pike cichlid (*Crenicichla lugubris*): Up to 30cm/12in
Pike cichlids are named for their streamlined shape and feeding habits: they hide amongst vegetation and ambush smaller fish. This fish (*above*) lives in the Amazon River basin and in the Uatumã, Branco and Negro Rivers in Brazil, in the Corantijn River in Suriname and in the Essequibo and Branco Rivers in Guyana.

Blackbelt cichlid (*Vieja maculicauda*): Up to 25cm/10in
This cichlid inhabits lakes and slow-moving rivers from Guatemala through Central America south to Panama. It feeds on the bottom, swallowing both rotting plant matter and small invertebrates that live amongst it. It also eats seeds and fruit that fall into the water. This fish varies greatly in colour but can be identified by the wide, belt-like black band around the middle of its body.

Orinoco peacock bass (*Cichla orinocensis*): Up to 62cm/24½in
This fish lives in the Orinoco River in Venezuela and Colombia and the Negro River basin in northern Brazil. It is notable for the eyespot near its tail, a feature it shares with several South American cichlids. This spot confuses the fin-nipping piranhas with which it shares its home, protecting its caudal fin from damage.

Angelfish

Pterophyllum scalare

To many people, this is the classic aquarium fish. Its distinctive shape means that it is one of the few cichlids most people could recognize and name. In the wild it lives in swamps and pools formed by the flooding of rivers. Its slender body enables it to move easily between the stems and leaves of aquatic plants. Most wild angelfish have stripes running down their bodies which help to camouflage them. Domestic angelfish, on the other hand, come in a huge variety of colours and patterns. This species has been more intensively bred to develop new strains than perhaps any other fish, apart from the goldfish. It is naturally common in the wild and is also bred in captivity in massive numbers.

Distribution: Amazon basin of Peru, Colombia and Brazil; also found in the Guyanas.
Habitat: Swamps, pools and slow-moving sections of rivers.
Food: Small aquatic invertebrates.
Size: Up to 7.5cm/3in.
Breeding: The female lays her eggs on the broad leaf of an aquatic plant or a similarly flat surface. Both partners protect the eggs and young.

Identification: The body is silvery, usually with three thick vertical stripes, one of which runs through the eye. The dorsal and anal fins are extremely long and pointed, and the pelvic fins trail like pennants beneath the body. The mouth is small and the snout pointed. The caudal fin is large and often almost transparent.

PIRANHAS AND PACUS

Mention fish and South America in the same sentence and most people would probably think of piranhas. Along with the anaconda and jaguar they are arguably the continent's best known predators and the subject of more than a few grisly tales and myths. While many piranhas are indeed fearsome predators, some are less vicious. Their lookalike cousins, the pacus, are comparatively docile.

Red-bellied piranha

Pygocentrus nattereri

Identification: The underside is red or orange. The back and sides are dark silver or grey. The dorsal and anal fins are black, and the pectoral fins the same colour as the belly. The lower jaw is large and protrudes in front of the snout. The eyes are set further forward than in most other fish.

This is the world's most infamous freshwater fish, a monster in the public imagination, supposedly capable of stripping the flesh from a man's skeleton in minutes. While the reputation of the red-bellied piranha has been exaggerated, there is no arguing that it is an extremely voracious and dangerous fish. It lives in schools and often attacks its prey in large numbers, going into a feeding frenzy so that schools can indeed strip their victims to the bone in no time at all. The usual prey of this fearsome piranha is other fish. Larger animals may be attacked, however, particularly when these piranhas are concentrated into pools during times of drought and if other food is scarce. There are no authenticated records of humans having been attacked and killed by this species, although there are plenty of stories.

Distribution: Found in the Amazon and Parana-Paraguay River basins. It also occurs in smaller rivers near the Atlantic coast.
Habitat: Rivers and streams.
Food: Other fish and, occasionally, larger animals.
Size: Up to 33cm/13in.
Breeding: Courting pairs circle one another in a ventral to ventral fashion. The eggs are laid in specially prepared nests, around 15cm/6in wide and 5cm/2in deep.

Black piranha

Serrasalmus rhombeus

Identification: A more gently sloped snout than most other piranhas and a slight hump where the head joins the body. The eyes are large and have red irises, which are particularly obvious in older individuals. The lower jaw is large and underslung. The general colour is dark grey but small scales on the sides often catch the light and shine like glitter.

This species, also known as the redeye piranha, is a formidable-looking fish. An inhabitant of rapids and the deeper waters of river channels, it has been little studied in the wild but is thought to live and hunt in loose schools. Like the slightly smaller red-bellied piranha, it has become popular as an exotic pet. For obvious reasons, it has to be kept in its own tank away from other fish. The black piranha exhibits diverse colour variations in the wild. The difference between the young and mature fish is even more extreme. Juvenile fish are light silver, with numerous grey spots on their sides. Confusingly, these fish are sometimes called white piranhas. It is only as they grow older that the darker coloration starts to develop.

Distribution: Occurs in the Amazon and Orinoco River basins, as well as smaller rivers draining into the Atlantic coast of Brazil and the Guyanas.
Habitat: The main channels of medium to large rivers.
Food: Other fish.
Size: Up to 41.5cm/16¼in.
Breeding: The breeding system of this species in the wild has not been observed. In captivity, black piranhas spawn in dense vegetation and appear to guard their eggs.

San Francisco piranha

Pygocentrus piraya

Distribution: Restricted to the Rio São Francisco in Brazil.
Habitat: Rivers.
Food: Other fish.
Size: Up to 50cm/19¾in.
Breeding: As with many piranhas, little is known about the breeding system of this species. However, it is thought that these fish are nest builders and that they do not guard their eggs.

This is the largest of all the piranhas. Sometimes known as the blacktail or piraya piranha, the San Francisco piranha is a typical carnivore. It has a large, protruding lower jaw and high, steep forehead, giving it a bulldog-like appearance. The teeth are large, triangular and exceptionally sharp, with serrated edges. This fish is named after the river in which it is found, the Rio São Francisco. Although rarely mentioned outside South America, this is the fourth largest river on that continent and the longest to flow entirely in Brazil (3160km/ 1964 miles). The San Francisco piranha is one of only two piranha species known from the river, the other being Brandt's piranha, *Serrasalmus brandtii*, which feeds mainly on the fins of other fish.

Identification: The pectoral fins, anal fin and belly are a vivid orange-yellow and this colour extends up the sides almost like flames. The upper half of the fish is purple. The scales are small and shimmer in the light. The jaw is underslung and the snout is very blunt.

Slender piranha (*Serrasalmus elongatus*): Up to 30cm/12in
This fish is also known as the elongated, or pike, piranha. Unlike other piranhas, it is very active, chasing down small fish or darting in to bite chunks from the fins of larger ones. It lives in the Orinoco and Amazon basins. Adults inhabit deep and fast-flowing waters in the middle of river channels, while juveniles prefer quieter eddies and pools.

Red pacu (*Piaractus brachypomus*): Up to 88cm/34½in
The red pacu (*above*) is a big fish, reaching up to 25kg/55lb. Young fish mimic the red-bellied piranha in coloration and are similar in size. Many people have bought and sold red pacus mistaking them for the latter. This fish is native to the Orinoco and Amazon River systems.

Wimple piranha (*Catoprion mento*): Up to 15cm/6in
This small piranha feeds by charging suddenly with its mouth open and ramming the sides of its prey, biting and knocking off scales which it then eats. It is able to open its mouth unusually wide, the two jaws making an angle of around 120° at the moment of impact. This species is found in Venezuela, Colombia, Bolivia and Brazil.

Black pacu

Colossoma macropomum

The black pacu – also known as the tambaqui, gamitana and the giant, or black-finned, pacu – is the largest member of the characin family in South America. Some fish may weigh more than 45kg/99lb. An omnivore with a gentle nature, it is a popular food fish in South America and is increasingly being bred and raised on fish farms. In the wild, adults tend to be solitary, feeding mainly on fallen seeds and fruit. Juveniles school and closely resemble the carnivorous piranhas, but feed mainly on aquatic invertebrates and decaying plants. This fish is native to the Amazon and Orinoco River systems but has been widely introduced elsewhere in South America. It has also been introduced to some rivers on the main island of Luzon in the Philippines.

Identification: A black to dark grey body, with black fins. The back is slightly arched. The pectoral fins are unusually small; the dorsal fin is large, with a curved rear edge. The snout is blunt but the lower jaw does not protrude. The eyes are large and set low down on the head.

Distribution: Native to the Orinoco and Amazon basins but widely introduced elsewhere in South America. Also introduced to the Philippines.
Habitat: Rivers.
Food: Young: aquatic invertebrates, decaying plant matter; adults: fallen fruit and seeds.
Size: Up to 1.1m/3½ft.
Breeding: Smooth, spherical eggs are scattered in open water and left to develop unguarded.

WOLF FISH, TRAHIRA, CHARACINS AND FRESHWATER BARRACUDA

The characin family, Characidae, to which most of these fish belong, is considered a somewhat 'catch-all' category by many ichthyologists. The freshwater barracuda – long thought to be a characin – was given a new family, Acestrorhynchidae, in 1998, and the classification of many other 'characins' is under review.

Wolf fish

Hoplias malabaricus

This fish has several names that emphasize its aggressive nature. Among them are 'tiger fish' and 'piranha eater'. It is an ambush hunter that does occasionally kill and eat piranhas. It strikes its prey hard, usually grabbing the middle of its body or tail end, then shaking it violently to stun or kill it before swallowing it head first. It lives in a variety of habitats, including shallow lakes in flooded forests. It may attack the feet and ankles of people wading through such waters, although it is not clear whether these attacks are serious feeding attempts, or made by males defending their nests.

Identification: The head is large and robust. Several pointed teeth protrude from both the upper and lower jaws, almost like those of a crocodile. The dorsal fin, when raised, is almost rhombic in shape, having straight front, rear and top edges. The stock at the base of the tail is deep and thick. The body is greenish above and silver-white below. A clear dark line separates the upper and lower halves.

Distribution: River basins from Costa Rica to Argentina.
Habitat: Streams, rivers, ponds, floodplain lakes, estuaries. Tolerates a wide range of temperatures so may be found in brackish as well as fresh waters.
Food: Aquatic invertebrates and fish.
Size: Up to 48.5cm/19in.
Breeding: Digs nest pits in shallow water. The male guards the nest, eggs and young.

Trahira

Erythrinus erythrinus

This species is known in the aquarium trade as the red-finned wolf fish. Although smaller than the true wolf fish it exhibits similar features. It is able to tolerate low oxygen levels due to its ability to gulp air and absorb oxygen through the walls of its swim bladder. It also lives and hunts in a similar way, spending most of its time lurking on the bottom in shallow water and then suddenly ambushing prey. In the wild, it feeds on small fish, aquatic invertebrates and insects which fall into the water. It tends to live in the margins of floodplain lakes and in small forest pools. If these dry out, it is able to travel some distance over the rainforest floor in search of new areas of still water in which to live.

Identification: The head is rounded and looks almost like that of a trout, but visible and quite vicious-looking teeth protrude from the lower jaw. The scales are quite large and clearly defined. The stock at the base of the tail is almost as deep as the caudal fin itself. The dorsal fin is large with an orange edge. The body is grey-gold above and silver below, with the two halves separated by a thick black stripe.

Distribution: Occurs east of the Andes from Venezuela to Argentina. It is also found in Trinidad and Tobago.
Habitat: Shallow lakes and pools in rain forest.
Food: Invertebrates and small fish.
Size: Up to 20cm/8in.
Breeding: Breeding has never been observed in this species, but it is thought likely to be a nest builder.

Glass headstander (*Charax gibbosus*):
Up to 12.5cm/5in
This fish (*above*) is popular with tropical freshwater fish enthusiasts because it is so easy to keep. In the wild it is restricted to the Essequibo River basin (Guyana), coastal rivers of Suriname and also Uruguay. It feeds mainly on insect larvae and other small invertebrates which it finds on the bottom, hence its name.

Trairacu (*Hoplias aimara*):
Up to 1m/3.3ft
This fish lives in the Amazon River and its tributaries, and in the Orinoco River, Venezuela. It feeds mainly on other fish but also takes small animals that fall into the water. It hunts at night and spends the day resting near the bottom. It can grow to quite a size – as much as 40kg/88lb.

Jeju (*Hoplerythrinus unitaeniatus*):
Up to 40cm/15¾in
This fish is also known as the aimara and the golden trahira. It lives in still and slow-moving waters throughout northern South America. An obligate air breather, it regularly surfaces to gulp air, although this makes it vulnerable to attacks near the surface by electric eels.

Silver dollar

Metynnis argenteus

The silver dollar is a popular aquarium fish with more than a passing resemblance to the piranhas and pacus. Its name is a reference to its distinctive shape as well as its colour – some look almost completely circular in profile. In the wild, these fish school in weedy areas near the banks of rivers and streams. Although it will occasionally take small invertebrates, it feeds mainly on aquatic plants and algae. This species is one of several in the genus, all of which look remarkably similar and behave in a similar way, schooling amongst the plants on which they feed. These other species are also sometimes sold in pet shops, usually under the same common name, silver dollar.

Identification: The body is very deep and vertically flattened. In many ways it resembles that of the angelfish, which lives alongside it. The fins, however, are much shorter, transparent and lack any ornamentation, except in the males, which have a red tinge to the front edge of the anal fin. The head is small compared with the rest of the body. The eyes are large and set almost directly behind the mouth.

Distribution: Restricted to the basin of the Tapajós River, a tributary of the Amazon River, in Brazil.
Habitat: Slow-moving waters with abundant vegetation.
Food: Aquatic plants, algae and, occasionally, small aquatic invertebrates.
Size: Up to 14cm/5½in.
Breeding: Eggs are scattered in open water, often near the surface. Once fertilized, they sink to the bottom and are left to develop unguarded.

Freshwater barracuda

Acestrorhynchus falcatus

Distribution: Occurs in the Amazon and Orinoco basins of Brazil, Colombia and Venezuela and smaller rivers in the Guyanas.
Habitat: Open water in rivers.
Food: Other fish.
Size: Up to 27cm/10¾in.
Breeding: Spawning occurs at the start of the rainy season in open water. The eggs are scattered and left to develop unguarded.

The name of this fish is something of an exaggeration. After all, the freshwater barracuda never grows more than a foot long. That said, it is a fierce and streamlined predator, capable of a good turn of speed when chasing prey. The freshwater barracuda feeds exclusively on other fish. Its jaws are lined with extremely pointed and well-separated teeth that are easily seen. The teeth are used for grabbing smaller fish, which are swallowed whole. It is a schooling fish, abundant in the open channels of slow and meandering rivers as well as those with moderate flow. It is widespread throughout the Amazon and Orinoco River basins and it is caught as a food fish across much of its range.

Identification: The mouth is large and the snout rather pointed. The eyes are also large and the face slightly forward. The fish is a pale gold colour over most of its body, although the back is darker than the rest. The scales reflect light extremely well, giving the fish a polished metallic appearance. The dorsal and anal fins are set quite far back. The caudal fin is large and has a black spot at its base. There is a small adipose fin.

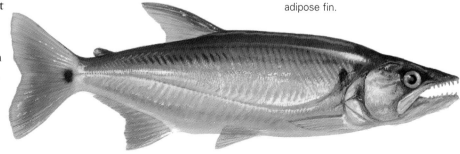

OTHER CHARACINS

The fish on these pages are popular aquarium species. Their small size, gentle habits and wide range of body shapes emphasizes the diversity of species currently classified as characins. All of these species are found within the Amazon basin, although some range more widely than others and can be found in other river catchments throughout South America.

Spraying characin

Copeina arnoldi

Identification: The body is slender and slightly compressed. The back is yellowish-brown in colour and the flanks and undersides yellow or green with a rusty sheen. A dark band, outlined with two parallel white bands, extends from the corner of the mouth to the eye. The dorsal fin has a black blotch and a red tip. The dorsal fin of the male is longer than that of the female. It tapers to a point and has a white spot at its base.

This little fish is famous among home aquarium enthusiasts for its breeding behaviour. The spraying characin, also known as the splash tetra, is the only freshwater fish to lay its eggs out of water and then spend time caring for its brood. In the wild, eggs are laid on the undersides of leaves overhanging the water. When the time comes to mate, the male and female select a leaf and make a few brief jumps out of the water towards it to judge its distance. They then lock their pectoral and caudal fins together and leap as one at the leaf, attaching themselves with their ventral fins, which act as suckers. Lying side by side they spawn, leaving their sticky eggs attached to the leaf before falling back into the water.

Distribution: Lower Amazon River basin of Brazil, Venezuela and the Guyanas.
Habitat: Rainforest streams beneath vegetation.
Food: Small aquatic invertebrates.
Size: Up to 3.4cm/1⅓in.
Breeding: Sticky eggs are laid on the undersides of leaves. The male guards the area below the eggs until they hatch, frequently splashing them with his tail to keep them moist.

Marbled hatchetfish

Carnegiella strigata

Identification: The body above the lateral line looks quite normal and is burnished gold in colour. Below the lateral line, which is marked by a black band, the body is exceptionally deep, giving the characteristic 'hatchet' shape. This part of the body is silver-white, like mother-of-pearl, and covered with black blotches and bands, giving a marbled effect.

The bold colours and unusual shape of this little fish have made it one of the most popular tropical freshwater aquarium species. It feeds on insect larvae and other small aquatic invertebrates at or near the surface. It also eats small insects that fall into the water.

In common with many surface feeders, it has an upward-pointing mouth, which makes grabbing prey easier. When it is not feeding it tends to lurk near the floating leaves of water lilies and other similar aquatic plants. Being a small fish, it is often targeted by predators and is easily startled, leaping from the water whenever it feels at risk. Jumping is an effective escape mechanism because as soon as it leaves the water it disappears from the view of larger fish and other underwater predators.

Distribution: Caqueta River in Colombia and the middle and lower Amazon River basin.
Habitat: Slow-moving forest streams.
Food: Small aquatic invertebrates and insects that fall into the water.
Size: Up to 3.5cm/1⅓in.
Breeding: The eggs are scattered in open water and drift to the bottom, where they are left to develop unguarded. They hatch after about 36 hours.

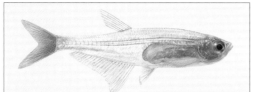

Glass bloodfin (*Prionobrama filigera*):
Up to 6cm/2in
The transparency of the glass bloodfin (*above*) provides a unique camouflage: the background can actually be seen through it. Non-transparent body parts, such as its intestines, are silvered to reflect light. The fish then spoils this camouflage somewhat with a red caudal fin. This shoaling fish is common throughout the Amazon basin.

Silver hatchetfish (*Gasteropelecus sternicla*):
Up to 3.8cm/1½in
This fish resembles the marbled hatchetfish in everything but colour. But whereas the marbled lives in small, quiet streams, the silver is usually found in open swamp waters. It is a shoaling fish that may jump to escape predators and to catch insects. It is found east of the Andes, from Peru to Venezuela and Brazil.

Twospot astyanax (*Astyanax bimaculatus*):
Up to 15cm/6in
This common fish inhabits large rivers, streams, ponds and lakes from Panama to the Amazon basin in Brazil. It eats everything from detritus and plant matter to invertebrates and the scales of other fish. It is named for the two large black spots on its side – one behind the eye, above the pelvic fin, the other at the base of the tail.

One-lined pencilfish

Nannostomus unifasciatus

This small fish is a common inhabitant of vegetated shores in streams and small rivers throughout the Amazon basin. Sociable by nature, it lives in small schools which may join up with schools of other, similar-sized fish for protection. The one-lined pencilfish feeds on tiny insect larvae and crustaceans which it snaps up from the water and plucks from the leaves of aquatic plants. When searching for food it swims slowly with its head up, its body tilted at an angle of 45°. When at rest, however, it keeps its body horizontal. At dusk it begins to change colour, taking on a nocturnal pattern of blotches. At dawn, the fish reverts to its bold, striped pattern. The reason for this is not clear, since it does not really need camouflage during the hours of darkness.

Distribution: Upper Orinoco basin and parts of the Amazon basin in Brazil, Bolivia, Venezuela and the Guyanas.
Habitat: Banks of rivers and streams with abundant aquatic vegetation.
Food: Small aquatic invertebrates.
Size: Up to 3.8cm/1½in.
Breeding: The eggs are scattered in open water and drift to the bottom where they develop unguarded.

Identification: The body is very long and slender and the snout pointed, hence the common name. A thin gold line extends along the side of the body, from the snout, through the eye and all the way to the tip of the caudal fin's lower lobe. Directly below this is a much broader black line that follows the same path along the body.

Banded leporinus

Leporinus fasciatus

Distribution: Throughout much of South America east of the Andes, from the Orinoco River to the Rio de la Plata in Uruguay and Argentina.
Habitat: Swift rivers and streams with rocky bottoms.
Food: Aquatic invertebrates, small fish and algae.
Size: Up to 30cm/12in.
Breeding: The female lays her eggs in a specially prepared nest. The male then guards them until they hatch.

A fish of fast-flowing rivers and streams, the banded leporinus feeds mainly on insect larvae and other aquatic invertebrates which it finds among the pebbles on the bottom. When the opportunity presents itself it will, however, also eat small fish. It supplements this diet with algae which it grazes off the rocks. When it searches for food it swims along with its head down but at rest it adopts a normal position, swimming against the current to hold its position in the water. It is a strong swimmer which escapes predators by jumping from the water. There are five different subspecies of this fish: *Leporinus fasciatus fasciatus*, *L. f affinis*, *L. f altipinnis*, *L. f tigrinus* and *L. f holostictus*. The banding and coloration of each subspecies is slightly different.

Identification: The head is quite small but the eyes are large. The body is elongated and has a base colour of lemon yellow to beige. This is overlaid with nine or ten thick black bars. The first of these passes through the eye and the last is right at the base of the tail. The fins are virtually transparent and the caudal fin is deeply forked.

TETRAS

Tetras include some of the smallest members of the characin family. They are among the most common fish in South America, as well as some of the most beautiful. They are shoaling fish that are often brightly coloured, and their beauty, together with their hardiness and adaptability, make them very popular with home aquarium enthusiasts.

Neon tetra

Paracheirodon innesi

Identification: The back is dark olive green and the flanks and underside silvery white. An iridescent blue-green stripe runs from near the tip of the snout through the upper part of the iris of the eye to the base of the adipose fin. Below that, a red stripe extends from the middle of the body to the base of the caudal fin. During the night, as the fish rests, the body colour fades. It glows again with the return of activity in the morning.

The neon tetra is probably the most popular of all aquarium fish. A small and gentle schooling fish, it is hardy, easy to keep and spectacular. Its colours are not an accident of evolution; they serve a clear purpose in the wild, helping it to find other individuals of the same species within the heavily tannin-stained, blackwater streams it inhabits. The neon tetra can also be found in clear water streams but is thought to have expanded into this habitat some time after it first evolved. Although it is restricted in what it can eat because of its small size, this tetra is a generalist feeder, catching tiny crustaceans and insect larvae both from open water and on the bottom. It also feeds on algae and, occasionally, the leaves of aquatic plants. This fish is bred and raised in captivity in great numbers for the aquarium trade.

Distribution: Restricted in the wild to the tributary streams of the Solimões River, which flows into the Amazon.
Habitat: Tannin-stained and clear streams.
Food: Small aquatic invertebrates, algae and plant matter.
Size: Up to 2.2cm/¾in.
Breeding: The eggs are scattered in open water and are washed downstream by the current. They hatch within 24 hours.

Cardinal tetra

Paracheirodon axelrodi

Identification: The back is olive green and there is an iridescent blue-green stripe running from the snout to the base of the adipose fin. The body beneath this is almost entirely red, apart from the front part of the belly, which is silver. All of the fins are transparent. As with the neon tetra, the eyes are very large compared with the rest of the head.

This fish is closely related to the neon tetra and even more spectacularly coloured. Like its relative, it uses its bright colours to recognise other members of its own species in the tannin-stained river waters where it lives. The cardinal tetra is a less common fish in the aquarium trade than the neon tetra, although it is just as abundant in the wild. The reason is that, until recently, the cardinal tetra was considered difficult to breed in captivity. As a result, almost all of those for sale were wild-caught specimens. In recent years, however, commercial operations have begun breeding cardinal tetras successfully, so it seems likely that this fish will soon become more widely available.

Distribution: Upper Orinoco and Rio Negro basins in Colombia, Venezuela and northern Brazil.
Habitat: Blackwater rivers and streams.
Food: Small aquatic invertebrates.
Size: Up to 2.5cm/1in.
Breeding Spawning occurs in shoals in open water. The eggs are left to develop unguarded.

Head-and-tail-light tetra

Hemigrammus ocellifer

Distribution: Throughout the Amazon basin of Brazil and Peru. Also found in smaller coastal rivers in the Guyanas.
Habitat: Backwater pools and other areas with little water flow.
Food: Aquatic invertebrates and plant material.
Size: Up to 4.4cm/1¾in.
Breeding: Spawning occurs in open water. The eggs sink down to the bottom, where they are left to develop unguarded.

Also known as the beacon fish, this tetra is named for its iridescent orange spots, one just behind the gill cover and the other at the base of the tail. In bright light these spots become hard to see but in the shaded, stagnant waters where the species lives they glow and help them to find other individuals. The head-and-tail-light tetra is a shoaling fish that feeds on small crustaceans, worms, insect larvae and plants. It is a prolific breeder and often breeds in home aquaria. As with many tetras, this species is a popular aquarium fish, being both hardy and attractive. The females are significantly larger and heavier than the males. Both sexes naturally shoal together in the wild.

Identification: The body is silvery-green to gold. A dark stripe runs down the middle, widening out into a blotch at the base of the tail. Some populations lack the stripe and retain the tail blotch alone. The anal fin is quite large and has a white mark at its tip. Other than this, all the fins are clear and virtually transparent. There is also a small adipose fin.

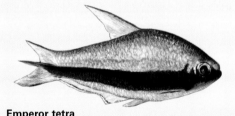

Emperor tetra
(*Nematobrycon palmeri*): Up to 6cm/2in
This fish (*above*) inhabits densely vegetated rivers in western Colombia. The males are unusual in having an extended ray in the middle of the caudal fin, which makes the tail look like a trident. Unusually for tetras, the eggs are laid one at a time, which means spawning takes several hours, rather than a few seconds.

Black phantom tetra (*Hyphessobrycon megalopterus*): Up to 3.6cm/1½in
This deep-bodied tetra lives in the Upper Paraguay, Mamore and Guaporé River basins in Bolivia and Brazil respectively. It is notable for its large dorsal and anal fins, both of which are edged in black, as is the caudal fin. The rest of the body is silver, apart from a large black blotch on its side. Unusually, the males are territorial.

Bleeding heart tetra (*Hyphessobrycon erythrostigma*): Up to 6cm/2in
This omnivorous fish, from the upper Amazon River basin in Colombia and Peru, is pinkish-violet to orange in colour, appearing purple in reflected light. There is a bright red spot just behind the gill cover, which gives this fish its name. The male has a long, sickle-shaped dorsal fin with a large black blotch on its rear edge.

Glowlight tetra

Hemigrammus erythrozonus

Compared with the other fish on these pages, the glowlight tetra might seem unspectacular. In the shaded waters in which it lives, however, the iridescent orange stripe along its side does literally glow. As with other iridescent tetras, this enables the fish to recognize one another and helps keep their shoals together. Although common in the wild, this fish is bred in large numbers in captivity – mainly in South-east Asia – for the aquarium trade. Gold and albino forms have been developed by breeders. The glowlight feeds mainly on worms and small crustaceans, and, occasionally, the leaves of aquatic plants.

Distribution: Essequibo River in Guyana.
Habitat: Rivers and streams.
Food: Aquatic invertebrates and some plant matter.
Size: Up to 3.3cm/1¼in.
Breeding: Spawning occurs in open water. The eggs are left to develop unguarded.

Identification: The body is almost entirely silver in colour, apart from an iridescent red to orange stripe, which runs from the snout to the base of the tail. The fins vary from silver to transparent. The dorsal fin has a mark at the base of its front edge the same colour as the stripe, and a white tip. The pelvic and anal fins both often have white marks at their edges.

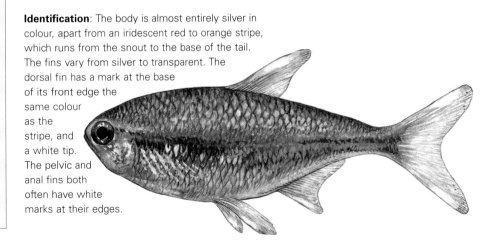

KILLIFISH, TOOTHCARPS AND TETRAS

The killifish of Central and northern South America are among the most abundant fish in the areas where they are found. Small, hardy and quick to reproduce, they support the populations of many larger species of fish, as well as other piscivorous fish. With the exception of the Argentine pearlfish, all of the fish on these pages are often kept in home aquaria.

Pike killifish

Belonesox belizanus

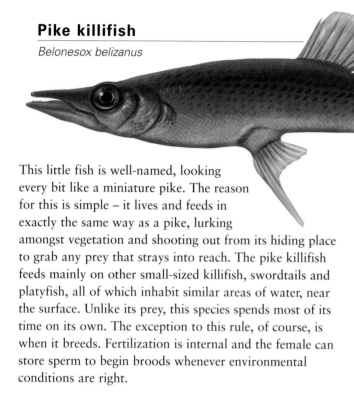

This little fish is well-named, looking every bit like a miniature pike. The reason for this is simple – it lives and feeds in exactly the same way as a pike, lurking amongst vegetation and shooting out from its hiding place to grab any prey that strays into reach. The pike killifish feeds mainly on other small-sized killifish, swordtails and platyfish, all of which inhabit similar areas of water, near the surface. Unlike its prey, this species spends most of its time on its own. The exception to this rule, of course, is when it breeds. Fertilization is internal and the female can store sperm to begin broods whenever environmental conditions are right.

Identification: The jaws are long and pointed and the eyes large and set near the top of the head. The mouth is filled with large teeth. The stock at the base of the tail is almost as wide as the rest of the body. The caudal fin is large and has a rounded rear edge. There is a dark spot at its base. The dorsal fin is set further back on the body than the anal fin. The male bears a modified anal ray that facilitates fertilization.

Distribution: Native to Central America, occurring from southern Mexico to northern Costa Rica. It has also been established in Florida since the late 1950s.
Habitat: Warm slow-flowing rivers, ponds and lakes.
Food: Other fish.
Size: Up to 14cm/5½in.
Breeding: Breeding occurs all year round. Fertilization is internal and the female gives birth to a brood of live young – as many as 300 at a time.

Yucatan molly

Poecilia velifera

Identification: The snout and mouth are turned upward. The male has an enormous dorsal fin which runs along most of the back and which can be raised like a sail. The fin colour ranges from orange to blue and is covered with iridescent spots. The sides of the male also vary, ranging from orange to blue-green and are covered with small, shimmering scales. The female is slightly larger but less brightly coloured.

The young of this species are among the fish preyed upon by the pike killifish, however the adults are too large. The male Yucatan molly is quite a spectacular fish with an enormous dorsal fin. It is a close relative of North America's sailfin molly (*Poecilia latipinna*), which has become a popular aquarium fish. As with other members of its genus, this fish is a live-bearer, with the females giving birth to broods of live young rather than laying eggs. This improves the survival chances of the young. By developing and hatching inside their mother's body they avoid the risks most fish eggs have to face, namely, being eaten before they can hatch.

Distribution: Confined to the Yucatan peninsula in the far south-east of Mexico.
Habitat: River estuaries and coastal lagoons.
Food: Aquatic invertebrates and plant matter.
Size: Up to 15cm/6in.
Breeding: Fertilization is internal and the female gives birth to live young, who number between 25–200.

Guppy

Poecilia reticulata

This tiny fish is undoubtedly the most popular aquarium species and it has been bred into a wide variety of forms. It is regarded as very easy to keep and breeds prolifically even in home aquaria. As well as being successful in captivity, the guppy has managed to spread far and wide in the wild. Like the mosquitofish, it has been widely introduced into different parts of the world, particularly in Africa and Asia, in an effort to control mosquito populations and hence malaria. Unfortunately, however, it has proved to have had no noticeable impact on either in any of the places where it has been introduced. Instead, it has often become a problem by out-competing native species for food and driving them towards extinction. The guppy feeds on aquatic insect larvae and flying insects, which it catches at the water's surface.

Distribution: Native to Trinidad, Barbados, the Venezuelan coast, the Guyanas and northern Brazil. Introduced both accidentally and deliberately to other parts of the world.
Habitat: Still or slow-moving water in a variety of habitats. Tolerates high salinity levels.
Food: Aquatic insect larvae and flying insects.
Size: Up to 3.5cm/1⅜in.
Breeding: Fertilization is internal. After 4–6 weeks, 20–40 live young are born.

Identification: In the wild, male guppies vary in colour and pattern a great deal, according to population. The mouth is always upturned and the head is small. Males are smaller than the females, although their caudal fins tend to be larger. Captive varieties may have even more ornate fins.

X-ray fish (*Pristella maxillaris*): Up to 4.5cm/1¾in
This tetra (*above*) lives in densely vegetated swamps and coastal rivers from Venezuela to Brazil. It is a shoaling species that feeds on aquatic invertebrates which it plucks from aquatic plants, finds on the bottom or snaps up in open water. Its transparency helps protect it from predatory fish and fish-eating birds.

Marbled headstander (*Abramites hypselonotus*): Up to 14cm/5½in
This fish gets its name from its habit of swimming with its head pointing downward. It feeds on worms, algae, insect larvae and crustaceans which it finds on the bottom of rivers and streams. It is widespread throughout much of northern South America.

Argentine pearlfish (*Cynolebias bellottii*): Up to 7cm/2¾in
This fish has evolved to live in habitats where standing fresh water is temporary, and so breeding must be accomplished before pools dry out. Eggs may lie dormant in the mud. They then begin, or resume, development as soon as rainwater fills the pools again. These fish grow rapidly and breed as soon as they are able.

Southern platyfish

Xiphophorus maculatus

The southern platyfish (or platy) shares much of its range with the pike killifish and Yucatan molly. It is best known, however, as an aquarium fish. Easy to keep and quick to breed, it is a popular choice for beginners to the hobby. Most of the platies sold in pet shops nowadays are captive-bred hybrids, produced by crossing this species with the green swordtail (*Xiphophorus helleri*). The latter lives in the same part of the world as the southern platyfish but rarely comes into contact with it in the wild, preferring swifter-flowing rivers and streams. As with many other live-bearers, the southern platyfish is quick to mature. Both sexes can breed when they are just four months old.

Distribution: South-western Mexico to northern Belize; introduced to other parts of the world.
Habitat: Swamps and slow-flowing streams with abundant vegetation.
Food: Insect larvae and other aquatic invertebrates.
Size: Up to 4cm/1½in.
Breeding: Fertilization is internal. Females give birth to broods of 20–80 live young around 4 weeks after mating.

Identification: Wild platies are much less colourful than aquarium fish – sandy yellow with a silver sheen. The scales are quite large and clearly defined. The mouth is small and upturned and the eyes are large compared with the rest of the head. The caudal fin is transparent, large and has a rounded edge.

CATFISH

Catfish are bottom-dwellers and are named for their whisker-like barbels – long, fleshy appendages used for locating prey and finding their way around. South American catfish vary greatly in shape, size and habit. Some are small invertivores (animals that feed on invertebrates) while others eat plants. The larger species are carnivorous and can be quite voracious predators.

Red-tailed catfish

Phractocephalus hemioliopterus

Identification: The head is broad and rounded. Seen from above, it is wider than the rest of the body. There are three pairs of barbels around the mouth. The belly and back are dark brown to black, as are the fins, apart from the caudal fin, which is orange or red. The sides and rear part of the underside are white. The upper tip of the dorsal fin may be red.

Right: Viewed from the front, the long barbels and wide snout of this species are very distinctive.

This is one of South America's larger species of catfish – old individuals can weigh in excess of 44kg/97lb. Compared with most large catfish, it looks quite striking, its dark belly and lower fins contrasting with the white of the underbelly, so it looks rather as if it has a large pale stripe down the side of its body. Amazingly, considering its voracity and potential size, it is often sold as a pet. As with many of its relatives, it is a nocturnal hunter. By day it lies on the river bed, motionless, often sheltering under a large object such as a sunken log.

Distribution: Native to the Amazon and Orinoco River basins of Colombia, Bolivia, Venezuela and Brazil.
Habitat: Deep channels and pools in rivers.
Food: Fish, large crustaceans and fallen fruit.
Size: Up to 1.34m/4.4ft.
Breeding: Spawning occurs mainly in January and February. The eggs are scattered over the bottom and left to develop unguarded.

Short-bodied catfish

Brochis splendens

This squat catfish inhabits well-vegetated, flowing waters but is normally found near the banks of rivers. Like most catfish it feeds on the bottom, but rather than searching the surface of the substrate for food, it grubs around in it to expose worms and other invertebrates. It is a small fish and travels in shoals to give it some protection from predators. Picking out an individual from a shoal is harder than catching one on its own and many pairs of eyes are more likely to spot prowling predators than one. In the wild this fish is brightly coloured, hence its other common names: the emerald green cory and the iridescent-plated catfish. In captivity, however, most individuals lose their emerald sheen, which suggests that colour may be linked to diet or water conditions in the wild.

Identification: The short-bodied catfish looks like the more commonly seen *Corydoras hastatus* species, but it has only six to eight rays in its dorsal fin, compared with the ten or more found in *Corydoras hastatus*. The body is deep and stubby and the back quite strongly arched. The caudal fin is quite big with the lower lobe larger than the upper. Wild individuals have a striking emerald green glow.

Distribution: Upper Amazon basin in Brazil and Peru and the Rio Napo in Ecuador.
Habitat: Slow-flowing sections of rivers and streams.
Food: Insect larvae, worms and other small, bottom-dwelling invertebrates.
Size: Up to 6cm/2⅓in.
Breeding: After laying the eggs, these are picked up with the aid of the pelvic fins and pasted individually on to water plants. They are left to develop unguarded.

Ripsaw catfish

Oxydoras niger

Distribution: Known to inhabit the Amazon, São Francisco and Essequibo River basins.
Habitat: The main channels of large rivers.
Food: Bottom-living invertebrates and detritus.
Size: Up to 1m/39½in.
Breeding: In the Amazon River spawning occurs in the lower reaches, before migration. Eggs are scattered and left to develop unguarded.

This catfish, also known as the cuiu cuiu or dolphin catfish, is widespread in the northern half of South America, occurring from the east coast of the continent to the foothills of the Andes and also at altitudes of up to 1,000m/3,280ft. It is one of around 40 fish species from the Amazon basin which engage in an annual migratory run known as the piracema. Every June, when water levels begin to drop, these fish begin to head upstream in vast numbers. The piracema lasts around four months, after which the rising water levels and increasing water current drive the fish back downstream again. The ripsaw is unusual among catfish in that it forms schools in the wild. Despite its size it poses no threat to other fish, feeding on detritus and invertebrates it finds on the bottom.

Identification: This fish is named for the sharp-edged scutes that run in a line down the side of its body. These structures are its most obvious distinguishing feature. The eyes are located on the sides of the head, rather than the top as in some other catfish, and they are set quite far back. The upper lobe of the caudal fin is pointed, while the lower lobe has a rounded edge.

Talking catfish (*Acanthodoras spinosissimus*): Up to 13cm/5¼in
This catfish is named for the grunting sounds it makes when taken out of the water. However, its defences are even more remarkable. Small erectible spines all over its body and tough spines at the front edges of its dorsal and pectoral fins make it a very unpleasant mouthful for any larger fish. It also produces a white, milky fluid when distressed, which is thought to be toxic.

Tiger shovelnose catfish (*Pseudoplatystoma tigrinum*): Up to 1.3m/4.2ft
This large catfish (*above*) is also known as the tiger sorubim. It lives in both fast and slow-moving sections of the Orinoco and Amazon River basins. It feeds mainly on fish and large crustaceans. Its name is justified since it is beautifully striped and has a head that is shaped like a shovel. Its meat is highly prized.

Raphael catfish (*Platydoras costatus*): Up to 24cm/9½in
Like the talking catfish, this has strong, pointed pectoral and dorsal spines that make it unpalatable to predators. It also uses these spines to wedge into rock cracks on the riverbed if under attack. It inhabits most of the river basins in South America east of the Andes and north of the Tropic of Capricorn. It feeds on molluscs and other aquatic invertebrates.

Suckermouth catfish

Pterygoplichthys pardalis

This handsome catfish is a popular addition to many home aquaria and has a relatively peaceful temperament. In the wild it feeds mainly on algae and plant material and it shows little interest in other fish. It is a bottom-dweller but has the ability to gulp air if oxygen levels drop too low. Its 'sucker' mouth is more an adaptation for grazing algae than holding on to rocks. In the aquarium trade, the suckermouth catfish is often confused with the similar looking common pleco (*Hypostomus plecostomus*), which, like the suckermouth catfish, is bred in large numbers in Hong Kong and Singapore. Both fish reach a significant size in time, which often comes as a shock to people who bought them as fingerlings.

Identification: The body is covered with beautiful marbling. The dorsal fin is large and can be raised like a sail, for the purpose of display. There are between eleven and thirteen dorsal rays, far more than the five to eight seen in the common pleco. The pectoral fins are long and have a tough spine along the front edge.

Distribution: Native to the Amazon basin of Colombia, Peru, Bolivia and Brazil. Introduced to other countries, notably the Philippines.
Habitat: Swamps, pools and slow-moving sections of rivers.
Food: Algae and plant matter.
Size: Up to 43cm/17in.
Breeding: Pairs spawn in hollows in riverbanks and near the edges of pools. The male remains with the eggs until they hatch.

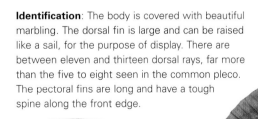

OTHER CATFISH

While large catfish are usually solitary predators, the smaller species either school or use camouflage to avoid predation. All seven species shown on these pages are relatively abundant in the areas in which they are found in the wild. Most of them are frequently bred in captivity to supply the international demand for attractive aquarium species.

Twig catfish

Farlowella acus

Identification: The shape makes this easy to distinguish from any other fish. Identifying individual species apart within the genus, however, is much more difficult; even experts cannot identify them unless they have two or more specimens to compare. The body is extremely elongated and covered with many small plates. The snout is pointed, with the mouth located on the underside.

This fish is also known as the whiptail or needle catfish. It is a beautifully camouflaged species that is difficult to spot in the wild. It feeds on algae and occasionally on aquatic plants, holding its body close to and in line with stems and leaves to avoid detection. When not feeding it hardly moves at all, unless it feels it has been seen. Then, it zips away at quite a speed to find a more secluded position and begin hiding again.

The unusual appearance of this fish has made it popular with home aquarium enthusiasts, although its very particular feeding requirements make it difficult to keep. Its camouflage is so good, particularly when young, that some people have found themselves bringing a fish home by accident, hidden away in the leaves of a plant bought for their aquarium. There are more than 30 different species of twig catfish in South America. This is one of the most common.

Distribution: Torito River basin and Lake Valencia in Venezuela.
Habitat: Shallow and well vegetated shore regions of still and slow-moving waters.
Food: Algae and plant matter.
Size: Up to 16cm/6¼in.
Breeding: Spawning occurs at dawn or dusk, with the female laying between 60 and 80 eggs. The male guards the eggs and helps the young free themselves from the eggs as they hatch.

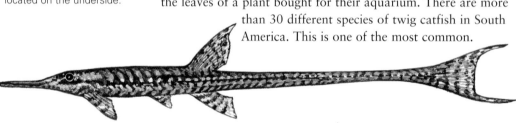

Armoured catfish

Callichthys callichthys

This popular aquarium fish has several common names – the bubblenest catfish, hassar and mailed catfish. In most parts of South America, where it occasionally finds itself on the menu, it is known as the cascarudo. It is a common and widespread species, occurring from Trinidad and Tobago to northern Argentina. The reason for its success is a combination of physical toughness and an ability to eat almost anything. If fish and aquatic invertebrates become scarce, it will consume plant matter. It can survive in low oxygen levels and may even travel short distances overland to find new sources of fresh water, gulping air and absorbing oxygen through its intestine walls.

Identification: The mouth is large and the barbels quite long. The eyes are small and set near the top of the head. The pectoral fins have strong, thick spines forming their leading edges. The body is long and, seen from the side, of virtually unchanging depth from the dorsal fin to the base of the tail. The caudal fin is strongly rounded. The flanks are armoured with tough, large, overlapping scales.

Distribution: Occurs throughout most of South America east of the Andes, from the far north to the area around Buenos Aires.
Habitat: Swamps, pools and slow-flowing streams.
Food: Small fish, aquatic invertebrates and plant matter.
Size: Up to 16.5cm/6½in.
Breeding: The male builds a bubble nest of saliva among floating plants and guards it fiercely once the female has laid her eggs.

Micro catfish
Corydoras hastatus

Distribution: Found in both the Amazon and Paraguay River basins.
Habitat: Well vegetated streams and small rivers.
Food: Aquatic invertebrates and some plant matter.
Size: Up to 3.5cm/1½in.
Breeding: The eggs are laid individually and attached to water plants. They are then left to develop unguarded.

This little catfish has several common names, most of which refer to its size. Among them are the dwarf catfish, tail spot pygmy catfish and dwarf corydoras. But its scientific name is perhaps most useful in terms of identification. The Latin word *hastatus* means 'spear-tip', referring to the spearhead-shaped mark at the base of its tail. This fish is unusual among catfish because it spends most of its time in mid water rather than on the bottom, holding its position in the current with rapid movements of its fins, particularly its pectoral fins. It hunts for small invertebrates among aquatic vegetation and often rests on the leaves of these plants in areas of low water current when not feeding.

Identification: The small size of this fish and the spear-shaped mark at the base of its tail are its two most distinguishing features. Compared with other members of its genus, the micro catfish has a relatively elongated body. It ranges in colour from olive to dirty white. A thin dark stripe runs from the rear edge of the gill cover to the base of the tail.

Banjo catfish
(*Bunocephalus bicolor*): Up to 15cm/6in
This unusual-looking catfish (*above*) is named for the shape its body makes when seen from above. It is camouflaged to live in forest streams beneath the Amazon rain forest canopy. Two long barbels extend from its upper jaw and four smaller ones are on the underside of its head.

Bronze catfish (*Corydoras aeneus*):
Up to 7.5cm/3in
This widespread species occurs from Colombia and Trinidad southward as far as the La Plata River basin in Argentina. It is also widely bred for aquaria in South-east Asia. Several colour variants have been developed in captivity, including gold, black, emerald green and albino forms. It lives in schools and prefers still or slow-moving shallow waters over mud.

Leopard catfish (*Corydoras julii*):
Up to 5cm/2in
This little fish resembles the bronze catfish, with its thickset, stubby body, large eyes and short barbels. However, it is covered in small spots and occurs less widely, confined to the lower Amazon basin and coast of north-eastern Brazil. It is often confused with the three-lined catfish (*Corydoras trilineatus*) although the latter has three distinct lines of spots down each side.

Midget suckermouth catfish
Otocinclus affinis

Also known as the golden otocinclus or oto cat, this catfish is a common addition to home aquaria, since it keeps the growth of algae at bay. In the wild it inhabits well-vegetated rivers with moderate currents, where it searches the bottom for food. Its range is relatively small compared with most other catfish. However, its small size and nocturnal habits make it difficult to observe and it may be more abundant than expected. As well as bottom-feeding, it also grazes algae from the leaves of water plants. It uses its sucker-shaped mouth to hold on when feeding and to attach itself to leaves or objects on the bottom when at rest.

Distribution: Known from a relatively small region around Rio de Janeiro in south-eastern Brazil.
Habitat: Well-vegetated rivers and streams.
Food: Algae.
Size: Up to 5cm/2in.
Breeding: Eggs are laid individually onto the leaves of aquatic plants. They are then left to develop unguarded.

Identification: The snout is pointed and slightly upturned. The mouth, which is shaped like a sucker, is on the underside of the head. The body is light brown to gold above with a dappling of darker brown. The underside is much paler – almost white. A thick dark band runs along the side from the snout to the base of the tail, where it widens into a rounded blotch.

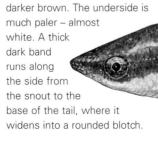

AQUATIC AMPHIBIANS AND TURTLES

The majority of South America's amphibians only enter the water to breed. The Surinam toad, however, is an exception, rarely leaving the water. The continent is home to dozens of turtle species. The six representatives shown here include the most common, widespread and interesting species.

Surinam toad

Pipa pipa

The Surinam toad is one of the weirdest looking amphibians on Earth. Its body is extremely flattened – so much so that it almost looks like an ordinary toad that has been trodden on or run over. It feeds on fish and aquatic invertebrates, which it catches on the bottoms of the swamps and murky pools it inhabits. It finds its prey by feeling for it with its outstretched front limbs. As soon as it touches something, it lurches forward to grab it in its mouth. Although it breathes air, the Surinam toad is almost completely aquatic. It has very unusual breeding behaviour. As the male fertilizes the female's eggs he spreads them over her back, where they are held in place and become surrounded by spongy tissue. The eggs are then carried around by the female until they hatch.

Identification:
This toad is quite unmistakable. Its entire body is extremely flattened and its head almost triangular. The eyes are unusually small. The front limbs end in feet without webbing but with four long fingers on each. These are tipped with fleshy, star-shaped tactile organs, which are used for locating prey. The rear feet are webbed and clawless.

Distribution: Trinidad and mainland north-eastern South America.
Habitat: Swamps and ponds.
Food: Fish and aquatic invertebrates.
Size: Up to 17cm/6¾in from head to rump.
Breeding: The eggs are carried on the female's back until they hatch. They hatch out as miniature toadlets, their tadpole tails having been absorbed while still in the egg.

Red-headed river turtle

Podocnemis erythrocephala

This little turtle lives mostly in backwater streams, although it is occasionally found in faster-flowing sections of some rivers. It is found in a relatively small area where the borders of Venezuela, Brazil and Colombia meet, and it is listed by the IUCN as Vulnerable. It is largely herbivorous, feeding mainly on aquatic plants and fallen fruits.

However, it will eat carrion too, if necessary, and it has been known to become hooked on lines baited with fish. The red-headed river turtle nests from August to November, with nesting activity peaking during September and October. Females lay small clutches of eggs and it is thought that they may lay more than one clutch every season. The hatchlings of this turtle are approximately 4cm/1.5in long when they emerge.

Identification:
The most obvious feature of this turtle is the one for which it is named. The head is bright red, with a mask of black over the eyes, on the cheeks and down the bridge of the snout. The upper jaw is distinctly notched. The carapace is oval, hard and slightly domed. It is chestnut brown in colour with a slightly lighter border around the rim.

Distribution: Occurs in the Rio Negro and Rio Casiquiare catchments of Colombia, Venezuela and Brazil.
Habitat: Rivers and streams.
Food: Plant matter and, occasionally, carrion.
Size: Carapace up to 32cm/12½in long.
Breeding: Nesting occurs in sandy, brushy areas near the water's edge. The female lays clutches of 5–14 eggs.
Status: Vulnerable.

South American snake-necked turtle

Hydromedusa tectifera

The long, flexible neck of this turtle serves two main purposes. Firstly, it enables the turtle to breathe without having to expose the whole of its body at the water's surface, thus helping to keep it hidden from predators. Secondly, it allows this carnivorous turtle to catch fish more easily. This species is an effective fish hunter, grabbing its prey from the water before it has time to react. Its method is simply to wait for unsuspecting fish to stray into its reach, then extend its neck suddenly, firing its head towards them, mouth open. As well as fish, it eats frogs and aquatic invertebrates such as water snails. In the more southerly parts of its range it may hibernate underwater, buried in the mud on the bottom and absorbing oxygen from the water through its skin. In coastal regions, this turtle may enter brackish water.

Distribution: South-eastern Brazil, Paraguay, northern Argentina and Uruguay.
Habitat: Slow-moving rivers and streams, lakes, ponds and marshes.
Food: Fish, amphibians and aquatic invertebrates.
Size: Carapace up to 30cm/12in long.
Breeding: Nests are dug on banks in spring. Clutches are small – around 4 eggs – and laid at intervals. Several clutches may be laid in a season.

Identification: The dark brown, relatively flat carapace is roughly oval but has nearly parallel sides. The neck is extremely long and, like the head, is dark brown above and yellowish-brown below. These two colours are separated by a dark brown line which runs from the snout, down the neck and into the shell. There are four claws on each foot. Females are larger than males.

Twist-necked turtle (*Platemys platycephala*): Carapace up to 18cm/7in long.
This turtle (left) lives in the far north of South America – Venezuela through the Guyanas and south-eastern Colombia to northern Brazil. It inhabits rainforest streams, pools and marshes, where it feeds on aquatic invertebrates and water plants. Compared with most freshwater turtles it is a relatively poor swimmer and it may sometimes be found wandering across the forest floor.

Tartaruga (*Podocnemis expansa*):
Carapace up to 89cm/35in long.
Also known as the arrau and the giant South American river turtle, this is the biggest turtle in Latin America. It lives in the larger Caribbean-draining rivers of Guyana and Venezuela, and the upper Amazon tributaries of Venezuela, Bolivia Colombia, Peru and northern Brazil. It feeds mainly on aquatic plants and fallen fruit. In the past, it has been heavily exploited for its meat and eggs, and is now quite rare.

Gibba turtle (*Phrynops gibbus*):
Carapace up to 23cm/9in long.
This small turtle lives in rivers, streams, pools and marshes in forests east of the Andes, in parts of Peru, Ecuador, Colombia and Venezuela, as well as similar habitats along the Atlantic coast in Venezuela, Trinidad, the Guyanas and Brazil. It forages at night and has two fleshy barbels on its chin, an unusual feature in turtles.

Matamata

Chelus fimbriatus

This bizarre-looking turtle is beautifully camouflaged to capture its prey. It spends most of its time lying still on the bottom, perfectly hidden among the fallen leaves and other debris. When a fish swims into reach it suddenly strikes, thrusting its head forward and engulfing its prey before it has time to react. It sucks in its victim by suddenly opening its mouth wide, then closing its jaws and expelling any water before swallowing the fish whole. The whole process takes a split second and can only be observed properly using slowed-down film. The matamata prefers to hunt in shallow water, where it can stretch its neck up to breathe without disturbing its position on the bottom.
Unlike most turtles, it is thought never to leave the water to bask.

Distribution: Widespread in the northern half of South America, in Ecuador, Peru, Colombia, Venezuela, Trinidad, the Guyanas and northern and central Brazil.
Habitat: Marshes, lakes, pools, slow-moving streams.
Food: Fish and amphibians.
Size: Carapace up to 45cm/17¾in long.
Breeding: Nesting occurs from October to December. Females lay 12–28 eggs in a clutch.

Identification: The carapace is black or brown and rather oblong in shape. Its front edge is straighter than rounded, as are its sides. There are three longitudinal rows of knobbly keels. The head is disguised to look, from above, like a leaf, with pointed, fleshy lobes on both sides and a narrow, pointed snout. In the wild, the carapace is often covered with algae.

CAIMANS AND CROCODILES

These large and often formidable reptiles are major predators of fish in the lakes, rivers and swamps of South and Central America. Caimans are only found in this part of the world. They belong to the same family as North America's alligator and differ from crocodiles in having only their top teeth visible when their mouths are closed.

Black caiman

Melanosuchus niger

Identification: The black caiman looks similar to the alligator, but its snout is much narrower. As the name suggests, it is darker in colour than other caimans. There are grey bands across the lower jaw: these turn brown as the animal ages. The eyes are relatively large and each sits beneath a bony ridge, which extends down the snout, as in other caimans.

This is the largest caiman and the biggest member of its family (Alligatoridae), out-growing even the North American alligator. It is a widespread species, found throughout the Amazon basin and beyond, in Colombia, Venezuela, Guyana, Brazil, Bolivia and Peru. Although once common, as with many other crocodilians it has been heavily hunted for its skin and is now listed as Conservation Dependent by the IUCN. The total world population is estimated at between 25,000 and 50,000 animals. The black caiman eats mainly fish. Its diet features some of the largest and most dangerous species in South America, including the bigger catfish and piranhas. Unusually, this species also hunts on land at night. It has been known to attack domestic animals and even humans.

Distribution: Northern South America, east of the Andes, ranging from Colombia to Bolivia and central Brazil.
Habitat: Rivers, streams, lakes, swamps and flooded savannah.
Food: Fish and other vertebrates.
Size: Up to 6m/20ft.
Breeding: Females lay 30–65 eggs in a specially-built nest mound near the end of the dry season. Eggs hatch as the wet season begins.
Status: Conservation Dependent.

Spectacled caiman

Caiman crocodilus

This is the world's most common crocodilian and by far the most commonly seen across its geographic range, which encompasses much of Central America and northern South America. It has actually benefited from the hunting its larger cousins have suffered, expanding into habitats in which they were once dominant. The spectacled caiman was once mainly found in still waters but proved extremely adaptable and is now found in most lowland freshwater habitats, from lakes and swamps to rivers. It feeds mainly on fish but is able to cope with food shortages and drought, burrowing into the mud and aestivating to save energy until the rains return. After they hatch, the juveniles stay with their mother for a few weeks, sometimes even following her over land to new areas of water.

Identification: The snout is broad and relatively short, making the head look almost abnormally small. The species is named for the bony ridge it has between the eyes, appearing to join them like a pair of spectacles. The upper eyelids each have their own bony ridge, which is triangular in shape. There are four recognized subspecies, each of which differs slightly in size, colour and the shape of the skull.

Distribution: Occurs from southern Mexico to Brazil and northern Bolivia.
Habitat: Most lowland freshwater habitats.
Food: Fish and other aquatic vertebrates; also water birds.
Size: Up to 3m/10ft.
Breeding: Eggs are laid in nest mounds, usually under the cover of vegetation, from July to August. Females sometimes share nests and guard them until the eggs hatch.

Jacaré caiman (*Caiman yacare*):
Up to 3m/10ft
This species (*below*) shares much of its range with the broad-snouted caiman but is usually found in faster-flowing waters. It is sometimes known as the piranha caiman because of its snaggletooth appearance: some of the lower teeth may entirely pierce the upper jaw and stick out through the skin when the mouth is closed. It is listed as Low Risk (Least Concern) by the IUCN.

Orinoco crocodile (*Crocodylus intermedius*):
Up to 6m/20ft
This species is listed as Critically Endangered by the IUCN. Perhaps fewer than 1,500 individuals are left alive in the wild as a result of over-hunting and habitat destruction. This crocodile is found in the middle and lower reaches of the Orinoco River system. Its head is relatively slender and its back is more heavily armoured than that of the American crocodile, which shares part of its range.

Morelet's crocodile (*Crocodylus moreletii*):
Up to 3m/10ft
The head has a relatively broad snout like the spectacled caiman, which shares its range, but it can be told apart by its protruding lower teeth (as well as those of its upper jaw when its mouth is shut). It occurs in Belize, northern Guatemala and south-western Mexico and is listed as Conservation Dependent by the IUCN.

Broad-snouted caiman

Caiman latirostris

Similar in size to the spectacled caiman, this caiman occupies a region further south. It is also found at higher altitudes, occurring in still and slow-moving waters at up to 600m/1,970ft above sea level. The young of this species specialize in feeding on water snails, crushing them before swallowing. As they grow larger their diet shifts to other prey such as fish and turtles. This species prefers to nest on isolated islands, out of reach of monitor lizards and other egg thieves. The male helps the female to build a nest mound, then leaves her to lay the eggs and guard them. Eggs are laid in two distinct layers to help ensure that an even number of males and females hatch. As with most crocodilians, sex determination is affected by the temperature of the egg.

Distribution: Southern Brazil, eastern Bolivia, Paraguay, northern Argentina and northern Uruguay.
Habitat: Freshwater and brackish swamps and marshes; mangrove forests.
Food: Snails and other aquatic invertebrates, fish, turtles and amphibians.
Size: Up to 3.5m/11½ft.
Breeding: During wet season. Female lays 20–60 eggs (which incubate and hatch in 70 days) then helps hatched young to the water.

Identification: An unusually broad snout – being short makes it appear even broader. A ridge runs from above each eye down each side of the snout. The back has many bony scales. The body is a pale olive green above and slightly lighter below.

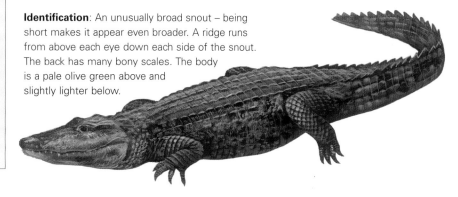

American crocodile

Crocodylus acutus

This is the largest crocodilian in the western hemisphere and one of the biggest reptiles in the world. It is found throughout Central America, the Caribbean and the far northern regions of South America. It is also found in the far south of Florida in the USA, where one population occupies the cooling canals of the Turkey Point nuclear power station. The American crocodile is a creature of both freshwater and brackish coastal habitats, being found in tidal estuaries, mangrove swamps and coastal lagoons, as well as lakes, reservoirs and rivers. It feeds mainly on fish and turtles, but also takes water birds. Unlike most crocodilians, it excavates nest holes wherever it can find banks that are suitably well drained. Otherwise it builds nest mounds.

Distribution: Southern Mexico through Central America to north Venezuela, north Colombia, Ecuador and north-west Peru. Throughout the Caribbean; also Florida.
Habitat: Lakes, swamps, rivers, coastal lagoons and mangrove forests.
Food: Fish and other vertebrates; water birds.
Size: Up to 7m/23ft.
Breeding: During dry season. The female lays 20–60 eggs which incubate in 90 days to hatch at start of wet season.

Identification: Relatively little dorsal armour compared with other crocodilians in its range. Its snout is long and narrows towards the tip. Teeth from both the upper and lower jaws are visible when the mouth is closed. The iris is silvery and there is a distinctive swelling in front of each eye. Adults are olive brown but younger individuals are lighter with banding on both the body and tail.

DWARF CAIMANS, ANACONDA, MANATEES AND RIVER DOLPHINS

The green anaconda is one of the world's most famous snakes, and it spends most of its time in the water. In addition to fearsome reptiles such as these, South America also has many aquatic mammals. The boto and tucuxi are dolphins that hunt fish, while manatees feed only on aquatic vegetation.

Cuvier's dwarf caiman

Paleosuchus palpebrosus

This is the world's smallest crocodilian species. Although the males reach a maximum length of 1.6m/5¼ft, the females rarely grow to more than 1.2m/4ft long. Cuvier's dwarf caiman is a predator of aquatic invertebrates and small fish. Its small, backward-curving teeth are well suited to gripping such slippery prey. As with all crocodilians, it has a special valve at the back of its mouth to prevent water flooding into its throat when swimming. In order to eat, it must lift its head above the surface and tip it backwards to move prey towards its throat so that it can be swallowed. Cuvier's dwarf caiman lives in rivers, streams and flooded areas in tropical rain forest. Due to its small size it has largely been spared the attentions of hunters and is relatively abundant across most of its range.

Identification: The body, including the belly, is covered with relatively heavy bony scales. These help to deter other, larger caiman and crocodile species from attacking it. The head is quite short and narrow for a caiman, and the snout is upturned. The lower jaw is dark but flecked with several white bands.

Distribution: Between the Amazon and Orinoco River drainages in the Guyanas, Venezuela, Colombia, Ecuador, Peru, Bolivia, Paraguay and Brazil.
Habitat: Forest rivers, streams and pools.
Food: Aquatic invertebrates and fish.
Size: Up to 1.6m/5¼ft.
Breeding: Females lay 10–25 eggs in a nest mound which is built in a secluded area. The eggs hatch after about 90 days.

Green anaconda

Eunectes murinus

Identification: The body is extremely thick and muscular, and covered with small, smooth scales. The eyes and nose are set on the top of the head, allowing the snake to both breathe and see prey above the water when the rest of its body is submerged. The general colour is dark green but large black spots with brown centres are scattered over the back. Similar spots occur near the underside but these have yellow centres.

This is the world's largest snake. Although the reticulated python (*Python reticulatus*) is officially longer, it is not as heavy. The green anaconda can weigh 225kg/500lb – as much as three full-grown men. The reason it is able to grow so large is that it spends most of its time in the water, lurking in the shallows of swamps or sluggish rivers and waiting for prey to come into reach. Animals coming down to drink are grabbed in its jaws and pulled into the water, where the snake coils around them, drowning them or killing them by suffocation. Because of its huge size, it can eat almost anything. Caimans are among its more common prey, caught in open water rather than at the shore.

Distribution: Lowland regions of the northern half of South America, east of the Andes.
Habitat: Swamps, sluggish rivers and flooded plains.
Food: Caimans, large mammals and water birds.
Size: Up to 9m/30ft.
Breeding: Mating occurs at the beginning of the rainy season. The green anaconda is viviparous, giving birth to between 20 and 40 live young. Once born, these are left to fend for themselves.

Amazonian manatee

Trichechus inunguis

Distribution: Amazon River and its larger tributaries in Guyana, Brazil, Colombia, Ecuador and Peru.
Habitat: Large, slow-moving rivers.
Food: Aquatic plants.
Size: Up to 2.8m/9¼ft.
Breeding: Females usually bear a single calf, which is born after a gestation period of about a year. There is no mating season: breeding occurs throughout the year.
Status: Vulnerable.

This aquatic, herbivorous mammal is hard to confuse with any other animal in South America, except the West Indian manatee, which has a different range. The Amazonian manatee has been described, quite accurately, as looking like a cross between a hippopotamus and a seal. Like many other herbivores, it spends much of its time eating, searching the waters of large rivers for aquatic plants. Incredibly, it may eat as much as eight per cent of its own body weight in plant matter every day. It is a gregarious animal: it was once known to occur in large herds but now is rarely seen in groups of more than eight, the result of serious over-hunting in the 1930s and 1940s for its hide. It is now listed as Vulnerable by the IUCN.

Identification: The Amazonian manatee has a large, stocky, dark grey body which ends with a large and perfectly rounded paddle-like tail. There are no hind limbs and the front limbs have evolved into flippers. These lack nails, unlike those of the West Indian manatee.

Schneider's dwarf caiman (*Paleosuchus trigonatus*): Up to 2.6m/8½ft
This is the second smallest crocodilian in South America – males usually grow to 2m/6½ft; females are smaller. It hunts in shallow forest streams at night. By day it shelters in burrows dug in the forest, often away from the water. Unusually, it spends much of its time alone. Its snout is longer and more pointed than that of its close cousin, Cuvier's dwarf caiman.

West Indian manatee (*Trichechus manatus*): Up to 4.5m/15ft
This is found mainly in inshore coastal waters, including mangrove forests and estuaries. It is occasionally found further upstream and rarely seen in any waters that are more than 6m/20ft deep. Like the Amazonian manatee, the West Indian manatee is entirely herbivorous, grazing on sea grasses and other aquatic plants. It ranges from Florida, where it is sometimes called the Florida manatee, to far north Brazil.

Tucuxi (*Sotalia fluviatilis*): Up to 2.2m/7¼ft
This dolphin (*above*) lives in the Amazon and Orinoco River basins and in tropical waters off the west coast of South America. River-dwelling tucuxi never enter the sea and tend to be smaller than their marine counterparts. The tucuxi looks more like a typical dolphin than the boto, with a stubby, inflexible neck and a triangular, backward-curving dorsal fin.

Boto

Inia geoffrensis

This is one of two dolphin species found in the larger rivers of South America and the only one to live exclusively in fresh water. It is incredibly well adapted to river life, with a flexible neck and a long, relatively sinuous body compared with other dolphins, which enables it to manoeuvre with ease. When the Amazon annually breaks its banks, the boto spends its time hunting for fish around the submerged trunks of trees. Like other dolphins, it is able to echolocate. It is most active in the early morning and late afternoon, and occasionally jumps from the water. Its bulging cheeks may block its downward view and, to compensate, it often swims upside down.

Identification: A long, slender, slightly down-curved beak, a bulging forehead and a long, plump body, ranging from off-white to vivid pink. It is notable for lacking a dorsal fin, instead having a long, low ridge running along much of its back. The eyes are unusually small and the cheeks are chubby.

Distribution: Found in the Amazon and Orinoco basins of Venezuela, Colombia, Ecuador, Peru and Brazil.
Habitat: Large rivers.
Food: Fish.
Size: Up to 2.7m/9ft.
Breeding: Females bear a single calf in July. As many as five years may pass between the birth of one calf and another.

AFRICA

With its dense rainforests and vast swamps, Africa has large areas of freshwater habitat that have yet to be studied closely. Some of its forest rivers have tributaries that have still not even been properly charted. On the other hand, Africa has some freshwater habitats that have been as closely examined by scientists as any of their equivalents on other continents. The fish of the Nile river and Rift Valley lakes, for example, are as well-documented as those of almost any other waterway or still body of fresh water on Earth.

Africa has giant fish, fish that breathe air and many other oddities. The Rift Valley lake cichlids also provide beautiful examples of adaptive radiation, the evolution of new species to take advantage of unoccupied niches in habitat. These and other, equally colourful, tropical African fish have found their way into the home aquaria of people around the world. Other familiar African freshwater creatures covered here include the Nile crocodile, which, though an aquatic species, spends much of its life out of the water.

Above, left to right: Gilled lungfish (Protopterus amphibius); blue lyrefish (Aphyosemion gardneri); slender-snouted crocodile (Crocodylus cataphractus).
Right: Map of Africa, showing major freshwater routes and bodies of water.

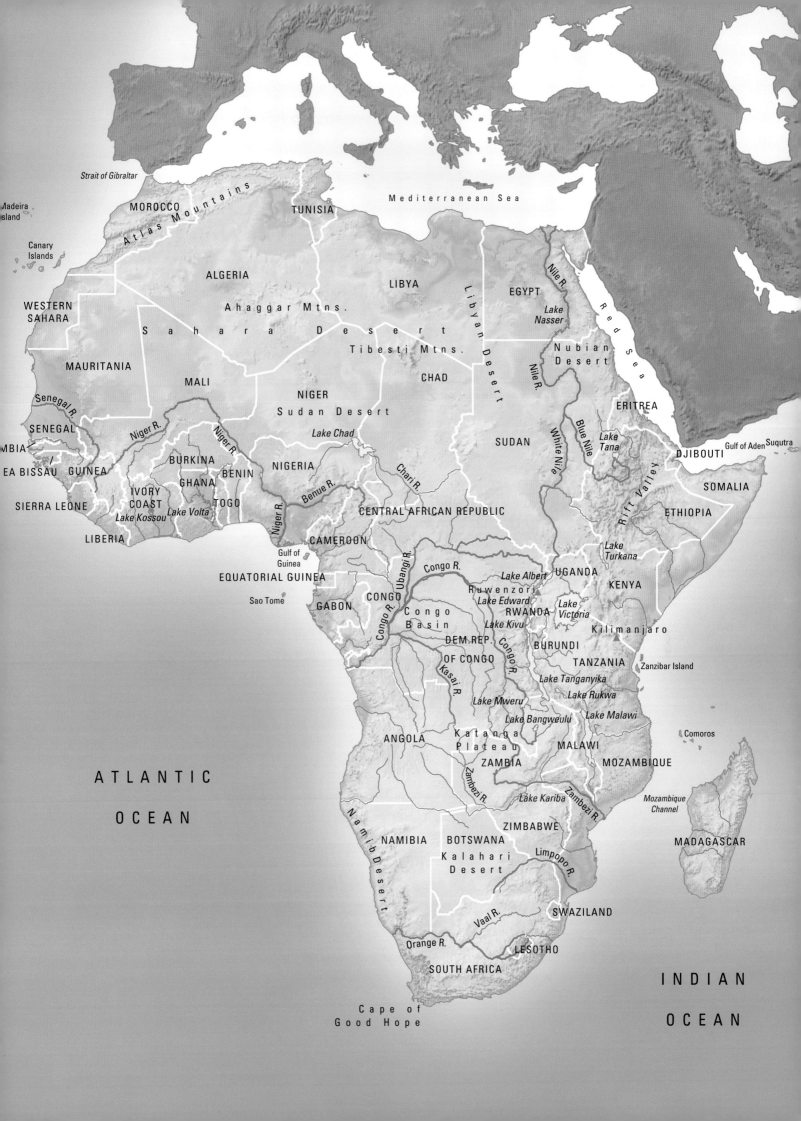

KNIFEFISH, ELEPHANTFISH, BICHIR AND LUNGFISH

All of these fish prefer still or slow-moving waters. The African knifefish and the elephantfish generate electric pulses to help them find their way around. The other five are all obligate air breathers with primitive lungs as well as gills, enabling them to inhabit waters with very low oxygen levels.

African knifefish

Xenomystus nigri

The African knifefish has a smooth-edged body (without a dorsal fin) which tapers to a pointed tip at the 'tail'. Its very long anal fin resembles the blade of a knife. This fish is a nocturnal species. It emerges from its lair at night to search the bottom of the well-vegetated waters where it lives for worms, insect larvae and other invertebrate prey. It finds most of these by touch, but emits weak electrical currents as it moves to help itself navigate in the dark. The African knifefish has no caudal fin and so is a weak swimmer, propelling itself through the water by undulating its long anal fin. What it lacks in speed, however, it makes up for in manoeuvrability. By reversing these undulations it can also swim backwards.

Identification: The body is laterally compressed and the back is arched and smooth with no trace of any fins. A single, long-based anal fin extends along the underside, running from a line just behind the gill covers to the tip of the missing 'tail'. The eyes are large and there are two transparent pectoral fins. This fish sometimes rises to the surface to swallow air, making a sound a bit like a chiming bell as it does so.

Distribution: Reported from the Chad, Nile, Congo and Niger River basins. Also found in coastal river basins in Cameroon, Benin, Togo, Liberia and Sierra Leone.
Habitat: Slow-moving rivers, streams and swamps.
Food: Aquatic invertebrates.
Size: Up to 30cm/12in.
Breeding: The female produces 150–200 eggs, each of about 2mm/⅛in diameter. It is not known whether this species guards its eggs or young.

Elephantfish

Gnathonemus petersii

The elephantfish is another African fish with an appropriate common name. Its long snout resembles an elephant's trunk. It uses this proboscis to probe around for invertebrate prey in the muddy bottoms of slow-moving rivers and streams. The end of the proboscis is flexible and loaded with touch sensors, making it extremely sensitive to movements and different textures within the mud. Like the African knifefish, the elephantfish is nocturnal and uses weak electrical currents to help it find its way around. *Gnathonemus petersii* is the most commonly seen elephantfish in the aquarium trade. However, it is just one of almost 200 similar-looking species in the family Mormyridae, all found in tropical Africa.

Identification: Distinguishing elephantfish from other fish is easy but identifying individual species is extremely hard. Elephantfish are characterized by a long, narrow, downward-pointing snout (or proboscis) and a small mouth. The caudal peduncle, or base of the tail, is much narrower than the rest of the body and the caudal fin is forked. *Gnathonemus petersii* is largely dark brown or black and occasionally has white markings near the rear of its body.

Distribution: This species is found in the Congo and lower Niger River basins in tropical west Africa.
Habitat: Slow-moving rivers and streams.
Food: Aquatic invertebrates: mainly worms and bottom-dwelling insects.
Size: Up to 35cm/13¾in.
Breeding: Electrical discharges increase during courtship, although their exact function is not properly understood. Eggs are left to develop unguarded.

Bichir

Polypterus ornatipinnis

Distribution: Congo River basin, in Lake Tanganyika and in Lake Rukwa, Tanzania.
Habitat: Swamps and slow-flowing rivers and streams.
Food: Aquatic invertebrates and fish.
Size: Up to 60cm/2ft.
Breeding: Spawning occurs during August and September after the rains. The female lays 200–300 eggs within vegetation. They are left to develop unguarded.

The bichir looks more like a salamander than a fish. Its head is broad and flattened, and its pectoral fins are fleshy and resemble legs. The bichir actually uses its pectoral fins to lift the front of its body off the bottom when at rest. It is a mainly solitary nocturnal carnivore. It spends the day hidden amongst dense vegetation and emerges at night to feed. Although it has gills, this fish is an obligate air breather, frequently rising to the surface to take a gulp of air. It absorbs oxygen through the wall of its swim bladder, which acts like a primitive lung. Breeding in this species occurs soon after the rains, when the waterways and pools in which it lives overflow and flood the surrounding plains. Adults then move into these temporary swamps to spawn.

Identification: The head is small but flattened, and the snout rounded like that of a salamander, with protruding tubular nostrils. The elongated body is covered with tough, rhombic scales. There are several dorsal finlets, which can be raised and lowered at will. The bases of the pectoral fins are fleshy and the fins themselves are large and rounded, like paddles.

Marbled lungfish (*Protopterus aethiopicus*): Up to 2m/6½ft
This large species is found in the Nile River basin and in and around Lakes Albert, Edward, Victoria, Tanganyika, Kyoga, Nabugabo and No in the Rift Valley. It can weigh up to 17kg/37½lb. Its cylindrical body is similar to the West African lungfish but is coloured dark slate-grey above and pinkish or yellowish grey below. It can also withstand desiccation by aestivating in cocoons.

Gilled lungfish (*Protopterus amphibius*): Up to 44cm/17¼in
All African lungfish have gills but this species (*above*) is the only one in which they are large and clearly visible in adults. This fish lives in swamps and floodplains in coastal regions of Somalia and Kenya, and the Zambezi River delta in Mozambique. Compared with other African lungfish, it has been relatively little studied.

Slender lungfish (*Protopterus dolloi*): Up to 1.3m/4¼ft
This fish lives in swamps and open river waters in the lower and middle regions of the Congo River basin, in the Ogowe River basin (Gabon) and the Kouilou-Niari River basin (Democratic Republic of the Congo). It is an obligate air breather but it does not dig burrows or aestivate because the regions where it lives have frequent rainfall and so never dry out completely.

West African lungfish

Protopterus annectens

This fish inhabits temporary swamps and floodplains. When these habitats start to dry, the fish buries itself in the mud and secretes a thin layer of slime around its body. This dries to form a fragile cocoon which helps to retain moisture. By slowing its body metabolism, it can live within this cocoon for a year or more, although it normally re-emerges within a few months, when the rains return. The fish digs its burrow with its mouth, eating through the substrate and expelling the mud through its gill slits. Once the water within its burrow has also evaporated away it relies entirely on its primitive lung to obtain oxygen.

Identification: The eyes are small and the snout is prominent. The pectoral and pelvic fins are long and filamentous. The body is grey to olive brown above, lighter below, and speckled with dark spots. The body tapers to a point at the end. There are two long fins, above and below the rear third of the body, that meet at the tail. Three external gills are located posterior to the gill covers and above the pectoral fins.

Distribution: Senegal, Gambia, Niger, Volta and Chad River basins; parts of western Sudan, the Ivory Coast, Sierra Leone and Guinea.
Habitat: Swamps and floodplains.
Food: Plant matter, invertebrates, fish and amphibians.
Size: Up to 1m/3⅓ft.
Breeding: The male digs a burrow in the substrate which the female enters to spawn. The male then guards the eggs and, later, the newly-hatched young.

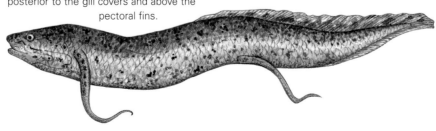

CATFISH, BUTTERFLYFISH AND AFRICAN LEAFFISH

These fish come from a variety of families and have quite different habits. The catfish are all bottom-feeders and most hunt at night. The butterfly fish is the only living member of its family, Pantodontidae, and is most active around dusk. The African leaffish feeds by day and belongs to the family Nandidae.

North African catfish

Clarias gariepinus

Despite its regional name, this species might also be called the pan-African catfish, since it is found throughout virtually the whole of the continent, from the Nile to Senegal and from Algeria to South Africa. It is also found naturally in the Middle East as far as Turkey and has been introduced to parts of Europe and Asia, where it is farmed on a large scale for its flesh. This catfish is not only widespread but is extremely tolerant of harsh conditions. As a result, it is often found in waters where few other fish can survive. It is able to tolerate both slightly acid and alkaline conditions and, being an obligate air breather, it can also live in habitats where oxygen levels are low. It is even able to survive short periods of drought by burrowing into the mud and secreting mucus around itself, which then dries into a protective crust.

Distribution: Most of Africa and parts of the Middle East. Also introduced to parts of Europe and Asia.
Habitat: Most freshwater habitats, from lakes and swamps to rivers and streams.
Food: Plant matter, invertebrates, fish and other small vertebrates.
Size: Up to 1.7m/5½ft.
Breeding: Spawns during the rainy season, particularly over freshly flooded areas. Eggs are scattered and left to develop unguarded.

Identification: The body is elongated with a flattened head and small eyes. It is coloured dark grey above and light cream below. The dorsal and anal fins stretch almost to the caudal fin. The large mouth is surrounded by four pairs of long barbels. The nasal barbels are shorter than the maxillary barbels, which can reach the origin point of the dorsal fin.

Giraffe catfish

Auchenoglanis occidentalis

The giraffe catfish is named for the striking pattern the adult fish have on their skin. In most of Africa the fish is known as the bubu. Although not quite as widespread as the North African catfish, it has an extensive range, occurring in the Nile and Congo-Lualaba River basins, Lake Chad, most Rift Valley lakes and the Omo and Giuba Rivers of Ethiopia and Somalia. It is also found in parts of West Africa. The giraffe catfish is a bottom-feeder, eating everything from invertebrates to fallen seeds and detritus. It tends to be found in shallower areas of water over mud.

Identification: The most distinctive feature of the species is the coloration. Adults have a beautiful pattern of reticulated spots over their backs, sides, upper and caudal fins, which closely resemble those of a giraffe. This may camouflage them against the bottom in shallow water, the pattern mimicking that of ripples struck by the sun. The underside is pale and lacks spots.

Distribution: Found across most of north-east and equatorial Africa.
Habitat: Large rivers and lakes.
Food: Invertebrates, plant matter and detritus.
Size: Up to 70cm/27½in.
Breeding: Nests are guarded by the male. Despite this, they are often also used by another catfish, *Dinotopterus cunningtoni*. The young of this species hatch faster than those of the giraffe catfish and often feed on the eggs and young of their host.

Electric catfish

Malapterurus electricus

Distribution: Occurs in the Nile, Niger and Senegal River basins, as well as smaller rivers in west Africa. Also found in Lake Turkana in Kenya and Lake Chad.
Habitat: Slow-moving rivers.
Food: Fish and large aquatic invertebrates.
Size: Up to 1.2m/4ft.
Breeding: Nesting occurs in holes made in river banks, up to 3m/10ft below the surface. It is thought that the male guards the young.

This fish can fire off electric charges using a specialized organ which now surrounds most of its body, but which originally evolved from the pectoral muscle. This organ is capable of discharging up to 350 volts – powerful enough to stun prey. The electric catfish is a nocturnal inhabitant of turbid waters and also uses this electrical organ for finding its way, continually firing off weaker electric pulses as it swims. It defends itself with the same organ. If it senses a fish larger than itself in the vicinity it fires off a third type of volley – shorter than the attack volley, but sufficiently strong to deter the intruder. Despite its ability to give shocks, this species never causes injury to people. In parts of Africa it is caught, smoked and eaten.

Identification: The body is elongated and sausage-shaped. All of the fins are small and rounded, apart from the caudal fin, which is very large. There is no dorsal fin. The mouth is fairly large and surrounded by three pairs of barbels. The back and sides are greyish-brown and there is usually a cream-coloured vertical bar near the tail with a dark brown or black bar directly behind it.

Upside-down catfish (*Synodontis multipunctatus*): Up to 27.5cm/10¾in
This handsome catfish (*above*) hails from Lake Tanganyika in the Rift Valley. It is often called the cuckoo synodontis because it deposits its eggs amongst those of the lake's many cichlids. The catfish eggs are then picked up by the mouth-brooding cichlids and carried around in the safety of their mouths until they hatch.

African leaffish (*Polycentropsis abbreviata*):
Up to 8cm/3¼in
This little fish lives in rainforest streams in Benin, Nigeria, Cameroon and Gabon. It is well camouflaged, being coloured and shaped just like a fallen leaf. Being small and well-disguised, it is easily overlooked and may be more common than previously assumed. In recent years it has become popular with aquarists.

Vundu (*Heterobranchus longifilis*):
Up to 1.5m/5ft
This is the largest freshwater fish species in southern Africa, reaching 55kg/110lb. It also inhabits large rivers across much of western and central Africa but is rarely common in these places. It preys on fish and other creatures, mainly at night. It also scavenges whenever it can, biting chunks from animal carcasses.

Butterflyfish

Pantodon buchholzi

The butterflyfish inhabits still and slow-moving waters. It is a surface dweller, feeding on mosquito larvae and flying insects that crash land and become trapped. The butterflyfish is named for its large pectoral fins, which resemble a butterfly's wings. When startled, it launches itself from the water. It also does this to snap up mayflies and other flying insect prey. It is not thought that the fish's pectoral fins increase the distance it travels, as they do in marine flying fish. Nevertheless, the butterflyfish is an extremely powerful jumper and it can seem to fly through the air. It is a popular aquarium fish and is now bred in captivity for the trade.

Distribution: Found throughout much of central and west Africa south of the Sahara.
Habitat: Swamps, and slow-moving rivers and streams.
Food: Aquatic insect larvae and flying insects.
Size: Up to 15cm/6in.
Breeding: Eggs are scattered in open water. After around 10 hours they turn dark and float to the surface, where they hatch 2 days later.

Identification: A boat-shaped body, with a flat head and back. The snout and mouth are upturned and the eyes sit high on the head. The pectoral fins are large and roughly triangular. The caudal fin is large and trailing. The long rays of the ventral fins hang down like streamers. Colour can vary a great deal between individuals: from drab brown or greyish green to silvery yellow. Fins are often vivid pink, tinged with violet.

CHARACINS, MADAGASCAR RAINBOWFISH AND CYPRINIDS

The classification of characins is a subject of much debate, but most biologists still place African and South American characins together, in the order Characiformes. Characins from Africa range from small shoaling fish to large predators. Africa's cyprinids are members of the carp family.

Pike characin

Hepsetus odoe

This long-bodied and large-mouthed fish is a typical ambush predator and very similar in appearance to the European pike. The pike characin, or Kafue pike, waits for its prey while hidden among submerged vegetation. It ambushes it at speed, grabbing it in its jaws before the prey has time to react. Although it looks like the European pike, the two are not related. Their similarities are the result of convergent evolution – the process by which two unrelated organisms look almost the same, after having evolved to fill similar ecological niches. The pike characin is relatively short-lived (four to five years) and breeds at the beginning of the rainy season, as water levels start to rise.

Identification: The body is long and torpedo-shaped with a rather large mouth. Both jaws are filled with sharp pointed teeth. These form a single row in the upper jaw and two parallel rows in the lower. Two teeth in each jaw are larger than the others, like canines. The body is dark brown or green above and silvery below, with pinkish to greyish fins. Prominent dark brown or black stripes radiate from each eye.

Distribution: Throughout much of western and central Africa, ranging from Senegal to Angola.
Habitat: Coastal rivers, lakes and floodplain lagoons.
Food: Fish.
Size: Up to 70cm/27½in.
Breeding: A multiple spawner, breeding during summer. The male builds a floating bubble nest of mucus, where the female lays her eggs. Both parents guard the eggs until hatching.

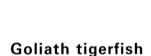

Goliath tigerfish

Hydrocynus goliath

Identification: The body is streamlined for speed, yet extremely solid. The scales are well defined. All fins are pointed, except the adipose fin. The body is pale green above and white below. Younger fish have darker horizontal stripes running down the length of the body, from the rear of the gill covers to the base of the caudal fin.

The Goliath tigerfish is the largest of the characins and a powerful predator with a vicious set of teeth. In many ways its head looks more like that of a crocodile than a fish, with its pointed, steak-knife teeth well separated and overlapping the sides of its mouth. This fish can weigh as much as 50kg/110lb. Its power, size and ferocious reputation make it one of the world's most sought-after freshwater game species; some people travel to Africa with the sole intention of catching one. The danger it poses is multiplied by the fact that it lives and hunts in shoals, much like the red-bellied piranha of South America.

Distribution: Lake Tanganyika and the Congo River basin.
Habitat: Lakes and large rivers.
Food: Fish.
Size: Up to 1.33m/4.4ft.
Breeding: The breeding system of this species has not been studied but it is thought likely to be an open water spawner that does not guard its eggs or young.

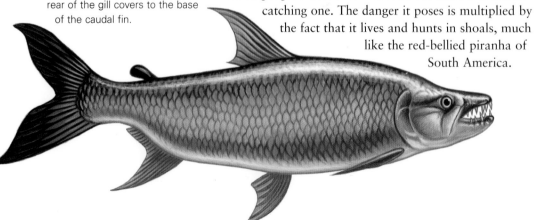

Congo tetra

Micralestes interruptus

Distribution: Congo River basin, primarily in the Democratic Republic of the Congo (formerly Zaire).
Habitat: Streams, quiet stretches of rivers.
Food: Aquatic invertebrates and plant matter.
Size: Up to 8cm/3¼in.
Breeding: The female scatters around 300 eggs into open water to be fertilized by the male. The eggs then sink to the bottom and are left to develop unguarded.

If the Goliath tigerfish is the beast of the Congo River, the Congo tetra might be considered the beauty. This fish is certainly admired by many freshwater aquarium enthusiasts and is exported in significant numbers to supply the trade. Like its far larger and somewhat distant relative the Goliath tigerfish, the Congo tetra lives in shoals, mostly searching the bottom for food rather than open waters. The bulk of its diet is made up of worms, insect larvae and crustaceans, although it will also eat plant matter when other food is scarce. Like many small tetras, the Congo tetra avoids fast-flowing waters and instead tends to be found in side streams and weedy areas along river banks. The males of this species are larger and more colourful than the females.

Identification: The body is laterally compressed with large eyes and scales. This fish may appear iridescent green, yellow, blue or sometimes even violet in colour, depending on the intensity and quality of the light falling on it. The dorsal and caudal fins may be transparent or brown, and the latter has a white fringe. All of the fins are delicate and flowing.

Largemouth yellowfish (*Labeobarbus kimberleyensis*): Up to 82.5cm/32½in
This long-bodied member of the carp family is South Africa's largest native fish. It is found in the Orange and Vaal River basins, preferring deep channels in flowing water. It is often found below rapids, although it also seems to do well in the artificial lakes formed behind dams. It feeds on aquatic invertebrates and small fish and is itself a popular food fish.

Purple labeo (*Labeo congoro*):
Up to 41.5cm/16¼in
This fish (*above*) occurs in rocky stretches of large rivers, including the Zambezi, Incomati and parts of the Congo. It feeds on algae and other encrusting organisms, scraping them from boulders and other hard surfaces such as the backs of hippos. It migrates upstream to breed when rivers are in flood.

Nile barb (*Barbus bynni bynni*):
Up to 82cm/32¼in
Another member of the carp family, this fish is confined to the Nile River and the lakes once linked to it but since cut off by dams. It is a large benthic feeder, eating insect larvae, crustaceans, molluscs and organic debris. It is common throughout much of its range and is an important food fish in these areas.

Madagascar rainbowfish

Bedotia geayi

This streamlined little fish is found in the clear mountain streams of Madagascar, off the south-east coast of mainland Africa. It is also known as the zona, or red-tailed silverside. It is a schooling species that feeds on insect larvae, worms, crustaceans and other aquatic invertebrates. It finds most of its prey on the bottom, searching for it among the sand and gravel. This species is a popular aquarium fish and is now bred in captivity. In the wild it is becoming increasingly rare, as a result of competition from introduced swordtails and platies, and predation of its young by introduced mosquitofish. It is listed as Vulnerable by the IUCN.

Distribution: Mananjary River basin, on the eastern side of Madagascar.
Habitat: Clear mountain streams.
Food: Aquatic invertebrates.
Size: Up to 9cm/3½in.
Breeding: Spawning occurs over a number of months. The female lays a few eggs each day which are attached by threads to water plants and develop unguarded.
Status: Vulnerable.

Identification: The body is long and streamlined, the head rather pointed. There are two dorsal fins, the second much longer than the first. The long anal fin runs from the mid-belly region to the base of the caudal or tail fin, which is rounded and fan-like. The back ranges from yellow to brown in colour and the flanks, which have a silvery-green iridescence, are marked by a broad, bluish band.

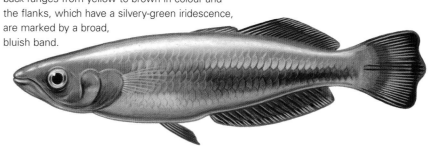

CICHLIDS FROM LAKE TANGANYIKA AND LAKE VICTORIA

Africa's Rift Valley lakes are famous for the variety of their cichlids, which evolved in isolation over a period of around 12 million years. The largest of these lakes is Lake Victoria but the second largest, Lake Tanganyika, is deeper and has a greater range of cichlids – more than 250 species.

King featherfin

Cyathopharynx furcifer

Identification: The male is iridescent green over most of his body. The head has a bluish-purple tinge. All of the fins are long and feather-like, for display. The caudal fin is crescent-shaped with long trailing tips. Females are smaller and silver all over. Their fins are functional rather than elaborate, the dorsal fin being low and rather small.

The king featherfin is endemic to Lake Tanganyika and the most spectacular fish to be found there. Its dazzling colours have made it a firm favourite with cichlid fans worldwide. As with most cichlids, the females are much less showy than the males and are smaller. Although best known for its colours, this fish is also notable for the impressive nests built by the males. These are made from sand which they pick up and move with their mouths. The nests resemble miniature volcanoes and may be more than 61cm/2ft across. The males then defend the areas around these nests and wait for females to approach to lay their eggs, which the males then fertilize.

Distribution: Lake Tanganyika.
Habitat: Relatively shallow waters.
Food: Aquatic invertebrates.
Size: Up to 21cm/8¼in.
Breeding: The male builds a nest, then guards it. As soon as the eggs are fertilized, the male picks them up one by one and keeps them in his mouth until they hatch.

Front cichlid

Cyphotilapia frontosa

Identification: Distinguished by a humped forehead, which grows more prominent with age. This is formed from a fatty deposit built up under the skin. Males are larger than females but otherwise the sexes look quite similar. The body is white or pale blue, with six or seven black vertical bars. The fins are pale and large. The pectoral fins are long and trailing.

Also known as the humphead cichlid, this is the only member of its genus and is endemic to Lake Tanganyika. Like the king featherfin it is a mouth brooder, but the females, not the males, carry and care for the eggs and young. It is a nocturnal predator, picking off small fish at night, when they are at rest. By day it often travels with shoals of *Cyprichromis* cichlids, which form the bulk of its prey. It also feeds on shellfish, such as water snails and freshwater mussels. A deep-water species, the front cichlid is difficult to find and catch alive, so it is uncommon in captivity. It is a popular food fish in areas around the lake.

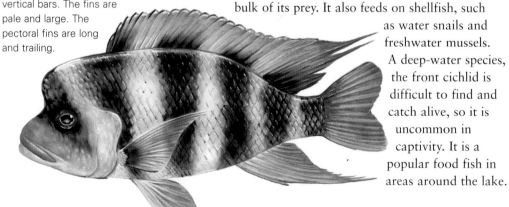

Distribution: Lake Tanganyika.
Habitat: Deeper waters.
Food: Fish and aquatic invertebrates.
Size: Up to 33cm/13in.
Breeding: Spawning occurs in a shallow pit on the bottom, which the male fills with his milt. The female then lays her eggs one by one in the pit and picks them up to be brooded in her mouth.

Moor's tropheus

Tropheus moorii

Distribution: Lake Tanganyika.
Habitat: Shore areas and reefs near the surface.
Food: Algae.
Size: Up to 14.5cm/5¾in.
Breeding: Males and females pair up to spawn. Females lay their eggs one at a time and take them up in their mouths for brooding.

This relatively small, shallow-water cichlid is another fish endemic to Lake Tanganyika. It is also known as the blunthead cichlid. More than 40 different colour morphs of this species occur in the wild. This fact, combined with the fish's size and relative ease of capture, makes it one of the most common cichlids in captivity. The shape of its skull and the position of its mouth is in part an adaptation to its lifestyle. In the wild, it feeds almost entirely on algae, which it grazes from the rocks in shallow water.

Most of its time is spent either feeding or swimming along slowly with its head down searching the rocks for food. When they are not feeding, males actively defend their small territories. Breeding takes place continuously throughout the year.

Identification: Sideways on, this fish is teardrop-shaped, with a large rounded head and a body that tapers down towards the tail. The eyes are positioned quite high and the mouth quite low on the head. The caudal fin has a straightish rear edge, making it appear almost triangular. Colour varies greatly between the different morphs. In most, the scales are clearly visible.

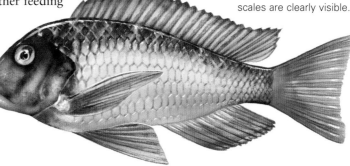

Burton's mouthbrooder
(*Haplochromis burtoni*):
Up to 15cm/6in
This cichlid (*above*) is found in Lake Tanganyika, Lake Kivu and the Ruzizi River, which joins them, as well as other rivers that flow into Lake Tanganyika. It is a common species of shallower waters and is widespread in the home aquarium trade. It is the well camouflaged females of this species that do the mouth brooding. The males are much brighter and slightly larger in size.

Green arrow haplochromis (*Haplochromis pellegrini*): Up to 10cm/4in
This fish, whose common name reflects its vivid green colour and streamlined shape, lives in the shallow waters of Lake Victoria's shores. It feeds on insect larvae and the eggs and young of other fish, which it finds in the sand and among the roots and stems of water plants. It is a mouth brooder.

Red pseudonigricans (*Lithochromis rufus*):
Up to 8.5cm/3¼in
This small cichlid from Lake Victoria feeds on insect larvae and snails, which it finds among rocks. It is known only from the Mwanza Gulf at the lake's southern end, and is listed as Critically Endangered (IUCN). However, it has been bred in captivity, so its future is thought to be safe.

Utinta cichlid

Xenotilapia ochrogenys

The Utinta cichlid is a schooling benthic feeder. Its mouth is positioned on the underside of its head, an adaptation to help it pick up mouthfuls of sand and sift through it for small invertebrate prey. It is mostly found in relatively shallow waters around the shores of the lake and thus is easily caught. Unsurprisingly, considering this and its attractive appearance, it is another species common in the home aquarium trade.

Identification: The head of this fish appears almost too big for the rest of its body. The eyes are large, positioned high up on the head and more oval-shaped than those of most fish. The dorsal and anal fins are relatively long and shallow. There is a silvery flap beneath the lower jaw which may be extended at will. Breeding males have distinctive spots and are brightly coloured while females are less showy.

Distribution: Lake Tanganyika.
Habitat: Sandy bottoms down to 20m/66ft.
Food: Aquatic invertebrates.
Size: Up to 11cm/4¼in.
Breeding: Males display in 'arenas' on the bottom and females then select their mates. Once the eggs have been fertilized the female picks them up in her mouth for brooding.

CICHLIDS FROM LAKE TANGANYIKA

Cichlids are notable for the protection they give to their eggs and young. Mouth brooders carry their eggs around to guard them until they hatch. Others use different methods. Many of the fish on these pages are so-called cave spawners, seeking out small caverns or crevices in which to lay their eggs to help protect them from predators.

Tanganyika Julie

Julidochromis marlieri

This streamlined cichlid inhabits crevices between boulders and smaller rocks in waters of between 5m/16½ft and 30m/98½ft deep. It also spawns within these crevices. Both parents fiercely guard the nests and the fry once they have hatched. The fry remain around the nest until they reach about 2.5cm/1in long. At this point, the parents start to see them as competition and chase them away. The Tanganyika Julie feeds on small aquatic invertebrates and algae. It rarely ventures far from its rocky home, which it uses as a bolt-hole whenever it feels threatened.

Identification: The body is patterned with black and white patches. The iris of the eye is white. The elongated dorsal fin runs from above the pectoral fins almost down to the tail base. The caudal fin is transparent but has a white then a black band marking its curved outer edge.

Distribution: The north-western part of Lake Tanganyika.
Habitat: Rocky shores and drop-offs.
Food: Algae and aquatic invertebrates.
Size: Up to 13cm/5in.
Breeding: Nests in rock crevices. Some pairs produce small clutches at regular intervals; others spawn less frequently, but produce more eggs each time they do so.

Princess of Burundi

Neolamprologus brichardi

Identification: The general body colour is sandy or tan, which blends in with the rocky substrate where the fish lives. There is a black T-marking from behind the eye to the gill-cover, and a yellow spot above this. The dorsal, anal and caudal fins all have long, trailing white tips.

This spectacular fish is also known as the lyretail cichlid, fairy cichlid and brichardi. It was one of the first cichlids from Lake Tanganyika to be imported into the USA to supply the aquarium trade, arriving in 1971. It was at this point that it earned both its scientific and common name. The original importer was Pierre Brichard and the area in which he collected his first specimens was the north-eastern shore of the lake, which is part of Burundi. This is a cave spawning cichlid, laying its eggs in the cracks and crevices between rocks on the bottom. It also spends much of its time hiding in similar crevices, or searching them for aquatic invertebrates to feed on.

Distribution: Lake Tanganyika.
Habitat: Rocky areas near the shore.
Food: Aquatic invertebrates.
Size: Up to 10cm/4in.
Breeding: The species forms monogamous pairs. The female lays her eggs in crevices and both parents guard the nest, eggs and newly-hatched young.

Lemon cichlid

Neolamprologus leleupi

The lemon cichlid is primarily a deep water species, rarely seen in the wild at depths of less than 40m/131ft. It is a small fish which feeds mainly on worms, insect larvae and other aquatic invertebrates, which it finds in the gaps between rocks or underneath debris on the lake bottom. It was first described in 1956. Before then it was completely unknown. Today it is a popular species with home aquarium enthusiasts and has been successfully bred in captivity.

This fish is unusual among cichlids in that the sexes can be difficult to distinguish. Older males develop a hump on the forehead, but until they do, they look virtually identical to the females.

Identification: The body is elongated and bright lemon yellow in colour, although orange and grey varieties also exist. The snout is quite pointed, with the mouth opening at its tip. The pelvic fins are long and have pointed tips, as do the anal and dorsal fins. The caudal fin is fan-shaped.

Distribution: The southern half of Lake Tanganyika.
Habitat: Rocky areas on the slopes and bottom.
Food: Aquatic invertebrates.
Size: Up to 10cm/4in.
Breeding: Spawning occurs in crevices with the female attaching her eggs to the underside of a large rock. She guards the nest until the eggs hatch, while the male, which may be twice her size, guards the vicinity around it.

Pearly lamprologus (*Altolamprologus calvus*): Up to 14cm/5½in
Also known as the pearly compressiceps or Congo blackfin, this fish (*below*) inhabits rocky areas in Lake Tanganyika. It nests in a crevice, just big enough for the female to enter and lay her eggs inside. The male then sheds his milt over the entrance and it drifts down to fertilize them. This fish was first scientifically described in 1988. Its name refers to the pale dots covering its sides.

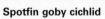

Spotfin goby cichlid (*Tanganicodus irsacae*): Up to 7cm/2¾in
This little fish from northern Lake Tanganyika has evolved the appearance and lifestyle taken on by gobies elsewhere in the world. It lives among pebbles near the shoreline, often within the low surf that builds up on the lake. It feeds on tiny crustaceans which live attached to the rocks. Like many true gobies, it can lift the front part of its body up using its pectoral fins.

Tanganyika tilapia (*Oreochromis tanganicae*): Up to 42cm/16½in
This is a relatively large cichlid that sometimes forms schools. It feeds on diatoms and blue-green algae, which it is thought to filter from open water using its gill rakers. The fish is coloured a rich but light green, overlaid with marbling and broken lines of darker green.

Neothauma shell cichlid

Lamprologus ocellatus

This fish shelters and nests inside the empty shells of neothauma snails that litter the bottom of Lake Tanganyika's shores. It uses them to create a ready-made, hard-walled burrow by burying its shell home within the mud or sand so that only the rim and opening of the entrance are visible. When it comes time to breed, the female entices a male to her shell. She enters to lay her eggs then emerges to let him in to fertilize them. The male then leaves, leaving the female to guard the eggs on her own. The neothauma shell cichlid defends its home from other fish (including larger cichlids) pugnaciously, charging out to harass them until they move away.

Identification: Sometimes called the frog-faced cichlid; the mouth is stubby and the eyes are high up and have ridges above them. Two stripes extend from the gill cover to the tail base. There is a black spot on the gill cover. Most fish are light brown or gold, although there are also white, blue, orange and yellow-finned varieties. The belly displays violet iridescence, but the fins are usually grey. The anal and caudal fins have small, pearl-coloured spots and dark edges. The dorsal fin has yellow edges (male) or white edges (female).

Distribution: Lake Tanganyika.
Habitat: Shallow waters close to shore.
Food: Small aquatic invertebrates.
Size: Up to 5cm/2in.
Breeding: The eggs are laid inside the empty shell of a neothauma snail. The female alone guards the eggs until they hatch.

CICHLIDS FROM LAKE MALAWI

Lake Malawi is the southernmost of the Rift Valley's three great lakes. Its shores are shared by the countries of Malawi, Mozambique and Tanzania. The lake is home to an incredible diversity of cichlid species, more than 500 of which are found nowhere else in the world. The few mentioned in this book include the most common and well-studied of these.

Rusty cichlid

Iodotropheus sprengerae

Identification: The body is oblong in shape and the forehead quite rounded. The caudal fin is large and triangular. In colour, this species ranges from rusty brown to violet, often with both colours present. The sexes are quite difficult to tell apart; the main difference is that the males have a longer anal fin which bears large white blotches known as egg spots.

The rusty cichlid, also known as the lavender mbuna or lavender cichlid, is found over a wide range of rocky habitats in Lake Malawi, occurring at depths of anything between 3m/10ft and 40m/131ft. It may be found singly or in small shoals; it is unusual among Lake Malawi cichlids in not being territorial, except for a short period before spawning. It can start breeding at a very young age, often within just 14 weeks of hatching, when it may still be less than 3cm/1¼in long. The species is better known than other Lake Malawi cichlids since it was one of the first to be collected alive for the aquarium trade and has long been kept and bred in captivity. The IUCN now lists it as Vulnerable.

Distribution: Lake Malawi.
Habitat: Near the bottom over rocks at various depths.
Food: Aquatic invertebrates, fish eggs and fish fry.
Size: Up to 11cm/4¼in.
Breeding: The female lays 5–60 eggs. Once these have been fertilized by the male, she takes them up in her mouth where they remain until hatching.
Status: Vulnerable.

Blue mbuna

Labeotropheus fuelleborni

Identification: This fish is almost impossible to identify by colour alone, as there are so many different natural morphs. The body is deep and its most distinctive feature is the head. The mouth is tucked underneath the protruding snout, a feature that enables the fish to scrape algae from rocky substrates while remaining in a horizontal position.

Mbuna is a local name given to many of Lake Malawi's cichlids living in rocky habitats. It translates literally as 'rock fish'. This fish is most abundant in shallow waters near the shore. As a result it is among the more commonly caught species for the aquarium trade. It feeds on algae, which it scrapes from the rocks. Although a herbivore, the blue mbuna is anything but peaceful. Males are highly territorial and can be extremely aggressive towards other males of their own kind, although they ignore fish of other species that pass through their area. Despite the name, this cichlid occurs in many different colour morphs throughout the lake. These are thought to represent distinct populations which, because of relatively sedentary habits, do not mix or interbreed in the wild.

Distribution: Lake Malawi.
Habitat: Rocky, shallow regions, particularly those near the shore.
Food: Algae.
Size: Up to 15cm/6in.
Breeding: A section of rock is carefully cleaned and up to 60 eggs laid on it. The eggs are fertilized by the male and then picked up by the female to be brooded in her throat cavity until they hatch.

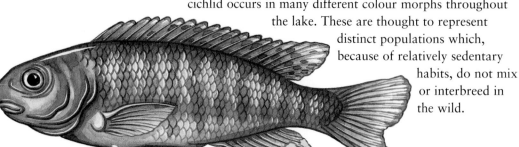

Malawi eyebiter
Dimidiochromis compressiceps

Distribution: Lake Malawi.
Habitat: Open water, usually over sand.
Food: Smaller fish.
Size: Up to 25cm/10in.
Breeding: The female lays 40–50 eggs which are fertilized by the male. She then takes the eggs up into her mouth where they are brooded until hatching.

One look at the Malawi eyebiter tells you that it is a predator. The long, streamlined body and large mouth are typical of fish built for sudden bursts of speed in attack. This fish usually hunts in open water, charging in with its mouth open to strike smaller fish quick and hard. If that first bite fails to kill its prey, it backs off and waits for it to die before moving in again to swallow it. Unusually, this species tends to hold its body at an angle in the water. This may be a behavioural adaptation to minimize its silhouette against the light streaming down through the water and make it less noticeable to its prey swimming below.

Identification: The body and the head are compressed. The mouth is large and the snout sharply sloped. Because of the elongated head, the eye appears to be set quite far back. Young fish and females are silvery-white with a single brown horizontal stripe running down the side of the body. Breeding males are electric blue with patches of red and orange on their fins.

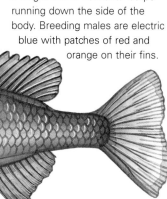

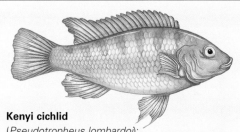

Kenyi cichlid
(*Pseudotropheus lombardoi*):
Up to 10cm/4in
This colourful cichlid (*above*) is found only around the Mbenji Islands in the centre of Lake Malawi. Juveniles are bright blue but the males turn vivid yellow, with blue dorsal fins, as they mature. It is an omnivore, surviving mainly on algae which it grazes from rocks, although it may also eat aquatic invertebrates and fish eggs.

Largemouth cichlid (*Tyrannochromis macrostoma*): Up to 30cm/12in
This predatory cichlid looks similar to the Malawi eyebiter but tends to be found in rocky areas rather than over sand. It hunts by probing the cracks between rocks in search of prey – other, smaller cichlids. It is most common in shallow water. It takes care of its eggs and guards its young for more than three weeks after hatching.

Powder blue cichlid (*Pseudotropheus socolofi*): Up to 10cm/4in
Also known as Eduard's mbuna, this fish looks like the electric blue johanni, but with vertical rather than horizontal stripes. It is found in the shallow waters along the east coast of Lake Malawi and around the Likoma Islands, in patches where sandy and rocky areas on the bottom meet.

Electric blue johanni
Melanochromis johanni

This is a popular and widely available aquarium fish. In the wild it lives in rocky areas in shallow water (6m/20ft deep or less) and is confined to the eastern side of Lake Malawi. It is an omnivorous fish and benthic feeder, with a diet of algae, insect larvae and other aquatic invertebrates. The males of the species are highly territorial. They build nests by picking rocks up one by one and dropping them to create a small pile. This is then defended and it appears to combine with the male's bright colours to attract females to spawn. Once eggs have been laid and fertilized, they are picked up by the female to be brooded in her mouth.

Distribution: The eastern half of Lake Malawi.
Habitat: Shallow water over rocks.
Food: Algae and aquatic invertebrates.
Size: Up to 13cm/5in.
Breeding: The male attracts the female to spawn. Once he has fertilized her eggs she picks them up and broods them in her mouth.

Identification: It is the male of this species that is electric blue; the female is a dull yellow with a brown stripe running down her side to the base of the tail. Breeding males have twin parallel stripes of lighter blue running down their sides as well as similarly coloured stripes running along the top and bottom edges of the dorsal fins. Their anal fins bear several 'egg spots'.

CICHLIDS FROM LAKE MALAWI AND ELSEWHERE

The bright colours and unusual breeding habits of African cichlids make them popular home aquarium fish and many species are bred in captivity. This helps safeguard their future – little strain is put upon wild populations, and reservoirs of fish are built up for reintroduction to the wild if necessary.

Sunshine peacock

Aulonocara baenschi

Identification: The forehead and nose are strongly curved, separating this species from other blue-headed peacocks. The males develop a large dorsal fin which is edged with white. The caudal fin also has streaks of white in it. Although the sides are golden yellow, they are crossed by six or seven faintly darker vertical stripes. The pectoral fins are clear and the pelvic fins trailing.

This species deserves its common name. Breeding males turn a burnished yellow gold – hence the 'sunshine' – with iridescent blue around their lower jaws. Females, as with avian peahens, are relatively dowdy. The sunshine peacock is a benthic feeder, preferring sandy areas with scattered rocks. It lies still on the lake bottom and senses the tiny movements made by its prey in the sand. It then strikes just once, accurately catching its prey. Unsurprisingly, this is a very popular species with cichlid enthusiasts, despite the fact that the males take more than two years to mature and attain their full breeding colours.

Distribution: South-western part of Lake Malawi.
Habitat: Sandy areas with scattered rocks.
Food: Aquatic invertebrates.
Size: Up to 13cm/5in.
Breeding: The male uses his bright colours to attract a female. Once the eggs have been laid and fertilized she takes them up in her mouth for brooding.

Malawi blue dolphin

Cyrtocara moorii

Identification: As the only member of its genus, its distinctive shape makes this fish hard to confuse with any other cichlid. The forehead is rounded and the snout slightly bottle-nosed in most individuals. The mouth is positioned right at the end of the snout and is quite thick-lipped. The eyes appear unusually large and the body is blue all over.

Despite its name, this fish is not a dolphin, nor is it a relative of the marine dolphinfish (family Coryphaenidae). Rather, it is a cichlid with a slightly bottle-nosed snout and, in the mature males, a hump on the forehead – enough for hobbyists to have settled on 'dolphin' for a common name. This fish is widespread throughout Lake Malawi but is relatively uncommon and thinly spread. It feeds on tiny invertebrates that live in the substrate, but rather than searching for them itself, it follows other bottom-feeders and picks off any small creatures they miss. Large benthic feeders are sometimes surrounded by groups of Malawi blue dolphins, hovering around them like scavengers around a carcass.

Distribution: Lake Malawi.
Habitat: Over sandy bottoms down to 15m/49ft.
Food: Aquatic invertebrates.
Size: Up to 20cm/7¾in.
Breeding: Spawning occurs approximately every two months. Once the male has fertilized the eggs, the female takes them up into her mouth for brooding.

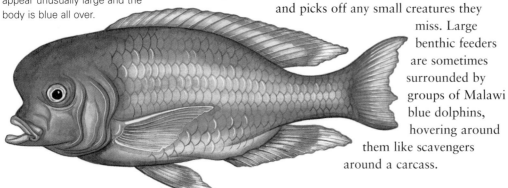

Jewel fish

Hemichromis bimaculatus

This handsome cichlid is widely distributed in West Africa, occurring from Senegal to the Democratic Republic of the Congo. It is also found in the Nile basin farther east. The jewel fish is an inhabitant of forest streams and small rivers, particularly those with sandy or muddy bottoms. It feeds on insect larvae and other aquatic invertebrates, as well as the eggs and fry of other fish. Breeding pairs form strong bonds and the males in particular become highly territorial during spawning. The eggs are laid on a flat rock or similar surface and closely guarded by both parents until hatching. The fry are also carefully protected until they are big enough to fend for themselves. This is a popular aquarium species and most fish found for sale are captive-bred.

Identification: Both males and females look similar, although males are subtly larger and darker. The body is elongated and the forehead sloping. The body is olive green above and orange or red below. There are two large black spots, one in the middle of the side and the other at the rear of the gill cover. The eyes are gold with a dark stripe running down through the middle.

Distribution: The Nile and lower Niger River basins, and coastal basins of West Africa from Senegal to Cameroon. Also inland as far as the Democratic Republic of the Congo (formerly Zaire).
Habitat: Forest streams and small rivers.
Food: Aquatic invertebrates, fish eggs and fry.
Size: Up to 13.5cm/5¼in.
Breeding: Sticky eggs adhere to the flat surface on which they are laid. Both parents guard eggs and young.

Butterfly peacock (*Aulonocara jacobfreibergi*): Up to 15cm/6in
This fish (*above*) is also known as the fairy cichlid. It is endemic to Lake Malawi, occurring in two populations with slightly different habitat preferences. Those from the north are found in rocky areas or near boulders. The southern population occurs in areas with both sand and rocks. It is a nest-guarding cave spawner.

Electric blue haplo (*Nimbochromis venustus*): Up to 25cm/10in
This cichlid is also endemic to Lake Malawi. Breeding males turn electric blue around the face and have a forehead of bright matt yellow. The body is patterned with blotches like a giraffe's spots. Despite its bright colours, it is an ambush hunter, darting out from sandy hiding places to capture other smaller cichlids.

Dwarf jewel fish (*Anomalochromis thomasi*): Up to 6.5cm/2½in
This tiny cichlid occurs across a small range in west Africa, in the coastal rivers and streams of Guinea, Liberia and Sierra Leone. A nest guarder, it lays its eggs on the bottom and watches over them until they hatch. It feeds mainly on insect larvae and other aquatic invertebrates.

Egyptian mouth brooder

Pseudocrenilabrus multicolor

The Egyptian mouth brooder is found in the Nile River system. It occurs all the way from Egypt, where the Nile empties into the Mediterranean Sea, to Lake Victoria, where it begins. While not the most colourful cichlid, it is small and easy to keep. This, together with the fact that it is a mouth brooder and breeds easily in a home aquarium, has made it one of the most popular of all cichlids. It feeds on both invertebrates and plant matter and lives in a wide range of freshwater habitats. However, it is most common in the Nile's tributary streams and the ponds that are filled when the river breaks its banks and floods. Virtually all of the fish sold in shops have been bred in captivity.

Distribution: The Nile River basin and lakes along its course.
Habitat: Mainly ponds and streams but also the fringes of lakes and quiet areas of rivers.
Food: Plant matter and aquatic invertebrates.
Size: Up to 8cm/3in.
Breeding: This species breeds every few months. The female broods the eggs in her mouth until hatching.

Identification: The snout is rounded and the head and body form a teardrop shape. The iris is gold with a vertical black stripe going through it. Breeding males are an iridescent lime green. The first half of the dorsal fin is edged with dark blue, red or purple, with a thin line of lighter blue beneath that. The pectoral, pelvic and caudal fins are largely transparent.

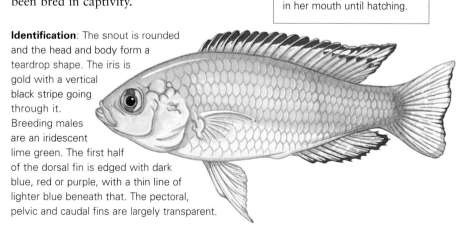

OTHER CICHLIDS AND TILAPIAS

Tilapias are cichlids in all but name, belonging to the same family, Cichlidae. They are best known as food fish and can be found on menus in many parts of the world. Kribs and the nudiceps are also types of cichlid. Like most members of their family, all of the fish on these pages exhibit a high level of parental care.

Common tilapia

Oreochromis mossambicus

Identification: The body is laterally compressed, the head and mouth large and the lips rather thick. The head is pointed and often makes an abrupt angle where it meets the back. The pectoral fins are fairly long and clear. The caudal fin is large with a rounded rear edge. The colour ranges from green to gold. In most individuals, the scales are large and well defined.

This is one of southern Africa's most widespread and abundant large fish. A prolific breeder with tasty flesh, it is now farmed as a food fish in many other parts of the world. In some places where it has escaped or been introduced into the wild, it has become a pest, establishing itself as the dominant species. Several colour varieties have been bred, some for the aquarium trade and some for the table. Red common tilapia are particularly popular as restaurant fish. The common tilapia is an omnivore, feeding on aquatic invertebrates, small fish and water plants. Its ability to survive on a wide variety of food is part of what has made it such an invasive species in the places where it has been introduced.

Distribution: Native to the lower Zambezi River basin and other rivers farther south. Widely introduced to other parts of Africa and tropical and subtropical countries around the world.
Habitat: Lakes, ponds, estuaries, rivers and streams.
Food: Aquatic invertebrates, small fish and plant matter.
Size: Up to 39cm/15in.
Breeding: A frequent breeder. Fertilized eggs are taken up by the female into her mouth for brooding.

Nile tilapia

Oreochromis niloticus

Identification: The mouth is large and the lips thick. The forehead and back slope evenly up to near the base of the dorsal fin. The body is large, oblong and laterally compressed. The dorsal fin stretches along the back, ending above the rear edge of the anal fin. The body varies from silver to olive green, with regular vertical bars across the caudal fin.

After the common tilapia, this is probably the most widely farmed cichlid in the world. Although not quite as prolific as the common tilapia it has the advantage of size, reaching up to 60cm/23½in long and weighing over 4kg/8.8lb – more than three times as much as its cousin. The Nile tilapia is mainly herbivorous, feeding largely on algae, which it grazes from the bottom. It also sifts phytoplankton (microscopic drifting algae) from the water and occasionally eats worms and other aquatic invertebrates. Its natural habitats are lakes and rivers but it is also common in irrigation channels and even sewage canals. As with the common tilapia, it has ousted native species where it has been introduced, by outcompeting for food.

Distribution: Native to the Nile River basin, the coastal rivers of Israel and also the Niger, Benue, Volta, Gambia and Senegal Rivers. Widely introduced elsewhere.
Habitat: Lakes, ponds, rivers and streams.
Food: Algae, phytoplankton and, occasionally, aquatic invertebrates.
Size: Up to 60cm/23½in.
Breeding: Spawning occurs several times a year. Once they are laid and fertilized, the female takes the eggs up into her mouth for brooding.

Spotted tilapia

Tilapia mariae

This is also known as the Niger cichlid, the black mangrove cichlid and the tiger cichlid. It lives in the coastal lowlands and lagoons around the Gulf of Guinea, where it is caught and eaten as a food fish. It has also become established in parts of the USA and Australia, after being released from commercial fish farms. In Australia it has multiplied to such an extent that it has started to become a pest, and attempts are currently being made to control its spread. In southern Florida, the South American peacock bass has been introduced to control it. In its native home the spotted tilapia is most common in streams and the lower reaches of rivers. It feeds on algae and the small invertebrates living within it, scraping mouthfuls from rocks and the leaves of water plants.

Distribution: Ivory Coast, Ghana, Benin, Nigeria and Cameroon. Introduced to Queensland, Australia, and Florida and Nevada, USA.
Habitat: Coastal lagoons, rivers and streams.
Food: Algae and small aquatic invertebrates.
Size: Up to 39cm/15in.
Breeding: Eggs are laid on the underside of a large flat rock. After 2 days, the female removes any fertile eggs, places them in a nearby pit, then eats the others.

Identification: Spots fade with age. Juveniles have five to seven dark spots in a line running along their sides, with the last at the tail base. The body is pale green above, with slightly darker vertical bands, and pale and unpatterned below. Fins are large and mottled.

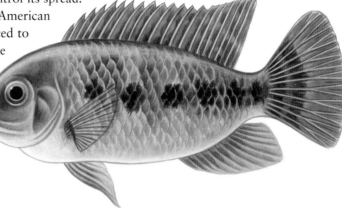

Nudiceps (*Nanochromis parilus*):
Up to 7.5cm/3in
This fish is native to the lower Congo River, being most common in and around rapids. It eats worms and other aquatic invertebrates. It is longer-bodied and has a stubbier face than most of its relatives, and looks more like a goby than a cichlid. Males are silvery grey to blue; females are golden brown. Both have a dark outer edge to the long dorsal fin.

Marakeli tilapia (*Paratilapia polleni*):
Up to 28cm/11in
This cichlid (*right*) is endemic to Madagascar. It has lived in isolation for around 20 million years, separated from the rest of Africa by the Mozambique Channel. This fish has more in common with the South American cichlids, suggesting that it and the South American families are closer to the ancestral cichlid line, and those in Africa have diverged.

Mouthbrooding krib (*Chromidotilapia guentheri*): Up to 16cm/6¼in
This fish lives in coastal rivers and streams from the Ivory Coast to Cameroon, and farther upstream in the Niger and Volta basins. It feeds mainly on aquatic invertebrates and plant matter but will occasionally take small fish. The male does the mouth brooding, but once the eggs hatch, both parents guard the young. This fish is also known as Guenther's mouth brooder.

Common krib

Pelvicachromis pulcher

This fish comes from the southern rivers and streams of Nigeria. It is most common over mud or sand and is rarely found far from stands of aquatic plants. In the past it was a very popular aquarium fish, but in recent years it has been overtaken by more colourful Rift Valley lake cichlids. It gives close attention to its eggs and its young. Pairs form strong bonds and tend to stick together through repeated spawnings. Eggs are laid in enclosed areas, then guarded by the female. When they hatch she leads her fry out into more open water, where the male joins her in protecting them.

Identification: The underside of the head is pale green. The body is beige with two lateral brown stripes: one from the snout to the caudal fin tip, the other from the forehead to the end of the base of the dorsal fin. The abdomen is often bright red to purple. The caudal fin is yellow with orange to red markings. The pelvic fins are red, purple and blue; the anal fins are yellow or blue and red. In some populations males have an eyespot at the rear of the dorsal fin; in others the spot is on the top half of the caudal.

Distribution: Restricted to south-western Nigeria.
Habitat: Coastal rivers and streams.
Food: Aquatic invertebrates.
Size: Up to 11cm/4¼in.
Breeding: Eggs are laid on the side or underside of a rock. The female protects the eggs for 2–3 days until they hatch. Both the male and female guard the young.

NILE PERCH, ANABANTOIDS AND LYREFISH

The Nile perch and anabantoids are members of the order Perciformes, the scientific term for perch-like fish. Anabantoids are also known as labyrinth fishes after the labyrinth organ, a supplementary breathing structure unique to their suborder. This organ enables anabantoids to absorb oxygen from air gulped at the surface, a capability displayed by some other fish but achieved in a different way.

Nile perch

Lates niloticus

Identification: Perch-like in shape, but can grow extremely large. The dorsal fin is deeply notched and looks like two separate fins. The body is silver; the fins are usually darker. The head is massive, the mouth very large and the forehead steeply sloped. The eyes are positioned near the top of the head and appear small compared with the rest of the fish.

The word 'perch' implies something quite small and innocuous, but this fish can grow to be a monster. Some individuals reach almost 2m/6½ft long and weigh up to 200kg/440lb – almost three times the weight of the average man. The Nile perch is fairly widespread in northern Africa, occurring in the Chad, Senegal, Volta and Congo Rivers as well as the Nile. It has been introduced elsewhere, sometimes with disastrous results for the local fish. Since it was introduced into Lake Victoria in 1954 it has contributed to the near extinction of possibly hundreds of endemic cichlid species through predation and competition for food. On the other hand, it has become the basis of a large and very lucrative fishery based around the lake.

Distribution: Native to the Nile, Chad, Senegal, Volta and Congo River basins; widely introduced elsewhere in Africa.
Habitat: Large rivers and lakes.
Food: Other fish.
Size: Up to 1.9m/6.25ft.
Breeding: Spawning occurs all year round but peaks in the rainy season. The eggs are scattered in shallow open water and left to develop unguarded.

African snakehead

Parachanna obscura

The African snakehead is an inhabitant of slow-moving and still waters, occurring in streams, rivers, lakes, lagoons, marshes and flood plains across most of equatorial Africa. Muscular and well-camouflaged, it is an ambush predator, lurking amongst submerged vegetation and waiting for prey to come into reach. This fish is a protective and caring parent. Whenever possible, it lays its eggs in a cavern or other enclosed space where, being buoyant, they float to the top. In open water they simply float at the surface. Both parents guard the eggs and the fry after hatching, carefully watching over them until they reach about 1.25cm/½in long. Both sexes of this species look similar, although the females are longer and a little plumper than the males.

Identification: The body is long and slightly vertically flattened. The head is depressed anteriorly, long and covered in scales – reminiscent of that of a snake. The mouth is also large and the lower jaw longer than the upper jaw. The eyes are near the front of the skull. The dorsal fin runs along two thirds of the body length, beginning just behind the pectoral fins and reaching almost to the base of the tail. The anal fin ends at a similar point but is slightly shorter, beginning farther back.

Distribution: Equatorial Africa, from Senegal to Ethiopia.
Habitat: Most areas of still or slow-moving water.
Food: Fish.
Size: Up to 50cm/19¾in.
Breeding: Spawning is thought to occur all year round. The eggs float and are guarded by both parents, as are the young.

Spotted climbing perch

Ctenopoma acutirostre

A rather unusual-looking fish, this species has a body shape that seems to have evolved to help camouflage it amongst the fallen leaves in the forest streams and rivers where it lives. It is also known as the Congo leaffish and the leopard bushfish. Some individuals have spots that closely resemble those of a leopard – dark rosettes with slightly paler centres, rather than simple blotches. The spotted climbing perch is a popular aquarium fish. Most of those sold are caught from the wild, although breeding has occasionally been achieved in captivity. Despite its common name, the fish is not known to climb.

Distribution: Restricted to the Congo basin in western central Africa.
Habitat: Forest rivers and streams.
Food: Aquatic invertebrates and small fish.
Size: Up to 15cm/6in.
Breeding: Eggs are laid on a floating bubble nest of mucus. Whether this is produced by the male or female is unknown. It is thought that the eggs are left to develop unguarded.

Identification: The body is laterally compressed and roughly leaf shaped. The head is very pointed – almost triangular – and the mouth is positioned at the point of the snout. The body is golden brown and covered with many dark-bordered spots. The eyes are quite large but less noticeable at first glance than the large, dark eyespot at the base of the tail.

Common lyrefish

Aphyosemion australe

The common lyrefish is one of the longer-lived species of killifish. Even so, it rarely reaches more than three years of age. A small species, it feeds on worms, insect larvae and other aquatic invertebrates, taking them from the open water, the bottom and also from the leaves of aquatic plants. It is found in the wild in Congo, Angola, the Democratic Republic of the Congo, Gabon and Cameroon. It is easy to breed and is widely kept in captivity, being a popular home aquarium fish. In common with many other types of killifish, the males are far more colourful and showy than the females. Several different colour morphs of this species have been bred in captivity and very few of those individuals now found for sale have been taken from the wild.

Distribution: Coastal regions of western equatorial Africa, from Cameroon to Angola.
Habitat: Slow-moving streams and still pools.
Food: Aquatic invertebrates.
Size: Up to 6cm/2¼in.
Breeding: Spawning occurs all year round. The eggs are scattered in open water and left to develop unguarded.

Blue lyrefish (*Aphyosemion gardneri*):
Up to 6.5cm/2½in
This species (*above*), also known as the gardneri killifish, inhabits the tributary streams and marshes of the Beno and Cross River basins of Nigeria. It occurs in both savanna and forested regions. Like the common lyrefish, it has become a popular aquarium species. It lays its eggs over the bottom and pairs stay close for some time, producing just a few eggs each day.

Playfair's panchax (*Pachypanchax playfairi*):
Up to 7.5cm/3in
This is the only species of freshwater fish endemic to the Seychelles. It is an egg scatterer, and breeds among floating water plants. This species is unusual in that the scales of the male become lifted during the breeding season, giving the skin a rough appearance. Like the lyrefish, it is a type of killifish and, as such, rarely lives for more than three years.

Ornate ctenopoma (*Ctenopoma ansorgei*):
Up to 8cm/3¼in
This fish belongs to the same genus as the spotted climbing perch but looks very different. Its body is more elongated and rounded – typical for a fish that spends a lot of time sitting on the bottom. It lives in slow-flowing forest streams in the Congo basin, where it feeds on worms, insect larvae and other aquatic invertebrates.

Identification: This fish is named for the male's lyre-shaped caudal fin. The upper and lower edges of the fin are orange with white tips. The dorsal fin, which lies far back on the body, also has an orange edge. The anal fin, positioned slightly farther forward, has a white edge with a line of black beneath it. The body is elongated and the eyes are rather large.

AQUATIC AMPHIBIANS AND SOFTSHELL TURTLES

The fish of Africa's lakes, rivers and swamps share their home with other aquatic vertebrates, most of which hunt them. While turtles might not spring to mind as predators, they take their toll on Africa's fish. Stealth and patience, rather than superior agility or speed, are the key to their success.

African clawed frog

Xenopus laevis

Identification: The body is plump and smooth-skinned; creamy white on the underside and patterned with olive brown and grey marbling on the back. The head is small, with the eyes near the top. There is no tongue. The front limbs are small, ending in clawless, unwebbed fingers. The large back legs have webbed feet with three clawed inside toes.

This strange species of frog is almost completely aquatic, only leaving the water during periods of rain to search for other pools. It eats a wide range of organic matter but feeds mainly on invertebrates, both living and dead. It tends to be rather inactive, only moving about slowly to find food. This relaxed lifestyle may be a contributing factor to its relative longevity – unusually for an amphibian it may live for 15 years or more. This frog occurs throughout much of southern Africa, living in warm and stagnant grassland ponds. It breeds throughout the year. Males attract females with a trilling call. The females answer, either with a quick, rapping acceptance call or a slow, ticking rejection. This behaviour is almost unique in the animal kingdom – it is very rare for the female to vocally answer male calls.

Distribution: Native to cool regions of sub-Saharan Africa, including higher altitudes between the African Cape, the plateau of Cameroon and Nigeria.
Habitat: Ponds in grassland.
Food: Aquatic invertebrates and carrion.
Size: Up to 12cm/4¾in from nose to rump.
Breeding: The eggs are released individually or in small groups over a period of 3–4 hours. The tadpoles live by filter feeding.

Zaire African dwarf clawed frog

Hymenochirus boettgeri

This little frog is unusual in being a suction feeder. Both the adults and tadpoles hunt aquatic invertebrates on the bottom and in open water, sucking them up suddenly by extending their tube-like mouths. The tadpoles have large, forward-facing eyes and rely mainly on vision to find their prey. The adults, by contrast, have poor eyesight and use smell and touch to find it instead. The Zaire African dwarf clawed frog is one of four species in its genus. Between them, these amphibians range across most of sub-Saharan Africa. Like the African clawed frog (*top*), this dwarf species spends its entire life in the water, unless forced to leave by overcrowding. Males also exhibit the behaviour of 'singing' underwater to attract mates. Although it must frequently rise to the surface in order to breathe, this frog is otherwise almost as aquatic as any fish.

Identification: The head and body shape are very similar to those of the African clawed frog. This frog also has no tongue. The skin, however, is warty with distinct bumps, unlike that of the African clawed frog. The easiest way to tell the two species apart is at the tadpole stage. Zaire African dwarf clawed frog tadpoles have bulbous, forward-facing eyes.

Distribution: Occurs naturally in the Congo River basin, Cameroon and Nigeria. It has been introduced to Florida in the USA.
Habitat: Pools, streams and marshes.
Food: Aquatic invertebrates.
Size: Up to 3.5cm/1⅜in from nose to rump.
Breeding: Eggs are laid singly near the surface of the water, usually at night. They are left to develop unguarded.

African softshell turtle

Trionyx triunguis

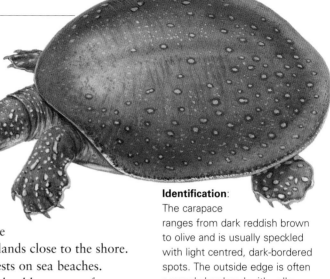

This is the most common and widespread softshell turtle in Africa, ranging over most of the continent apart from the far south and north-west. It prefers slow-moving or still fresh waters but also lives in brackish waters where rivers meet the sea. The African softshell turtle digs its nests in the earth or sand on the banks of lakes and rivers, or on islands close to the shore. Near river mouths it sometimes nests on sea beaches. This species occasionally basks on land but more often soaks up the sun while floating at the water's surface. A carnivore, it feeds on a wide variety of prey, including large invertebrates, fish, amphibians and other reptiles. It also eats carrion when the opportunity arises.

Distribution: Most of Africa. Also Israel, Lebanon, Syria and parts of Turkey.
Habitat: Lakes and large rivers.
Food: Aquatic invertebrates, fish, amphibians, reptiles and, occasionally, carrion.
Size: Carapace up to 101cm/39¾in long.
Breeding: Nests March to July. Several clutches of 8–34 eggs may be produced in a season. Eggs are spherical with brittle shells.

Identification: The carapace ranges from dark reddish brown to olive and is usually speckled with light centred, dark-bordered spots. The outside edge is often narrowly bordered with yellow. The front edge of the carapace thickens over the neck. The head is relatively small and ends with a short tubular snout. The toes are webbed and the feet paddle-like.

Aubry's flapshell turtle (*Cycloderma aubryi*): Carapace up to 55cm/21½in long
This turtle (*above*) is a rain forest species, occurring in the Central African Republic, Gabon, Congo and the Democratic Republic of the Congo. It is well camouflaged in the leafy pools and streams it inhabits. Its appearance and the habits of its close relatives suggest that it is probably an ambush hunter of fish, lying in wait for unsuspecting prey to swim into range.

Nubian flapshell turtle (*Cyclanorbis elegans*): Carapace up to 60cm/23½in long
This turtle inhabits marshes and slow-moving rivers from Ghana eastward to Sudan. It is the largest member of its genus and the second largest turtle in Africa, after the African softshell turtle, which occurs across much of its range. It can be distinguished from the African softshell turtle by the presence of large turbercles, or lumps, on the front edge of its carapace.

Senegal flapshell turtle (*Cyclanorbis senegalensis*): Carapace up to 50cm/19½in long
This turtle occurs in lakes, rivers and streams, usually within dry gallery forests. During the rainy season it may also be found in marshes and ponds on adjacent savanna. Senegal forms the westernmost extremity of this species' range, which reaches as far east as Sudan. Like many African turtles, it is little understood. It is listed as Near Threatened by the IUCN.

Zambezi flapshell turtle

Cycloderma frenatum

This is another carnivorous turtle. It catches most of the fish it eats by ambush, but sometimes chases small fish over short distances to catch them. It spends much of its time buried in mud or sand on the bottom, lying in wait for prey, although it has to come up to the surface occasionally to breathe. Nesting occurs from December until March. The females dig pits for their eggs in the banks of lakes, streams and rivers. They then cover these pits up and return to the water, leaving their eggs to incubate and hatch alone. Because of its habit of burrowing in the mud, this turtle is less commonly seen than some other species. It is listed as Near Threatened by the IUCN.

Distribution: East Africa, from the Save River basin, Mozambique and south-eastern Zimbabwe, to the Rufiji River basin, Tanzania.
Habitat: Lakes, ponds, rivers and streams.
Food: Aquatic invertebrates and fish.
Size: Carapace to 56cm/22in.
Breeding: Clutches of 15–25 eggs. These are spherical and have brittle shells.
Status: Near Threatened.

Identification: The carapace is oval, soft and dark green, sometimes with brown blotches. The underside is cream with faint blotches of grey. The grey-green head has five horizontal stripes which run from the crown and the area behind the eyes to the base of the neck. The chin and throat are pure white in most individuals, although in some this is crossed with darker streaks.

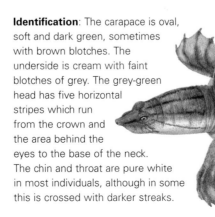

OTHER TURTLES, CROCODILES AND THE WEST AFRICAN MANATEE

As reptiles, turtles and crocodiles come out of the water to lay their eggs. Most species will also bask in the sun on land. The West African manatee is a mammal that spends its whole life in the water. It not only feeds but also mates and gives birth in the rivers and mangrove swamps where it lives.

African helmeted turtle

Pelomedusa subrufa

This creature, like all of Africa's inland turtles, inhabits fresh water but it is able to survive conditions of drought better than most. If the pool in which it is living starts to dry up, it buries itself in the soft mud and waits for the rains to return. This enables it to survive in drier, less stable habitats than the African softshell turtle or any of the flapshell species. As well as the usual marshes, ponds and rivers, it is also found in the water holes used by the large hoofed mammals of the African plains. The African helmeted turtle is carnivorous and has a wide-ranging diet, feeding on everything from water snails and worms to fish, birds and even small mammals. Once it has grabbed prey in its jaws, it rips it to shreds using its powerful front feet.

Identification: The carapace is brown to olive in colour and smooth or with some serrated posterior edges. It is oval, wide and rather flattened. The underside of the shell is usually cream or yellow, but may sometimes be darker. The head is rounded and the snout very slightly protruding, with two almost perfectly circular nostrils at the tip. The head is brown or olive above and, usually, cream or yellow below.

Distribution: Most of tropical and subtropical Africa, except Sahara region. Also present in Madagascar, southern Saudi Arabia and Yemen.
Habitat: Rivers, streams, marshes, ponds and temporary water holes.
Food: Invertebrates, fish, amphibians, reptiles, birds and small mammals.
Size: Carapace up to 32.5cm/12¾in long.
Breeding: Nesting occurs in spring or early summer with a single clutch of 13–42 eggs.

Nile crocodile

Crocodylus niloticus

The name of this crocodile is slightly misleading. Although it was once found throughout the Nile River it is now absent from its lower reaches. It is common, however, throughout much of the rest of Africa outside the Sahara and Namib Deserts. The Nile crocodile is Africa's largest and most dangerous reptile, responsible for hundreds of human deaths every year. It hunts large mammals by lying still in the water and waiting for them to come down to drink. As soon as its senses a victim it lunges out of the water, grabs the unfortunate animal in its jaws and pulls it under, rolling its prey over and over until it has drowned. These crocodiles also eat large numbers of fish and will even turn to cannibalism if other food becomes scarce.

Identification: The head and body are massive and the snout relatively broad, particularly near the base. The teeth of both the upper and lower jaws are long, pointed and clearly visible when the mouth is closed. The skin lacks the bony plates seen in many other crocodilians and the scales on the back are large and roughly square or rectangular.

Distribution: Most of sub-Saharan Africa and in the Nile basin as far as southern Egypt.
Habitat: Lakes, swamps, rivers, water holes and estuaries.
Food: Fish and other large vertebrates.
Size: Up to 6m/20ft.
Breeding: The female lays 40–60 eggs in a hole nest dug in sandy areas above the waterline. Once the eggs hatch, she helps her young down to the water.

African dwarf crocodile

Osteolaemus tetraspis

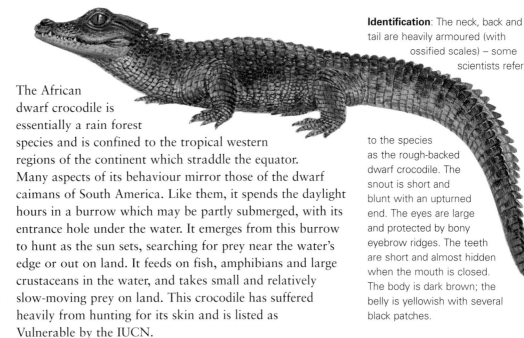

Distribution: From Guinea-Bissau eastward to the Central African Republic and the Democratic Republic of the Congo.
Habitat: Rain forest swamps, pools and slow-moving rivers and streams.
Food: Fish, amphibians and large invertebrates.
Size: Up to 1.9m/6¼ft.
Breeding: A nest mound is built in May or June and 10–20 eggs are laid in it, then guarded by the female.
Status: Vulnerable.

The African dwarf crocodile is essentially a rain forest species and is confined to the tropical western regions of the continent which straddle the equator. Many aspects of its behaviour mirror those of the dwarf caimans of South America. Like them, it spends the daylight hours in a burrow which may be partly submerged, with its entrance hole under the water. It emerges from this burrow to hunt as the sun sets, searching for prey near the water's edge or out on land. It feeds on fish, amphibians and large crustaceans in the water, and takes small and relatively slow-moving prey on land. This crocodile has suffered heavily from hunting for its skin and is listed as Vulnerable by the IUCN.

Identification: The neck, back and tail are heavily armoured (with ossified scales) – some scientists refer to the species as the rough-backed dwarf crocodile. The snout is short and blunt with an upturned end. The eyes are large and protected by bony eyebrow ridges. The teeth are short and almost hidden when the mouth is closed. The body is dark brown; the belly is yellowish with several black patches.

Slender-snouted crocodile (*Crocodylus cataphractus*): Up to 4.2m/13¾ft
This rare, little known crocodile (*below*) has a similar range to the African dwarf crocodile and is also found in rain forests. It prefers large rivers and lakes, however, so the two species rarely compete directly for territory or food. It feeds mainly on fish – its narrow specialized snout helps it catch and hold on to this small, slippery prey.

African forest turtle
(*Pelusios gabonensis*): Carapace up to 30cm/12in
This turtle inhabits rain forest rivers, streams, swamps and pools and is found throughout equatorial Africa west of the Rift Valley. It feeds mainly on aquatic invertebrates and small fish. Its carapace ranges from buff to dull yellow, with a thick black line running from behind the head to the base of the tail.

African dwarf mud turtle (*Pelusios nanus*): Carapace up to 12cm/4¾in long
This tiny turtle is the smallest member of its genus, with an elongated oval carapace. It inhabits streams and rivers in moist savanna in southern Africa, from Angola eastward along the southern border of the Congo basin to northern Zambia. Females are capable of sperm storage, enabling them to fertilize eggs and begin development for laying long after mating occurs.

West African manatee

Trichechus senegalensis

This large, peaceful aquatic mammal lives in coastal lagoons, mangrove swamps and major rivers from Senegal to Angola. Like its close cousins the Amazonian and West Indian manatees, it is strictly herbivorous. It feeds on aquatic plants, but occasionally lifts its head above the surface to browse land plants growing over the water's edge. It spends most of its waking hours feeding; plants are quite low in energy so it needs to consume a great deal in order to survive. When not feeding it is often seen sleeping at the surface or resting on the bottom. Being a mammal, it must come to the surface to breathe. It rarely stays completely submerged for more than 20 minutes at a time. It has very few competitors for food and no natural predators.

Distribution: Coastal waters from Senegal to Angola and all of the major rivers that empty into the sea between these points.
Habitat: Mangrove swamps, coastal waters and large rivers.
Food: Aquatic plants and overhanging leaves.
Size: Up to 4.5m/15ft.
Breeding: Gives birth to a single calf every 2 or 3 years. As with all mammals, the mother produces milk for her young.

Identification: The body is massive and very rounded, and the grey or brown skin is hairless and leathery. The upper lip is extremely large and flexible, and bears thick, bristly whiskers. The front limbs are paddle-like, but may be used for gathering plants. The tail flipper is large and has a rounded outer edge.

EUROPE

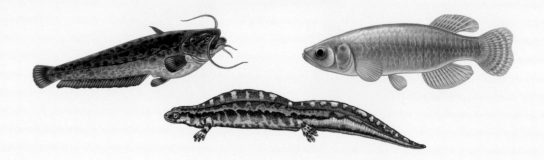

The freshwater fish of Europe are well-documented. Perhaps more than on any other continent, most lakes, rivers and streams here are easily accessible. There is little forest cover and the majority of land has been turned over to farming. Roads run along lake shores and cross most waterways. Nearly all of the major rivers pass through towns and several bisect capital cities.

The freshwater fish of Europe are not the most brightly coloured or varied in the world, but they are perhaps the best known and their populations the most closely studied. A great many of them are well-known as angler's favourites and food fish, factors that have caused species such as the brown trout, a salmonid, to be introduced to widely different parts of the world.

Europe's freshwater fish might be some of the best known but they are also among the most threatened. The large concentration of people on this continent, together with the number and industry of its conurbations, mean that many of the waterways are badly polluted, particularly in eastern Europe. However, fish have adapted to live in some of the cleaner man-made waterways. Zander and pike for instance, which live naturally in slow-flowing rivers, also favour the still waters of canals.

Above, left to right: Aristotle's catfish (Parasilurus aristotelis); *great crested newt* (Triturus cristatus);
Valencia toothcarp (Valencia hispanica).
Right: Map of Europe, showing the main freshwater routes and bodies of water.

PRIMITIVE FISH

Lampreys and lamperns are the most primitive living vertebrates. Like sharks and rays, they have skeletons made of cartilage rather than bone, but unlike them they lack jaws and true teeth. Sturgeons are an ancient group of fish that have barely changed since the time of the dinosaurs. Their skeletons are made partly of cartilage and partly of bone.

Lamprey

Petromyzon marinus

This fish spends part of its life in fresh water and part in the sea. In many ways its life cycle is a mirror image of that of the eel, which it resembles. Adult lampreys enter fresh water to breed, swimming up rivers to spawn over gravel shallows before returning to the sea. The young fish, known as prides, are filter feeders, sifting algae and tiny invertebrate animals from the silt on the river bottom. They remain prides for six to eight years, before developing into sub-adults and heading downstream to the sea. Adult lampreys are parasitic, attaching themselves by means of their sucker-shaped mouths to the bodies of other fish and feeding on their blood. In Europe, this species has become uncommon, due to pollution in the rivers where it breeds.

Identification: The body is long and eel-like but the mouth is a sucker-shaped disc. The tooth plate of the adult, at the front of the disc, has between seven and nine large, sharp cusps. There are seven separate gill openings, which run in a horizontal line on the side of the head. There are no paired fins. The upper side is olive to yellow-brown and heavily blotched with darker brown. The underside is much lighter.

Distribution: Most of coastal Europe; many of the Atlantic-draining rivers of North America's east coast.
Habitat: Large rivers and coastal waters.
Food: Young: filter feeders; adults: blood of other fish.
Size: Up to 1.2m/3.9ft.
Breeding: Spawning occurs in the middle of summer. Each pair makes a pit in the riverbed, where the eggs are laid. They are then left to develop unguarded.

Brook lamprey

Lampetra planeri

This fish closely resembles the larger lamprey (*top*), but can be told apart from it by its smaller size and the places where it is found. As its name suggests, the brook lamprey is an inhabitant of small streams and is usually found in the upper reaches of rivers. Unlike the lamprey, it spends its entire life in fresh water. The young are filter feeders, eating tiny organisms sifted from the mud, but the adults do not feed at all. They live just long enough to breed and then die, their rotting bodies returning nutrients to the streams in which their young will grow up. The brook lamprey spawns in nests dug on the bottom in shallow water. Wherever possible, these tend to be positioned in shade and sites under bridges are often used. Sometimes several pairs will spawn in the same nest.

Identification: Closely resembles the lamprey but has a smaller sucker disc containing small, blunt teeth. The colour ranges from dark brown to dark grey above and lighter below, usually yellowish but sometimes white. There are seven gill openings and no paired fins. During spawning, the areas around the mouth and anus turn rusty red.

Distribution: Throughout northern Europe as far south as central France.
Habitat: Streams and, rarely, lakes.
Food: Algae and small invertebrates.
Size: Up to 25cm/9¾in.
Breeding: Larvae become adults at 6 or 7 years old. Spawning usually occurs in sandy or gravelly areas.

Sturgeon

Acipenser sturio

Distribution: Once widespread in Europe's Atlantic coastal rivers, now confined to Gironde River.
Habitat: Large rivers and coastal marine waters.
Food: Bottom-dwelling invertebrates and small fish.
Size: Up to 3.5m/11½ft.
Breeding: Spawning occurs in spring or early summer. Females, often accompanied by 2–3 males, lay black, sticky eggs in deep pools over gravel.
Status: Critically Endangered.

This fish is most famous for its eggs (caviar). The extremely high price of this product has led to the fish being hunted to the verge of extinction. It has disappeared completely from many of the rivers where it once spawned and is now extremely rare in those where it remains. The only western European river in which it is now found is the Gironde, which flows through south-west France and empties into the Bay of Biscay. The sturgeon is listed as Critically Endangered by the IUCN. Although it breeds in fresh water, it spends much of its adult life in the sea. Young fish migrate downstream and move into salt water when they are around three years old. The sturgeon is one of Europe's largest freshwater fish, weighing as much as 315kg/695lb.

Identification: The belly is white and the upper body olive to black. The body is elongated and lacks scales, but does have five rows of bony scutes – large plates that look like primitive armour. The snout is long and narrow, and has a pointed tip. There are no teeth: prey is located using the sensitive barbels on the lower jaw and then sucked into the mouth.

Lampern (*Lampetra fluviatilis*):
Up to 50cm/19½in
Halfway between the lamprey and the brook lamprey in size, the lampern has a similar life cycle to the former, spending its adult life at sea and entering fresh water to breed. Despite this, it is sometimes called the river lamprey (and the lamprey, in turn, the sea lamprey). It inhabits coastal waters and rivers of north-western Europe, but is now rare as a result of pollution.

Sterlet (*Acipenser ruthenus*):
Up to 1.25m/4.1ft
This fish (*above*) belongs to the same family as the sturgeon and beluga but is much smaller – rarely exceeding 6kg/13.25lb. It can be told apart from its young relatives by its much longer snout and more slender, streamlined body. It lives in the Danube and other rivers that flow into the Black Sea, and tributary rivers of the Caspian Sea.

Danubian lampern (*Eudontomyzon danfordi*):
Up to 30cm/12in
This fish spends its whole life in fresh water. Despite its name, it actually lives in the tributary streams of the Tisza River (a tributary of the Danube). The adult fish is parasitic and feeds on the blood of other fish. Occasionally it gnaws all the way into the body cavity of its prey. The young are filter feeders which find their food at night. By day, they lie hidden, buried in silt on the bottoms of the streams.

Beluga

Husu huso

This is the largest member of the sturgeon family and the largest European fish to enter fresh water, weighing as much as 2,072kg/4,568lb. It is even more prized than the sturgeon (*top*), producing top quality caviar in large quantities. It is listed in the Guinness Book of Records as the world's most valuable fish. The beluga spends most of its adult life in salt water but enters fresh water to breed. A long-lived fish, it may take 18 years to reach sexual maturity and even then only breed every two to four years. The beluga is listed as Endangered by the IUCN. As well as fishing, it is threatened by habitat destruction and the damming of the rivers in which it spawns.

Identification: The snout is flattened and slightly upturned. The body is long and, in older fish, massive. There are five rows of scutes, one running along the back, one on each of the flanks and two on the underside of the body. The barbels are positioned in front of the mouth and are short, fleshy and feathered at the ends. The body is mainly dark grey or greenish. The belly is white.

Distribution: Adriatic, Black and Caspian Seas, being most common in the latter.
Habitat: Large rivers and shallow seas.
Food: Invertebrates and small fish.
Size: Up to 5m/16½ft.
Breeding: Migrates upstream to breed in spring or autumn. Spawning occurs in shallow pools, mainly in the Volga River. A large female produces at least 300,000 eggs at each spawning.
Status: Endangered.

SALMON, TROUT AND THEIR RELATIVES

All of the fish on these pages belong to the family Salmonidae. They are shoaling fish and, in the main, migratory breeders. Some of them spend part of their lives in the sea. The salmon and brown trout in particular are prized by both anglers and the restaurant trade. In western Europe, these two species are more common on restaurant menus than any other freshwater fish.

Salmon

Salmo salar

The salmon, or Atlantic salmon, as it is known in North America, is one of the world's most familiar fish. It is caught wild and also widely farmed. It is an important sports fish too, particularly in Scotland. The salmon also has its own place in mythology. In Ireland's ancient Celtic myths, for example, Bradán Feasa (the Salmon of Knowledge) was caught by the poet Finn Eces and prepared by the hero Fionn mac Cumhaill (Finn McCool). When hot fat from the fish was sucked off his thumb, the knowledge Finn gained thereby enabled him to become leader of the fabled Fianna tribe.

Identification: The tail fin is slightly forked and has clear, well defined rays. There is a small adipose fin. The corner of the mouth extends to directly below the rear edge of the eye. Adults and large juveniles (smolts) are silvery with small x-shaped marks on the flanks. The underside is white. Young fish (parr) have between eight and eleven dark rounded marks on each flank, with orange spots between these marks.

Distribution: Northern Europe, Iceland, southern Greenland and the east coast of North America.
Habitat: Rivers and seas.
Food: Invertebrates and small fish.
Size: Up to 1.5m/5ft.
Breeding: Adults enter rivers from the sea. Spawning occurs in November or December in shallow riffles.

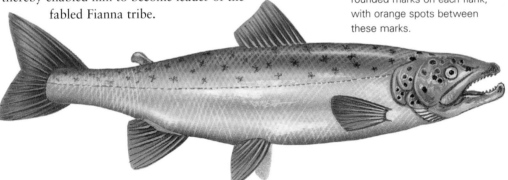

Brown trout

Salmo trutta

Identification: The base of the tail is thick compared with that of other trout and the caudal fin has a relatively square rear edge. There is also a small adipose fin present. The corner of the mouth extends behind the rear edge of the eye. Although called the brown trout, the colour of this species varies: freshwater individuals tend to be brownish with numerous black and rusty red spots. Sea trout are silvery with an orange-edged adipose fin.

The brown trout is another very familiar fish. Although native to Europe it has been widely introduced to other parts of the world as far distant as North America, Australia and the Falkland Islands. In Europe, this is the species most often caught by fly fishermen. They use lures made to look like mayflies, which they dance over the surface of the water. This fact betrays the brown trout's predilection for flying insects. It can often be seen jumping or breaking the surface of lakes and slow-flowing rivers, particularly at dawn and dusk when these insects are most abundant. The brown trout is considered good eating and in some places is farmed as a food fish.

Distribution: Native to Iceland, the British Isles, mainland Europe and parts of Russia. Widely introduced elsewhere.
Habitat: Rivers, streams, lakes and the sea.
Food: Invertebrates and small fish.
Size: Varies: in fresh water around 30cm/12in; in the sea up to 1.4m/4½ft.
Breeding: Females dig shallow depressions in which they spawn. Marine individuals (sea trout) enter fresh water to spawn.

Huchen

Hucho hucho

Distribution: Danube River and its tributaries.
Habitat: Rivers.
Food: Invertebrates, small fish, amphibians, occasionally aquatic mammals.
Size: Up to 1.5m/5ft.
Breeding: Spawning occurs in early spring over gravel. As with the brown trout and salmon, the female digs a shallow nest (redd). The eggs are left to develop unguarded and hatch after 5 weeks.
Status: Endangered.

This large fish is native to the Danube River. Once common, it is now quite rare, as pollution has led to a reduction in its numbers. No fewer than four capital cities are built on the banks of the Danube and it is a major route for cargo vessels. The huchen today occasionally reaches lengths of around 1.5m/5ft and weights of 18kg/40lb, but historically it grew much larger. It is a protected species across most of its range and fry raised in captivity are frequently released to boost the wild stock. This fish has been introduced to parts of France and, less successfully, Britain. It is listed as Endangered by the IUCN.

Identification: Similar in appearance to the salmon, but with a thicker tail base. The huchen has very small scales and a slightly pointed head. The corner of the mouth extends beyond the rear edge of the eye. There is an adipose fin and the caudal fin is shallowly forked. During the breeding season both sexes turn coppery red.

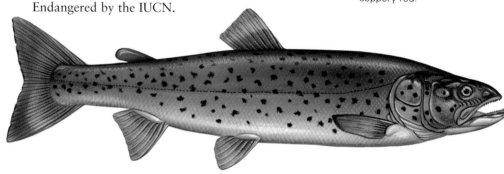

Vendace (*Coregonus albula*):
Up to 35cm/14in
This fish looks very similar to the schelly, but its mouth opens higher up on the snout. It inhabits mountainous lakes and northerly rivers and estuaries. In Britain it is found only in a few of the lakes of the Lake District, although it was formerly also found in a few Scottish lochs. An open water shoaling fish, it feeds almost exclusively on planktonic crustaceans.

Schelly (*Coregonus laveretus*):
Up to 30cm/12in
The schelly (*above*) inhabits a few isolated highland lakes in England, Scotland and Wales, as well as lakes in the Alps and rivers flowing into the Baltic Sea. It feeds mainly on planktonic invertebrates, filtering them from the water using its gill rakers. It was formerly found in the eastern North Sea but is now thought to be extinct there, due to pollution and over-fishing.

Pollan (*Coregonus autumnalis*):
Up to 25cm/9¾in
In Europe, this shoaling fish is only found in two Irish loughs, Lough Neagh and Lough Erne. Another land-locked population lives in Lake Baikal in Siberia, where it is known as the omul. The pollan also has a more northerly form that spends much of its life in the sea. This fish also goes by a third common name, the Arctic cisco.

Arctic charr

Salvelinus alpinus

Two forms of this fish exist in the wild. One inhabits deep mountain and highland lakes in central and northern Europe (including Britain and Ireland). It shoals in open waters not far above the bottom. The other form, found in the northernmost reaches of Europe, is migratory, breeding in rivers but spending its winters at sea. The two forms look quite different. Landlocked Arctic charr are darker and smaller, and rarely exceed 30cm/12in long. The Arctic charr is one of Britain's rarest freshwater fish but it is quite common in the rest of its range. In Siberia it is known as golets.

Identification: The base of the tail is relatively narrow. The caudal fin is large and can be deeply forked. There is a small adipose fin. The scales are very small. Fish that spend the winter at sea are silvery, with bellies of orange or red. Lake fish are greeny-brown, with red and white spots on their sides. Both forms have white edges to their pectoral, pelvic and anal fins.

Distribution: Lakes in Europe and rivers and the sea around the Arctic, from Scandinavia and Russia to Alaska and Canada.
Habitat: Lakes, rivers, sea.
Food: Aquatic invertebrates and small fish.
Size: Up to 1m/3½ft.
Breeding: Mostly in tributary streams of their river homes; winter or early spring. Eggs are laid in gravel redds and develop unguarded.

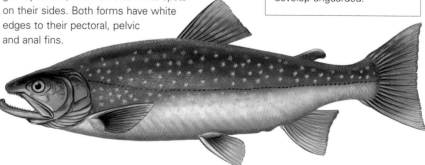

LOACHES, CATFISH AND BURBOT

All of the fish on these pages are bottom-dwellers and as a consequence are rarely seen in the wild, even where they are common. Although they vary greatly in size and diet, they have similar patterns of behaviour, hiding out by day and becoming active at night. This helps them to avoid herons, otters and other visual predators, which do their hunting by day.

Spined loach

Cobitis taenia

Identification: The body is long, slender and slightly compressed in the vertical plane. The head is small with the eyes placed high on the sides. The mouth is small and surrounded by six fleshy barbels. There is a short but sturdy backward-pointing spine beneath each eye (hence the name). This has two pointed tips and is usually retracted into the skin. The sides are marked with conspicuous rows of dark, oblong blotches.

This little fish is widespread throughout Europe but rare in most of the places where it is found. It also occurs in Asia, where it is thought to be more common. The spined loach is an inhabitant of still and slow-moving waters. It lives on the bottom, where it feeds on tiny invertebrates and other particles of organic matter. These are removed with the help of mucus as it filters water, laden with sediment, through its mouth. This fish tends to be most active at dawn and dusk. It spends the daylight hours hidden beneath mats of algae on the bottom or buried in the mud. It has large gills, an adaptation which helps it survive in waters with low oxygen levels. It is also able to absorb oxygen through its gut wall and occasionally gulps air.

Distribution: Most of Europe, apart from northern Scandinavia. It is absent from Ireland and in Britain is restricted to a few eastward-flowing English rivers.
Habitat: Swamps, ponds, lakes, rivers and streams.
Food: Detritus and tiny invertebrates.
Size: Up to 13.5cm/5¼in.
Breeding: Spawning occurs during May and June. Eggs are usually laid on mats of algae or around the bases of aquatic plants.

Stone loach

Nemacheilus barbatulus

Identification: The body is relatively long and slender, but the front is more rounded than the rear half, which is vertically flattened. The head is quite large compared with most other loaches but the eyes are quite small. There are six barbels around the mouth but no spines beneath the eyes. In colour it is olive-brown above, with darker blotches, and yellow below.

The stone loach is a fish of streams and small, fast-flowing rivers. It is often found in the same stretches of water as bullheads. It spends the day hidden amongst the stones and other rubble on the bottom, hence its common name. Like the spined loach, it becomes active as the sun goes down. It hunts throughout the night, seeking out mayfly larvae, stonefly larvae and other invertebrate prey while most of its own predators are inactive. Although a common fish, it is rarely seen, being beautifully camouflaged even when it is out in the open. Although several individuals may be found within the same area of river, this fish tends to be solitary, only gathering with others to breed.

Distribution: A huge range, being found throughout most of Europe and as far east as China. Introduced into Ireland.
Habitat: Streams and rivers.
Food: Small aquatic invertebrates.
Size: Up to 15cm/6in.
Breeding: Spawning occurs from April until June. The eggs are laid in two or three batches over the same spot, often among vegetation or gravel. They are guarded by the male until they hatch.

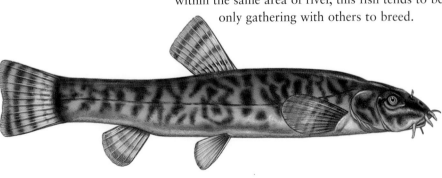

Wels

Silurus glanis

This gigantic creature holds the title of world's largest exclusively freshwater fish. One individual, caught in Russia's Dnieper River in the 19th century, measured 4.6m/15ft long and weighed an incredible 336kg/720lb. No freshwater fish caught anywhere since has come close to beating this record. The wels is a type of catfish that lives in large, slow-flowing rivers and areas of still water. It is mainly nocturnal, spending the day lying still amongst tree roots or beneath overhanging river banks. Not all wels are giants but most older individuals are very large fish. It is a carnivore. The bulk of its diet is made up of other fish but it also eats amphibians, waterfowl and small mammals.

Distribution: Native to larger rivers of northern Europe and Russia. Introduced into England, France, Spain and northern Italy.
Habitat: Large rivers, lakes and marshes.
Food: Fish and other aquatic vertebrates.
Size: Up to 4.6m/15ft.
Breeding: Spawning occurs from May until July. The female lays her eggs in a shallow depression made by the male, who then guards the eggs.

Identification: The body is long and relatively slender in younger fish, tapering towards the tail. The head is massive and very broad. There are three pairs of barbels: two on the underside of the head and the third arising from the upper lip – this pair is much longer than the others. The dorsal fin is very small and there is no adipose fin. The anal fin is very long, more than half the whole length of the fish.

Golden loach (*Cobitis aurata*):
Up to 12cm/4¾in
This fish lives in the Danube River basin and other eastern European rivers flowing into the Black Sea. It is also found in the Aral Sea and its tributaries. Its name is an accurate description of its colour. An inhabitant of sandy river beds, it is well camouflaged against the bottom and only rarely strays on to patches of mud. Most individuals spend the day buried in the sand, emerging at dusk to feed.

Aristotle's catfish (*Parasilurus aristotelis*):
Up to 1.5m/5ft
This large fish (*above*) is confined to Greece and Macedonia, being native to the former and introduced into the latter. Like the wels, which it resembles in many respects, it spends its time on the bottom of large rivers and lakes, resting by day and becoming active at night. It spawns from June to August; the male builds a nest and guards the eggs.

Weatherfish (*Misgurnus fossilis*):
Up to 30cm/12in
This loach is normally nocturnal but is said to become active by day prior to large storms, and this is a habit that earned it its common name. It is widespread through central continental Europe, from Belgium to the edge of the Caspian Sea. It inhabits oxbow lakes, marshes, ditches, ponds and the backwaters of rivers.

Burbot

Lota lota

This fish is the only member of the cod family to live in fresh water. It has an enormous range, occurring right across the northern parts of Europe, Asia and North America. It was once found in eastern England but is now extinct there (it is the only freshwater fish known to have become extinct in Britain in recent centuries). It is mainly nocturnal and spends the day lying still in a sheltered nook on the bottom. By night it scours the beds of rivers and lakes for invertebrates and small fish. In North America it is also known as the eelpout and the lawyer, although the origins of these curious names are sadly lost in history.

Identification: The body is long and rounded at the front but flattened towards the tail. There are two dorsal fins, the second much longer than the first, stretching along half the length of the body. The anal fin is only slightly shorter. The head is broad, with a large mouth and prominent barbel on the chin. The nostrils extend out into short tubes.

Distribution: Found across most of the temperate and sub-polar regions of the Northern Hemisphere.
Habitat: Slow-flowing rivers and lakes.
Food: Aquatic invertebrates and fish.
Size: Up to 1m/3¼ft.
Breeding: Spawning occurs in mid-winter, often under ice. The eggs are scattered over gravel and left to develop unguarded.

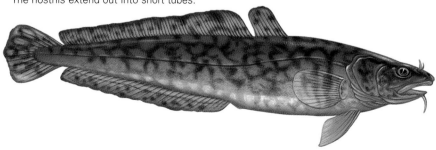

STICKLEBACKS, BULLHEADS AND MUDMINNOW

Apart from the mudminnow, which is named after its habitat, all of these fish are named for physical characteristics. Sticklebacks are named for their spines – stickle is Old English for 'thorn'. Bullheads are so called because their prominent eyes and flattened heads give them a slightly bovine appearance.

Three-spined stickleback

Gasterosteus aculeatus

Identification: The three spines that give this fish its name are its most obvious distinguishing feature, running along the back in front of the second, more complete, dorsal fin. The body is torpedo shaped and quite streamlined, and the eyes are large. The pelvic fins, like the first dorsal fin, are reduced to spines. The general colour of freshwater individuals is greenish brown, but the male's belly turns red during the breeding season.

The three-spined stickleback is a great fish to watch in the wild. Its preference for still shallow water and its fearless nature make it easy to observe, and its breeding behaviour is quite absorbing. In spring and early summer, males build nests from algae and plant fibres on the bottom. These nests are shaped like little tunnels and the males entice the females into them to lay their eggs. The males then guard the eggs and keep them well-oxygenated until they hatch by fanning them with their fins. During the breeding season males become quite territorial but at other times of the year these fish can often be found in small shoals. Interestingly, the three-spined stickleback is also found in coastal marine waters. There the males make their nests from seaweed.

Distribution: Throughout Europe, from Iceland to the Iberian Peninsula, southern Italy and the Black Sea. Also found in North Africa; widely introduced throughout other parts of the world.
Habitat: Rivers, lakes, ponds, ditches and coastal waters.
Food: Aquatic invertebrates and fish fry.
Size: Up to 10cm/4in.
Breeding: The male builds a nest into which he entices the female. He then guards the eggs until they hatch.

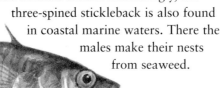

Ten-spined stickleback

Pungitius pungitius

Identification: The body is relatively slender and the base of the tail long and narrow. Eight to ten spines run along the back, in front of the more complete second dorsal fin. The anal fin is almost a complete mirror image of the second dorsal fin. The body is dark olive green to brown above and lighter below. During the breeding season, in spring and summer, the males become darker and their throats turn black.

Slightly smaller and less cosmopolitan in its distribution than the three-spined stickleback, the ten-spined stickleback is less well-known to most Europeans. Nevertheless, it is a relatively common fish with similarly fascinating breeding habits. This stickleback tends to be found in areas more choked with the stems of water plants than its three-spined relative, and it can survive in waters with much lower oxygen levels. It ranges through the coastal regions of most of the temperate and sub-polar northern hemisphere, including North America. There it is known as the Newfoundland stickleback or nine-spined stickleback. The latter name is telling. This species can have as few as eight spines along its back and does not always have ten, as might be expected.

Distribution: Europe, Russia and North America. This species is rarely found far inland.
Habitat: Pools, marshes, rivers and ditches.
Food: Aquatic invertebrates.
Size: Up to 7cm/2¾in.
Breeding: The male builds a nest in vegetation a little way off the bottom. One or more females are enticed in to lay their eggs, which are then guarded by the male.

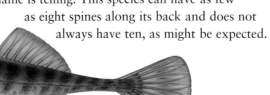

Distribution: Ranges from southern Scotland to the Black Sea. More common in Britain than on the continent; absent from most of Spain and Portugal.
Habitat: Streams and small rivers with rocky bottoms.
Food: Aquatic invertebrates and fish eggs.
Size: Up to 17cm/6¾in.
Breeding: Spawning occurs March to May. The female attaches her eggs to the underside of a rock. The male guards them until they hatch.

Bullhead

Cottus gobio

This fish lives in rocky streams and small rivers. By day it usually hides beneath large stones or in the gaps between pebbles, its dappled colours making it virtually invisible unless it moves. As the sun starts to set it emerges to find insect larvae and the eggs of other fish, holding itself steady in the rushing current with its large pectoral fins. The bullhead is rarely active throughout the night, usually settling after an hour or two of feeding, and then foraging for another hour or two around dawn. This crepuscular behaviour is driven by the fact that it is a visual predator that is itself quite vulnerable to predation. Although it can grow larger, the bullhead rarely exceeds 10cm/4in long. In parts of England it is called the 'miller's thumb'.

Identification: The body is slightly flattened, a typical adaptation of bottom-dwelling fish in swift water. The head is quite broad and the body, seen from above, tapers from the temples to the tail. There are two relatively long dorsal fins. The anal fin is positioned directly below the second dorsal fin and is slightly shorter. The pectoral fins appear unusually large.

Greek ten-spined stickleback (*Pungitius hellenicus*): Up to 5cm/2in
This little fish closely resembles the ten-spined stickleback but it lacks its spiny pelvic and dorsal fins. This fish is found in small tributary streams in the Sperchios River basin in central eastern Greece. Water removal for human use from these places has reduced its numbers and it is now listed as Critically Endangered by the IUCN.

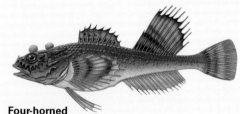

Four-horned bullhead (*Myoxocephalus quadricornis*): Up to 36cm/14in
Four bony lumps on its head make this bullhead (*above*) a strange looking fish. Mainly a marine species, there are also freshwater populations in the deeper lakes of Sweden, Finland and western Russia, relics from before the last Ice Age when sea levels were higher and these lakes were linked to the sea. It is a bottom dweller, feeding on invertebrates and small fish.

Siberian bullhead (*Cottus poecilopus*): Up to 7.5cm/3in
As well as Siberia, this fish is also found in the Baltic states, Sweden, Denmark, Poland and the western half of Russia. It looks similar to the bullhead but is slightly smaller, with a more rounded caudal fin. It is similar in its habits too, being most active around dawn and dusk.

Mudminnow

Umbra krameri

This is a fish of stagnant waters with dense vegetation – mostly places with thick black silt on the bottom, created from decaying leaves. Such waters are often low in oxygen in summer and frozen over in winter, making them very difficult places to live. Among the few other fish that can survive here are the Crucian carp and the weatherfish, which are often found living alongside the mudminnow. Despite its ability to tolerate tough conditions, this fish has started to become rare. The floodplain pools in which it once thrived have begun to disappear as the plains themselves have been drained. It is now listed as Vulnerable by the IUCN.

Identification: A stout little fish with scales that extend over the head as well as the body. It is greenish-brown on the back and yellowish below, with dusky vertical bars on the flanks. The caudal fin is quite large and rounded. The dorsal fin extends from directly above the base of the pelvic fins to a point above the rear of the anal fin.

Distribution: Limited to Austria, Hungary, Romania, Slovakia and the Czech Republic.
Habitat: Swamps, stagnant ponds and oxbow lakes.
Food: Small insect larvae and other aquatic invertebrates.
Size: Up to 13cm/5in.
Breeding: Spawning occurs in spring, with the female laying around 150 eggs in a hollow made near plant roots. She guards the eggs until they hatch.
Status: Vulnerable.

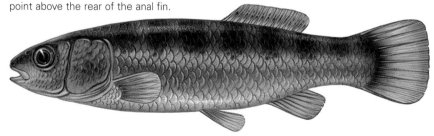

MINNOWS AND OTHER SMALL CYPRINIDS

The species on these pages include some of Europe's smallest freshwater fish. Most are too small to be of interest to anglers, but they play an important role as food for larger fish in the rivers, streams, lakes and other ecosystems where they live. Although not showy, they are interesting fish to watch and most are easy to observe in the wild.

Minnow

Phoxinus phoxinus

Identification: The head and the body are both rounded and the snout is blunt. The body is covered with small scales and there is an obvious lateral line, curving down towards the belly. A line of dusky blotches runs along the side – these become darker towards the tail. During the breeding season the male's belly reddens and his throat turns black.

The minnow is famous for being small. It is not the smallest freshwater fish but it is the smallest native fish in Britain to spend its whole life in fresh water. A shoaling fish of streams and small rivers, it is most common in waters where the temperature is quite low and the oxygen levels are high, although it is sometimes found in the shallows of slower-flowing, warmer waters. It is an omnivore, feeding on everything from algae and water plants to insect larvae. It is itself prey for a wide range of larger fish and an important food source for the brown trout and the kingfisher (*Alcedo atthis*). This fish is considered a good indicator of water quality in rivers and streams, being absent where pollution levels are high.

Distribution: Widespread throughout Europe, including Ireland, where it has been introduced. Also found in Russia, where its eastern range extends to Siberia.
Habitat: Streams and rivers.
Food: Algae, plant matter, aquatic invertebrates.
Size: Up to 12cm/4¾in.
Breeding: Spawning occurs from April to June. The eggs are shed into open water over gravel and left to develop unguarded.

Swamp minnow

Phoxinus percnurus

Identification: The body is similar in shape to that of the minnow but slightly less rounded. The body is covered with many small scales which are more visible than those of the minnow. The flanks, rather than being blotched, have many small, irregular spots, each about the size of three or four individual scales. The belly is creamy and the sides have a green-gold sheen.

This fish, as its name suggests, is most common in still waters with abundant vegetation. As well as in swamps and marshes, it is also found around the edges of lakes where reeds and other plants grow. The swamp minnow, like its cousin, is a small schooling fish that lies near the middle of the food chain. While it preys on insect larvae and other small aquatic creatures it also provides food for many larger fish and birds such as the bittern (*Botaurus stellaris*). The swamp minnow is more able to cope with low oxygen levels than many other fish and can also tolerate very shallow and slightly acidic water. It is one of the few fish relatively common in peat cuttings, for example. Despite its hardiness it has become scarce in many parts of its range, due to land drainage for agricultural use.

Distribution: Eastern Germany and Poland through north-eastern Europe to Russia.
Habitat: Bogs, swamps and lakes.
Food: Aquatic invertebrates and land insects blown into the water.
Size: Up to 12cm/4¾in.
Breeding: Spawning occurs at the beginning of summer. The eggs are deposited on the leaves of water plants and are then left to develop unguarded.

Soufie

Leuciscus souffia

Distribution: Most common in the Alps but also found in some lower tributaries of the Danube, Rhône and Rhine.
Habitat: Over sand or gravel in swift, clear streams and some lakes.
Food: Aquatic and terrestrial invertebrates that fall into the water.
Size: Up to 25cm/9¾in.
Breeding: Spawning occurs from April until July. The eggs are shed over gravel and left to develop unguarded.

Also known as the varione, the soufie is a small schooling fish which lives in clear, fast-flowing streams. It is most abundant in hilly and mountainous areas, in the headwaters of larger rivers, but is also found in some sub-alpine lakes. Several isolated populations are known from different parts of Europe and some of these have been assigned their own subspecies. It feeds on aquatic invertebrates and insects, but has few natural predators of its own, mainly because it lives at such high altitudes. Despite its small size, it is sometimes caught as a food fish by anglers. The soufie is not thought to be in any danger of extinction, but it has become rare in parts of its range.

Identification: The head is relatively small, scaleless and slightly pointed. The body is slender and covered with moderately large silvery scales – there are 45 to 48 in the lateral line, which is clearly visible. There is a dark stripe running along the middle of the body. In colour this fish is grey-green to bluish on the back and silvery below. The rear edges of the dorsal and anal fins are straight or slightly convex.

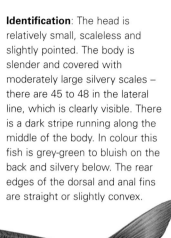

Bogardilla (*Iberocypris palaciosi*):
Up to 18.5cm/7½in
This fish is known from just a single river – the Guadalquivir in Spain. It lives in the middle reaches, where water flow is moderate and oxygen levels are high. It is thought that the females greatly outnumber the males. This may indicate that the species changes sex. This is known to occur in some other fish, with only the largest individuals turning into males when the previous locally dominant male is killed or dies.

Iberian minnow
(*Anaecypris hispanica*): Up to 8cm/3¼in
This small schooling fish (*above*) feeds on algae and a variety of small invertebrates. Much of its tiny prey is filtered out of the water using densely packed gill rakers. The Iberian minnow is found only in the Guadina and Guadalquivir Rivers of southern Spain and Portugal, and is listed as Endangered by the IUCN.

Albanian minnow (*Pachychilon pictum*):
Up to 17cm/6¾in
This fish lives in the shallows of large lakes in Albania and the former Yugoslavia. Although it resembles the minnow it is thought to be more closely related to the roach. The Albanian minnow spawns from March until June, swimming up the tributary streams of its lake homes to lay its eggs. It is a schooling fish that feeds on invertebrates and plant matter.

Bitterling

Rhodeus sericeus

This fish has a very unusual but successful method for protecting its eggs – it lays them inside a living freshwater mussel. As the breeding season begins, the male sets up a territory around a mussel, which he defends from other males. He attracts a female who then lays her eggs in the mussel's inhalant siphon, which leads into its gills. (She does this using an ovipositor, a delicate tube which she develops during the spawning season.) The male then sheds his sperm over the inhalant siphon, which sucks it in.

Identification: The body is deep, with large scales. The mouth is small. The dorsal, caudal and anal fins are significantly larger than the others. The lateral line is visible only in the first five or six scales behind the gill cover. The body is greyish-green on the back and silver on the sides and belly. Breeding males turn purple and develop small turbercles on the forehead and snout.

Distribution: Native to the Danube basin and central Europe but has been widely introduced into western Europe, including England.
Habitat: Lakes, ponds and overgrown, slow-flowing rivers.
Food: Planktonic crustaceans and insect larvae.
Size: Up to 9cm/3½in.
Breeding: April to August. The female lays 30–100 eggs inside a mussel. The fertilized eggs remain here until they hatch 3–4 weeks later.

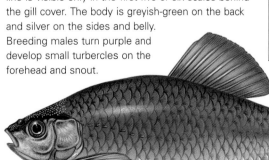

ROACHES AND RUDDS

Roaches and rudds are commonly found in weedy lakes and rivers, where they live in shoals.
Medium-sized members of the carp family, they are most often seen on the end of a hook.
A few populations are fished commercially for food but generally speaking they are considered
sport fish and of more interest to anglers.

Roach

Rutilus rutilus

Identification: This fish is moderately deep bodied with a relatively small head. The body has fairly large, almost diamond-shaped, scales but the head is scaleless. The flanks and belly are intensely silver and the back blue-green to brown. The pelvic and anal fins range from orange to bright red. The iris of the eye is also red.

This common and easy-to-catch fish is very familiar to European anglers. It has been introduced to many parts of the continent where it is not native, including Ireland, Scotland and Wales. It is a schooling fish, most common in still or very slow-flowing waters. An omnivore, it eats large amounts of plant matter and tends to be particularly abundant in areas of thick weed growth. It is no giant but it can grow to quite a respectable size – as much as 1.8kg/4lb. It is rarely eaten, however. Angling for roach is mostly a sporting pastime and fish tend to be put back in the water after they have been unhooked and, possibly, weighed.

Distribution: Native to eastern England and most of Europe, including Russia as far east as the Ural Mountains.
Habitat: Ponds, lakes and slow-flowing rivers.
Food: Plant matter and aquatic invertebrates.
Size: Up to 53cm/21in.
Breeding: Spawning occurs from April until June. Eggs are shed over vegetation, which they stick to, and are left to develop unguarded.

Escalo

Chondrostoma arcasii

This fish is also known as the panjorca or red roach. Unlike the true roach it is entirely carnivorous, eating insect larvae and other aquatic invertebrates, fish fry and insects caught at the surface. The escalo is confined to the western half of the Iberian Peninsula, where it schools both in upland streams and more sluggish lowland rivers. It is not found in the rivers of the far south. This species is threatened across much of its range by pollution, habitat destruction and competition from introduced species, and is listed as Vulnerable by the IUCN. The escalo can grow up to 25cm/9¾in long but more commonly grows to lengths of about 13cm/5in.

Identification: The head is small and the body relatively slender. Like the roach, the head is scaleless and the body covered with diamond-shaped scales. The end of the snout is rounded and the mouth down-turned. The eyes are relatively large and have pale irises. The back is greenish and the sides and belly silver. A dark slender line runs from the top of the gill cover to the base of the tail.

Distribution: Restricted to Portugal and the western parts of Spain.
Habitat: Streams and rivers.
Food: Invertebrates and fish fry.
Size: Up to 25cm/9¾in.
Breeding: Spawning occurs from the end of April until early June. The eggs are scattered in open water and left to develop unguarded.
Status: Vulnerable.

Rudd

Scardinus erythrophthalmus

Distribution: Occurs throughout Europe, ranging from England to the Ural Mountains. Introduced to Ireland and Wales.
Habitat: Sluggish rivers, ponds, lakes and other areas of still water.
Food: Invertebrates and plant matter.
Size: Up to 45cm/17¾in.
Breeding: Spawning occurs from April to June. Eggs are shed over vegetation, which they stick to, and are left to develop unguarded.

The rudd was named, in the seventeenth century, for the colour of its fins. The word for red has obviously changed a little in England since then (although the word ruddy, meaning reddish, is still in use.) This is a schooling fish, found in oxbow lakes and large, slow-flowing rivers. Its popularity with anglers has seen it introduced to a wide range of freshwater habitats, including ponds, lakes, reservoirs and canals. It survives in waters with fairly low oxygen levels so tends to thrive wherever it is introduced but, it requires abundant vegetation and a gentle flow of water.

Identification: Resembles the roach in many respects and is often confused with it. The rudd, however, has its dorsal fin set farther back and has a keel on its belly (the belly of the roach is rounded). The dorsal and pectoral fins are grey with a reddish tint. All of the other fins are bright red. The back is bluish green; the sides and belly are silver.

Italian roach (*Rutilus rubilio*):
Up to 20cm/8in
In its general appearance and habits this roach closely resembles most of the other European members of its genus. Like them, it inhabits still or slow-moving water with abundant vegetation. It is notable, however, for having larger scales, with just 36 to 44 in the lateral line. As the name suggests, it is found throughout Italy. It also occurs in the Adriatic rivers of Albania, Greece and the former Yugoslavia.

Greek rudd (*Scardinus graecus*):
Up to 40cm/15¾in
This rudd (*above*) is restricted to just two lakes – Lake Yliki and Lake Paralimni, in the far east of mainland Greece. It has an unusually slender body for a rudd and a very shallow sloping head. Like the Acheloos rudd, it is entirely herbivorous: the young eat planktonic algae and the adults feed on water plants.

Acheloos rudd (*Scardinus acarnanicus*):
Up to 30cm/12in
This fish is found only in the Acheloos River system in western Greece. Outwardly it is identical to the rudd in everything but size. It is classified as a separate species because of its internal anatomy – having a different number of vertebrae from other rudd – and its geographical range. It is commercially fished.

Danubian roach

Rutilus pigus

The Danubian roach forms two separate subspecies. One, *Rutilus pigus virgo* lives in the upper and middle reaches of the Danube River basin. The other, *Rutilus pigus pigus* is found in the lakes and rivers of the Po basin of northern Italy. The Danube population is believed to have shrunk in recent decades but the species as a whole is not thought to be threatened. The Danubian roach is a fish of still and slow-flowing waters. In the lakes it inhabits, it tends to spend most of its time at some depth but it migrates into shallower waters to breed. Spawning occurs in large schools amongst water plants.

Identification: Similar in appearance to the roach but less deep-bodied and with slightly smaller scales. The dorsal fin has 10 to 13 branched rays, rather than the roach's 9 to 11, and the lateral line has 45 to 49 scales (the roach has 42 to 45). Danubian males also develop numerous tubercles on the back and head during the breeding season.

Distribution: The Po and Danube River basins.
Habitat: Lakes and rivers.
Food: Aquatic invertebrates and plant matter.
Size: Up to 40cm/15¾in.
Breeding: Spawns late spring. Eggs stick to water plants and develop unguarded. Each female lays 35,000–60,000 eggs.

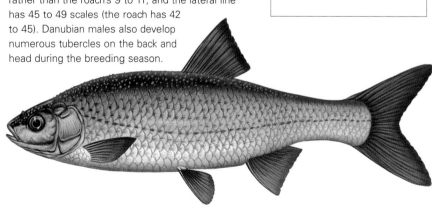

CARP, CHUB, DACE AND TENCH

These fish include some of the larger members of the carp family found in Europe. Some are regularly stocked in lakes, reservoirs and flooded gravel pits, and are familiar to anglers. Others are less commonly seen. Considering their size, all of these fish eat relatively small creatures. With the exceptions of the chub and dace, they also feed on plant matter.

Carp

Cyprinus carpio

Identification: The mouth is toothless, with two pairs of barbels emerging from the upper lip – those nearer the corner of the mouth are longer. In most wild fish the body is fully scaled but there are varieties such as the leather carp and mirror carp in which most of the scales are absent. The head is always scaleless. The dorsal fin is long, stretching along more than half the length of the back.

The carp is a potentially large and long-lived fish that thrives in still and slow-flowing waters around the world. It is a sport fish for anglers as well as a source of food. Its preference for plant matter and invertebrates means that it poses no threat to other fish, which has made it a popular choice for stocking new ponds and lakes. In some areas where it has become established, however, it is considered a nuisance. In captivity it has been known to reach 47 years old and a weight of 36kg/80lb.

Distribution: Native to the Danube basin and much of Asia as far east as China. Widely introduced in western Europe (including Britain) and elsewhere around the world.
Habitat: Lakes, large ponds and slow-flowing rivers.
Food: Aquatic invertebrates and plant matter.
Size: Up to 1.5m/5ft.
Breeding: Spawns spring and summer in shallow water. Scattered eggs are left to develop unguarded.

Chub

Leuciscus cephalus

Identification: The body is thickset and rounded with the head and 'shoulders' unusually broad. The mouth is wide and the snout quite blunt. The dorsal and anal fins have relatively short bases and are similar in shape and size, although the outer edge of the anal fin is more rounded. The scales on the back and sides are green to greyish-brown and clearly outlined.

The chub is a truly European fish, being found throughout the continent apart from the very far north, from Wales to the Ural Mountains. It is sometimes found living alongside the carp in still or slow-flowing waters but is more common in large rivers with moderate flow. Young chub form schools for protection, but the adult fish are usually solitary. The chub is a carnivorous fish and extremely adaptable, feeding on a wide range of small creatures. Prey varies from insect larvae and crustaceans such as crayfish to frogs, small fish and even young water voles. Although not as large as the carp, the chub can reach a respectable size and is often caught by anglers. The largest specimens landed have weighed around 7.25kg/16lb.

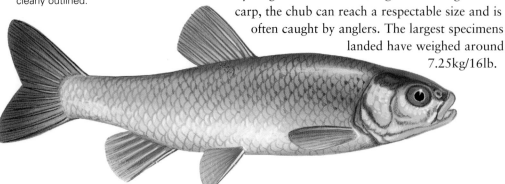

Distribution: Absent from Ireland but otherwise found throughout Europe, apart from the very far north.
Habitat: Rivers and, less commonly, lakes.
Food: Aquatic invertebrates and small vertebrates.
Size: Up to 61cm/24in.
Breeding: Spawning occurs in May and June in shallow water. The eggs are scattered over water plants, which they stick to, and left to develop unguarded. The hatch after around 8–10 days.

Dace

Leuciscus leuciscus

Distribution: From Britain through northern Europe and Russia, as far east as Siberia; no farther south than the Alps. Introduced to Ireland.
Habitat: Rivers and large streams.
Food: Invertebrates, particularly insects.
Size: Up to 30cm/12in.
Breeding: Spawning occurs in shallow waters early in spring. Eggs are deposited over gravel and left to develop unguarded.

This northern Eurasian fish is found in rivers, most commonly in the relatively clean water of their middle and upper reaches. That said, it may also be found in slower-flowing stretches downstream and has even been known to enter brackish water at the edge of the Baltic Sea. It is a shoaling fish and feeds on invertebrates, particularly insects, eating both the aquatic larval forms and adults as they lay their eggs at the surface. It also eats other invertebrates that fall into the water. The dace is a very active and relatively fast-moving fish. In some places it is known by the alternative common names of dart or dare.

Identification: The body is slim and the head and mouth are relatively small. The lateral line is clearly visible, beginning at the back of the gill cover, level with the centre of the eye, and curving downward then back up again, mirroring the curve of the belly. The iris of the eye is yellowish and the pectoral, pelvic and anal fins pale orange or yellow. The other fins are grey.

Crucian carp (*Carassius carassius*): Up to 51cm/20in
This widespread fish ranges from eastern England to central Russia. It is smaller and more deep-bodied than the carp and lacks barbels. Purebred fish are quite rare as this species interbreeds with the carp and also with the goldfish (*Carassius auratus*). It is a fish of still or slow-flowing water. It can tolerate low oxygen levels and is often found in waters with heavy plant growth.

Ide (*Leuciscus idus*): Up to 1m/3¼ft
The ide (*above*) is similar in appearance to the dace but grows much larger. It lives in schools in the lower reaches of northern Europe's rivers, including their estuaries, and is also common in flood plain lakes. Young ide are plankton feeders. Adults feed on invertebrates and, occasionally, small fish.

Balkan dace (*Leuciscus svallize*): Up to 25cm/9¾in
This fish looks similar to the dace but is known only from rivers flowing into the Adriatic Sea. It can be told apart from the dace by the rays in its anal fin (11 or 12 rather than the dace's 8 or 9). It is a schooling fish, most common in quite clear waters. It feeds on invertebrates – insect larvae, worms and freshwater shrimps.

Tench

Tinca tinca

This fish is able to tolerate much higher temperatures and lower oxygen levels than most of its relatives. It is found mainly in still water, although it also inhabits very slow-flowing backwaters of rivers. It is usually the most common large fish in very silty or overgrown bodies of fresh water in its range. It is a favourite of anglers, with record fish measuring 70cm/27½in and weighing around 6.4kg/14lb. Fishing for tench is a summer pursuit; the species tends to lie inactive near the bottom in winter.

Identification: Most easily told apart from its relatives by its very small scales. These are deeply embedded in very thick skin, the surface of which is often slippery, like that of an eel. The eyes are small and have reddish irises and there is a single pair of barbels, one at each corner of the mouth. The body is rounded and the base of the tail rather deep.

Distribution: Native to most of Europe, including England and the western part of Russia. Introduced to Ireland, Wales, parts of the USA and Australia.
Habitat: Lakes, marshes and the backwaters of rivers.
Food: Invertebrates and plant matter.
Size: Up to 70cm/27½in.
Breeding: Spawns late spring and early summer. Eggs are shed over vegetation and develop unguarded.

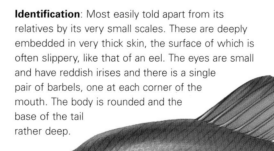

BARBELS

Barbels are members of the carp family. They have many features in common with catfish, having evolved to live in a similar way. Like catfish, barbels are bottom feeders that find their food mainly by touch. This is evident in the fleshy tentacles that give them their name. These tentacles enable them to detect the slightest movement in the sediment as they search for prey.

Barbel

Barbus barbus

Identification: The body is long and almost circular in cross section, although the belly is flattened. The snout is pointed and the eyes rather small. The lips are thick and have two pairs of barbels. The body is a soft greenish brown on the back, golden yellow on the flanks and lighter on the underside. The scales are fairly small and well embedded in the skin.

The barbel was known in medieval times as the pigfish, for its habit of rooting around for food. It hunts for invertebrate prey at night and is relatively inactive by day, although it will happily take bait during daylight if offered it. It is a great favourite of anglers, being renowned for its fighting spirit once hooked. This popularity has led to it being introduced into many rivers. Once caught, it is usually weighed and then put back in the water, as it is not generally considered good to eat. Despite its size and the fact that it often schools, the barbel can be difficult to spot; its coloration camouflages it against the bottom.

Distribution: Native to eastern England and most of continental Europe. Introduced to other parts of England and Wales.
Habitat: Clean rivers with good stretches of gravel.
Food: Aquatic invertebrates.
Size: Up to 91cm/36in.
Breeding: Males and females congregate in shallow water and spawn as a group. The eggs are scattered over clean gravel and are left to develop unguarded.

Southern barbel

Barbus meridionalis

Identification: The body is long and the back smoothly curved. The lips are thick and there are two pairs of barbels, the second, at the corners of the mouth, being longer than the first. The anal fin has a short base but the front rays are long, reaching the base of the caudal fin if held flat against the underside. Coloration is similar to the barbel, but there are numerous black spots on the back and sides and on the dorsal and caudal fins.

This species shares part of its range with the barbel but tends to be found in slightly faster waters farther upstream. Like the barbel, it feeds on bottom-dwelling invertebrates, particularly insect larvae and small crustaceans. It is also known as the Mediterranean barbel, a name that accurately describes the west of its range but not the east. As well as countries with Mediterranean coastlines it is also found in Bulgaria, Romania, Moldova, Ukraine and Belarus. The southern barbel is smaller than the barbel, an adaptation to life in shallower, narrower rivers. It migrates upstream to breed. By doing this it avoids competing with its own offspring for food, since the young fish move slowly downstream as they grow.

Distribution: Common in southern Europe from Spain to Greece. Also found in parts of eastern Europe.
Habitat: Rivers and streams.
Food: Aquatic invertebrates.
Size: Up to 30cm/12in.
Breeding: Spawning occurs in May and June. Eggs are scattered in open water over sand or gravel and left to develop unguarded.

Portuguese barbel

Barbus comizo

Distribution: The Tajo, Jarama, Guadiana and Guadalquivir Rivers in the southern half of Portugal and south-western Spain.
Habitat: Rivers.
Food: Aquatic invertebrates.
Size: Up to 35cm/13¾in.
Breeding: The breeding system of this species has not been studied closely. However, it is known to scatter its eggs and leave them to develop unguarded.
Status: Vulnerable.

This bottom-dwelling fish is known from just four rivers, the Tajo, Jarama, Guadiana and Guadalquivir, all of which are in the south-western corner of the Iberian Peninsula. In common with many fish from that part of the world it is threatened by water extraction for irrigation purposes from the rivers in which it lives. It is listed as Vulnerable by the IUCN. The Portuguese barbel is most common in the slow-moving, silty waters of the lower reaches of rivers, although it is also found in smaller numbers farther upstream. This species is sometimes, confusingly, called the Iberian barbel. That common name is correctly applied to another fish, *Barbus bocagei (see box below).*

Identification: The body shape of this species is typical for a barbel, being elongated and roughly circular in cross section. The head, however, is unusually long and large, vaguely resembling that of a pike. There are two pairs of barbels, the second being longer than the first. The mouth is large, opening at the front of the snout. The dorsal fin is positioned directly above the pectoral fins.

Iberian barbel (*Barbus bocagei*):
Up to 61cm/24in
This fish occurs throughout Spain and in parts of Portugal. Compared with the Portuguese barbel the head is relatively small and the dorsal fin is positioned in front of the pelvic fins, rather than level with them. This barbel lives in rivers, lakes and reservoirs, being most common where the water is cloudy and warm. Like the Portuguese barbel, this species has relatively large scales.

Peloponnesian barbel (*Barbus peloponnesius*):
Up to 30cm/12in
This small barbel (*above*) lives throughout central and western Greece, in parts of Albania and the former Yugoslavia, and has been introduced into the Isonzo River, northern Italy. It lives in lakes and areas of still or slow-moving water, feeding on invertebrates. Although little studied, it is known to breed from May until July.

Greek barbel (*Barbus graecus*):
Up to 45cm/17¾in
This fish is endemic to Greece, occurring only in the Sperchios River and two lakes, Lake Yliki and Lake Paralimni. Its appearance is similar to that of the barbel but it has slightly larger scales and bigger eyes. Its internal anatomy is also somewhat different. The Greek barbel is under threat due to the removal of water from its habitats. It is listed as Endangered by the IUCN.

Po barbel

Barbus plebejus

Although found in the Po River, this fish is also found in most other rivers in Italy. It is even known from Sicily, although whether it is native there or was introduced is uncertain. The Po barbel lives in the upper reaches of rivers where the current is strong. It is a relatively sedentary fish, rarely travelling far: most individuals spend their whole life in the same short section of river. Like other barbels it feeds at night. It spends daylight hours hidden beneath a large rock or in the shade of an overhanging river bank, only emerging to search for food once the sun has set. The adults of this species tend to be solitary, but the young form schools.

Identification: A similar shape to the barbel, but the eyes are bigger and the scales slightly smaller. The colour is also similar to that of the barbel, but there are many small, faint black spots on the back and flanks, as well as on the dorsal, caudal and anal fins. As with all barbels, the head is scaleless.

Distribution: Common in Italy; range extends into neighbouring Switzerland, Croatia and Slovenia.
Habitat: Rivers.
Food: Invertebrates and, occasionally, algae.
Size: Up to 61cm/24in.
Breeding: Spawning occurs in May and June. The eggs are scattered over sand and left to develop unguarded.

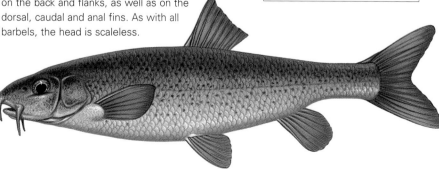

OTHER BARBELS AND GUDGEONS

All of these fish are members of the carp family, Cyprinidae. Generally speaking, barbels are larger than gudgeons. The two can also be told apart by the fact that gudgeons have just a single pair of barbels, whereas barbels have two pairs. The Dalmatian barbelgudgeon is gudgeon-like in size but it has two pairs of barbels around its mouth.

Thracian barbel

Barbus cyclolepis

This is a relatively common and widespread bottom-dwelling river fish. Like other barbels, it finds its food primarily by touch, rummaging around in the rubble on the bottom to expose small prey. It does most of its foraging at night. By day it often hides itself beneath fallen leaves on the bottom. Like other fish of its size it often falls prey to otters and herons, both of which are visual predators that hunt by day. In some parts of its range this barbel is also eaten by people. It is not caught commercially but is fished on a small scale by individuals, a practice that does no more harm to its populations than do its natural predators.

Identification: This is a typical barbel in many respects and one that is only easily identified by experts. The most distinguishing characteristic is its barbels, which are shorter than those of other members of its genus. There are two pairs, the first, front pair being less than half as long as the rear pair. The rear barbels are about equal in length to the diameter of the eye.

Distribution: South-western Europe: native to Greece, Turkey, Bulgaria, Romania and Ukraine. Introduced into Italy.
Habitat: Rivers and streams.
Food: Aquatic invertebrates, fish eggs and algae.
Size: Up to 35cm/13¾in.
Breeding: An extended spawning season lasts over 3 months, from late spring into early summer. The eggs are shed in open water and left to develop unguarded.

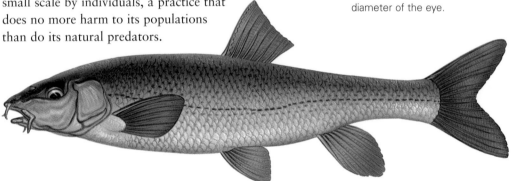

Dalmatian barbelgudgeon

Aulopyge huegeli

As its name suggests, this fish – the only member of its genus – has physical features in common with both barbels and gudgeons. It lives in the karst limestone areas of Croatia and Bosnia-Herzegovina (the region which was once known as Dalmatia), inhabiting lakes, reservoirs and streams. Some of these streams have underground branches and it is thought that this fish retreats into these during the winter, when conditions above ground can become harsh. Pollution, water extraction and general degradation of its habitat have led to the Dalmatian barbelgudgeon decreasing in numbers and it is now listed as Endangered by the IUCN.

Identification: The snout is long, narrow and pointed and bears two pairs of barbels. The eyes are large and positioned near the top of the head. Both the head and body are completely devoid of scales. The lateral line is unusually wavy but clearly visible on the silvery flanks. The first spine of the dorsal fin extends above the others. The females of this species are deeper-bodied than the males.

Distribution: Parts of former Yugoslavia near the northern end of the Adriatic Sea.
Habitat: Lakes, reservoirs and streams.
Food: Uncertain, but thought to include aquatic invertebrates.
Size: Up to 13cm/5in.
Breeding: Spawning begins once water temperatures rise above 20°C/68°F and lasts for about a month. It is not known whether the adults care for the eggs or young.
Status: Endangered.

Gudgeon

Gobio gobio

Distribution: Native to the whole of Europe apart from Ireland and the Iberian Peninsula. It has been introduced to both of these places.
Habitat: Lakes, rivers and canals.
Food: Aquatic invertebrates.
Size: Up to 20cm/8in.
Breeding: Spawning occurs in shallow water at night in early summer. The eggs are scattered, usually over gravel, and are then left to develop unguarded.

Although unfamiliar to most people, the gudgeon is a relatively common little fish. It lives in a wide range of habitats, including canals, and is much more tolerant of disturbances than most fish, such as regular boat traffic. As a result, it is often the first type of fish caught by budding anglers. It prefers still or slow-moving waters but may be found in areas with moderate or even relatively rapid currents. As its body form suggests, it is a bottom-dwelling species, locating small invertebrate prey partly by touch as it grubs around in the silt. (In still waters young gudgeon feed on planktonic organisms in open water.) Gudgeon tend to form small shoals. Unusually for fish, they are capable of producing squeaking sounds, which they appear to use to maintain contact within the shoal.

Identification: The body is long and slender and the back slightly curved. In cross section it is almost circular, but compressed somewhat towards the tail. There is a single barbel at each corner of the mouth. The head is scaleless but the body is covered with rather large scales, with between 38 and 44 in the lateral line. The dorsal, anal and caudal fins are covered with small, dark spots.

Danubian gudgeon (*Gobio uranoscopus*): Up to 12cm/4¾in
This fish is found in the upper tributaries of the Danube in Slovakia, Hungary, Romania and parts of the former Yugoslavia, but not the Danube River proper. It has a more slender and rounded base to its tail than other gudgeons, and conspicuous bars on its caudal fin. It prefers fast-flowing waters with high oxygen levels. Like the white-finned gudgeon, it is little studied.

Kessler's gudgeon
(*Gobio kessleri*): Up to 12cm/4¾in
This small, slender gudgeon (*above*) is another inhabitant of the Danube's upper tributaries. While the Danubian gudgeon has scales on its throat, between its pectoral fins, the underside of this gudgeon's body is completely scaleless. It is also poorly known, but is thought to be mostly solitary, only gathering to breed.

Euboean barbel (*Barbus euboicus*): Up to 25cm/9¾in
This fish is a very close relative of the Thracian barbel. It is named after the island of Euboea in the Aegean Sea, where it lives exclusively. One of the world's smallest barbels, it inhabits small streams with rocky bottoms. Naturally at risk of extinction due to its tiny range, it has become further threatened by the extraction of water for human use on the island. It is now listed as Critically Endangered by the IUCN.

White-finned gudgeon

Gobio albipinnatus

Like the gudgeon, this is a bottom-dwelling fish that forms small shoals. It is found in the slow-moving lower reaches of rivers that flow into the Black and Caspian Seas, but is also common in still waters, including oxbow and flood plain lakes. In common with many other fish from these habitats it can survive in waters where levels of oxygen are low. In fact, it is better able to tolerate reduced oxygen levels than any other gudgeon. The white-finned gudgeon is not uncommon but it has been little studied. It is known to prefer waters where the bottom is muddy, and bloodworms (midge larvae) are high on its list of prey.

Identification: The clear dorsal and caudal fins that give this species its name are its most obvious feature. In other respects it resembles the gudgeon, having a long body, roughly rounded in cross section, a flat belly and a gently curving back. The upper side of the body is dusky green and there are eight to ten bluish blotches on each side of the body.

Distribution: South-eastern Europe from Austria eastward to Russia and Kazakhstan.
Habitat: Slow-flowing rivers and shallow lakes.
Food: Aquatic invertebrates.
Size: Up to 12cm/4¾in.
Breeding: The breeding system of this species has not been studied. However, it is thought likely to spawn in open water and not guard its eggs.

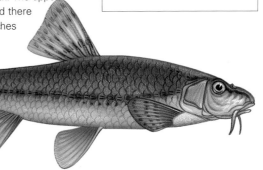

NASE, SOIFFE, ASP AND ZIEGE

These members of the carp family are notable for their relatively plain coloration. Fish of clear, open water, they are silvered to reflect light rather than camouflaged to blend in with vegetation or the river bottom. Most of these fish are entirely herbivorous, apart from the asp and ziege, which are both active hunters.

Nase

Chondrostoma nasus

This fish is also known as the sneep. It is a bottom feeder and a shoaling fish. It is found in swiftly flowing streams and rivers throughout most of continental Europe north of the Alps, ranging from western France to the edge of the Caspian Sea. It tends to be most common in shallow water, especially near the swirls created where water flows past large rocks or the piles of bridges. It lives on algae, which it scrapes from the rocks using the horny lower lip of its underslung mouth, but when not feeding holds its position in the water above the bottom. Schools migrate upstream to spawn in small, fast-running tributaries.

Identification: The body is slender and laterally compressed. It is covered with relatively small scales. These are greenish-grey on the back and lighter on the sides. The belly is silvery in colour. The snout of this fish is fleshy and protrudes from the front of the head. The mouth is small and underslung. The upper lip is soft but the lower lip is hard, with horny tissue forming a cutting edge.

Distribution: Most of Europe between the Alps and the Baltic Sea. Absent from Britain, Ireland, the Iberian Peninsula and Scandinavia.
Habitat: Swift rivers and streams.
Food: Algae.
Size: Up to 50cm/20in.
Breeding: Spawning occurs between February and April (the season starting earliest in the south of its range). The eggs are shed in open water over gravel and left to develop unguarded.

Soiffe

Chondrostoma toxostoma

This fish is about half the size of the nase (*top*) but it resembles it in many other respects. Like the nase, the soiffe is an algae eater, scraping its food from the stones in the small rivers where it lives. It is most common where the current is moderate and the water is clear. In a few places it is also found in lakes. The soiffe is not a rare fish but it is in decline. Water extraction, pollution and hybridization with the nase have all been identified as contributing factors to this. The decline is more serious than it might otherwise be because the range of the soiffe is relatively small. In 2005, the IUCN upgraded the soiffe's status from Lower Risk/Least Concern to Vulnerable.

Identification: The body is slender and laterally compressed. Seen from below, the mouth looks curved. As with the nase, the upper lip is soft but the lower lip is hard, with a relatively sharp edge formed from horny tissue. The head is small and the fleshy snout slightly protruding. The scales are small but there are never more than 56 in the lateral line (the nase has 57–62).

Distribution: Central and southern France and eastern Spain. It is most common in hilly areas.
Habitat: Rivers and streams; also some lakes in mountainous regions.
Food: Algae and occasionally water plants.
Size: Up to 25cm/9¾in.
Breeding: The adults migrate upstream to spawn in spring. The eggs are scattered in open water over gravel and left to develop unguarded.
Status: Vulnerable.

Asp

Aspius aspius

Distribution: From the Baltic states to the Caspian Sea and Iran. Isolated populations live in lakes in southern Sweden.
Habitat: Rivers and, less often, lakes.
Food: Aquatic invertebrates and fish.
Size: Up to 80cm/31½in.
Breeding: Spawns April and May in running water over gravel. The sticky eggs become attached to the river-bed and develop unguarded. They hatch after 2 weeks.

This fish favours open water, inhabiting lakes and the middle reaches of rivers. Young asp feed on aquatic invertebrates and tend to gather in schools for protection, but adult fish are mainly solitary, hunting other fish in mid-water or near the surface. The asp migrates upstream to spawn. Its eggs hatch and the fry then drift downstream, settling in pools of slower-moving water, where they develop and grow. It takes four or five years for an asp to reach sexual maturity and even longer to reach its full size. Most fish grow to 40–60cm/16–23½in long but a few become bigger. The heaviest individuals weigh around 9kg/20lb.

Identification: The body is slender and laterally compressed. There is a sharp keel on the underside between the pelvic fins and the vent. The mouth is large, reaching almost to below the level of the eye. The lower jaw is slightly hooked and reaches farther forward than the upper jaw, fitting into a notch within it when the mouth is closed. The scales are small and the lower fins are red.

Boga (*Chondrostoma polylepis*): Up to 41cm/16in
The boga lives in Portugal and far west Spain. There are two subspecies: *C. polylepis polylepis* occurs in the north-west of the Iberian Peninsula and *C. polylepis wilkommi* is found farther south. The boga lives in fast-flowing mountain streams and rivers. It feeds on algae growing on rocks. It does this in the same way as its close relatives the nase and soiffe, using its horny-edged lower lip.

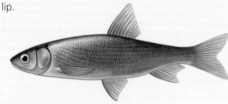

Savetta (*Chondrostoma soetta*): Up to 40cm/16in
The savetta (*above*) is the Italian equivalent of the nase, although this fish has a deeper body and less prominent snout. Like the nase, it is an algae eater. It is found only in the River Po. As well as the main channel and large tributaries, it also lives in alpine lakes along the river's course.

Lasca (*Chondrostoma genei*): Up to 25cm/9¾in
This fish is very closely related to the soiffe and is almost identical in both its habits and appearance, with only minor anatomical differences. The lasca is an exclusively Italian fish. It is most common in the upstream tributaries of the Po but is also found in other rivers in the north of the country. The soiffe, by contrast, is confined to France and Spain.

Ziege

Pelecus cultratus

Distribution: There are two geographically separated populations: one around the Baltic basin of Poland, southern Sweden, Finland and the Baltic states; the other in the Danube and other tributaries of the Black and Caspian Seas.
Habitat: Rivers, estuaries and lakes.
Food: Aquatic invertebrates and small fish.
Size: Up to 60cm/23½in.
Breeding: Spawning occurs from May until July. The eggs are scattered in open water near the surface and left to develop unguarded.

The shape of the ziege's body and its exceptionally wavy lateral line make it quite unmistakable. The adults live in brackish lakes, estuaries and the lowest reaches of rivers but they migrate farther upstream into fresh water to spawn. Young ziege eat tiny crustaceans which they snap up from the water column. As they grow they move downstream and their diet alters to include larger prey. Adult ziege can grow fairly large and feed on other fish, particularly small schooling species which they catch near the surface. The ziege is the only living member of its genus. It is also known by another common name – the sabrefish.

Identification: The body is slender and laterally compressed with the back almost straight and the underside strongly curved. The mouth points upwards at such an angle that it appears almost vertical. The dorsal fin is small and set quite far back. The anal fin is much larger and has a strong concave curve to its outer edge. The lower lobe of the caudal fin is usually longer than the upper.

BREAMS AND BLEAKS

These members of the carp family tend to be found in running water, particularly the lower reaches of rivers. They all feed on small prey and some are an important food source for larger fish. Although most of these species feed in relatively deep open water, they tend to spawn in the shallows, usually where the bottom is covered with weeds.

Bream

Abramis brama

Identification: This fish has flat sides and a high, arched back. Its head is small with a mouth that can extend to become tubular. The head is scaleless but the body is covered with many small scales. The back is grey or dark brown and the flanks more golden brown. The fins are greyish-brown: those on the underside are tinted with red.

The bream is a schooling fish that spends the day in deep water. At night it moves into the shallows to feed. Like many members of the carp family this fish is a bottom feeder, eating insect larvae, crustaceans, worms and other small invertebrates. It catches its food by sucking it up from the bottom, using its down-turned, tubular mouth. Despite the size of its prey it can grow into quite a large fish – the biggest may weigh as much as 9kg/20lb. It is found throughout much of Europe and is popular with anglers. Bream spawn in shallow water amongst dense vegetation, mostly at night.

Distribution: Native range extends from Wales eastwards to the Ural Mountains and from the northern Baltic to the Alps. Widely introduced elsewhere, including Scotland and Ireland.
Habitat: Lakes and deep, slow-flowing rivers.
Food: Aquatic invertebrates.
Size: Up to 80cm/31½in.
Breeding: Spawns late spring and early summer. Yellowish sticky eggs adhere to stems and leaves and are left to develop unguarded.

Zope

Abramis ballerus

Identification: The body is laterally compressed but not especially deep. The head is small and the eyes moderate in size. The anal fin is quite long, reaching from just behind the centre of the belly to near the base of the tail. The caudal fin's lower lobe is longer than the upper. The back is deep turquoise and the flanks are silvery with a golden sheen on their upper part.

The zope is a close relative of the bream and resembles it in many respects, although the zope is smaller. It also tends to be lighter in colour. Like the bream, the zope is a schooling fish but it finds most of its food in open water. It feeds mainly on tiny swimming crustaceans and other planktonic creatures, although it also occasionally snaps up insect larvae from the leaves of water plants. In cold weather this fish gathers near the bottom but generally it is found swimming higher up in the water column. The zope migrates to spawn, moving to areas of shallower water, with vegetation.

Distribution: Basins of the Danube and Volga Rivers. Also found in rivers flowing into the Baltic Sea, but is less common in these.
Habitat: Flood plain lakes and slow-flowing rivers.
Food: Aquatic invertebrates.
Size: Up to 41cm/16in.
Breeding: Spawning occurs April and May. Lake dwellers move to thickly vegetated shallows; river fish swim upstream to shallow waters with vegetation and gravel. Eggs develop unguarded.

Silver bream

Blicca bjoerkna

Although it belongs to a different genus and is smaller, this fish closely resembles the bream in shape, hence its common name. In feeding habits it lies somewhere between the bream and the zope, eating planktonic creatures in open water but also searching for larger invertebrates on the bottom. The silver bream is a schooling fish like its namesake. It may reach weights of up to 1kg/2⅓lb but is usually smaller. Its size has made it unpopular with commercial fishermen, who complain that it competes for food with larger, more profitable freshwater fish. This fish is also known as the white bream or flat bream. In the Danube it has been known to hybridize with the zährte.

Distribution: Widely distributed throughout Europe from eastern England to the Caspian Sea, between the Baltic states and the Alps.
Habitat: Large rivers.
Food: Aquatic invertebrates.
Size: Up to 36cm/14in.
Breeding: Spawning occurs in small schools in summer. The eggs are shed among water plants and will stick to their leaves. They are left to develop unguarded.

Identification: The body is predominantly brilliant silver in colour, although the top of the back is usually light olive-brown. The pectoral and pelvic fins are orange with grey tips; all of the other fins are dusky. The body shape is similar to that of the bream but the scales are larger and the mouth is not tubular. The head is small and, as with other cyprinids, scaleless.

Danubian bream (*Abramis sapa*):
Up to 30cm/12in
This fish is similar in shape to the zope but has a more rounded snout and a slightly smaller mouth. The Danubian bream is a bottom feeder, eating invertebrates such as midge larvae and small molluscs. It is a schooling fish and is found in the lower reaches of the Danube basin and other rivers flowing into the Black Sea, as well as rivers that feed the Caspian and Aral Seas.

Danubian bleak (*Chalcalburnus chalcoides*):
Up to 30cm/12in
Despite its name, this fish (*above*) belongs to a different genus than the bleak. It is also bigger and darker. It is found in the basins of most rivers flowing into the Black and Caspian Seas, including the Danube. It is also found in several Austrian subalpine lakes. This species spawns in the mouths of streams that empty into these lakes. River-dwelling shoals migrate upstream to spawn in shallow water over gravel.

Alborella (*Alburnus albidus*):
Up to 20cm/8in
The alborella is a close relative of the bleak, which it resembles; it differs only subtly, with a shorter anal fin and fewer scales. Like its cousin it is a schooling fish that feeds mainly on plankton. It is found only in northern Italy and the Adriatic-draining rivers of the Balkans.

Bleak

Alburnus alburnus

The bleak is a relatively small shoaling fish. It is often found in turbid waters and slow-moving reaches of rivers where there is little oxygen. It is also found in clear waters in some lakes and streams. It feeds on planktonic animals in the water column. It also takes advantage of its upward-pointing mouth to take flying insects that land on the surface. Shoals often spend much of their time near the surface during the day and head down into deeper waters at night. Because of its size, the bleak is not really sought after by anglers. Nevertheless, it is frequently caught, being quicker than many other fish to take bait in open water. Despite its ability to tolerate low oxygen levels, it is very sensitive to pollution and has declined in many European rivers as a result.

Distribution: Found throughout most of Europe apart from the Iberian Peninsula. It is native to eastern England and has been introduced into some rivers in the west.
Habitat: Lakes, rivers and, occasionally, streams.
Food: Aquatic invertebrates.
Size: Up to 20cm/8in.
Breeding: Spawning occurs in shallow water during May and June. The eggs are scattered, often over weeds, and are left to develop unguarded.

Identification: A relatively shallow, slender body. The head is slightly pointed with the opening of the mouth on its upper side. The eyes are large and the lateral line clearly visible. The scales are quite big, but are thin and fragile, and are easily dislodged. The back and upper flanks are turquoise in colour and the underside is white.

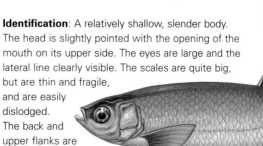

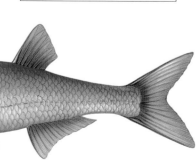

OTHER CYPRINIDS AND TOOTHCARPS

Three of these fish, the sunbleak, schneider and zährte, belong to the carp family. The rest all belong to another family, the toothcarps or Cyprinodontidae, which translates as 'carp teeth'. Apart from their dentition, toothcarps have little in common with cyprinids. They are small fish and tend to be found in places where few other freshwater fish could survive.

Sunbleak

Leucaspius delineatus

Identification: The body is small and slender, and the head is relatively large. The scales are large but thin and are easily detached. The eyes are large and the mouth points slightly upward. The anal fin is longer at the base than the dorsal fin and is set farther back. The back is olive in colour and the flanks and belly are silver. An extremely bright blue-silver strip runs along each side of the body.

The sunbleak is a small schooling fish found in still or slow-moving waters, usually in or around weeds. The schools it forms can be quite large and are at their most numerous in autumn, boosted by the year's surviving youngsters. As winter approaches, these schools, now depleted by predators, break up and the fish, previously most common near the surface, head into deeper waters. The sunbleak is also known as the white aspe or belica. It feeds mainly on planktonic creatures and other small invertebrates. Occasionally it takes insects from the surface. Unusually for a cyprinid, it guards its eggs. The female lays her eggs on the stem of a water plant. Once he has fertilized them, the male watches over the eggs and keeps them oxygenated by nudging the plant to move them through the water.

Distribution: Common throughout continental Europe north of the Alps. Also found in central Asia.
Habitat: Shallow lakes and pools, canals and slow-flowing rivers.
Food: Aquatic invertebrates and, occasionally, flying insects.
Size: Up to 12cm/4¾in.
Breeding: Spawning occurs April until July. The female lays a sticky string of eggs on a water plant. These are guarded by the male.

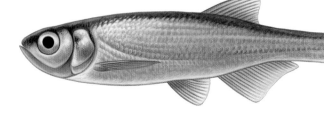

Schneider

Alburnoides bipunctatus

Identification: The eyes of this fish are rather large, as is the mouth, opening at the tip of the snout and extending back to beneath the eye. The scales are small and the lateral line clearly visible, curving downwards towards the belly before rising back up again to the base of the tail. The anal fin has a concave outer edge and is longer at the base than the dorsal fin.

The carp family is usually associated with still or slow-moving waters but the schneider is an exception to this rule. It prefers the swifter waters of small rivers and streams, and is often found living alongside trout and minnows. Where it is found in slower waters it tends to be uncommon. The schneider is a schooling fish that feeds both on the bottom and in open water. Much of its prey is made up of insect larvae but it also eats crustaceans, such as freshwater shrimps, and flying insects that fall into the water. In North America, where it is sometimes kept as an aquarium fish, the schneider is known as the chub. In reality it is only distantly related to the true chub (*Leuciscus cephalus*). It also goes by the common name of spirlin.

Distribution: Ranges throughout most of continental Europe apart from Scandinavia and the Iberian Peninsula. Also found in Iran, Turkmenistan, Afghanistan and Uzbekistan.
Habitat: Rivers and streams.
Food: Aquatic invertebrates and insects that fall into the water.
Size: Up to 15cm/6in.
Breeding: Spawning occurs in May and June over sand or gravel. The eggs adhere to the bottom and are left to develop unguarded.

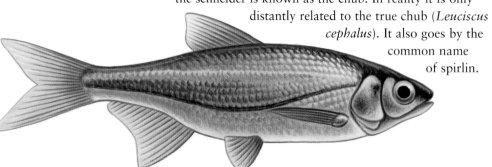

Zährte

Vimba vimba

Distribution: Sweden to Iran: rivers flowing into the Baltic, Black and Caspian Seas.
Habitat: Rivers.
Food: Plant matter, algae and aquatic invertebrates.
Size: Up to 50cm/20in.
Breeding: Migrates upstream to spawn in shallow water from May to July. Eggs are shed over gravel and left to develop unguarded. Dams and weirs in parts of range have affected migrations and, hence, ability to reproduce.

The zährte is a bottom-feeding, schooling fish found in the middle and lower reaches of rivers. It tolerates brackish water and is often found in river mouths at the edge of the sea. It occurs in two distinct populations: one inhabits the rivers that feed the Baltic Sea and the other is found in rivers feeding the Black and Caspian Seas. The Baltic population has become sparse in recent decades, particularly in Poland, southern Sweden and Germany. Elsewhere the zährte is relatively stable. It is most studied and best known from the Danube River system. It is an unfussy feeder, eating both aquatic invertebrates and plant matter.

Identification: A protruding, fleshy snout and an underslung mouth. The anal fin is much longer at the base than the dorsal fin and both have a concave outer edge. The leading edge of the anal fin begins slightly behind the rear edge of the dorsal fin. The scales are small and are absent from the small keel, which stretches from the rear edge of the anal fin to the base of the caudal fin.

Spanish toothcarp (*Aphanius iberus*):
Up to 5cm/2in
This fish occurs where the Mediterranean toothcarp does not – southern coastal Spain and north Morocco. Its small range means that it is much more threatened, and the IUCN lists it as Endangered. It has larger eyes, a flatter head and a bigger caudal fin than its relative. Males have 15 pale blue bars on each flank.

Valencia toothcarp (*Valencia hispanica*):
Up to 8cm/3¼in
This species (*above*) is found only in Valencia and Cataluña in north-eastern Spain. It has lost much of its natural habitat (coastal marshes and streams) to developers and is threatened by pollution and introduced predators. The IUCN upgraded it from Endangered to Critically Endangered in 2005, after an 80 per cent drop in numbers over the previous decade.

Greek toothcarp (*Valencia letourneuxi*):
Up to 5cm/2in
This species shares its range with the Mediterranean toothcarp – coastal regions of Albania and north-western Greece. It is found in marshy pools and drainage ditches, usually over silt and amongst thick vegetation. It is able to tolerate low oxygen levels and in some of the places it inhabits it may be the only fish. It is listed as Critically Endangered by the IUCN.

Mediterranean toothcarp

Aphanius fasciatus

This little fish belongs to the same family as the pupfish of North America. Like them, it is short-lived and able to tolerate high levels of salt. It tends to be found in brackish lagoons, swamps, ponds and ditches, particularly where there is abundant vegetation. It has also become common in the Suez Canal. It feeds on both aquatic invertebrates and plant matter. This species is found throughout the coastal regions of Europe's Mediterranean countries, excluding Spain. It is also widespread in north Africa, from Egypt to eastern Algeria, and is found on many islands in the Mediterranean Sea. In Europe the Mediterranean toothcarp has become scarce as a result of coastal development, but elsewhere it thrives.

Identification: Small and rather dumpy in shape, being broad across both the head and back. The dorsal and anal fins are positioned well back on the body and are relatively long at the base. The caudal fin is rounded. The back is brownish-green, the flanks bronze and the belly yellow. Males have between 10 and 15 brownish bars running down each flank.

Distribution: From southern France right around the Mediterranean to Algeria. Also occurs on many islands.
Habitat: Swamps, ditches, lagoons and other areas of still or very slow-flowing water.
Food: Algae, plant matter and aquatic invertebrates.
Size: Up to 6cm/2½in.
Breeding: Spawning occurs in dense vegetation from April until September. The eggs are scattered and left to develop unguarded.

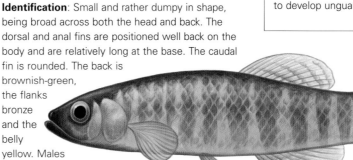

PERCH, ZANDER, RUFFE AND RELATIVES

With its large, distinctive dorsal fins, the perch is one of the most familiar of Europe's freshwater fish.
It is also the one that gives its name to the family to which all of the fish on these pages belong,
Percidae. All of the fish in this family are predatory but most eat relatively small creatures.
The zander, however, is a large and formidable hunter of other fish.

Perch

Perca fluviatilis

Identification: The body is usually slender and the head quite short (making up about a quarter of the total length). There are two dorsal fins; the first has spines protruding from its upper edge. The pelvic fins are set close together and each has a spine on its leading edge. The back is greenish-brown and there are dark vertical bars on the sides. The underside fins are deep orange.

The perch is widespread within northern Eurasia, with a range extending from Ireland as far eastward as Siberia. It is naturally a fish of lowland lakes and slow-flowing rivers but has been widely introduced into other areas of still fresh water. Young perch feed on planktonic creatures and form shoals for protection from predators, but as they grow older they become more solitary. Adult perch hunt small fish, including other members of their own kind. They also eat insect larvae and other invertebrates. The perch is a popular fish with anglers. It rarely exceeds 2kg/4½lb in weight but occasionally may reach up to 4.75kg/10½lb. It is relatively long-lived, sometimes reaching 22 years of age.

Distribution: Most of Europe north of the Alps and Pyrenees. Also occurs throughout much of Russia.
Habitat: Lakes and rivers.
Food: Young: plankton; adults: aquatic invertebrates and small fish.
Size: Up to 51cm/20in.
Breeding: Spawning occurs in April and May in shallow water. Strings of eggs are laid and woven around aquatic plants. They are left to develop unguarded.

Zander

Stizostedion lucioperca

Identification: The body is long and slender and the head rather pointed. The mouth is large and filled with many small, sharp teeth. There are several longer fangs at the front. The two dorsal fins are clearly separated. The front fin, like that of the perch, has spines emerging from its top edge. The anal fin is about half as long at the base as the second dorsal fin.

This large, streamlined fish is a solitary predator, hunting other fish in large rivers and lakes. It tends to be more common in cloudy waters than clear ones and is most active around dawn and dusk. It lives and hunts in open water and tends to avoid the weed beds favoured by other predators, such as the pike. Larvae feed on tiny planktonic creatures but move on to larger invertebrates and small fish as they grow older. This fish was introduced into England in the 1960s and has since spread, possibly to the detriment of native fish. Like the pike it is a favourite target of experienced anglers. Large zander can weigh as much as 19kg/42lb.

Distribution: Native to parts of Sweden and Finland, eastern Europe and western Asia. Introduced into English rivers, lakes and canals.
Habitat: Lakes, rivers and canals.
Food: Aquatic invertebrates and fish.
Size: Up to 1.3m/4¼ft.
Breeding: Spawning occurs from April until June. The eggs are scattered over stones or vegetation and left to develop unguarded.

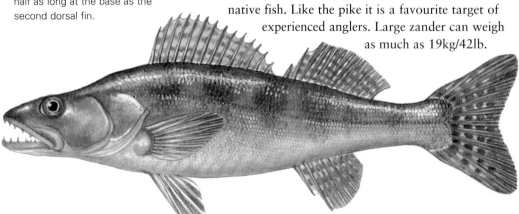

Ruffe

Gymnocephalus cernuus

Distribution: Native to most of Europe north of the Alps. Occurs through Russia and central Asia as far as China. Introduced to Scotland and North America.
Habitat: Lakes and slow rivers.
Food: Aquatic invertebrates and fish eggs.
Size: Up to 30cm/12in.
Breeding: Spawning occurs from March until May. The sticky eggs are scattered over plants or stones and left to develop unguarded.

This is a schooling fish of slow and still waters, usually over soft mud. It only occurs naturally where the flow is very gentle. It feeds mainly on aquatic invertebrates, which it snaps up from the bottom, both during the day and at night. Bloodworms (midge larvae) make up the bulk of its diet but it also eats other insect larvae and, sometimes, fish eggs. It is widespread in continental Europe and western Asia, but in Britain it is native only to eastern England. It has been introduced to Scotland and parts of North America. In the Great Lakes of the latter it has become a pest, out-competing local fish for food. It is a prolific breeder, which has made it impossible to eradicate where it has been introduced, accidentally or otherwise.

Identification: The body form is not a great deal different from that of the perch and is similarly slender. The first and second dorsal fins, however, are fused to form one, long, continuous fin. Another distinguishing feature of this fish are the several large cavities visible beneath the skin of the lower part of the head, lying on the lower gill cover and beneath the jaws.

Volga zander (*Stizostedion volgensis*):
Up to 45cm/17¾in
This fish is very similar in appearance to the zander but is much smaller. It is found in the Volga River, but also occurs in other rivers that flow into the Caspian and Black Seas, including the Danube. The Volga zander has been little studied, although it is known to prefer open water away from vegetation and tends to hunt in the half-light around dawn and dusk.

Asprete (*Romanichthys valsanicola*):
Up to 12cm/4¾in
This fish (*above*) is found only in the Vislan River of Romania. Although unrelated, it resembles the bullhead which shares its small range. It hides beneath stones on the bottom during the day, emerging at night to feed on aquatic invertebrates. Unknown until 1957, the asprete has since become rare and is now listed as Critically Endangered by the IUCN.

Balon's ruffe (*Gymnocephalus baloni*):
Up to 20cm/8in
Balon's ruffe is found only in the Danube basin. A schooling fish, it lives mainly in slow-flowing waters but is also found in smaller numbers in some of the faster flowing tributaries of the Danube. It resembles the ruffe, but is darker and has a higher, more triangular shaped first dorsal fin (which runs into the second dorsal fin).

Schraetzer

Gymnocephalus schraetzer

This fish is similar to the ruffe in its habits but is more slender-bodied and far less widespread. It is native only to the Danube River basin. Like many other fish from here, it is becoming much rarer, having declined as pollution and heavy shipping have altered its habitat. It is listed as Vulnerable by the IUCN. It is a schooling fish of relatively deep flowing water and is usually found over sand or gravel. It feeds on the bottom on insect larvae and other invertebrates, being most active during the dawn, dusk and at night. This fish is also known as the striped ruffe or, sometimes in the USA, the striped ersh.

Identification: The head is similar in shape to that of the ruffe but is slightly more pointed and lacks the pits beneath the skin. The body is also more slender and is marked on each side by three or four dark brown, broken horizontal stripes. As with the ruffe, the first and second dorsal fins are fused together.

Distribution: Confined to the Danube basin, occurring in Austria, Bulgaria, the Czech Republic, Germany, Hungary, Romania, Ukraine and parts of the former Yugoslavia.
Habitat: Rivers.
Food: Aquatic invertebrates and fish eggs.
Size: Up to 30cm/12in.
Breeding: Spawning occurs over sand or gravel during April and May. Each female sheds up to 10,000 eggs, which are fertilized and left to develop unguarded.
Status: Vulnerable.

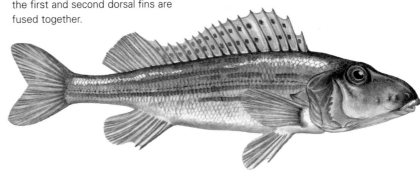

PIKE, GRAYLING, EEL AND FRESHWATER BLENNY

Apart from the zingel and strebers, which belong to the perch family, all these fish have the distinction of being the sole representatives of their families in Europe's freshwater habitats. Their shapes vary greatly, reflecting their different homes and habits, as well as the great versatility of the general fish body form.

Pike

Esox lucius

The pike is the archetypal freshwater predator. Its huge mouth and long, streamlined, yet powerful body mark it out as a hunter, and it is very good at what it does. It catches other fish unawares, holding its position in the water column amongst weeds so that it blends in with the background. As soon as its prey swims into range it strikes, darting out from cover to snap it up. The pike can reach quite an impressive size. Females may grow to as much as 1.3m/4¼ft long and weigh up to 24kg/53lb. The males are significantly smaller, rarely exceeding 69cm/2¼ft long. The pike is one of the most widespread fish in the northern hemisphere and also occurs in North America, where it is known as the northern pike.

Identification: The body is long and muscular and the mouth very large. The lower jaws contain several massive fangs while the palate has hundreds of much smaller sharp teeth. Seen from the side, the head is pointed. From above, the snout appears flat. The dorsal and anal fins lie very far back on the body, which is greenish-brown on the back and green on the flanks. Patterning varies between individuals.

Distribution: Throughout Europe (north of the Alps and Pyrenees) and northern Asia, from Ireland to eastern Siberia. Also found Canada, northern states of the USA.
Habitat: Lakes, canals and slow-flowing rivers.
Food: Fish, amphibians, small mammals and water birds.
Size: Up to 1.3m/4¼ft.
Breeding: Spawns early spring. Females may spawn with more than one male. Eggs are shed over water plants and develop unguarded.

Grayling

Thymallus thymallus

Identification: The most striking feature of this fish is its flag-like dorsal fin, which is particularly large in the males. The other fins are relatively small and unspectacular. There is an adipose fin present. The head is quite small and the snout rather pointed, with the mouth on its underside. The greenish-brown to steel blue body is covered with moderately large scales.

This is a shoaling fish of cool, clean, well-oxygenated rivers and lakes. It feeds on invertebrates that live on the bottom as well as insects that fall into the water. Some authorities classify the grayling as a salmonid, putting it in the same family as salmon and trout. Most, however, give it and its close relatives a family of their own, Thymallidae. Indeed, its appearance more closely resembles some cyprinid fish rather than trout or salmon. The grayling has quite a wide natural distribution but its range has been extended by anglers. Unlike many fish caught by anglers, the grayling is often eaten and its flesh is said to have an excellent flavour.

Distribution: Found naturally from Wales to as far east as the Ural Mountains and from southern Sweden south to France. Introduced elsewhere.
Habitat: Lakes and rivers.
Food: Invertebrates.
Size: Up to 50cm/20in.
Breeding: Spawning occurs in pairs from March until May. The eggs are shed into a shallow depression dug by the female in sand or gravel and are left to develop unguarded.

Eel

Anguilla anguilla

Distribution: Coastal regions of Europe from Iceland to the Mediterranean. Also found in north Africa as far west as Morocco.
Habitat: Lakes, rivers and the ocean.
Food: Bottom-dwelling invertebrates and carrion.
Size: Up to 1m/3¼ft.
Breeding: Adults migrate downstream and breed in the ocean (Sargasso Sea). Newly-hatched larvae then drift slowly back to Europe with the Gulf Stream.

With its long, sinuous body, the eel looks more like a snake than a fish. Since it sometimes comes out of the water in wet weather to travel short distances over land, it might even occasionally be confused for one. The eel is remarkable in its behaviour as well as its appearance. Although it spends most of its life in fresh water, it spawns in the Sargasso Sea, on the far side of the Atlantic Ocean. The young then make their way back to Europe's fresh waters, entering rivers as young, transparent 'glass eels' and migrating upstream. As they travel they grow darker (then called 'elvers'). They then spend anything from 6 to 20 years growing to sexual maturity before heading downstream and into the ocean to begin the cycle again.

Identification: The body is extremely long and snake-like. The head is small and the mouth quite large, with the lower jaw longer than the upper. The gill slit is small and positioned directly in front of the pectoral fin. The dorsal fin begins about a third of the way along the back, reaching down and joining the caudal fin. The anal fin begins farther back but also reaches and joins with the caudal fin.

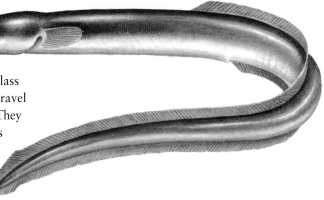

Streber (*Zingel streber*):
Up to 22cm/8¾in
This fish is a smaller relative of the zingel and has a similar distribution, being found in the tributaries of the Danube and other rivers in Bulgaria. The streber tends to be found in smaller rivers and streams than the zingel. It spends the day in the shallows and moves to deeper midstream waters at night to hunt for aquatic invertebrates. It is listed as Vulnerable by the IUCN.

Zingel (*Zingel zingel*): Up to 40cm/16in
The zingel (*above*) occurs in the Danube, Prut and Dnestr River systems of south-eastern Europe. Slightly bulkier than the streber, it has similar habits, hunting aquatic invertebrates in shallow water at night. Although less rare than either of the streber species, it too has suffered from modification and pollution of its habitat. It is listed as Vulnerable by the IUCN.

Rhône streber (*Zingel asper*):
Up to 20cm/8in
Like its namesake from farther east, the Rhône streber is a very slender-bodied fish. Its shape is an adaptation to the relatively fast-flowing waters in which it lives. The Rhône streber mimics the streber in its food habits and behaviour. Damming and other changes to the Rhône have greatly impacted its numbers and it is listed as Critically Endangered by the IUCN.

Freshwater blenny

Salaria fluviatilis

Blennies are generally marine fish, with around 20 species found in Europe's coastal waters. The freshwater blenny, as its name suggests, is an exception. It is found only in lakes and large rivers and never occurs in the sea. It has slender pelvic fins, each with just two rays, which it uses to prop the front part of its body up when at rest. It is most common in areas with rocky bottoms, and it seems to deliberately seek out larger rocks to sit on, apparently to give it a better view of its surroundings. The freshwater blenny is generally solitary and actively hunts invertebrates and, occasionally, smaller fish. Although quite short-lived, it is sometimes kept by freshwater aquarium enthusiasts.

Distribution: Rivers and coastal lakes around the Mediterranean, from Spain and Morocco to Israel.
Habitat: Lakes and rivers.
Food: Aquatic invertebrates and small fish.
Size: Up to 15cm/6in.
Breeding: Spawning occurs from April until June. The female lays her eggs in a small cave beneath a rock, which is then guarded by the male.

Identification: The head slopes steeply up from the snout. The large mouth has fleshy lips and contains two rows of strong teeth, one on each jaw. The teeth near the corners of the mouth are the longest. The dorsal fin is long and large, beginning just behind the head and running to the base of the tail. The pectoral fins are also large. The small pelvic fins are used as props.

GOBIES

Although they have their own family, Gobiidae, gobies resemble blennies in many respects. Like blennies, they have strong, downward-pointing pelvic fins, which they use to prop themselves up. They also have large pectoral fins and eyes set at the top of the head. The main difference between the two groups is that gobies have two dorsal fins, whereas blennies have one.

Lagoon goby

Knipowitschia panizzae

Identification: Although small, this fish has a thickset body. The head is large, the eyes bulging and the lips rather thick. Although there are scales on the sides, these are absent from the front half of the back and are sometimes missing as far back as the rear of the second dorsal fin. As with other gobies, the pelvic fins are joined to form a single body, which is shaped like a sucker.

This little fish lives in both fresh and brackish water, inhabiting the inland lakes of northern Italy and lagoons and estuaries around the Adriatic coast. Like most gobies it is easy to spot but very difficult to catch. When at rest it sits propped up on its modified pelvic fins so that it has an almost panoramic view around it. Well camouflaged, it stays still until it thinks it has been spotted. It then darts off a metre or two before stopping and propping itself up again, keeping its eye on the perceived source of danger. The lagoon goby becomes sexually mature at just one year old and then spawns frequently. Its eggs are laid on the inner surface of an empty cockle shell and then watched over until they hatch, a few days later.

Distribution: Italy, Albania, Greece and parts of the former Yugoslavia.
Habitat: Estuaries, brackish lagoons and freshwater lakes.
Food: Aquatic invertebrates.
Size: Up to 3.7cm/1½in.
Breeding: Breeding occurs from April until August, with females spawning once every couple of weeks.

Tube-nose goby

Proterorhinus marmoratus

Identification: The most obvious feature of this fish is the one that earned it its name – the tube-shaped nostrils. These extend out beyond the end of the snout, overhanging the thick upper lip. The head of this fish is broad and the body rather stout. The second dorsal fin is rather long for a goby: it is mirrored by an anal fin which is about two-thirds as long.

The tube-nose goby is found in the east of Europe and the western part of Central Asia. Like the lagoon goby, it is a fish of both fresh and brackish water, inhabiting the tributary rivers and estuaries of the Black, Caspian and Aral Seas. The tube-nose goby feeds on insect larvae, worms and small crustaceans, which it finds among the stones and beds of algae common in the shallow waters where it lives. Although not at any great risk of extinction, it has become rare in some parts of its range due to pollution and water extraction. This fish breeds at the beginning of summer, with the females laying their eggs in secluded spaces beneath rocks or shells. In common with many other gobies, this species guards its eggs until they hatch.

Distribution: Ranges from the Czech Republic and Austria to Kazakhstan. Also introduced to Germany, Uzbekistan, the USA and Canada.
Habitat: Rivers and estuaries.
Food: Aquatic invertebrates.
Size: Up to 11cm/4⅓in.
Breeding: Spawning occurs during May and June. The eggs are guarded by the male until they hatch.

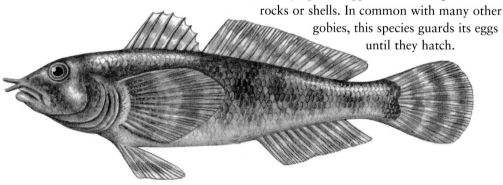

Monkey goby

Neogobius fluviatilis

Distribution: Ranges from Bulgaria to Iran, inhabiting tributaries of the Black and Caspian Seas.
Habitat: The lower reaches of rivers, estuaries and brackish lagoons.
Food: Aquatic invertebrates and small fish.
Size: Up to 20cm/8in.
Breeding: Spawning occurs from May until July. The male guards and protects the eggs from other fish for the 3–4 days they take to hatch.

This fish shares much of its range with the tube-nose goby and in some places can be found living alongside it. However, unlike the tube-nose goby it rarely penetrates far upstream. Instead it is most common in brackish estuary waters and lagoons, over mud or sand. It is particularly abundant in the salt marshes near the mouth of the Danube. Being larger than most gobies, the monkey goby also takes larger prey. The majority of its diet consists of invertebrates but it also occasionally hunts small fish. The monkey goby spawns in early summer. The female lays her small, oval eggs over algae, water plants or stones. They are then watched attentively by the male.

Identification: The body is stout and the head quite pointed. The lips are thick and the rather large eyes are positioned on the top of the head. Ordinarily this fish is sandy brown with darker marbling but during the breeding season the males change colour, becoming a deep blue that in some lights can look black. The rear edge of the caudal fin in breeding males is pale yellow.

Dwarf goby (*Economidichthys trichonis*):
Up to 3cm/1¼in
This fish is found only in small streams running into Lake Trichonis, near the upper reaches of the Acheloos River in Greece. Unlike most gobies, which tend to be solitary, it lives in loose schools. It was only discovered in 1990. With adult females measuring just 1.8cm/¾in long, it is Europe's smallest freshwater fish. Its tiny range and small population means it is listed as Endangered by the IUCN.

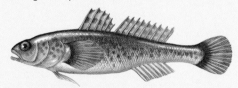

Canestrini's goby (*Pomatoschistus canestrinii*):
Up to 6.7cm/2¾in
Canestrini's goby (*above*) lives in both fresh and brackish waters. It is native to the rivers and estuaries of the northern Adriatic. It feeds on invertebrates. Although it has been known of since 1883, it has been little studied. It is thought to lay its eggs on the underside of rocks or shells, and guard them until they hatch.

Louros goby (*Economidichthys pygmaeus*):
Size: Up to 5.4cm/2¼in.
This fish is found in Lake Trichonis and in the Louros, Arahthos and Vlyho Rivers of western Greece. It is most common in areas where there is abundant vegetation and detritus, which it searches through for invertebrates to feed on. Its body lacks stripes, but there is a dark spot on its first dorsal fin.

Common goby

Pomatoschistus microps

The common goby is a marine fish that enters estuaries and the lower reaches of rivers. It is also found in brackish coastal marshes but tends to spend the winter in deeper waters a little way out to sea. Like most other gobies it is a mainly solitary creature that feeds on aquatic invertebrates, seeking them out between rocks or snapping them up from the muddy bottom. Most people who have seen this fish in the wild have seen it in rock pools, where it is often trapped by the retreating tide. The common goby breeds throughout spring and summer, with females laying their eggs beneath the empty shells of bivalve molluscs, such as mussels. When at rest this goby often burrows into the sediment to avoid predators.

Distribution: Around Britain and along the Atlantic coast of Europe and north-west Africa, from southern Norway to Morocco.
Habitat: Estuaries, brackish marshes and the sea.
Food: Aquatic invertebrates.
Size: Up to 6.5cm/2½in.
Breeding: Spawning occurs from April until August. The female lays her eggs beneath hollow, empty mollusc shells. The male guards them for 9 days or so until they hatch.

Identification: A stout body and a broad head, with thick lips and protruding eyes. The bases of the second dorsal fin and anal fin are of similar lengths, although the former is just slightly longer. Colour varies between individuals from sandy fawn to light grey with a paler underside. Mature males have a dark spot on the first dorsal fin and up to 10 dark vertical bars on each flank.

SHADS, SMELT, THIN-LIPPED GREY MULLET AND SEA BASS

All of the species here are marine fish that enter fresh water. The flounder is a bottom-dwelling fish, but all of the others tend to be found swimming in open water. Some have populations that are entirely land-locked. Some, such as the sea bass, are sought-after game fish or are hunted commercially for food.

Allis shad

Alosa alosa

Identification: The body is flattened and the underside has a greater curve than the back. The belly has a keel made up of sharp, backward-pointing teeth. The head is relatively large and all of the fins, apart from the caudal fin, are small. The back is metallic blue in colour, and the flanks golden, shading into silver. There is usually a dark blotch just behind the gill covers at the same level as the eye.

This fish spends most of its adult life in the sea, only entering large rivers to breed. In spring it gathers at river mouths in shoals which then journey upstream, usually travelling some distance upriver, before spawning at night. They never leave the main channel. Once hatched, the young fish remain in fresh water, moving down to the brackish water of estuaries during autumn. They feed on planktonic crustaceans and other tiny invertebrates living in the water column. Adults eat larger invertebrates and small fish. The Allis shad can grow to a significant size; weights of 2.7kg/6lb are not uncommon. Its size and the fact that it shoals have made it a target for commercial fishermen.

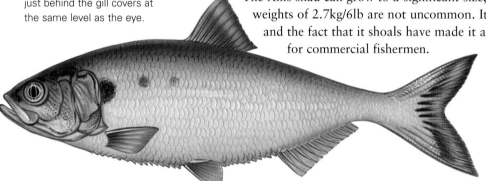

Distribution: Coastal waters from Norway to Morocco, as well as the western Mediterranean. It spawns in the rivers that flow into these areas.
Habitat: Rivers and the sea.
Food: Aquatic invertebrates and small fish.
Size: Up to 60cm/24in.
Breeding: Spawning occurs in May in swift water over gravel. The eggs are shed in open water and left to develop unguarded.

Smelt

Osmerus eperlanus

Identification: The smelt looks not unlike a trout or salmon in its general form but is much smaller. The mouth is relatively large, with the lower jaw longer than the upper. Both jaws contain sharp, backward-pointing teeth: these are larger in the lower jaw. There is an adipose fin. The back is light olive brown and the flanks metallic purple to silver. The underside is white.

In terms of habitat, the smelt is an unusual fish. Some populations are confined to freshwater lakes, which they never leave. Others are marine and only enter fresh water to breed. Like the Allis shad, the smelt is a shoaling fish and one that is caught commercially. Smelt is often smoked before being sold for consumption. It is also used to make fish oil. All smelt tend to spawn over sand banks or gravel. Occasionally they shed their eggs over plants. Once the eggs have hatched (after three to five weeks) the larvae make their way downstream. Rather than entering the sea straight away they spend some time in the brackish waters of estuaries, feeding on planktonic invertebrates, then moving on to shrimps and other larger crustaceans as they grow.

Distribution: Occurs from the west coast of Ireland to the Baltic states. Abundant in parts of the North and Baltic Seas.
Habitat: Lakes, rivers and coastal marine waters.
Food: Aquatic invertebrates and small fish.
Size: Up to 30cm/12in.
Breeding: Spawning occurs late winter and early spring over sand or gravel, and occasionally vegetation. Eggs are shed in open water and left to develop unguarded.

Thin-lipped grey mullet

Liza ramada

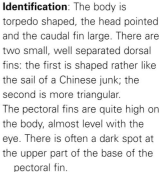

Distribution: Throughout the Black Sea, Mediterranean and western Atlantic as far north as Scotland and southern Sweden.
Habitat: Coastal marine waters, estuaries and rivers.
Food: Algae and aquatic invertebrates.
Size: Up to 60cm/24in.
Breeding: Spawning occurs at sea in coastal waters from September until February. The young then colonize shoreline habitats and estuaries.

The thin-lipped grey mullet is essentially an ocean fish but adults often enter estuaries and the lower reaches of rivers to feed. This species eats a variety of small invertebrates as well as algae, often grazed from pilings sunk into the bottom, such as those used to support jetties. Invertebrates are usually sifted from mud, although they may occasionally be snapped up in open water. Despite the small size of its prey, this can be quite a sizable fish, weighing up to 2.9kg/6½lb. It is a popular game fish among sea anglers. It is also caught commercially and, in some places, farmed as a food fish. In the wild, the thin-lipped grey mullet tends to form small schools, which move slowly as they search for food.

Identification: The body is torpedo shaped, the head pointed and the caudal fin large. There are two small, well separated dorsal fins: the first is shaped rather like the sail of a Chinese junk; the second is more triangular. The pectoral fins are quite high on the body, almost level with the eye. There is often a dark spot at the upper part of the base of the pectoral fin.

Twaite shad (*Alosa fallax*): Up to 55cm/22in
This fish looks similar to the Allis shad but is less deep-bodied and has a distinct notch in its upper jaw. It is a predominantly marine species that enters rivers to breed. There are also land-locked freshwater populations in some Irish and Italian lakes. It feeds on planktonic crustaceans and small fish. It occurs from Iceland and southern Norway to Morocco as well as throughout the Black and Mediterranean Seas.

Flounder (*Pleuronectes flesus*): Up to 51cm/20in
The flounder (*right*) is the only flatfish found in fresh water in

Europe. Large adults live on the bottom of the sea at depths of 25–40m/82–131ft, but young fish enter rivers and migrate upstream, beyond the reach of tidal waters. Flounders found in rivers are rarely more than 20cm/8in long. When over this size, they move downstream and re-enter the sea.

Big-eyed sandsmelt (*Atherina boyeri*): Up to 9cm/3½in
This little fish is best known from populations in brackish lakes and lagoons along the coast of the Mediterranean, but it also occurs in the sea. As well as the Mediterranean it is found near the shore in Atlantic waters, ranging north to the Netherlands and the southern coast of Wales. It forms large, tightly packed shoals for protection.

Sea bass

Dicentrarchus labrax

This large species is probably known to most people in Europe as a food fish. A predominantly marine species, it is fished commercially off the south coast of England and also, in larger numbers, off France, Spain and Italy. It often enters estuaries and is occasionally found quite far up tidal rivers. The young in particular may be found schooling in estuaries, hiding from predators in the murky water and feeding on the shrimps and other crustaceans that are often abundant here. Adults are less gregarious than the young and often search alone for larger invertebrates and fish.

Identification: The body is torpedo-shaped and the head rather large. There are two well separated dorsal fins: the first has eight or nine strong, slender spines and is longer at the base than the second. The anal fin lies almost directly beneath the second dorsal fin and is similar in both shape and size. The mouth is large and the rear edge of the gill cover has two flattened spines.

Distribution: Throughout the Black and Mediterranean Seas and in Atlantic coastal waters from Denmark to north Africa.
Habitat: Coastal marine waters and estuaries.
Food: Aquatic invertebrates and small fish.
Size: Up to 1m/3¼ft.
Breeding: Spawning occurs from March to May in coastal waters. The eggs are buoyant and the larvae tend to head for estuaries soon after hatching.

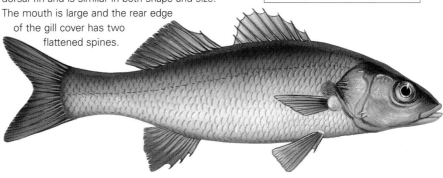

NEWTS, SALAMANDERS AND POND TURTLES

With its northerly position and mainly temperate climate, Europe has fewer amphibian and reptile species than other continents. Of those that do occur, most spend the majority of their time on land. However, the creatures shown here live a predominantly aquatic lifestyle. The olm never leaves the water at all.

Great crested newt

Triturus cristatus

Identification: This newt is most often seen and most easily recognized during the breeding season. The males at this time look like little dragons with a long, ragged crest running along the back from just behind the head to the base of the tail. Both sexes have warty skin and a bright orange underside. This is broken up by a pattern of black markings which varies between individuals.

Sometimes called the warty newt or the northern crested newt, this is one of Europe's most aquatic amphibians. In some parts of its range it rarely leaves the water, although in others it hibernates on land. It is one of Europe's largest newts and among the most widespread. It occurs from Great Britain as far east as the Ural Mountains. In parts of its range (including Britain) it has become rare due to the disturbance and drainage of its natural habitats, but in other places it continues to thrive. At night it hunts for aquatic invertebrates. By day it tends to lie hidden on the bottom or amongst vegetation. Like many amphibians, it can absorb oxygen from the water through its skin.

Distribution: Most of northern Europe north of the Alps, from Britain east to Russia. Absent from Ireland.
Habitat: Large ponds with abundant weeds.
Food: Aquatic invertebrates.
Size: Up to 18cm/7in.
Breeding: The first eggs are laid in early April but breeding may continue until July. Eggs are laid individually and each is wrapped in the leaf of an aquatic plant by the female.

Olm

Proteus anguinus

This bizarre looking amphibian is also known as the cave salamander, white salamander and human fish. It lives in subterranean freshwater habitats, where it feeds on invertebrates. Its natural home is blanketed in perpetual darkness and over millions of years of evolution its eyes have become extremely reduced, leaving it blind. As with many other cave-dwelling creatures, it completely lacks body pigment, having no need for camouflage.

The olm finds its food by sensing chemical cues in the water. It also uses its extremely heightened sense of touch. Adults develop lungs but retain their feathery gills throughout life. During the breeding season, which varies in different areas, the males become highly territorial. This creature is listed as Vulnerable by the IUCN.

Identification: The body is long and the limbs are reduced. The head is flattened and the snout rounded. There are three pairs of small, red, feathery gills. The rest of the body is a very pale and pasty pink, with the skin being translucent enough for the outlines of many of the internal organs to be visible. The eyes are tiny and barely visible. Male olms are smaller than the females.

Distribution: Italy, Slovenia and parts of the former Yugoslavia.
Habitat: Subterranean rivers in limestone formations.
Food: Aquatic invertebrates.
Size: Up to 30cm/12in.
Breeding: Fertilization is internal. Some females then lay up to 70 eggs, which are guarded by both parents. Others carry their eggs inside them, a few hatching as larvae and growing inside the females' bodies, feeding on the unhatched eggs.
Status: Vulnerable.

European pond turtle

Emys orbicularis

Distribution: Spain through southern France and northern Italy to Turkey and Russia.
Habitat: Ponds, lakes, streams, rivers and canals.
Food: Aquatic invertebrates, small fish, amphibians and plant matter.
Size: Carapace up to 23cm/9in long.
Breeding: Mates March to May (later in northern parts of range). Eggs are buried in soil or sand close to the water's edge and develop unguarded.

Sometimes known as the European pond terrapin or the European pond tortoise, this reptile is found in the south and east of the continent, and also in northern Africa and western central Asia. It lives mainly on a diet of invertebrates, small fish and amphibians, but it also eats plant material when prey becomes scarce. The European pond turtle lays eggs from May to June and the sex of the young is influenced by the temperature at which they incubate. Below 28°C/82.5°F only males are produced but if the temperature rises to more than 30°C/86°F for long periods, all the hatchlings are females. In the north of its range this turtle hibernates through the winter, emerging towards the end of March.

Identification: The overall colour varies from olive through darker brown to black. Many individuals have bright yellow or gold speckling across their carapace, a feature that has made this species popular in the pet trade. Individuals from the northern range for this species tend to be larger and darker.

Spanish ribbed newt (*Pleurodeles waltl*):
Up to 30cm/12in
This relatively large amphibian is found only in Portugal, Spain and Morocco, in ponds and other still-water areas. It has pointed ribs that can emerge through specialized tubercles and push through the skin of its sides when it is under attack. This defence mechanism leaves the newt itself unharmed and has led to another common name, the sharp-ribbed newt. This newt is almost entirely aquatic.

Marbled newt (*Triturus marmoratus*):
Up to 17cm/6¾in
With its beautifully patterned skin the marbled newt (*above*) is well named. It lives in western France, Spain and Portugal, just overlapping the western edge of the great crested newt's range. The two species are closely related and where they co-exist they often hybridize. The marbled newt tends to be found in wooded areas. During the breeding season it is entirely aquatic but at other times it may be found out of water.

Pyrenean brook salamander (*Euproctus asper*):
Up to 16cm/6¼in
Found only in the cold mountain streams of the Pyrenees, this amphibian hardly ever leaves the water. By day it hides beneath stones on the bottom, emerging at night to hunt invertebrate prey. It breeds very soon after the snows start to melt. After hatching, the larvae can take as long as two years to develop into adults.

Mediterranean turtle

Mauremys leprosa

This species is also known as the Spanish terrapin. In truth it is neither confined to Spain nor ranges around the Mediterranean. It is actually more widespread in Africa than Europe, occurring from Morocco to Libya and then south as far as Senegal and Niger. It has an omnivorous diet, eating everything from algae and carrion to live fish and other prey. Large adults may even eat the young of their own species. Perhaps as a result, the young tend to be rather shy, spending most of their time hiding amongst rotting leaves and other debris on the bottom. The adults, on the other hand, may often be seen basking in the sun.

Identification: Compared with the European pond turtle, this has a rather flattened carapace. It also has a longer neck, which is marked with yellow stripes. The carapace is tan to olive and the underside of the shell is yellow. Females grow larger than the males, and have wider heads and shorter tails.

Distribution: Ranges from south-western France through Spain to parts of Portugal. Also found in Africa.
Habitat: Ponds, lakes, oases, rivers, streams and canals.
Food: Plant matter, carrion, invertebrates, fish and other small animals.
Size: Carapace up to 18cm/7in long.
Breeding: Mates March to April. After 2 months females emerge from the water to lay eggs in shallow nests dug in sand or between tree roots. Eggs develop unguarded.

ASIA & OCEANIA

The world's largest continent, Asia is home to a wealth of aquatic animals. Among them are some of the biggest freshwater fish on the planet. Most of the big species are found in the continent's rivers, some of which stretch inland for thousands of miles. The names of Asia's largest rivers are familiar but exotic to most of us, names such as Ganges, Indus, Mekong and Yangtse. Many of the fish they contain also appear familiar but exotic to Europeans. Linked to Europe by land, Asia shares some species and several fish families with its western neighbours.

Dominated by Australia, Oceania has far less variety when it comes to freshwater fish. Much of Australia itself is desert: its longest river is the Murray, which rises in the Snowy Mountains of South Australia and is approximately 2,520 km (1,566 miles) in length. The lack of diversity in freshwater life has resulted in the introduction of a number of freshwater species from Europe and Asia. However, the isolation of Oceania from the rest of the world's land masses has also given rise to some unique freshwater life. Its creatures have evolved along their own lines, in the same way as have Australia's marsupials and New Zealand's flightless birds.

*Above, left to right: Bumblebee goby (*Brachygobius doriae*); Ceylon killifish (*Aplocheilus dayi*);*
*Indo-Pacific hump-backed dolphin (*Sousa chinensis*).*
Right: Map of Asia and Oceania, showing main freshwater routes and bodies of water.

SHARK, SAWFISH, RAYS AND EELS

Sharks, sawfish and rays are cartilaginous fish. The Ganges shark is one of six members of its genus, all of which inhabit rivers. Three of the other species are found in Australia, a fourth is found in Myanmar (Burma) and the fifth in Borneo. All are very little known. The three eels featured here each belong to different families. Only the shortfin eel is a true eel, from the family Anguillidae.

Ganges shark

Glyphis gangeticus

The Ganges River is one of the few rivers in the world to have its own species of shark. This is a formidable fish. In size it is rivalled only by the bull shark (*Carcharhinus leucas*), also found in the Ganges, the goonch and tapah and Ganges river dolphin. Like most sharks it is a predator that also eats carrion. Its main prey is fish. It has been claimed that it attacks humans, although most attacks seem more likely to have been carried out by bull sharks, which hunt larger prey and are more aggressive. This shark has become rare as heavy fishing has depleted its natural prey and the IUCN lists it as Critically Endangered.

Identification: The eyes of this species are extremely small, suggesting that it relies on smell and other senses to find its prey. The first dorsal fin is large and triangular, and there is a second, smaller dorsal fin close to the tail. The pectoral fins are long, as is the upper lobe of the caudal fin. The head is very pointed and the body highly streamlined. There are five gill slits.

Distribution: Known only from the Hooghly-Ganges River system. Reports of it from the Indus River have not been confirmed.
Habitat: Rivers.
Food: Fish and other vertebrates.
Size: Up to 2m/6½ft.
Breeding: Breeding has never been observed in this species. However, it is known to give birth to live young rather than producing eggs or mermaid's purses.
Status: Critically Endangered.

Small-tooth sawfish

Pristis pectinata

Identification: The long flattened snout makes the fish hard to confuse with any other. As its name suggests, it has much smaller teeth on its snout than the large-tooth sawfish (*Pristis perotteti*). It also has more of them – between 50 and 64, as opposed to the maximum of 42 found on the large-tooth sawfish. The large-tooth does not occur in Asian or Australian waters.

This large and unmistakable fish mainly occurs in coastal marine waters, but it also enters estuaries, lagoons and rivers. The small-tooth sawfish looks rather like a cross between a ray and a shark. The underside of its body is flattened, like that of a ray, but it has triangular dorsal fins and moves by sweeping its tail from side to side. It searches for its bottom-dwelling prey with a sideways swipe of its tooth-edged snout. Widespread in coastal regions of southern Asia, the small-tooth sawfish is also found around Arabia, most of Africa and in the Caribbean Sea. In the far north of its western Atlantic range it occurs up the eastern seaboard of the USA, as far as Virginia.

Distribution: Throughout most of southern Asia, including Indonesia. Also found in northern Australia.
Habitat: Coastal waters, estuaries, lagoons and rivers.
Food: Fish.
Size: Up to 7.5m/24½ft.
Breeding: Females give birth to 15–20 live young. In some places, this species has been observed entering estuaries to pup. Normally it gives birth at sea.

Swamp eel

Monopterus albus

Distribution: India, China and most of South-east Asia, including Japan and Indonesia.
Habitat: Swamps, ponds, paddy fields, ditches, canals and slow-flowing streams.
Food: Large aquatic invertebrates, fish and amphibians.
Size: Up to 1m/3¼ft.
Breeding: Spawning occurs in shallow water. The male builds a bubble nest in vegetation and guards both the eggs and larvae.

With its long, sinuous body and slimy skin, the swamp eel might not appear to be the most appetizing of fish. Nevertheless, it is highly prized as a food fish in China, so much so that Chinese emigrants have often taken it with them when they have moved overseas. This process may have introduced the swamp eel into Hawaii, where it is now considered a pest. In its native Asia, it is found in a variety of still and slow-moving freshwater habitats. It is more tolerant of polluted water and low oxygen levels than many other fish, and it can even gulp air, enabling it to travel short distances over land. Despite its name, the swamp eel is not related to true eels at all; it belongs to the family Synbranchidae. Swamp eel larvae may change sex and become males as they grow older.

Identification: The long, snake-like body is rounded in cross-section and completely lacks scales. The head is quite large and the snout blunt. The eyes are small. The fins are greatly reduced, so much so as to be virtually non-existent. There is a single v-shaped gill opening on the underside of the throat but no gill openings on the side of the head, like on most other fish.

Cowtail stingray (*Pastinachus sephen*):
Up to 1.83m/6ft across
This stingray is a marine fish of coastal waters, but it is also found in estuaries and occasionally ventures into fresh water farther upstream. It lives right around the Indian Ocean and in parts of the western Pacific. It feeds on fish and invertebrates on the bottom. Like some other rays, it can detect its prey even when it is hidden beneath the sand, by picking up subtle electrical pulses.

Zig-zag eel
(*Mastacembelus armatus*): Up to 90cm/35½in
This fish (*right*), often called the tire-track eel in North America, is a popular aquarium species. It belongs to the spiny eel family, Mastacembelidae, and occurs from Pakistan to Indonesia, in rivers, streams and marshes. By day it usually lies still on the bottom, becoming active only as dusk falls. It feeds mainly on aquatic invertebrates but it also occasionally eats plant matter.

Freshwater whipray (*Himantura chaophraya*):
Up to 2.4m/7¾ft across
This fish is also known as the giant freshwater stingray – it may grow to 5m/16½ft long. Despite its great size, it is rarely seen and so is little known. It is thought to occur in large rivers and estuaries in Australia's tropical north, as well as in New Guinea, Borneo and parts of Thailand. It holds a venomous sting on its whip-like tail.

Shortfin eel

Anguilla australis

The shortfin and the longfin eel (*Anguilla dieffenbachii*) are the antipodean equivalents of the European eel, to which they are closely related. The shortfin eel is the more common and widespread. Like the European eel, both species live in fresh water but breed in the sea, migrating out into the Pacific. Their leaf-shaped larvae (leptocephali), drift back to the coastal waters of New Caledonia, New Zealand and Australia with the prevailing ocean currents. There they change into glass eels and make their way upstream. Females may reach 35 years of age before they enter the ocean to breed. The males, which are smaller, migrate when they are younger. Both sexes are thought to die at sea.

Distribution: Found in New Zealand, New Caledonia and the eastern coastal regions of Australia.
Habitat: Lakes, swamps, streams and the sea.
Food: Aquatic invertebrates, fish and, occasionally, plant matter.
Size: Up to 1.3m/4ft.
Breeding: Adults move downstream to spawn at sea. Their exact spawning grounds are unknown.

Identification: The body is long and sinuous and the head rather small. The mouth extends back to just beyond the eyes. The dorsal and anal fins are of roughly equal length and meet at the tail, where they join. Colour can vary significantly between individuals, ranging from yellowish to dark olive brown. The underside, however, is always paler and usually silvery, hence this fish's other common name, the silver eel.

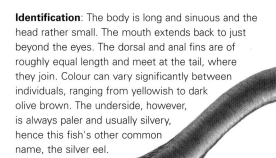

LUNGFISH, GARFISH, GUDGEON, SCULPIN, HALFBEAK AND GOBIES

The fish on these pages occupy a variety of niches. The position a fish occupies in the water column infuences its shape more than where it occurs. The slimy sculpin and bumblebee goby, for instance, are similarly shaped, even though one lives at the equator and the other at the edge of the Arctic Circle.

Australian lungfish

Neoceratodus forsteri

Identification: The long, heavy body is covered with large scales. The mouth is large and the forehead sloping. The snout is slightly pointed and the eyes are small. The pectoral and pelvic fins of this fish are paddle-like and have fleshy bases. The dorsal fin begins around halfway along the back and runs to the tail, where it merges with the caudal fin.

All lungfish look primeval but the Australian lungfish could almost be the missing link between fish and amphibians. Although it is a modern species, it resembles the lobe-finned fish that are thought to have given rise to the first land vertebrates. Like the primeval fish it has large, fleshy fins where an amphibian's legs would be. In addition, of course, it can breathe air. It is an extremely long-lived species. One individual, kept in Queensland's Shedd Aquarium, reached 82 years of age in 2007, making it possibly the world's oldest captive fish. Unlike some other lungfish it is unable to survive for more than a few days out of water and does not bury itself in the mud to survive drought.

Distribution: Naturally restricted to the Burnett and Mary River systems in the southern part of Queensland, Australia. Introduced into other eastern Australian rivers.
Habitat: Slow-flowing rivers and deep, permanent pools.
Food: Aquatic invertebrates, fish, amphibians and fruit that falls into the water.
Size: Up to 1.7m/5½ft.
Breeding: Spawning occurs from August until October. The eggs are scattered and left to develop unguarded.

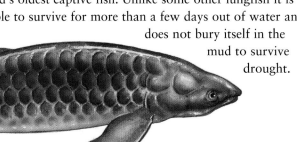

Freshwater garfish

Xenentodon cancila

Also known as the needlenose fish, the freshwater garfish is the only member of its genus. It is also one of the very few needlefish found in fresh water: most members of this family live in the sea. The freshwater garfish lives primarily in rivers but also inhabits some canals and still pools. It hunts in open water, often chasing its small prey at great speed. In rivers this streamlined predator tends to swim against the current rather than with it. As well as aquatic creatures, it sometimes feeds on insects that fall or crash into the surface. The freshwater garfish may be found living alone or in shoals. An elegant species, it is often found for sale in shops that supply home aquaria. However, compared with many aquarium fish, it is nervous and somewhat difficult to keep.

Identification: This fish is highly streamlined, being shaped rather like the blade of a knife. The body is long and flattened, and the fins rather small. The delicate, narrow jaws extend out from the front of the head like precision pincers. The lower jaw is slightly longer than the upper. The body is light brown above and silver below, with a dark brown band running along each flank. The eyes are large, with gold irises.

Distribution: Sri Lanka and mainland southern Asia, from India as far east as the Mekong River.
Habitat: Rivers, canals and still pools.
Food: Insects, aquatic invertebrates and small fish.
Size: Up to 40cm/15¾in.
Breeding: The eggs are produced and fertilized singly. They attach to submerged vegetation and are left there to develop unguarded.

Purple-spotted gudgeon

Mogurnda mogurnda

Distribution: Confined to Australia and New Guinea but is found virtually throughout both.
Habitat: Most freshwater habitats.
Food: Aquatic invertebrates, fish fry and plant matter.
Size: Up to 17cm/6¾in.
Breeding: Spawns in rainy season, November to March. The female lays 100–150 eggs on a submerged rock or log. The male guards and fans them until hatching.

This handsome little fish is widespread in the freshwater habitats of Australia and New Guinea. It can be found everywhere from desert bores and billabongs to humid swamps and clear rainforest streams. In flowing water it tends to be most common where the current is sluggish and is often found in or around vegetation, although it may also be seen on bare rocks. The purple-spotted gudgeon feeds on a wide range of small prey, including insect larvae, worms, molluscs, fish fry and crustaceans. It has also been known to eat plant matter when other food is scarce. This fish is also known as the trout mogurnda or northern trout gudgeon.

Identification: The head of this fish is moderately-sized and the mouth, which points slightly upwards, is rather large, with thick lips. There are two dorsal fins, the first much smaller than the second. The second dorsal fin is almost mirrored, both in size and position, by the anal fin. The caudal fin has a rounded rear edge. This species is highly variable in colour. The spots on the flanks are often more red than purple.

Wrestling halfbeak (*Dermogenys pusillus*): Up to 7cm/2¾in
This fish looks just like a miniature freshwater garfish, but with a much shorter upper jaw. The halfbeak also gives birth to live young rather than laying eggs. It is found in Thailand, Laos, Vietnam, Malaysia, Singapore and Indonesia. During the breeding season the males become territorial and often fight, hence the 'wrestling' part of its name.

Bumblebee goby (*Brachygobius doriae*): Up to 4cm/1½in
This tiny species (*above*) comes from Malaysia and Indonesia, and is a popular aquarium fish. The bumblebee goby is a bottom dweller most common in areas with rocks and is found in both fresh and brackish waters, where it hunts invertebrate prey. Females lay up to 200 eggs which are guarded by the male until hatching.

Common bully (*Gobiomorphus cotidianus*): Up to 15cm/6in
This fish is found only in New Zealand, in freshwater habitats. It feeds on insect larvae and other invertebrates. For much of the year it forms small schools, but during the breeding season, males become territorial, building and defending nests. They also turn almost black with an orange-edged first dorsal fin.

Slimy sculpin

Cottus cognatus

The slimy sculpin is a close relative of the European bullhead and it lives in a similar way. It is most common in fast-moving rivers and streams with rocky bottoms, although it also lives in lakes. By day it hides beneath large rocks and gravel to avoid the attention of otters, herons and other diurnal predators. As night falls it emerges to feed, scouring the nooks and crannies between stones to find benthic invertebrate prey. This fish is a nest builder that takes good care of its eggs. In spring the male cleans out a suitable cavity beneath a large rock for the female to spawn in. Once enticed in, she lays her eggs in clusters on the ceiling of the little cave. The male then guards the eggs and fry until they are big enough to tackle the current alone.

Identification: Seen from above, the head is large and frog-like. The body tapers from the gill covers towards the tail. The pectoral fins are large and fan-shaped. The pelvic fins have few rays and may be used by the fish to lift the front part of its body up from the bottom. There are two dorsal fins, the second much longer than the first. During the breeding season, males turn almost black.

Distribution: Throughout eastern Siberia. Also occurs northern North America, including much of Canada.
Habitat: Lakes, rivers and streams.
Food: Aquatic invertebrates and fish eggs.
Size: Up to 12cm/4¾in.
Breeding: Spawning occurs in April and May. The male builds a nest and fiercely guards the eggs until they hatch up to 4 weeks later.

CATFISH

The catfish of Asia include some of the largest freshwater fish to be found anywhere in the world.
A few of these giants are rare, but others are widespread and common. Some are even bred as a source
of food. As with most other catfish, the majority are bottom feeders, searching for meals with the help
of their sensitive barbels.

Mekong giant catfish

Pangasianodon gigas

Although official weight and length records show that European wels can grow larger, it seems likely that this monstrous species from South-east Asia is, in fact, the biggest living, exclusively freshwater (as opposed to partially salt-water) fish on Earth. In the wild, this fish is vegetarian, feeding on water plants and fallen fruit, but it has been known to take other food in captivity. It is unusual among catfish because it lacks teeth and has only tiny barbels. Over-fishing and the declining quality of its habitat have led to it becoming rare and it is now listed as Critically Endangered by the IUCN.

Identification: The head is wide and flattened, with the eyes positioned rather low down on each side. The mouth is large and completely lacks teeth. The caudal fin is massive and the anal fin roughly triangular, being longer at the base than any of the other fins. There is an adipose fin present. Juvenile fish have much longer barbels than the adults.

Distribution: Found only in the Mekong River and its larger tributaries, in China, Myanmar (Burma), Thailand, Laos, Cambodia and Vietnam.
Habitat: Rivers.
Food: Water plants and other vegetable matter.
Size: Up to 3m/10ft.
Breeding: The breeding system of this species has not been studied. However, it is known to migrate, possibly for breeding purposes.
Status: Critically Endangered.

Paroon

Pangasius sanitwongsei

Identification: Similar in appearance to the Mekong giant catfish, with a large caudal fin, triangular anal fin and small adipose fin on the back towards the tail. Its pectoral, dorsal and pelvic fins, however, are longer, with long trailing ends on them. The anal and other fins on the paroon also have areas of dark pigmentation.

This huge creature runs a close second to the Mekong giant catfish in the big fish stakes. In 2006 a 2.75m/9ft monster was caught in Thailand that weighed over 550lb/250kg. The paroon is a carnivore. Juveniles feed mainly on fish and crustaceans. Adults hunt similar prey but they are also scavengers, feeding on the flesh of dead animals that fall into the water. The paroon is found in the Chao Phraya River basin and also shares most of the Mekong giant catfish's habitat range. It is much more abundant, however, and is frequently caught for sale as a food fish. This fish also goes by the names of paroon shark (despite being completely unrelated to sharks) and giant pangasius.

Distribution: The Mekong and Chao Phraya River basins, in China, Thailand, Laos, Cambodia and Vietnam.
Habitat: Rivers.
Food: Fish, crustaceans and carrion.
Size: Up to 2.75m/9ft.
Breeding: Spawning occurs just before the rainy season. Like the Mekong giant catfish, this species is migratory, although whether its migrations are linked to breeding is not known.

Iridescent shark

Pangasius hypophthalmus

Distribution: Native to the Mekong and Chao Phraya River basins, but has also been introduced to other parts of southern and South-east Asia.
Habitat: Rivers and lakes.
Food: Aquatic invertebrates, fish and plant matter.
Size: Up to 1.3m/4.2ft.
Breeding: Spawning occurs from May until July. The eggs are scattered in open water and are left to develop unguarded.

Also known as the Siamese shark, Sutchi catfish, Swai and striped catfish, this species is native to the Mekong and Chao Phraya River basins of South-east Asia. It is a popular food fish and has been introduced to other countries, including Bangladesh and the Philippines. It is named for the sheen exhibited by juvenile individuals. This aspect of its appearance has brought it to the attention of home aquarium suppliers, although its rapid growth rate and eventual large size make it an unsuitable choice. In the Mekong River it is migratory, moving downstream from May to August, and then travelling back upstream from October to February. This migration may be linked to spawning as the majority of smaller fish are found far downstream.

Identification: The head is wide and flattened, and the eyes point slightly downwards. The body of the adult fish is bulky and there is a slight hump just in front of the base of the dorsal fin. Juveniles are much more svelte and streamlined, with the dorsal fin appearing longer and more pronounced. The anal fin is long at the base but not as deep as that of other pangasius species. There is a very small adipose fin.

Glass catfish (*Kryptopterus bicirrhis*): Up to 15cm/6in
This small schooling catfish is one of the few freshwater fish which is almost completely transparent. Those parts of the body which are not transparent are silvered and reflect the light. It lives in rivers with turbid waters, where its 'camouflage' makes it very hard to see. It feeds on fish fry and aquatic invertebrates, which it locates with its long barbels.

Goonch (*Bagarius yarrelli*): Up to 2m/6½ft
The goonch (*above*) is another large catfish. Its body is flattened and tapers back from a wide head to a very slight and narrow tail base. It is often found in fast-flowing waters and feeds mainly on crayfish and other aquatic invertebrates, as well as fish. It is relatively widespread, occurring in the Indus and Ganges River basins and large mainland rivers as far east as the Mekong. It is also found in Indonesia.

Tapah (*Wallago attu*): Up to 2.4m/7¾ft
This large catfish inhabits the lakes and slow-flowing rivers of much of southern and South-east Asia, from Afghanistan as far east as Indonesia. A voracious predator, it feeds on large invertebrates, fish, water birds and small aquatic mammals. One of its distinguishing features is its mouth – full of fearsome conical teeth, and with the corners lying far back behind the eyes.

Walking catfish

Clarias batrachus

As its name suggests, this catfish can move across land, albeit slowly and over relatively short distances. This has enabled it to spread quickly in places where it has been introduced. It was introduced, for instance, to two locations in Florida in 1968, and it has since spread across half the state. The walking catfish is native to much of southern and South-east Asia, including the islands of Sumatra, Java and Borneo in Indonesia. There it is common in swamps, paddy fields and other habitats with low levels of dissolved oxygen. It is able to survive in these places because it can absorb oxygen from the air, rising to the surface every so often to take a gulp before swimming down to the bottom again.

Identification: The head is broad and flat, ending with a wide mouth. The lips are fleshy and surrounded by four pairs of long, forward-pointing barbels. The dorsal fin is very long, reaching from not far behind the head almost to the base of the tail. The anal fin is just over half the length of the dorsal fin. The eyes are small and situated on the top part of the head, rather than the sides.

Distribution: Occurs India to Indonesia. Introduced to Japan, the Philippines, New Guinea and elsewhere.
Habitat: Swamps, streams, paddy fields, ponds, ditches.
Food: Aquatic invertebrates and plant matter.
Size: Up to 47cm/18½in.
Breeding: Spawning occurs between individual pairs rather than in shoals. Eggs are laid in a hollow, dug by both partners, then guarded until they hatch. Breeding occurs during the rainy season in seasonal parts of range; year-round elsewhere.

KNIFEFISH, FEATHERBACKS AND BONYTONGUES

All of the fish on these pages belong to the order Osteoglossiformes, a primitive and ancient group commonly known as the bonytongues. As the common name suggests, they all have tongues covered with bony projections, which they use to help them grip prey.

Asian knifefish

Notopterus notopterus

Identification: The body is elongated and strongly laterally compressed, shaped like the blade of a dagger. The anal and caudal fins join to form one continuous fin which runs along three-quarters of the underside of the fish. The dorsal fin is very small. The body is covered with tiny scales, as are the gill covers. In colour this fish ranges from silver to bronze. The fins are sometimes darker than the rest of the body.

With its unusual shape and metallic colour, this fish could hardly look more like the blade of a dagger or knife. The 'cutting edge' of the blade is formed by its long ventral fin, which it undulates to propel itself through the water. The Asian knifefish is found in a wide variety of freshwater and brackish habitats, where it feeds on smaller fish, invertebrates and, less often, plant matter. It becomes active at dusk and searches for food through the night. Unlike the South American knifefish, which belongs to a different scientific order (Gymnotiformes), it does not have any electrosensory apparatus, but finds its prey by vision or touch. Also known as the bronze or grey featherback, the Asian knifefish is common across much of its range and is caught as a food fish in significant numbers.

Distribution: Throughout most of southern and South-east Asia from India to Indonesia. Absent from Borneo and north Vietnam.
Habitat: Streams, rivers, estuaries, lakes, flood plains, ponds and canals.
Food: Fish, invertebrates and plant matter.
Size: Up to 60cm/23½in.
Breeding: Spawning occurs at night. The eggs are laid in small clumps on aquatic plants and are guarded until they hatch.

Clown featherback

Chitala ornata

This fish looks quite similar to the slightly smaller Asian knifefish (*top*), but it is less widespread, being confined to Indochina and parts of Indonesia. Like the Asian knifefish, it is active at twilight and during the night. It feeds on smaller fish and invertebrates, which it hunts near the surface. The clown featherback, or clown knifefish, as it is also known, is a popular aquarium fish in Europe and the USA. It has become established in parts of Florida, following the release of oversized home aquarium fish there. In its native Asia it is a common food fish, often found for sale in markets.

Identification: The body is long and laterally compressed with a single fin running along between two-thirds and three-quarters of the underside. The dorsal fin is small and positioned about halfway along the back. There is a distinct hump on the back above the head. The mouth is large and extends far back behind the eyes. The fish is silver in colour with a line of six to nine large black dots or blotches above the base of the anal fin.

Distribution: Known from Thailand, Laos, Cambodia, Vietnam and southern Borneo. It may also exist in other parts of Indonesia.
Habitat: Rivers.
Food: Fish and invertebrates.
Size: Up to 1m/3¼ft.
Breeding: Spawning occurs from March until July. The male guards and fans the eggs until hatching.

Dragonfish

Scleropages formosus

This fish has several common names, such as Asian bonytongue, kelesa, Malayan bonytongue and Asian arowana. The name dragonfish comes from its resemblance to the mythical Chinese dragon and in many parts of Asia this fish is considered lucky. The large scales and double barbels are features it shares with depictions of the dragon, and it is often found in tanks positioned in Chinese buildings for positive Feng Shui. The popularity of this fish among Chinese communities has led to it becoming rare in the wild and it is now listed as Endangered by the IUCN. However, the future of the species seems safe, as it is bred in significant numbers in captivity to supply the trade.

Distribution: Native to Thailand, Cambodia, Vietnam, Malaysia, Indonesia and the Philippines. Introduced to Singapore.
Habitat: Tannin-stained streams.
Food: Invertebrates and fish.
Size: Up to 90cm/35½in.
Breeding: Pairs form several weeks before spawning. Once the eggs have been laid and fertilized, the male takes them up into his mouth until they hatch.
Status: Endangered.

Identification: The body is elongated and covered with large, hexagonal scales. The pectoral fins are long and elegant; the pelvic fins are shorter. The upward-pointing mouth is large, with two short pairs of barbels on the lower lip. The dorsal fin is positioned well back on the body, with its front edge farther back than that of the larger anal fin.

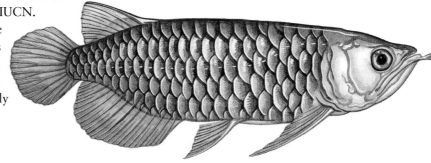

Giant featherback (*Chitala lopis*):
Up to 1.5m/4¾ft
This predatory fish is found in the Mekong and Chao Phraya River basins in Laos, Thailand, Cambodia, Vietnam and peninsular Malaysia. Like other Asian featherbacks and knifefish, it hunts from dusk until dawn and is inactive during the day. It is much larger than its relatives. It also has a larger mouth, with its corners far back behind the eyes.

Australian bonytongue
(*Scleropages jardinii*): Up to 1m/3¼ft
This large predatory fish (*above*) is also known as the Gulf saratoga, since it lives in many of the rivers which empty into the the Gulf of Carpentaria in north Australia. It is also found in New Guinea. It is solitary and highly territorial like its close relative, the saratoga. It feeds near the surface, on various invertebrates and small fish. It is a mouth brooder.

Royal knifefish (*Chitala blanci*):
Up to 1.2m/4ft
This fish lives in the main channel of the Mekong, from Thailand through Laos and into Cambodia. It feeds at night on invertebrates and small fish. It is closely related to the more common clown knifefish, but has different rear-body patterning. Rather than a few large spots, the royal knifefish has many small blotches, which combine to form bands near the tail.

Saratoga

Scleropages leichardti

A close relative of the dragonfish, the saratoga is confined to Australia, where it lives in still and slow-flowing waters. A solitary species, it is highly territorial and aggressive, particularly towards other members of its own kind. In the wild, many of these fish bear scars from previous fights. The saratoga is also known as the spotted barramundi. A carnivorous fish, it feeds on small fish and invertebrates, including insects that fall into the water. Like the dragonfish, it is a mouth brooder. However, it is the female rather than the male that carries the eggs. While she is carrying them, she loses all interest in feeding and spends much of her time near the surface. The fry also use their mother's mouth as a refuge for the first few days after hatching.

Distribution: Native to the Fitzroy River system of Queensland. Introduced into other rivers in southern Australia.
Habitat: Slow streams and rivers.
Food: Fish and invertebrates.
Size: Up to1m/3¼ft.
Breeding: Spawning occurs September until December. The female lays 70–100 eggs, each 1cm/½in diameter, and broods them in her mouth.

Identification: Very similar to the dragonfish, with large, hexagonal scales, a flat back and an upward-pointing mouth. However, the saratoga has just one pair of small barbels. In colour it varies from dark brown to olive green on the back, with lighter sides and a white belly. Each scale has a small red or orange dot at its centre.

GOURAMIS

All of these fish belong to the gourami family, Osphronemidae, part of the order Perciformes (perch-like fish). Gouramis are found only in Asia and are characterized by the fact that they all have an elongated first ray to the pelvic fins. Some gouramis are mouth brooders while others build bubble nests. The males of many species are aggressive and highly territorial.

Paradise fish

Macropodus opercularis

Identification: The head is slightly pointed and the body lozenge-shaped. The mouth slopes upward and has thick lips. The male has long, trailing dorsal and anal fins and feathery trailing ends to both lobes of the caudal fin. The male has a purple spot at the rear of the gill cover while the female is smaller and plainer, with much less spectacular fins. Several colour forms of this species have been bred in captivity.

This beautiful and colourful fish was one of the first species ever kept as a home aquarium fish in Europe. The first examples were imported from Asia in the late 1800s. Nowadays, it is much less commonly seen. Although it is easy to keep, it is very aggressive towards other fish and best kept in a tank all on its own. Its popularity began to wane as soon as other, less temperamental fish became available on the market. In the wild it inhabits man-made ditches and paddy fields, as well as naturally formed streams and small rivers.

It tolerates a much wider range of physical conditions than most fish and so is one of the most commonly found fish across much of its range.

Distribution: Occurs in China from the Yangtze River basin southward. It is also found in Laos, Vietnam, Cambodia, Taiwan and Japan.
Habitat: Still and slow-flowing waters, from paddy fields to rivers.
Food: Invertebrates and fish fry.
Size: Up to 6.5cm/2½in.
Breeding: The male builds a nest of bubbles at the surface, where the female lays her eggs. The male guards them until hatching.

Siamese fighting fish

Betta splendens

Identification: The snout is pointed and ends with an upward-sloping mouth, which has thick lips. The body is lozenge-shaped. As with the paradise fish, there is significant sexual dimorphism. The males are larger, more colourful, and have more spectacular fins than the females. In both sexes the scales, which cover the body, are clearly visible.

After the goldfish, the Siamese fighting fish is probably the best-known Asian freshwater fish outside its own continent. The males are notoriously aggressive and highly territorial. Even if kept alone in fish bowls or tanks they often end up fighting their own reflections in the glass. In the wild this fish lives in standing waters, including paddy fields, where it feeds on mosquito larvae and other invertebrates. Able to gulp air, it can tolerate waters with much lower levels of dissolved oxygen than many other fish. Before going into battle, the male splays out his fins to impress and intimidate his rival. Wild individuals have relatively short fins but decades of captive breeding have led to them becoming much larger. Several colour forms of this species have also been developed.

Distribution: Native to Thailand, Laos, Vietnam and Cambodia. It has been introduced into Malaysia, Colombia and Brazil, and elsewhere.
Habitat: Rivers, canals, flood plains, ditches and paddy fields.
Food: Invertebrates.
Size: Up to 6.5cm/2½in.
Breeding: The male builds a nest of bubbles at the surface, where the female lays her eggs. The male guards them until hatching.

Giant gourami

Osphronemus goramy

Distribution: Native to southern China, Thailand, Laos, Vietnam, Cambodia, Malaysia and Indonesia. Introduced to other countries as a food fish.
Habitat: Swamps, lakes, ponds and rivers.
Food: Plant matter, fish, invertebrates, amphibians and carrion.
Size: Up to 70cm/27½in.
Breeding: Male builds a nest of vegetation, then guards the eggs and young for up to 3 weeks after hatching.

In its native Indochina and Indonesia the giant gourami is a common and widespread fish. It inhabits most freshwater habitats, both still and flowing, and is an opportunistic omnivore, feeding on a wide range of foods. Its attractive appearance and placid temperament have made it a popular aquarium fish. Some owners report that it makes a very personable pet, even allowing people to stroke it. In Australia the giant gourami is bred as an ornamental fish that is used to stock ponds. Golden and white colour forms have been developed. In its native range it is often caught for food. It is a relatively long-lived species, with some individuals living to well past 20 years old.

Identification: Deep bodied, with the curve of the belly extending far below the bottom of the head. The snout is pointed, the mouth upturned and there is a slight bump on the forehead. The anal fin has a long base and expands outward towards the rear. The pelvic fins are long and trailing and the pectoral fins paddle-like. The scales are diamond-shaped and clearly visible, as they are outlined in black.

Pearl gourami
(*Trichogaster leeri*):
Up to 12cm/4¾in
A native of Thailand, peninsular Malaysia, Sumatra and Borneo, this fish (*above*) is named for the many round white spots that pepper its sides. It is a popular aquarium fish. In the wild it lives in lowland swamps with acidic water. A bubble nester, it feeds mainly on aquatic invertebrates. As with many other gouramis, the male is larger and more colourful than the female.

Kissing gourami (*Helostoma temmincki*):
Up to 30cm/12in
The males of this species 'kiss' as they lock their mouths together in fights over territory. Unlike some other gouramis, the kissing gourami does not build a nest but rather leaves its eggs – which float to the surface – to develop unguarded. In the wild it inhabits paddy fields and muddy, well vegetated lakes and ponds throughout Thailand, Malaysia and Indonesia.

Croaking gourami (*Trichopsis vittata*):
Up to 7cm/2¾in
This little fish occurs throughout Indochina and most of Indonesia, where it lives in still freshwater habitats. It feeds on invertebrates and is a bubble nester. Its croaking noises are made by a structural adaptation of its pectoral fins and are used during courtship and to help establish dominance hierarchies amongst males.

Dwarf gourami

Colisa lalia

Also known as the red lalia and sunset gourami, this is a popular aquarium fish native to the Indian subcontinent. It has also become established in Palm Beach County, Florida, and in Colombia, following accidental introductions. In its native range, the dwarf gourami inhabits lakes and slow-moving streams and small rivers with abundant vegetation. Like the giant gourami, it is an omnivore, feeding on algae and other plant matter as well as invertebrates and fish fry. The male builds a bubble nest and the female releases her eggs just beneath it. Being buoyant, these float upwards into the nest, where they are then guarded by the male until they hatch.

Distribution: Native to India, Bangladesh and Pakistan. Introduced into Singapore, Colombia and the USA.
Habitat: Lakes, ponds, streams and rivers.
Food: Plant matter, invertebrates and fish fry.
Size: Up to 9cm/3½in.
Breeding: The male builds a bubble nest at the surface, sometimes adding twigs and other bits of vegetation. He guards the eggs until they hatch after 12–24 hours.

Identification: The head and body are teardrop-shaped, with the snout forming the pointed end. Compared with the rest of the body, the head and mouth are quite small and the mouth slopes upwards. The dorsal and anal fins are long at the base and fan-like. The pelvic fins are slender and trailing. In his breeding colours the male is spectacular, each side bearing more than 20 alternating bars, which drop from the back to belly at a slight angle. The female is much less colourful, being mainly silver.

SNAKEHEADS

Snakeheads are primitive members of the order Perciformes. They are unusual among fish in being obligate air breathers: despite the fact that they still have gills, if they are denied access to the surface they die from oxygen starvation. All snakeheads are solitary predators. Some are important food fish in the countries in which they are found.

Giant snakehead

Channa micropeltes

Few fish end up on wanted posters but the giant snakehead is one of them. This tough survivor has several US websites dedicated to its eradication. It was accidentally introduced into parts of the country and is now considered a serious threat to native fish – so much so that its sale as an aquarium fish is illegal in California. It is a voracious predator, capable of reaching a significant size: large individuals may weigh 20kg/44lb. Parents guard their eggs fiercely and have been known to attack humans that approach too closely. In its native Asia it inhabits a wide variety of freshwater habitats. Its ability to obtain oxygen by gulping air enables it to survive even in very shallow, stagnant waters.

Identification: The body is long, thick and muscular, and covered with many small scales. The head is slightly flattened and pointed at the snout. The mouth is large, extending back beyond the eye. There are several large pointed teeth in the lower jaw: those in the upper jaw are smaller. The dorsal fin extends from a line above the base of the pectoral fin almost to the tail. The caudal fin is rounded.

Distribution: Native to Thailand, Laos, Cambodia, Vietnam, peninsular Malaysia and the islands of Sumatra and Borneo.
Habitat: Canals, lakes, ponds, swamps and slow-moving streams and rivers.
Food: Fish and other small vertebrates.
Size: Up to 1.3m/4.2ft.
Breeding: Spawning occurs between pairs in a circular area cleared of vegetation. Eggs float to the surface, and are guarded until hatching.

Cobra snakehead

Channa marulius

If the giant snakehead is a big fish, this species is a monster. The cobra snakehead can reach 1.83m/6ft long and weigh up to 30kg/66lb. It is also known as the great snakehead or bullseye snakehead. Like the giant snakehead, this species is a formidable predator. It lives mainly on fish but has also been known to kill and eat water birds, rodents and snakes. In Thailand it is widely believed to be venomous. Although this belief is erroneous, the cobra snakehead does have a fearsome bite and often turns on anglers that haul it in. It is a solitary fish that inhabits still and sluggish waters, usually with abundant vegetation. In rivers it tends to be confined to deep pools.

Identification: The body is long and muscular and the head is flattened. The mouth is large and filled with fearsome pointed teeth. The eyes are red and there is a distinctive black eyespot rimmed with orange on the top part of the base of the caudal fin. The anal fin is about two-thirds the length of the dorsal fin. Both the caudal fin and the pectoral fins are rounded.

Distribution: Widspread in southern Asia, occurring from Pakistan to Indonesia. Introduced into parts of the USA.
Habitat: Canals, lakes, ponds, swamps and slow-moving streams and rivers.
Food: Fish and other vertebrates.
Size: Up to 1.83m/6ft.
Breeding: Both parents build a floating nest of weeds, where the eggs are deposited. The nest and fry are guarded for around a month.

Chevron snakehead

Channa striata

Distribution: Native to most of southern Asia, from Pakistan to Indonesia. It has been widely introduced elsewhere.
Habitat: Most still and slow-flowing waters.
Food: Fish, amphibians and aquatic invertebrates.
Size: Up to 1m/3.3ft.
Breeding: Spawning occurs throughout the year. The eggs float after fertilization and are guarded by both parents, as are young.

The chevron is the most common and widespread of all the snakeheads. It has several other names, among them the common snakehead, snakehead murrel, striped snakehead and aruan. In its native Asia it is caught for food and it is thought to be one of the main food fish in Indochina. It occurs in a wide range of freshwater habitats. It is most common in waters that are a metre or more deep but it is able to survive in shallower pools. In regions that are prone to drought it buries itself in the mud and waits for the rains to return, living off its fat reserves and absorbing oxygen by gulping air. The popularity of this fish for food has led to it being introduced into many other parts of the world, including Madagascar, Hawaii, Fiji, the Philippines, and Mauritius.

Identification: The common name refers to the characteristic diagonal lines on the dorsal and anal fins. In other respects, this fish resembles most other snakeheads, having a long, muscular body, a flattened, snake-like head and a large mouth, containing several long, pointed teeth. The scales are larger than those of most other snakehead species.

Emperor snakehead (*Channa marulioides*): Up to 65cm/25½in
This species is native to southern Thailand, peninsular Malaysia, Sumatra and Borneo. It feeds on fish, amphibians and other aquatic vertebrates. At the base of their caudal fin, juveniles have an obvious eyespot outlined with light green, the same colour as the underside of the body. As they mature the eyespot all but disappears as the fins and body darken.

Golden snakehead (*Channa stewartii*): Up to 25cm/10in
Native to the Himalayan foothills of northern India and southern Nepal, this small snakehead (*above*) is found at altitudes over 1,500m/4,921ft. It lives in ponds and streams and feeds on small fish and aquatic invertebrates. It is a popular aquarium fish but, as with other snakeheads, is best kept on its own due to a tendency to attack and even eat smaller fish that share its tank.

Orange-spotted snakehead (*Channa aurantimaculata*): Up to 40cm/15¾in
This fish is endemic to the middle Brahmaputra River basin of Assam, India, and is most common in its tributary streams and occasional swamps. It is named for the seven or eight large, irregular blotches on each side of its body. This fish was only scientifically described in the year 2000 and has yet to be properly studied.

Splendid snakehead

Channa lucius

This relatively small snakehead has a long, tapering head compared with most other species. It is also known as the forest snakehead, reflecting its main habitat – tropical rainforest rivers and streams. In contrast with most of its relatives, it is just as common in relatively swift-flowing waters as it is in sluggish streams. Wherever it occurs, it is rarely found far from submerged vegetation. It hunts fish and large invertebrates in mid water or close to the surface, relying on its camouflage to keep it hidden from prey until ready to strike. Much of its hunting is done around dawn and dusk. The splendid snakehead is also able to change colour to a limited extent to match its surroundings.

Distribution: Native to southern China, Thailand, Laos, Cambodia, Vietnam, Malaysia and Indonesia.
Habitat: Rainforest rivers, streams and pools.
Food: Fish and aquatic invertebrates.
Size: Up to 40cm/15¾in.
Breeding: Spawning occurs throughout the year. Both parents guard the eggs and young.

Identification: The body is relatively long and thick, and the head is tapering. The mouth is large but does not extend beyond the eye. Seen in profile, the forehead is slightly concave. Two lines, often broken, run along either side of the head, dipping at a slight angle from the eye to the edge of the gill cover. A line of large blotches runs along the side of the body, the first of these being positioned on the gill cover and the last near the base of the tail.

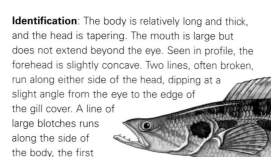

SNAKEHEADS AND TIGERFISH

All of the fish on these pages are ambush predators. Snakeheads prefer to target their prey from below, often lunging upwards from the bottom to grab fish and other creatures. Tigerfish, on the other hand, attack their prey by darting straight at them through the water. They are named for the stripes which help to camouflage them against submerged vegetation.

Black snakehead

Channa melasoma

This is a nocturnal predator that feeds on large invertebrates and small fish. Once it has located its prey it rushes towards it, snapping it up before it has time to escape. Like other snakeheads, the black snakehead is an obligate air breather and is capable of travelling short distances over land to find new sources of water and food. It prefers clear but shaded forest streams with muddy bottoms, although it is also sometimes found in turbid water. Although abundant throughout its geographical range it is rarely seen for sale in food markets, unlike some other snakeheads. It is reportedly very difficult to find, burrowing into the mud at the first sign of danger.

Identification: The head is rounded and, with its protruding eyes, looks almost frog-like. Seen from above the body tapers from the temples back towards the tail. The pectoral fins have narrow fleshy bases and are usually held out from the sides of the body like paddles. The back is greenish and mottled with irregular darker patches, distinguishing it from other snakeheads.

Distribution: Found in Thailand, Laos, Vietnam, Cambodia, Malaysia, Indonesia and the Philippines.
Habitat: Streams and rivers.
Food: Invertebrates and fish.
Size: Up to 30cm/12in.
Breeding: Spawning is thought to occur throughout the year. The eggs are guarded by one of the parents until they hatch.

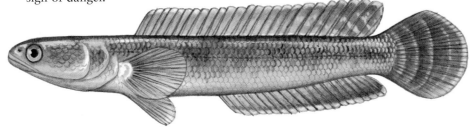

Rainbow snakehead

Channa bleheri

As its name suggests, this snakehead is extremely colourful. This fact, combined with its relatively small size, has made it a popular fish with home aquarium enthusiasts. In the wild, it is confined to the subtropical far north-eastern corner of India, where it lives beneath forest in ponds, swamps and streams. Being common in captivity, the rainbow snakehead's breeding habits have been quite well studied. Like other snakeheads, this species closely guards its eggs and young. The eggs each contain an oil globule, which helps them float to the surface. Here they stick together and are carefully watched. Both parents periodically take the eggs into their mouths and expel them from their gills, presumably to remove algae or other material that may stick to them.

Identification: The mouth is wide and the head slightly flattened. As with other snakeheads, both the dorsal and anal fins are very long at the base and virtually reach the tail. The caudal fin is rounded and there are no pelvic fins. There are one or two large scales on the underside of the lower jaw. The body is covered with large, irregular orange or red blotches.

Distribution: Restricted to the Brahmaputra River basin of Assam, in north-eastern India.
Habitat: Ponds, streams and swamps.
Food: Aquatic invertebrates and fish fry.
Size: Up to 13.5cm/5¼in.
Breeding: The transparent eggs float to the surface, stick together and are guarded by both parents until hatching. The fry are also guarded until big enough to fend for themselves.

Malay snakehead (*Channa bankanensis*):
Up to 23.5cm/9¼in
This little fish (*above*) inhabits backwaters and dark, tannin-stained streams in the rain forests of peninsular Malaysia, Sumatra and Borneo. Due to the remoteness of its habitat it has been little studied but it is known to be a predator of smaller fish and invertebrates and thought likely to be protective of its eggs and young.

Silver tigerfish (*Datnioides polota*):
Up to 30cm/12in
This popular food fish resembles the Siamese tigerfish, but is slightly smaller and more widespread, ranging from India to Papua New Guinea. It lives in both fresh and brackish water – in rivers, lakes, estuaries and coastal lagoons. It feeds on smaller fish and invertebrates, including prawns, crabs and insect larvae. It is also known as the barred tigerfish, the four-banded tigerfish and the four-banded ripple-tail.

Thinbar tigerfish (*Datnioides undecimradiatus*):
Up to 40cm/15¾in
This fish looks similar to the other tigerfish but has just two or three thin bars on its body and a small one at the base of its tail. Like the other tigerfish, it is an ambush predator, and widely available as a home aquarium fish. It is restricted to the middle and lower Mekong basin, being most common in Laos, Cambodia and Vietnam.

Dwarf snakehead

Channa gachua

This is one of the smaller snakeheads, although not the smallest of all: that title belongs to *Channa orientalis*, the green snakehead, which comes from Sri Lanka. The dwarf snakehead is one of the most widespread members of this family, ranging from Iran to Sumatra in Indonesia. It is also found throughout India and alongside the green snakehead in Sri Lanka. The dwarf snakehead is most common in forested areas and seems to prefer the clear water of shallow streams, pools and swamps. However, like other snakeheads it is extremely tolerant of low oxygen levels and is sometimes found in very stagnant, turbid water. It can migrate short distances over land – those who have watched it do so describe its movement as exceedingly active, progressing by a series of small leaps.

Distribution: Throughout most of mainland southern and South-east Asia. Also occurs in Sumatra.
Habitat: Most freshwater habitats.
Food: Invertebrates and small fish.
Size: Up to 20cm/8in.
Breeding: This species is a mouth brooder, with the male holding the eggs in his oral cavity until they hatch.

Identification: There are scales on the upper part of the head to just behind and above the eyes, but no scales on the underside of the jaw. The pelvic fins are small. Colour varies slightly throughout its range. Some individuals have an eyespot at the rear of the dorsal fin, while others lack this feature.

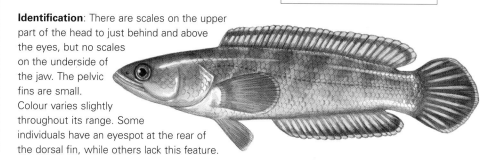

Siamese tigerfish

Datnioides microlepis

This fish is also known as the ringan, tiger datnoid and finescale tigerfish. It is a fast-moving ambush predator of rivers and lakes and is usually found lurking near submerged branches or other cover, waiting for smaller fish or invertebrates to swim into its visual range. Before striking, it sways slowly from side to side, perhaps to help judge the distance between itself and its victim before it lunges into attack. In Thailand and many other parts of its range, it is a prized food fish. Its striking appearance has also made it a popular aquarium fish. As well as freshwater habitats it may sometimes be found in estuaries and other areas of brackish water.

Identification: The body is almost leaf-shaped, with a pointed head and a large mouth. There are two dorsal fins: the first has rays formed from large, thick spines; the second is much more delicate and rounded. The back and sides are gold and the underside white. There are five to seven black bars running down either side of the body.

Distribution: Found in the Chao Phraya and Mekong River basins of Thailand, Laos, Vietnam and Cambodia. Also found in Borneo and Sumatra.
Habitat: Lakes and rivers.
Food: Fish and aquatic invertebrates.
Size: Up to 45cm/17¾in.
Breeding: The breeding system of this species has not been studied, although capture of gravid females suggests that spawning occurs from June until August.

OTHER PERCH-LIKE FISH

The order Perciformes contains more species of fish than any other. In Asia and Australia they include some of the largest freshwater fish. The barramundi and Murray cod are giants and, like most giant fish, they are predators. Other members of this order, such as the catopra, are largely herbivorous, feeding on algae and seeds and fruits that fall into the water.

Barramundi

Lates calcarifer

Identification: A pointed snout and concave forehead. The mouth is large, with its corners behind the eyes. The anal fin is rounded. The first dorsal fin has seven to eight strong spines; a smoother second dorsal has ten or eleven. The caudal fin has a rounded rear edge. The back is silvery grey, fading almost to white on the lower flanks and belly.

This is probably Australia's best known freshwater fish. But in fact it is neither restricted to fresh water nor to the continent of Australia; it is also found in brackish and coastal marine waters, ranging as far west as Pakistan. In Australia it is a highly prized sports fish, reaching weights of 60kg/132lb or so. It is also an important food fish, and is farmed for its flesh in Australia as well as Thailand and Indonesia. This fish is a 'protandrous' hermaphrodite, which means the hatchlings are born male but some turn into females later in life, depending on how many females there already are in the area.

Distribution: Fresh, brackish and coastal waters, northern Australia to Pakistan.
Habitat: Coastal marine waters, estuaries, lagoons and rivers.
Food: Aquatic invertebrates and fish.
Size: Up to 2m/6½ft.
Breeding: Spawning occurs in summer. Barramundi living in rivers move downstream to spawn in estuaries. All hatchlings are male; some turn into females later in life.

Murray cod

Maccullochella peelii

Identification: The body is elongated and deep. The snout is pointed, the eyes small and the mouth large. The first dorsal fin is relatively low in profile and has six or seven thick spines. The second dorsal fin is larger and rounded. The upper part of the body is olive to yellowish and covered with a beautiful reticulated pattern of darker green markings. The underside is white, as are the pelvic fins.

The Murray cod is Australia's largest exclusively freshwater fish, capable of reaching weights of 113.5kg/250lb. It is named after its main habitat range – the Murray River, along with its tributary the Darling River, in the south-east of the country. Once abundant, the Murray cod is now quite rare. It began to decline in the late 19th and early 20th centuries, when it was fished commercially for food. After the 1930s, when this practice ended, its numbers continued to drop, partly as a result of over-exploitation by anglers and partly due to declining water quality in the river catchment. Today, sadly, the Murray cod is listed as Critically Endangered by the IUCN.

Distribution: Confined to the Murray-Darling River system in the Australian states of Queensland, New South Wales, Victoria and South Australia.
Habitat: Rivers.
Food: Aquatic invertebrates, fish and other vertebrates.
Size: Up to 1.8m/6ft.
Breeding: Spawning occurs in pairs from September until January following migration upstream. The male guards the eggs until hatching.
Status: Critically Endangered.

Climbing perch

Anabas testudineus

The climbing perch is named for its ability to move out of water. Although it does not actually climb as such, it does travel over land to reach new pools. These short migrations usually occur at night, either during or immediately after heavy rain, and are triggered by overcrowding. This fish is native to most of southern and South-east Asia. It has been introduced to Papua New Guinea and Florida in the USA. In western countries it is occasionally kept as an aquarium fish but across most of its native range it is caught for food. Its ability to remove oxygen from gulped air means that it is often still alive when sold in markets. In the wild it gulps air to supplement the small amounts of oxygen to be found in the shallow pools it often inhabits. It also enables the fish to survive drought, lying buried in the mud until the rains return.

Distribution: Pakistan to Indonesia. Also occurs throughout most of Nepal and much of southern China.
Habitat: Swamps, ponds, pools, puddles and other areas of still water.
Food: Algae, invertebrates and fish fry.
Size: Up to 25cm/10in.
Breeding: Spawning occurs from March until October. The eggs float to the surface, where they are guarded until they hatch.

Identification: A rounded head in profile and large eyes. The strong pectoral fins are sometimes used to prop the fish up on the bottom. The two dorsal fins are joined: the first is very long and low. The caudal fin is rounded. There is an eyespot at the base of the tail. The body is greenish grey, with several broken bars of darker scales down the flanks.

Blue threadfin (*Eleutheronema tetradactylum*): Up to 2m/6½ft
This primarily marine species is also found in fresh and brackish waters. It is also known as the blue salmon and four-fingered threadfin (its pectoral fins have four long filaments and no webbing). It is a schooling species that feeds on other fish and open water invertebrates. Like the barramundi, with which it shares its range, it is a protandrous hermaphrodite.

Catopra (*Pristolepis fasciata*): Up to 20cm/8in
This handsome member of the perch family (*right*) is primarily vegetarian, feeding

on algae, submerged land plants, seeds and fruit. It also occasionally catches aquatic invertebrates. The catopra, or Malayan leaffish as it is also known, is native to the islands of Sumatra and Borneo, as well as Indochina and the Malay Peninsula. It lives in sluggish rivers and still waters on their surrounding floodplains.

Marbled sand goby (*Oxyeleotris marmorata*): Up to 65cm/25½in
Despite its name, this fish is not a true goby at all but a member of the sleeper goby family, Eleotridae. It lives in rivers and swamps in Indochina, Indonesia and the Philippines. It feeds on small fish and aquatic invertebrates. It is considered a delicacy in China and other parts of eastern Asia and large fish sell for high prices.

Archerfish

Toxotes chatareus

This is one of nature's wonders: a fish that has evolved to shoot insects from overhanging branches. The upper part of its tongue has a ridge which fits into a deep groove in the roof of its mouth. By quickly closing its gill covers and dropping its tongue slightly it is able to fire a small jet of water from its mouth. This can be shot accurately to a distance of around 1.5m/5ft – more than enough to reach many of the leaves that overhang the mangrove swamps and forest rivers and streams it inhabits. Once it has knocked its target into the water it darts across to snap it up. The archerfish also eats aquatic invertebrates and small fish, as well as floating aquatic plants.

Identification: The snout is very pointed and the mouth slopes upwards. The eyes are large and positioned near the top of the head. This species is sometimes called the seven-spot archerfish and there are indeed seven large dark spots on either side of the upper part of its body, three larger than the rest. The back is gold, fading into silver on the flanks and underside.

Distribution: Throughout India, Sri Lanka and South-east Asia, as well as New Guinea and northern Australia.
Habitat: Mangrove swamps, rivers and streams.
Food: Insects, aquatic invertebrates, small fish and plant matter.
Size: Up to 40cm/15¾in.
Breeding: Spawning occurs during the wet season. The eggs, which are buoyant, are shed into open water and left to develop unguarded.

CICHLIDS, BLUE PERCH, RAINBOWFISH, PANCHAX AND KILLIFISH

Most of these fish will be familiar to home aquarists. With the exception of the green chromide, all are small and relatively easy to keep. In the wild they are constantly in danger of attack from larger fish and other predators, so they tend to be jittery at first. However, they soon settle into a well-maintained tank.

Green chromide

Etroplus suratensis

Identification: The body is oval and laterally flattened, the forehead steeply sloping and the back and belly rounded. The two dorsal fins are linked; the first contains several thick spines. The body colour is dark green but the sides are covered with many lighter dots. The mouth is small and the eyes are positioned near the front of the head. The caudal fin has a very slightly v-shaped rear edge.

This shoaling fish is most common in estuaries and other areas of brackish water, although it is sometimes found farther upstream in rivers. It feeds mainly on algae and when kept in an aquarium tends to consume all of the water plants. The green chromide is a cichlid and like most cichlids takes good care of its young. Pairs form close bonds and work together to defend their offspring. The female lays around 500 eggs which she attaches to a submerged rock or log in still or very sluggish water. Both parents guard them and after the fry have hatched they form a small shoal which remains close to the adults for several weeks. During this period the parents largely refrain from feeding.

Distribution: Confined to the western Indian Ocean, ranging from Gujarat in India to Sri Lanka.
Habitat: Estuaries, coastal lagoons, rivers and the sea.
Food: Algae, water plants and aquatic invertebrates.
Size: Up to 40cm/15¾in.
Breeding: Spawning occurs year round. Pairs break away from shoals to lay eggs. Both parents guard and fan them to keep them oxygenated for 4 days until they hatch.

Indian glass fish

Parambassis ranga

Identification: The body is almost completely transparent – even the bones let light through. Some breeders inject dye into these fish, altering their colour, but in nature they lack pigment: only the eyes and the area around the brain are silvered. The eyes are large and the head is pointed. The mouth is small. The fins are transparent. The caudal fin is deeply forked.

As its name suggests, this species is almost transparent. It is a shoaling fish from the Indian subcontinent and Indochina. Compact, attractive and easy to keep, it has become popular with home aquarium enthusiasts. It is often sold under different names, such as the Indian glassy fish, Siamese glass fish and ghost fish. In the wild, it inhabits areas of sluggish and standing water. It is an extremely prolific breeder and an important source of food for many larger fish, such as snakeheads. Its transparent body has evolved to help it avoid being eaten, rather like the camouflage of many other fish. Rather than mimicking its surroundings to blend in, the Indian glass fish has done its best to become invisible, letting the background appear through its body.

Distribution: Natural range extends from Pakistan to peninsular Malaysia. Introduced into Japan.
Habitat: Backwaters, lakes and ponds.
Food: Aquatic invertebrates.
Size: Up to 8cm/3in.
Breeding: Breeding occurs all year round but increases during the rainy season. The eggs are scattered into open water and are then left to develop unguarded.

Blue perch

Badis badis

Distribution: Found from Pakistan, through northern India and Nepal to Bhutan. A separate population occurs in Thailand.
Habitat: Pools, swamps, streams and rivers.
Food: Aquatic invertebrates.
Size: Up to 8cm/3in.
Breeding: The eggs are laid in a rocky crevice beneath stones on the bottom and guarded by the male. The male also guards the fry after hatching.

This little fish is native to the Ganges River basin. It is also found in the Mahanadi River basin farther east. For most of the year the blue perch is anything but blue, being a nondescript brown, patterned with faint bars of red, brown or black. During the breeding season, however, the males change colour, taking on the azure hues that give this species its common name. The change is so considerable that this fish has earned itself another name, the chameleon fish. Although small, the blue perch is generally solitary. It inhabits rivers, streams, pools and swamps, where it searches for worms, insect larvae and other invertebrates to feed on. The blue perch is commonly kept in home aquaria – males are territorial, but they rarely attack other fish.

Identification: The body is elongated and slightly laterally compressed. The dorsal fin is long and fan-like, stretching from just behind the gill covers almost to the base of the tail. The anal fin has a shorter base but is almost as flamboyant. The caudal fin is large and has a rounded outer edge. The scales on the body are well defined, clearly visible and extend on to the fleshy bases of the dorsal, anal and caudal fins.

Canara pearlspot (*Etroplus canarensis*): 11.5cm/4½in
This fish was discovered in 1877, then promptly disappeared. Long thought to be extinct, a new, previously hidden population was found in 1997, in India's Netravati River. This is one of the few Asian cichlids to live only in fresh water. Due to its long disappearance and a lack of study since redisovery, its life history remains mysterious. It has yet to breed in captivity, but specimens are now available through the aquarium trade.

Ceylon killifish
(*Aplocheilus dayi*):
Up to 9cm/3½in
This little fish (*above*) is very easy to keep and is therefore a popular species with home aquarists. It is endemic to Sri Lanka and inhabits shallow forest streams over silt, where it feeds on aquatic invertebrates and fish fry. It is also found in mangrove swamps, often schooling with dwarf panchax (*Aplocheilus parvus*).

Striped panchax (*Aplocheilus lineatus*):
Up to 10cm/4in
The striped panchax is native to India and Sri Lanka. A hardy fish, it can be found in a wide range of habitats, from mountain streams and rivers to low-lying paddy fields. It feeds on invertebrates, particularly mosquito larvae, and has been introduced into Hawaii to help with mosquito control there.

Australian rainbowfish

Melanotaenia nigrans

This colourful species is a widely kept fish, common in the home aquarium trade. In the wild it is confined to the northern part of Australia, ranging from the Cape York Peninsula in Queensland westward through the coastal regions of the Northern Territory. The Australian rainbowfish lives in lagoons and small streams, where it feeds mainly on insects and their larvae. It is common in rainforest waterways and is sometimes found in the brackish waters of river mouths. Wherever it lives, however, it seems to prefer clear, slightly acidic waters. The sexes differ in appearance, with the male being pale purple above and the female an iridescent green. In both sexes the hexagonal scales are clearly visible.

Distribution: Found only in northern Australia and a few nearby offshore islands.
Habitat: Lagoons, billabongs and streams.
Food: Insects and their larvae, algae.
Size: Up to 10cm/4in.
Breeding: Spawning occurs throughout the year. Pairs form, with the female laying her eggs on the stems and leaves of water plants.

Identification: The head is pointed and the body streamlined. The mouth is small but the eyes are relatively large. There are two dorsal fins, the first shorter at the base than the second. The anal fin is similar in length at the base to both of the dorsal fins put together. A dark band runs along the side of the fish all the way from the snout to the caudal fin.

DANIOS AND BARBS

Asia is the original source of many of the world's tropical freshwater aquarium fish. All of the species on these pages fall into that category, being widely collected and in some cases bred for the trade. Some, such as the Java barb, are also caught for food and eaten within their native range. Danios and barbs belong to the carp family, Cyprinidae.

Zebra danio

Brachydanio rerio

Identification: The body is fairly long and streamlined with the dorsal fin positioned quite far back. The eyes are large and the mouth slopes upwards. This species is most easily identified by its horizontal stripes, which run from the rear edge of the gill cover along the body right to the caudal fin. The anal fin is also striped.

With its striking black and white stripes, the zebra danio could hardly be better named. This handsome little fish is often seen in pet shops and is resident in tanks in many homes around the world. The leopard danio is a spotted colour morph of this species. In the wild the zebra danio naturally inhabits streams, ponds and ditches in and around the Indian subcontinent. It is also often found in man-made bodies of fresh water, including reservoirs, canals and paddy fields. It is a shoaling fish and feeds on small invertebrates, including mosquito larvae. As with many fish, the males are more colourful than the females. They are also slightly smaller. The zebra danio also goes by several alternative names including rerio, striped danio, anju, lauputi and zebrafish.

Distribution: Native to India, Nepal, Bangladesh, Bhutan and Myanmar (Burma). Introduced into Japan, Colombia, Martinique, Sri Lanka and the USA.
Habitat: Streams, ditches, ponds, canals, reservoirs and paddy fields.
Food: Aquatic invertebrates.
Size: Up to 4cm/1½in.
Breeding: Spawning usually occurs at night. The eggs are quite large for a small fish, and are scattered into open water and develop unguarded.

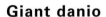

Giant danio

Devario aequipinnatus

Identification: The body is streamlined and the snout is pointed. The mouth is small and the eyes are large. In colour this fish is a greenish silver. There are two or three broken horizontal stripes and several blotches of almost luminous lime green on each of the flanks. The fins are clear and delicate-looking. The caudal fin is v-shaped.

This fish is one of the largest of the danios and one of the most commonly kept, after the zebra danio. Although they start out small, giant danios have the potential to grow, which comes as a shock to some beginners in the home aquarium hobby. In the wild, the giant danio is a shoaling fish of fast-flowing streams, usually found in hilly areas. It prefers clear, shaded water running over gravel or sand, and tends to spend most of its time near the surface, where it snaps up flying insects. This diet is supplemented with aquatic invertebrates, including worms and crustaceans such as freshwater shrimps. Spawning of this species has often been observed in captivity but has not been studied in the wild.

Distribution: Native to the Indian subcontinent (including Sri Lanka) and most of Indochina, ranging from Pakistan to Cambodia.
Habitat: Fast-flowing streams.
Food: Flying insects and aquatic invertebrates.
Size: Up to 15cm/6in.
Breeding: Females lay over 1,000 eggs in a season. The eggs are laid at short intervals in batches of 5–20. They are scattered into open water to develop unguarded.

Rosy barb

Puntius conchonius

This fish could easily be confused for a goldfish. It is similar in size and often close in colour, ranging from copper to greenish gold. Like the goldfish, the rosy barb is often kept as an ornamental fish. It is hardy and can tolerate relatively low temperatures. In the wild this fish inhabits lakes and swift-flowing hill streams. It is an omnivore, feeding on worms, insect larvae and other invertebrates, as well as plant matter. Unlike the goldfish, however, the rosy barb changes colour through the year. The males turn a much stronger rosy red (hence the common name) and the females, which are larger, also acquire more of a luminous glow. These fish are prolific spawners, with each female producing hundreds of eggs at a time.

Distribution: Native to Afghanistan, Pakistan, India, Nepal and Bangladesh. It has been introduced to Australia, Colombia, Mexico, Puerto Rico and Singapore.
Habitat: Lakes and streams in hilly areas.
Food: Aquatic invertebrates and plant matter.
Size: Up to 14cm/5½in.
Breeding: Large numbers of eggs are scattered among water plants and are left to develop unguarded. They hatch after 1–2 days.

Identification: Males in particular closely resemble goldfish. The main difference between the species is the presence of a large, dark eyespot at the base of the tail in the rosy barb. The rosy barb also shows slight sexual dimorphism, the females being both larger and paler. The head is quite small, the snout pointed and the eyes rather large.

Pearl danio (*Brachydanio albolineatus*): Up to 7cm/2¾in
This small, pearl-coloured fish inhabits clear, fast-flowing streams throughout western Indochina, from Myanmar (Burma) to Vietnam. It is also native to Sumatra, and introduced to Japan. Like other danios it feeds near the surface, picking off insects that fall into the water. Although the sexes look similar, the females are larger.

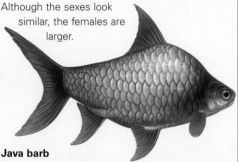

Java barb
(*Barbonymus gonionotus*):
Up to 40.5cm/16in
Despite its name, the Java barb (*above*) is not confined to Java but is also native to Sumatra, Indochina and the Malay Peninsula. It has been introduced into India, Bangladesh and the Philippines and it is widely caught as a food fish. It is a large shoaling fish of slow-moving waters and feeds on plant matter and invertebrates.

Cherry barb (*Puntius titteya*): 5cm/2in
This cherry-coloured little fish is native to Sri Lanka but has also been introduced to Mexico and Colombia. It lives in slow-flowing streams, usually shaded by trees and with silt and rotting leaves on the bottom. It feeds on a wide range of tiny invertebrates as well as algae.

Tiger barb

Puntius tetrazona

This fish, also known as the Sumatra barb, is native to the islands of Sumatra and Borneo, but has been introduced into other parts of the world. It is one of the world's most popular home aquarium fish. In one year, more than two and a half million tiger barbs were imported into the USA. This is naturally a fish of tropical forest streams and swamps. It is found in both clear and turbid water, and is thought to be quite tolerant to changes in water quality. It is an omnivore, feeding on aquatic invertebrates, but also eating plant matter when animal food is scarce. These fish are quick to mature. Females can spawn when they are as young as six weeks old. Tiger barbs live for six years on average – quite a long life span for such a small fish.

Identification: Shaped like an arrowhead, with the dorsal and anal fins erect. The snout is pointed, the mouth small and the eyes quite large. Wild specimens are silver to golden brown in colour with four thick, black, vertical bars. One of the bars crosses the base of the tail and another runs down through the eye. The dorsal fin's rear edge is red.

Distribution: Native to Sumatra and Borneo. Also introduced into Australia, Colombia, Singapore and Suriname.
Habitat: Forest swamps and streams.
Food: Aquatic invertebrates and plant matter.
Size: Up to 7cm/2¾in.
Breeding: Spawning occurs all year round. The eggs are scattered over water plants and are then left to develop unguarded.

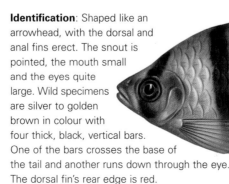

BARBS, MAHSEERS, ROHU AND RIVER CARP

All of the fish on these pages belong to the carp family. Carp and their relatives are a favourite target of anglers and those from Asia are no exception. Some draw sports fishermen from around the world to seek them out. Unfortunately their popularity has led to many populations declining in numbers. Commercial fishing for food has also had an impact.

Giant barb

Catlocarpio siamensis

Identification: A large head and mouth, with the eyes positioned low down on the head. The back slopes upwards to a hump at the base of the dorsal fin. The dorsal fin itself is triangular and looks almost shark-like when raised. The anal fin is also triangular and longer along its front edge than along its base. The head is scaleless but the body is covered with very large, well defined scales.

This enormous fish is the largest freshwater member of the carp family in the world, weighing up to 300kg/660lb. It is also known as the Pla Kaho or Siamese giant carp. The giant barb lives in the Mekong, Maeklong and Chao Phraya River basins of Indochina. As its large size might suggest, the adults prefer deep pools in large rivers, although the young are often found in smaller tributaries and swamps fed by these rivers. The giant barb is a herbivore, feeding on algae and fruit that fall into the water. It is itself a highly desirable food fish and has been heavily exploited for its flesh. Nowadays, few individuals reach their potential maximum size before being captured and sold. As well as being caught from the wild, the giant barb is raised in ponds as a food fish.

Distribution: Native to Thailand, Laos, Vietnam and Cambodia.
Habitat: Rivers and swamps.
Food: Algae and fallen fruit.
Size: Up to 3m/10ft.
Breeding: Spawning occurs throughout most of the year. The eggs are shed into open water and are then left to develop unguarded.

Isok barb

Probarbus jullieni

Identification: The body is relatively streamlined. The head is roughly triangular in shape, and the snout seen sideways on is slightly rounded. The mouth is quite small and the eyes set up towards the top of the head. The dorsal fin is equally long along its front edge as it is at its base. The rear edge is notched in the middle. The caudal fin is deeply forked, with the rear edges of each lobe rounded.

Although small compared with the giant barb, the Isok barb is a large fish by most other standards. Old individuals can reach weights of 70kg/154lb – almost as much as a fully grown man. Sadly, as with the giant barb, monsters like this are now exceedingly rare; the Isok barb is heavily fished for its flesh and is now listed as Endangered by the IUCN. This species feeds on aquatic plants, insect larvae and freshwater shellfish. It is most abundant in the deeper waters of river channels, particularly where there are large populations of freshwater molluscs. Shoals travel upstream to breed in winter and spring, and it is during this period that they are most often caught, using gill nets spread across river channels.

Distribution: Thailand, Laos, Vietnam, Cambodia and peninsular Malaysia.
Habitat: Found in the deeper, larger rivers with sand and gravel substrates.
Food: Aquatic plants, insect larvae and freshwater shellfish.
Size: Up to 1.5m/5ft.
Breeding: Spawning occurs from October until April. The eggs are scattered into open water and are then left to develop unguarded.
Status: Endangered.

Himalayan mahseer

Tor putitora

Distribution: Native to Afghanistan, Pakistan, India, Nepal, the Himalayas of China and Bhutan. Introduced into Bangladesh.
Habitat: Mountain rivers.
Food: Algae, plant matter, invertebrates and fish.
Size: Up to 2.75m/9ft.
Breeding: Spawning occurs from April until October. Orange, sticky eggs are shed into open water over rocks and gravel and are left to develop unguarded.

This large, long-bodied fish lives in the fast-flowing streams and rivers of the Himalaya Mountains and their foothills. It is a powerful swimmer, as it needs to be in this environment, and is highly sought after as a sports fish by serious anglers. When hooked, the Himalayan mahseer tends to swim rapidly downstream, combining its own strength with the power of the moving water. This makes it a very difficult fish to land. It is an omnivore, feeding on everything from algae and plant matter to insect larvae and fish. As with many fish, it swims upstream to breed. Spawning occurs when the water-levels of the rivers in which it lives are relatively low, in advance of the coming monsoon.

Identification: The body is long and muscular, and covered with large, well defined scales. The head, which is also long, is scaleless. The mouth is relatively large but the eyes are small and positioned near the top of the skull. The small, triangular dorsal fin is almost exactly halfway along the body. In colour it ranges from silvery white to dull gold.

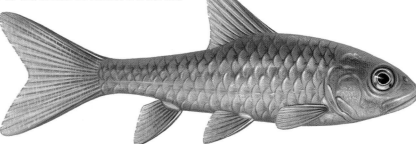

Thai mahseer (*Tor tambroides*): Up to 1m/3¼ft
This fish, from Indochina, the Malay Peninsula, Sumatra, Java and Borneo, is smaller than the Himalayan and humpback mahseers, but is still quite sizeable. It is also omnivorous, feeding on plant matter as well as invertebrates and small fish. It inhabits rivers and large streams with rocky beds in undisturbed forests, preferring clear water.

Humpback mahseer (*Tor mussullah*): Up to 1.5m/5ft
This large omnivore (*above*) lives in the deeper parts of forest rivers and streams in hilly areas of India. Like the Himalayan mahseer it is a popular game fish, renowned for the strong fight it puts up once hooked. The humpback mahseer is little studied but is known to produce large numbers of eggs, which it scatters into open water. Large individuals weigh up to 90kg/200lb.

River carp (*Tor douronensis*): Up to 35cm/13¾in
Despite its name, this fish belongs to the same genus as the mahseers. Like them it has a long body, a shark-like triangular dorsal fin and large, well-defined scales. It is told apart from them by size and by its caudal fin (the upper lobe is much longer than the lower). It is native to southern China, Indochina and parts of Indonesia.

Rohu

Labeo rohita

Compared with other Indian subcontinent carp species, the rohu is a common fish. It is also known as the rawas, rui and rou. It is widely farmed, so wild populations remain relatively unexploited. It is the most important freshwater food fish in India and an essential ingredient in several regional dishes. It has been introduced into other parts of India, including the Andaman Islands, as well as many other countries with large Indian communities, and several without, including Madagascar, Mauritius, Sri Lanka and Zimbabwe. It is a herbivore, usually found singly rather than in shoals.

Distribution: Native to India, Pakistan, Bangladesh and Nepal. Introduced to several other Asian countries, such as Thailand, Laos, Vietnam.
Habitat: Rivers.
Food: Algae and plant matter.
Size: Up to 2m/6½ft.
Breeding: Gathers in large numbers to breed. Spawning occurs April to September, before the monsoon. Eggs are scattered in open water and develop unguarded.

Identification: The body is roughly teardrop-shaped, although the head is pointed. Due to the depth of the body the head looks rather small. The mouth is right at the end of the snout and the eyes are very small. The dorsal fin is triangular but almost twice as long at the base as along its leading edge. The base of the tail is thick and fleshy and the caudal fin deeply forked.

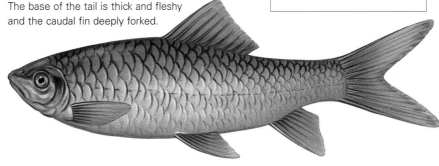

GOLDFISH, CARP, RASBORAS AND MINNOWS

All of the fish on these pages are cyprinids. Some, such as the goldfish, are more familiar to most of us than the majority of our own native fish. Others, such as the silver carp and false rasbora, are perhaps less well known, despite the fact that they have been introduced all over the world.

Goldfish

Carassius auratus

Identification: The mouth is rather small, opening forwards rather than downwards. The head is rounded in shape. The dorsal fin and anal fins each have a saw-edged spine at the leading edge. The caudal fin is large and forked, with the tips of the lobes rounded. The head is scaleless but the body is covered with clearly defined scales. The eyes are fairly large.

The goldfish must be the world's best-known freshwater fish. Its small size, attractive appearance and hardiness have helped it become the most commonly kept ornamental fish. It can survive outdoors through the winter in temperate countries, even if the ponds in which it is kept become covered with ice. As an indoor fish it requires very little maintenance and can survive in the relatively small area of water provided by the traditional goldfish bowl. In the wild the goldfish inhabits rivers, streams, lakes and ponds. Its natural colour is olive brown rather than the orange-gold most of us are familiar with. This colour, along with many other more unusual traits, such as bobble eyes and long, ornate fins, has been selectively bred into ornamental stock.

Distribution: Native to China, Japan, Myanmar (Burma) and Laos. It has been introduced in many more countries worldwide.
Habitat: Lakes, ponds and slow-flowing rivers and streams.
Food: Algae, plant matter and invertebrates.
Size: Up to 59cm/23¼in, but usually smaller.
Breeding: Spawning occurs in spring amongst water weeds. The eggs are left to develop unguarded.

Grass carp

Ctenopharyngodon idella

Identification: The body is broad and oblong in shape and longer than in most types of carp. It ranges from silvery to olive in colour. The head is scaleless but there are moderately large, well defined scales all over the rest of the body. The mouth is quite small, reaching only half the distance from the end of the snout to the eye. The dorsal fin, which is roughly rectangular, is short and pointed, with eight fin rays. The caudal peduncle is short and deep.

As its name might suggest, this fish is a herbivore. It is also known as the white amur, a reference to the Amur River system of China and Siberia, where it lives in the wild. The grass carp has long been farmed in China as a food fish and in the 1960s was introduced into the USA to control the growth of water weeds. Today it is widely farmed outside China as well as within it and has found its way into the natural waterways of numerous countries, from Uruguay to the Ukraine and Sudan to Sweden. In most of the places where it has escaped it is considered a pest, often virtually destroying water plant communities. It is a very hardy species, capable of tolerating very low dissolved oxygen levels and temperatures of 0–38°C/32–100°F.

Distribution: Native to the Amur River basin of Siberia and China. It has been widely introduced elsewhere.
Habitat: Rivers.
Food: Large quantities of plant matter and, occasionally, aquatic invertebrates.
Size: Up to 1.5m/5ft.
Breeding: Spawning occurs throughout spring and summer. The eggs are shed into open water near the bottom and are left to develop unguarded.

Silver carp (*Hypophthalmichthys molitrix*):
Up to 105cm/41¼in
This large shoaling fish feeds on planktonic algae and invertebrates, filtering its food from the water with its gill rakers. Originally from China and eastern Siberia, it has been introduced elsewhere, including the USA, to help control algal blooms, particularly in reservoirs. It is also widely farmed as a food fish. If disturbed or frightened, it instinctively leaps from the water.

Scissortail (*Rasbora trilineata*):
Up to 13cm/5in
One look at this fish (*above*) and the reason for its name is clear. Its deeply forked caudal fin has two long lobes which are pointed like a pair of scissor blades. It comes from Indochina, the Malay Peninsula, Sumatra and Borneo and can be found in a wide range of slow-moving and still freshwater habitats. It feeds mainly on insects which land on or crash into the surface.

False rasbora (*Pseudorasbora parva*):
Up to 11cm/4¼in
This little fish is also known as the topmouth gudgeon and the stone moroko. It is native to Japan, Taiwan, Korea and the Amur River basin in China and eastern Siberia, and introduced in other Asian and European countries. Quick to breed, it is now often considered a pest. It feeds on aquatic invertebrates, fish fry and fish eggs.

Harlequin fish

Trigonostigma heteromorpha

This popular little aquarium fish is also called the harlequin rasbora or, simply, the rasbora. Although often sold individually, it is best kept in groups of five or more, being a shoaling fish. In the wild it inhabits streams and peat swamps in and around tropical rain forests. It feeds on worms, insect larvae and other invertebrates. Other rasboras shed their eggs into open water; the female harlequin fish attaches her eggs to the undersides of waterplant leaves. Once she has found a suitable leaf she swims upside down beneath it and rubs her belly against it, laying her eggs while the male simultaneously fertilizes them. Formerly known as *Rasbora heteromorpha*, this fish was reclassified and given its own genus, Trigonostigma, in 1999.

Identification: The body is lozenge-shaped, being slightly elongated towards the tail. The mouth is small but the eyes are large, dominating the head. The dorsal fin, which is clear, is roughly triangular but has a concave rear edge. The head and front part of the body are gold, the rest is silver. There is a large black wedge-shaped mark on the rear half of each flank.

Distribution: Native to Thailand, Malaysia, Singapore and Indonesia.
Habitat: Rainforest swamps and streams.
Food: Aquatic invertebrates.
Size: Up to 5cm/2in.
Breeding: Spawning occurs all year round. The eggs are attached to the leaves of water plants and left to develop unguarded.

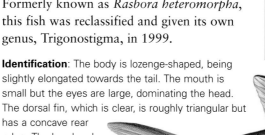

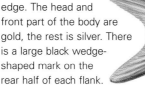

White cloud mountain minnow

Tanichthys albonubes

Distribution: Known from the far south of China and northern Vietnam.
Habitat: Streams.
Food: Invertebrates and organic detritus.
Size: Up to 4cm/1½in.
Breeding: Spawning has not been studied in the wild but this species breeds easily in captivity. The eggs are scattered and are left to develop unguarded.

Today this little fish can be found in pet shops all over the world. A hundred years ago, however, it was not even known to science. The white cloud mountain minnow was discovered in 1930 by a Boy Scout leader called Tan (hence *Tanichthys* – 'Tan's fish'). He found it living in a stream on White Cloud Mountain (*albonubes* means 'white cloud') in the Chinese province of Guangdong. It is now known to occur in many other places in southern China and in the north of Vietnam. The white cloud mountain minnow is often considered a good fish for newcomers to the home aquarium hobby, being very hardy compared to most subtropical and tropical fish. It can cope with water temperatures as low as 5°C/41°F. It feeds on detritus and tiny planktonic invertebrates.

Identification: The eyes are very large, dominating the head. The body is relatively elongated and covered with small, barely visible scales. The most striking aspect of this fish's appearance is its coloration. A thin dark line, stretching from just behind the eye to the base of the tail, neatly divides the flanks. Below it the body is orange, while above it is silver and gold.

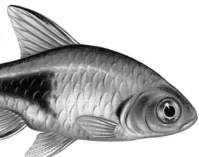

LOACHES

Loaches are bottom-living fish that tend to be solitary, although a few species form shoals. Loaches are members of the carp family, Cyprinidae, but in many ways they resemble catfish. Like those fish they search for their food on the bottom and several species also have sensitive barbels to help them locate their small prey.

Oriental weatherfish

Misgurnus anguillicaudatus

This creature is quite large by the standards of most loaches. It is farmed for its flesh both within and outside its natural range. A tough survivor, it has become established in many countries where it has been deliberately or accidentally introduced, and it is now considered a pest in some places. In Queensland, Australia, its import has been banned completely, even as an aquarium fish, with high fines for those who break the law. This fish occurs naturally in lakes, ponds and rivers in north-eastern Asia, including much of China. It prefers places with silty bottoms, burying itself in the mud by day with only its head sticking out. Its name refers to its habit of becoming more active with the onset of storms.

Identification: The body is long and cylindrical. The small dorsal fin lies slightly more than halfway along the back and the caudal fin has a rounded rear edge. The small mouth is narrow and surrounded by two to three pairs of delicate barbels. The body varies in colour from olive to sandy brown, and it is covered with numerous irregular dark blotches.

Distribution: A wide natural range, occurring from India, through China to Russia, Korea and Japan. It is also native to the countries of Indochina.
Habitat: Lakes, ponds and slow-moving rivers.
Food: Aquatic invertebrates.
Size: Up to 25cm/10in.
Breeding: Spawning occurs from April until June. The eggs are scattered over the bottom and left to develop unguarded.

Clown loach

Chromobotia macracanthus

Identification: The body is almost triangular in cross section, the belly being flattened and the flanks curving up towards the top of the back. The caudal fin is deeply forked and the dorsal fin is rounded but shark-like. There are three pairs of small barbels around the mouth and a sharp, erectile spine beneath each eye which is raised in defence if threatened. The pectoral fins are red and the body gold with three thick black bars.

This fish is a popular home aquarium fish, perhaps more popular than it should be given its full-grown size. It is usually sold in its juvenile stages, but over time grows into quite a large fish. More stocky and less sinuous than most loaches, the clown loach is the sole member of its genus. In many ways it looks like an intermediate stage between the typical loaches and most other cyprinid fish. The clown loach is a truly tropical species, hailing from the islands of Sumatra and Borneo. In the wild it inhabits rivers running through tropical rain forest, where it feeds at the bottom on plant matter and invertebrates. Although not completely inactive by day, the clown loach is primarily a nocturnal fish, becoming more animated as light levels drop. Unusually for a loach, it lives in small shoals.

Distribution: Found only on the islands of Sumatra and Borneo.
Habitat: Rivers and streams.
Food: Plant matter and aquatic invertebrates.
Size: Up to 41cm/16in.
Breeding: Breeding occurs with the onset of the heaviest seasonal rains. The eggs are concealed but left to develop unguarded.

Chain loach

Botia sidthimunki

Distribution: Restricted to Thailand, Laos and Cambodia. In Thailand the chain loach is a protected species.
Habitat: Rivers, streams, lakes and paddy fields.
Food: Plant matter and aquatic invertebrates.
Size: Up to 5.5cm/2¼in.
Breeding: Captive breeding is achieved using hormones (details are a closely guarded trade secret). Spawning has not yet been observed in the wild.
Status: Critically Endangered.

This beautiful little fish is also known as the dwarf loach, the dwarf botia and the chipmunk botia. It is the smallest member of its genus. In the wild it inhabits a variety of freshwater habitats, ranging from large rivers to paddy fields. However, it is now extremely rare, having been over-collected to supply the home aquarium trade. As a wild fish, it is listed as Critically Endangered by the IUCN. Most chain loaches now sold in pet shops are bred in captivity. This is a shoaling fish that naturally gathers in quite large numbers. Although these fish feed on the bottom they often travel a little way above it, descending when they spot a good area to search for a meal.

Identification: The body is relatively elongated and the caudal fin is forked. The forehead slopes towards the snout, which is slightly pointed. There are three pairs of very small barbels. The coloration of this fish is split along its lateral line. Above this line it is black with blotches of white or silver (the 'chain'), while below it is white with pale bars of grey-black.

Yoyo loach (*Botia almorhae*):
Up to 15cm/6in
This fish inhabits rocky streams in the Himalayas of India and Nepal. It is named for the alternate pattern of y- and o-shaped markings along the flanks of juveniles. It is also known as the tiger loach or jabo and can be identified by the pattern of black lines running down the body. In the wild it may be found both alone and in small shoals.

Coolie loach (*Pangio kuhlii*):
Up to 12cm/4¾in
This loach (*above*) is native to Thailand, Malaysia and Indonesia. It lives in hill streams and lowland rivers flowing through rain forest. It feeds on aquatic invertebrates, finding them by grubbing around beneath stones and in leaf litter, using its barbels to sense their movements. Like the clown loach, it has spines beneath each eye, which it uses for defence. These have earned it another common name – prickly eye. It is also known, for obvious reasons, as the leopard eel.

Zebra loach (*Botia striata*):
Up to 8cm/3¼in
This little fish inhabits the clear streams of the Western Ghats, a hilly region of southern India. Like the yoyo loach, it is sometimes exported as an aquarium fish. It is a shoaling fish usually found over sand. It feeds on worms and other aquatic invertebrates, which it finds with the help of its delicate, sensitive barbels. It has numerous vertical black stripes down its body.

Chinese hillstream loach

Pseudogastromyzon cheni

This loach inhabits fast-flowing streams in upland areas of China. It feeds on algae, which it grazes from pebbles and boulders, clinging on with its concave belly, which it lifts upwards to create a kind of suction pad. Common in the wild, this species is often exported for sale to the home aquarium trade. Providing it is kept under the right conditions, with a steady flow of clean water running from one end of its tank to the other, the Chinese hillstream loach adapts well to life in captivity. Breeding has often been observed, with the male digging a nest hole in the substrate and then attracting the female by swimming around her and fluttering his fins.

Distribution: Found only in China.
Habitat: Streams and small rivers.
Food: Algae.
Size: Up to 6cm/2¼in.
Breeding: The male digs a nest in which the pair spawn. The eggs are covered up and left to develop unguarded.

Identification: Seen from above, the front of the head is rounded, with the body tapering back from the pectoral fins towards the tail. The belly is flattened and pale in colour, and the mouth is situated on the underside of the head. Males have prominent nasal tubercles. The base colour of the back and flanks is pale green. This is mottled with darker green, providing camouflage against algae-covered rocks.

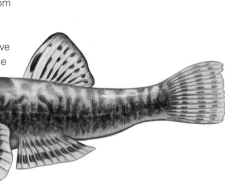

AQUATIC AMPHIBIANS AND SOFTSHELL TURTLES

Asia's fish have no shortage of enemies. All of the creatures on these pages count them as prey. The two giant salamanders are unique to Asia. Softshell turtles are more cosmopolitan. Rarely emerging from the water, they are the most aquatic of all freshwater reptiles.

Japanese giant salamander

Andrias japonicus

This strange-looking creature is the world's second largest living amphibian, after the Chinese giant salamander. Although it lacks gills as an adult, it is entirely aquatic, absorbing the oxygen it requires through its skin. The Japanese giant salamander lives in fast-flowing hill and mountain rivers and streams. It is nocturnal, spending the day hidden in an underwater cavern or amongst large rocks and only emerging at night to find food. This huge amphibian is predatory, feeding on everything from snails and invertebrates to fish. Its eyes are tiny and it locates its prey using smell and touch, lunging suddenly with a sideways swipe of its head to grab fish before they have time to react and escape.

Identification: This creature looks quite unlike any other wild animal in Japan. The skin is heavily wrinkled, to increase the surface area for oxygen uptake, and is mottled grey, black and cream in colour. The body is long and the tail is broad. The relatively short, stubby legs have round-ended, tactile toes. The eyes are tiny and positioned on the top of the head. The mouth is large and the nostrils are clearly visible, being lighter in colour than the rest of the head.

Distribution: Restricted to the cold, swift rivers of Kyushu Island and western Honshu in Japan.
Habitat: Rivers and streams.
Food: Aquatic invertebrates, other amphibians and fish.
Size: Up to 1.5m/5ft.
Breeding: The female lays a string of 400–500 eggs in August. Males fight to gain access to these eggs and to fertilize them. They then guard the eggs until they hatch.

Asiatic softshell turtle

Amyda cartilaginea

Identification: The snout is long and tubular and the feet are strongly webbed. The carapace ranges in colour from brown or grey to black. It differs from that of similar species by the fact that it has small knobbly lumps (tubercles) along its front edge, just behind the head. Younger individuals have yellow speckles on the head and limbs. These fade as they grow.

This large softshell turtle is mainly nocturnal. By day it spends much of its time buried in the mud or sand at the bottoms of ponds, lakes and streams, rising occasionally to the surface to take a gulp of air. It feeds on a wide variety of plant and animal matter, eating everything from fish and amphibians to fallen fruit. It is the most common softshell turtle found across most of its range but is nevertheless far from being a common animal. Caught for food and used as an ingredient in several types of Chinese medicine, the Asiatic softshell turtle is now listed as Vulnerable by the IUCN.

Distribution: Found in Vietnam, Laos, Thailand, Myanmar (Burma), Cambodia, Malaysia and Indonesia.
Habitat: Lakes, ponds, rivers.
Food: Fish, amphibians, aquatic invertebrates and plant matter.
Size: Carapace up to 83cm/32½in long.
Breeding: Nests in mud banks. The female lays 6–30 eggs in a clutch, 3–4 times a year. These take 135–40 days to incubate before hatching.
Status: Vulnerable.

Indian narrow-headed softshell turtle

Chitra indica

Distribution: Native to Pakistan, India, Nepal and Bangladesh.
Habitat: Rivers.
Food: Fish, aquatic invertebrates and plant matter.
Size: Carapace up to 1.15m/3.8ft long.
Breeding: A flask-shaped nest is dug in sand at the river's edge and 100 or more eggs are laid.

As its name suggests, this species has a soft shell, with the carapace almost merging into the skin of the neck, and lives on the Indian subcontinent. It inhabits the clear, sandy sections of large rivers, notably the Coleroon, Ganges, Godavari, Indus, Mahanadi and Padma Rivers. The Indian narrow-headed softshell turtle is highly aquatic and only leaves the water to lay its eggs – in late August or early September each year. Although omnivorous, this turtle gets most of its food by hunting. It catches fish by ambush, lying buried in the sand at the bottom then snapping them up with a sudden lunge of its head as they swim past. Fish that are too big to swallow whole are torn apart with the jaws and clawed forefeet.

Identification: The carapace is leathery and grey – the same colour as the rest of the turtle's skin. Juveniles are tan coloured and have lighter markings that resemble splashes and swirls. These fade with age. The head is unusually narrow and rather small for such a large animal. The oversized paddle-shaped feet, however, are large, making this turtle a powerful swimmer.

Chinese giant salamander (*Andrias davidianus*): Up to 1.8m/6ft long
This is the world's largest salamander – weighing up to 65kg/143lb. It is completely aquatic, absorbing oxygen through its wrinkled, porous skin. It lives at high altitudes, in the mountain tributaries of the Pearl, Yangtze and Yellow Rivers. Hundreds of individuals gather in late August to breed at traditional sites. Males compete fiercely for access to females, with some dying from battle injuries.

Burmese peacock softshell turtle (*Nilssonia formosa*): Carapace up to 65cm/26in long
This handsome turtle (*above right*) is found wild only in the Irrawaddy, Sittang and Salween Rivers of Myanmar (Burma). It is also sometimes seen in pools in Buddhist temples, where it is well fed and treated with great respect, being thought lucky. It is one of the more common softshell turtles in Asia and, unlike larger species, is rarely caught for food.

Malayan softshell turtle (*Dogania subplana*): Carapace up to 26cm/10in long
This small turtle occurs from Myanmar (Burma) through Thailand to the Malay Peninsula and on the islands of Sumatra, Java and Borneo. Most common in swift upland streams with rocky bottoms, it is also found in slow forest streams over mud. It has been little studied but it is thought to eat fish and aquatic invertebrates.

Cantor's giant softshell turtle

Pelochelys cantorii

This is an enormous freshwater turtle, growing to lengths of more than 2m/6½ft, including its neck and head. Cantor's giant softshell turtle is an omnivore but, like the Indian narrow-headed softshell (*top*), gets most of its nourishment from fish and other animal prey which it catches by ambush, lying buried within the sand. Cantor's giant softshell is highly aquatic and able to absorb oxygen from the water through its pharynx. As a result of this adaptation it can stay submerged for hours at a time, sometimes only rising to the surface twice a day to breathe. As with other Asian softshell turtles, it is often caught for food and has become rare in recent decades. The IUCN lists it as Endangered.

Distribution: India through southern China and Indochina to Malaysia, Indonesia, New Guinea and the Philippines.
Habitat: Streams, rivers, estuaries; may go out to sea.
Food: Fish, amphibians, aquatic invertebrates, plants.
Size: Carapace to 2m/6½ft long.
Breeding: Females lay small clutches (about 28 eggs) in sandy river banks in February and March.
Status: Endangered.

Identification: The carapace is smooth, lacking patterns and tubercles. It ranges from a uniform olive green to brown in colour. The paddle-shaped limbs and neck are a similar colour. Juveniles have a yellow rim around the carapace and dark spots on the head, but these fade with age. The base of the neck is quite broad, making the head look smaller than it really is.

OTHER TURTLES

In many ways, turtles are the reptile equivalents of fish. Rather than fins they have webbed feet or, occasionally, paddles. Unlike most fish, however, turtles must breathe air. The species shown on these pages include some of the most common turtles from Asia and Australia. All have hard, horn covered carapaces, apart from the pig-nose turtle, which is related to the softshell turtles.

Giant Asian pond turtle

Heosemys grandis

This is one of the largest hard-shelled freshwater turtles in Asia. Although much shorter than the biggest softshell turtles it is more bulky and can weigh up to 12kg/26½lb. It is semi-aquatic and is often found in and around Buddhist temples, where it is fed and cared for almost like a pet. In the wild it inhabits rivers, streams, lakes and swamps as well as ponds, often emerging from the water to bask on land. This turtle is omnivorous but, not being particularly agile, tends to feed mainly on plant matter. It is often found amongst the leaves of water lilies and other floating aquatic plants. Its breeding system has evolved to coincide with the driest times of the year. Eggs are laid just as the rainy season ends then hatch just before the next one begins.

Identification: The face has orange spots, hence this species' other common name, the orange-headed temple turtle. The skin of the forelimbs is scaly and there is webbing between the toes. The carapace is arched and has a single, well defined keel running along the middle, from the head to the tail. The skin of the head, neck and limbs is darker than that on the rest of the body.

Distribution: Ranges throughout Indochina, from Myanmar (Burma) to Vietnam and southward to the Malay Peninsula.
Habitat: Ponds, lakes, swamps, rivers and streams.
Food: Plant matter, fish and aquatic invertebrates.
Size: Carapace up to 43.5cm/17in long.
Breeding: Females emerge to lay as the rainy season ends, late November to early December. A clutch consists of 2–6 oval eggs.

Spiny turtle

Heosemys spinosa

Identification: The carapace is broad and oval in shape, with numerous sharp, tooth-like projections around its edge. The slightly dark brown coloration of the caparace is interrupted by a well defined lighter ridge running along the centre from the neck to the tail. The forelimbs have large, overlapping scales. The scales on the club-like hind limbs are spiny. The toes are only partially webbed.

This striking reptile is also known as the cogwheel turtle, a reference to the serrated edge of its carapace. The young are particularly spiky, having spines along the ridge of their carapace as well as at the edges. The spiny turtle lives in clear, shallow mountain streams in forested areas. Although the adults spend the majority of their time in the water they are also sometimes found on land, wandering through the undergrowth. Juveniles are even more terrestrial and spend more time out of the water than in it. This turtle is almost entirely herbivorous, feeding on fallen fruit, leaves and other vegetable matter. Although it is fairly widespread it has declined in numbers as a result of collecting for the pet trade and is now listed as Endangered by the IUCN.

Distribution: Native to Myanmar (Burma), Thailand, peninsular Malaysia, Sumatra, Borneo and many smaller Indonesian islands.
Habitat: Forest streams.
Food: Fallen fruit and leaves.
Size: Carapace up to 23cm/9in long.
Breeding: Eggs are laid three times a year. A clutch contains only 1–2 eggs. Eggs are large, white and oblong.
Status: Endangered.

Asian yellow pond turtle (*Mauremys mutica*): Carapace up to 19cm/7½in
This little turtle is found in ponds, marshes, swamps and slow-flowing streams in China, Vietnam and Japan. The yellow in its name refers to a broad line on its head and neck which stretches from just behind the eye up over the ear. The carapace is dark brown or black. This turtle is also known as the moss-backed or green haired turtle. Many wild specimens have thick mats of algae growing on their shells.

Pig-nose turtle (*Carettochelys insculpta*): Carapace up to 56cm/22in
This species (*above*) is one of the most completely aquatic of all freshwater turtles and is unusual among them in having paddle-like forelimbs. It is found in Australia's Northern Territory and the southern rivers and lakes of New Guinea. It feeds mostly on plants, but also eats a range of animal matter, including carrion.

Asian leaf turtle (*Cyclemys dentata*): Carapace up to 26cm/10¼in
This small, hard-shelled turtle is very widely distributed, ranging from India through Indochina and most of Indonesia east to the Philippines. It lives in shallow streams and feeds on invertebrates, small fish and plant matter. Gentle and lively for a turtle, it is a popular pet.

Common snake-necked turtle

Chelodina longicollis

This strange-looking creature comes from south-eastern Australia, where it lives in swamps, lakes, slow-moving rivers and billabongs (stagnant pools). It is commonly kept both in its home country and elsewhere as a pet. New owners may be concerned by its smell – it emits a repellent musk when agitated. This behaviour soon stops, however, as the turtle settles in. The common snake-necked turtle is carnivorous, feeding on small fish, tadpoles, frogs and large invertebrates in the wild. It catches its prey with a sudden sideways sweep of its neck, grabbing it firmly in its sharp jaws. Although mainly aquatic, this turtle is sometimes found wandering over land on overcast days, particularly in the summer when some of the pools it inhabits dry up.

Distribution: Endemic to Australia, occurring in the states of Queensland, New South Wales, Victoria and South Australia.
Habitat: Swamps, lakes, pools and rivers.
Food: Fish, amphibians and invertebrates.
Size: Carapace up to 26cm/10¼in long.
Breeding: The females emerge to lay their eggs in sand during summer. Up to 10 eggs are laid in a clutch.

Identification: The most obvious distinguishing feature of this species is the long, snake-like neck, which is around half as long as the carapace. When the turtle is alarmed this is folded against the shell, with the head tucked against one of the legs. The neck is covered with pointed tubercles. The musk glands are located around the groin and in the 'armpits' where the front legs join the rest of the body.

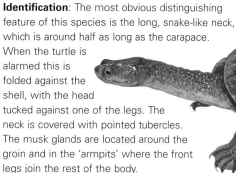

Northern Australian snapping turtle

Elseya dentata

Distribution: Throughout northern Australia, from the Kimberley district of Western Australia to Queensland's Burnett River.
Habitat: Rivers, billabongs and lagoons.
Food: Fallen fruit, leaves and algae.
Size: Carapace up to 45cm/17¾in long.
Breeding: A single clutch of 3–5 elongated, brittle-shelled eggs is laid annually at the end of the wet season.

Despite its common name, this turtle is not related to the snapping turtles of North America. It is largely herbivorous, living on a diet of fallen fruit, leaves and algae. The Northern Australian snapping turtle inhabits large rivers and the lagoons and billabongs. It spends most of its time in the water but emerges every morning to bask on a half submerged branch or similar platform. Once it has warmed its body up sufficiently to become active it re-enters the water to feed. This is a slow-growing species that is late to mature. Being heavily dependent on overhanging trees for food it is highly vulnerable to development and disturbance, disappearing from wherever river banks are cleared.

Identification: The carapace is oval and flattened, broadest towards the back. The head is large and the nostrils prominent, sticking out a little on a rounded, button-like nose. The jaws are powerful and the upper jaw is often slightly notched. There are two small barbels on the chin. The top of the head is capped with a smooth horny shield, rather than skin.

CROCODILES AND CHINESE ALLIGATOR

Crocodiles and alligators are major predators of fish. These formidable reptiles are native to most tropical parts of Asia and Australia, although in many places they are now much rarer than they once were. Crocodiles and alligators differ subtly in their anatomy. Alligators have more rounded snouts and, unlike crocodiles, all the teeth of their lower jaws are hidden when their mouths are closed.

Estuarine crocodile

Crocodylus porosus

This creature, also known as the saltwater crocodile or 'saltie', is the biggest reptile in the world. Large males can reach lengths of 7m/23ft and weigh more than 1 metric ton/ 1.1 US short tons. The estuarine crocodile is a formidable predator thought to be responsible for the deaths of up to 2,000 people every year. Although humans are not its natural prey, it will attack anything that enters or comes close to the edge of the water. Like other crocodiles it also feeds on other aquatic animals such as fish. As its name suggests, this crocodile can tolerate brackish and salt water, and is sometimes spotted far out at sea. It also lives in swamps, rivers and other freshwater habitats. It is in these places that it most often comes into contact with humans.

Identification: A pair of ridges run from the back of the head over the eyes and along the centre of the snout. The scales on the flanks are more oval in shape than those of other crocodiles. The scales on the belly are rectangular and relatively small. The head is massive and the jaws lined with fearsome, cone-shaped teeth. The snout is broader than that of other crocodiles that share its range, apart from the mugger.

Distribution: Occurs around the coastal regions of the Indian Ocean, from Sri Lanka to northern Australia.
Habitat: Swamps, rivers, estuaries and the sea.
Food: Fish and other large vertebrates.
Size: Up to 7m/23ft.
Breeding: Females lay 40–60 eggs in nest mounds built from vegetation. Once the eggs hatch the female digs the young out and carries them to the water.

Mugger

Crocodylus palustris

Identification: The snout is unusually broad, almost more like that of an alligator. There are very large, armoured scales on the throat that may serve as protection. Adults range from plain grey to brown in colour. Juveniles are light tan with black bands on the body and tail. Despite its intimidating name (a corruption of the Hindi word *magar* – 'water monster') this species almost never attacks humans.

The mugger is India's most common crocodile. It is also found in several adjoining countries, including Sri Lanka. It lives in still and slow-moving freshwater habitats and is also occasionally found in saltwater lagoons. It prefers areas of relatively shallow water and has adapted to live in irrigation canals, reservoirs and other man-made bodies of fresh water. Like most crocodiles, it hunts both within and from the water, bursting up on the shore to grab unwary creatures that have come down to the edge for a drink. Once it has pulled its prey in it drowns it by rolling over and over. It then rips chunks of flesh from it with a violent sideways movement of the head. In the morning, the mugger emerges from the water to bask. It has been known to dig burrows for shelter.

Distribution: Eastern Iran, Pakistan, India, Nepal, Bangladesh and Sri Lanka.
Habitat: Rivers, lakes, swamps, reservoirs and lagoons.
Food: Fish and other vertebrates.
Size: Up to 5m/16½ft.
Breeding: The female digs a nest hole in the dry season (from December to February), usually on a sloping bank. Between 10 and 48 eggs are laid, and these hatch after 55–75 days.

Australian freshwater crocodile

Crocodylus johnstoni

Distribution: Restricted to the northern part of Australia, ranging from north-western Queensland to the state of Western Australia.
Habitat: Lakes, rivers, billabongs and swamps.
Food: Fish and other small vertebrates.
Size: Up to 3m/10ft.
Breeding: Nesting occurs from July until September. Between 4 and 20 eggs are laid. They take up to 95 days to incubate and hatch.

Identification: The snout is long and narrow – far more so than that of the estuarine crocodile, the only other species found in Australia. The body is relatively small and lightly built and the ridges on the skull end over the eyes. The scales on the flanks and legs are rounded and pebble-like, whereas the body scales are large with armoured plates. The general colour is light brown, with darker bands on parts of the body and tail.

Compared with the infamous 'saltie' (*opposite page*) of northern Australia, the Australian freshwater crocodile is virtually harmless. Attacks on people by this species are almost unknown. Those that have occurred usually happened after the animal was provoked. The Australian freshwater crocodile is a fish-eating specialist, its long, narrow snout having evolved to help it catch fast-moving, slippery prey. It hunts by lying still on the bottom and waiting for fish to swim into reach. As soon as they do, it snaps them up with a sudden sideways swipe of its head. Although it mostly eats fish, this species occasionally takes other small vertebrate prey, including lizards, amphibians, water birds and small mammals. This species is also known as Johnston's crocodile.

Chinese alligator

Alligator sinensis

Siamese crocodile (*Crocodylus siamensis*): Up to 4m/13ft
The Siamese crocodile (*above*) is farmed for its skin and is now listed as Critically Endangered by the IUCN. It once ranged widely over Indochina and parts of Indonesia but is now only relatively common in Cambodia. Elsewhere it is either extremely rare or extinct in the wild. A reintroduction programme is under way in Thailand using animals from captive populations.

Philippine crocodile (*Crocodylus mindorensis*): Up to 3m/10ft
As its name suggests, this crocodile is confined to the Philippines. It is also listed as Critically Endangered by the IUCN. It has a broad snout, and a heavily armoured body. It feeds mainly on large aquatic invertebrates and fish. Unlike the estuarine crocodile, which shares its range, it is found only in freshwater habitats, including lakes, ponds, rivers and marshes.

New Guinea crocodile (*Crocodylus novaeguineae*): Up to 3.5m/11½ft
Unlike those of many other Asian crocodilians, populations of this species are healthy in numbers. The island of New Guinea, where it is found, remains relatively wild and there are few pressures on its wild populations. It inhabits freshwater lakes, swamps and rivers but is rare in coastal areas, which are dominated by the estuarine crocodile. It eats fish and other aquatic vertebrates.

This is Asia's smallest crocodilian and also the rarest. The estimated wild population of this species is less than 200 and it is listed as Critically Endangered by the IUCN. It feeds on shellfish such as water snails and mussels, and has short powerful jaws especially evolved for the task. Like other crocodilians, however, it is an opportunistic predator and will also take fish and other small vertebrates when it has the chance. The Chinese alligator is threatened in the wild by habitat destruction, including the draining of marshes to create agricultural land. Although its future as a wild animal is doubtful, there are several populations in captive breeding programmes around the world which are thriving.

Identification: The snout is short, broad and slightly upturned. There are bony plates on each upper eyelid. Juvenile Chinese alligators are black with bands of bright yellow running across their bodies and tails. Adults lack this banding and are dark all over. The teeth are relatively blunt, being adapted for crushing rather than puncturing prey.

Distribution: Restricted to the lower Yangtze River basin in China.
Habitat: Lakes, ponds, swamps and slow-moving rivers and streams.
Food: Shellfish, fish and other small vertebrates.
Size: Up to 2m/6½ft.
Breeding: The female builds a nest mound from plant matter during July or August and lays 10–50 eggs.
Status: Critically Endangered.

GHARIALS, DOLPHINS AND PORPOISES

All of these creatures are air breathers that survive on a diet of fish. The gharial and false gharial are reptiles that spend most of their time in the water but emerge to bask and lay their eggs on land. Dolphins and porpoises are mammals, and entirely aquatic. They give birth to their young in the water and feed them on milk until they are big enough to catch fish for themselves.

Gharial

Gavialis gangeticus

This bizarre-looking creature is a highly efficient and effective predator of fish. Its long, narrow snout and needle-like teeth are especially adapted to grab its fast-moving, slippery prey. The gharial lives in the northern part of the Indian subcontinent, inhabiting the Indus, Ganges, Mahanadi, Brahmaputra, Kaladan and Irrawaddy Rivers. Once abundant, it is now very rare due to hunting and over-fishing in the rivers it inhabits, and it is now listed as Critically Endangered by the IUCN. The gharial is a highly aquatic creature, only leaving the water to bask and nest. Both of these activities usually take place on sand banks within the main channel of the river or along the shore.

Identification: With its long, narrow snout, this crocodilian is unmistakable. The only creature that looks anything like it is the false gharial, but that species has a different range. Mature male gharials have a bulbous lump on the tip end of the snout, which may be used as a vocal resonator, a stimulus for female attraction or for courtship. The body and tail are long and sturdy. Typically crocodilian, they are covered with tough leathery scales.

Distribution: Pakistan, India, Bhutan, Bangladesh and Myanmar (Burma).
Habitat: Rivers.
Food: Fish.
Size: Up to 6m/20ft.
Breeding: Nesting occurs from March until May. Between 30 and 50 eggs are laid, hatching 87–94 days later.
Status: Critically Endangered.

Irrawaddy dolphin

Orcaella brevirostris

Identification: The dorsal fin is small and roughly triangular, with a blunt tip. The head is rounded, the beak almost non-existent. The upper side of the body is bluish grey; the underside paler. The flippers are large and strongly curved on their leading edges. The mouth line is almost straight, leading back almost to the eye. When diving, the tail flukes are raised above the water's surface. Like many river dolphins, the flexible neck enables it to inhabit shallow waters.

This round-headed dolphin lives in some of the larger rivers of southern and South-east Asia, including the Irrawaddy, Mekong, Brahmaputra, Ganges and Mahakam (in Borneo). It is also found in estuaries, mangrove swamps and coastal waters as far south and east as Queensland, Australia. It is sometimes seen alone but is more common in small groups, ranging from 2 to 15 individuals. It feeds on fish and, like many other dolphins, often hunts cooperatively, working together to round up and contain shoals for feeding. In the Irrawaddy and Mekong Rivers it is said to help fishermen by driving fish into their nets. It is a slow swimmer for a dolphin, and breaks the surface gently. As a result it can be hard to spot and is often overlooked.

Distribution: This species occurs in rivers and coastal waters from eastern India to northern Australia.
Habitat: Larger rivers, estuaries, mangrove swamps and the sea.
Food: Fish and large invertebrates, such as squid.
Size: Up to 2.6m/8½ft.
Breeding: The breeding system of this species is not well studied. It is thought the calves are born after a gestation period of 14 months.

Finless porpoise

Neophocaena phocaenoides

Distribution: Coastal waters and rivers from the Arabian Gulf to New Guinea and Honshu Island, Japan.
Habitat: Mangrove swamps, estuaries, rivers and the sea.
Food: Fish and swimming invertebrates.
Size: Up to 1.9m/6¼ft.
Breeding: This species becomes sexually mature at between 3 and 6 years of age. Calving occurs at different times of the year in different parts of its range. Gestation takes 10–11 months.

This is one of the smallest members of the Cetacea, the order that contains the world's porpoises, dolphins and whales. It lives in small family groups but it may gather in larger numbers where there are rich sources of prey. It lives in both fresh water and the sea. It is commonly spotted in the Yangtze River, and has become accustomed to boat traffic here. Elsewhere, although not rare, it is seldom seen, being shy and tending to avoiding contact with people. Other rivers it inhabits include the Indus, Brahmaputra, Ganges and Mekong. It has recently been reported in the Mekong from Laos, a landlocked country some distance from the sea. This porpoise seems to prefer murky waters and makes very little disturbance when rising to the surface.

Identification: This species looks not unlike a smaller version of the Irrawaddy dolphin, being similar in colour and virtually lacking a beak. The finless porpoise, however, lacks a dorsal fin and instead has a low ridge along its back covered with circular, wart-like tubercles. The flippers are long and pointed, and are narrow at the base. The tail rarely breaks the surface when this species dives.

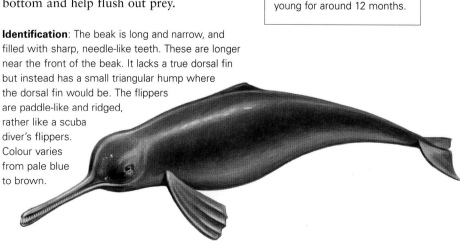

False gharial (*Tomistoma schlegelii*):
Up to 5m/16½ft
This reptile, like its larger and better known cousin the gharial, specializes in preying on fish. It lives in lakes, rivers and swamps in Malaysia and Indonesia. It was once known in Thailand but is now thought to be extinct there. It prefers areas of water with abundant vegetation. This species has suffered from hunting and habitat loss and is listed as Endangered by the IUCN.

Indo-Pacific hump-backed dolphin (*Sousa chinensis*): Up to 2.8m/9¼ft
This dolphin (above) is a marine species that inhabits coastal waters and sometimes enters rivers. It is often seen in mangrove swamps and estuaries around the Indian Ocean and far south-west Pacific. It is a schooling dolphin. The best studied population lives around the Pearl River delta, where it is known as the pink dolphin.

Indus river dolphin (*Platanista minor*):
Up to 2.5m/8¼ft
This dolphin looks almost identical to the Ganges river dolphin and was long considered to be the same species. Closer study in the 1970s, however, showed this dolphin to have important differences in the shape of its skull and it was allocated a species of its own. It is found only in the Indus River. Its lifestyle is virtually identical to that of the Ganges river dolphin.

Ganges river dolphin

Platanista gangetica

This is an entirely freshwater mammal, found only in the Ganges and Brahmaputra Rivers. Less sociable than other dolphins, it is usually seen alone or in pairs, although groups of up to ten may congregate where feeding is good. It is adapted for life in murky water. Its eyes are small and its vision poor but its ability to echolocate helps it to find fish and negotiate obstacles. Although it prefers deeper water, this species may sometimes be seen in water less than a metre deep. When travelling through the shallows it tends to swim on its side with its tail held slightly higher than its head. Sometimes, it may drag one of its flippers through the mud as it goes, to stir up the bottom and help flush out prey.

Distribution: Only found in the Ganges and Brahmaputra Rivers and their tributaries.
Habitat: Rivers.
Food: Fish.
Size: Up to 2.5m/8¼ft.
Breeding: Calves are born between October and March. The mothers nurse their young for around 12 months.

Identification: The beak is long and narrow, and filled with sharp, needle-like teeth. These are longer near the front of the beak. It lacks a true dorsal fin but instead has a small triangular hump where the dorsal fin would be. The flippers are paddle-like and ridged, rather like a scuba diver's flippers. Colour varies from pale blue to brown.

GLOSSARY

Aestivation
A slowing down of the metabolism to survive through times of drought or extreme heat. The process of aestivation is equivalent to hibernation.

Apex predator
A predator at the very top of the food chain or food pyramid, with no natural predators of its own.

Backwaters
Still or very slow moving areas of rivers and river systems: regions which are bordering on becoming marshland or swamp.

Barbels
Fleshy, whisker-like projections around the mouth of bottom-feeding fish. Like whiskers, barbels enhance the sense of touch.

Benthic
Name for a fish or other organisms which feed on the bottom of lakes, or bodies of water.

Carapace
The domed part of the shell of turtles, tortoises or crustaceans.

Convergent evolution
The evolution of similar physical features in unrelated animals, due to both occupying the same ecological niche.

Crepuscular
Active during the hours of dawn and dusk to avoid the attention of predators which hunt by day.

Cryptically coloured
Coloured in such a way as to blend in with the surrounding environment. Cryptic coloration is the most common form of camouflage amongst fish.

Desiccation
Drying out.

Diurnal
Active only during the hours of daylight. In biological terminology, diurnal is the opposite of nocturnal.

Drainage basin
The area of land drained by a particular river and its tributaries.

Drop-off
An underwater cliff or similar feature which causes a very sudden increase in a body of water's overall depth.

Echolocation
Using sound and echoes to navigate and find prey. Animals which use echolocation include dolphins.

Ecological niche
The role of an animal or other living organism in its habitat and the community of species it is part of.

Ecological niches among freshwater fish include open water predator or insect-eating bottom-feeder, for example.

Filamentous
Made up of thin, hair-like fibres.

Filter feeder
An animal which sieves its food from the water, using specialized structures, such as gill rakers.

Fry
The newly hatched offspring of a fish.

Gallery forest
Forest bordering a river and backed by open country.

Gill rakers
Projections of cartilage or bone which stick out from the gill arches and cross the gaps on either side of the back of a fish's mouth, which lead to the gills. Gill rakers prevent food escaping from the mouth through the gill slits.

Gills
Organs by which fish and other aquatic organisms breathe, by removing dissolved oxygen from water. Gills are the aquatic equivalent of lungs.

Gravid
Laden with eggs: female fish are said to be gravid in the few days before spawning.

Headwaters
The source of a river: the farthest point from its mouth.

Hibernation
A slowing down of the metabolism to survive through winter, or other periods of cold.

Ichthyologist
A scientist who specializes in the study of fish.

Inhalant siphon
A tube-like fold of the mantle of molluscs, such as mussels, along which water, oxygen and food particles can be drawn into the mantle cavity.

IUCN
The International Union for the Conservation of Nature; responsible for assigning organisms to agreed categories of rarity.

Meander
A looping curve in a river's course. Meanders are most common where rivers run over flat ground.

Milt
The sperm (sex cells) and semen (fluid which carries the sex cells) of male fish, released during the process of spawning.

Nocturnal
Active by night: nocturnal fish and other animals usually have

adaptations to help them find food in the dark. Many are more reliant on the sense of touch than they are on vision.

Oviparous
Egg-laying: most fish are oviparous, laying eggs rather than giving birth to live young.

Oxbow lake
A small lake, created from a former meander of a river but now cut off from the main channel by land.

Papillose
Nipple-like: many fish have small papillose projections on the surface of their skin.

Parr
Young salmon during the first two years of their lives, which they spend in fresh water.

Pelagic
Name given to fish that feed in open water.

Piscivorous
Fish-eating: birds, mammals and other creatures are said to be piscivorous if their diet is made up predominantly of fish.

Plankton
Tiny animals and other organisms which live in open water, drifting with the currents.

Predation
The hunting of one organism by another for food.

Rays
A set of spines which give support to a fish's fin.

Redds
Shallow nests dug during the breeding season by some fish in the bottoms of the rivers and streams they inhabit. For the purpose of receiving eggs and containing them until hatching.

Riffles
Areas of choppy water in rivers, caused by the presence of sandbars or bars of rubble just beneath the surface. Large riffles in areas of intense water flow are known as rapids.

Runs
Small, fast-flowing streams or brooks.

Sandbar
A bank of sand formed by currents in water.

School
A group of fish, or other aquatic animals, swimming together.

Scutes
Hard bony plates that form part of the skin of animals such as tortoises, and fish such as sturgeons.

Sediment
Small particles carried by water that build up on the bottom. Different types of sediments include sand and silt.

Sexual dimorphism
A difference in body shape, size or colour between the two sexes in one species. In most cases the males are more brightly coloured than the females, since it is they which have the job of attracting a mate.

Shoal
A multitude of fish swimming together.

Spawning
The release of eggs and milt into the water, during which the eggs are fertilized.

Spiracles
Holes into which water is drawn, so that it can pass over the gills of some cartilaginous fish. The spiracles of rays are positioned just beneath the eyes.

Stock
The part of a fish's body which makes up the base of its tail and to which the caudal (tail) fin is attached.

Tributary
A stream or river which flows into a larger one. The Rio Negro, for example, is a tributary of the Amazon.

Troglodytic
Cave-dwelling: troglodytic fish inhabit underground rivers, which are particularly common in limestone regions.

Viviparous
Live-bearing: a small proportion of the world's freshwater fish species are viviparous, giving birth to fully developed, live young, rather than laying eggs.

Watershed
A ridge of high land dividing two regions which are drained by different river systems.

INDEX

PICTURE ACKNOWLEDGEMENTS

t=top; m=middle; b=bottom; l=left; r=right

Photographs
6t Image Quest; 6b Image Quest; 7t Image Quest; 7b Image Quest; 8
Image quest; 9 (all images) Image Quest; 10l Image Quest; 10r (panel)
Image Quest; 11 (all images) Image Quest; 12t Image Quest; 13 (all
images); Image Quest; p15 (all images) Image Quest; 16l Image Quest;
16r Image Quest; 17t Image Quest; 17b Image Quest; 18–19 (all
images) Image Quest; 20/21 (all images) Image Quest; 22/3 (all images
(Image Quest); 22/23 (all images) Image Quest; 24/25 (all images)
Image Quest; 26t Image Quest; 27bl Image Quest; 28t (panel) NHPA;
28bl NHPA; 29t NHPA; 29b Image Quest; 30tl NHPA; 30tr Image quest;
30bl (panel) Image Quest; 30br Image Quest; 31t Image Quest; 31b
Image Quest; 32 (all images) Image Quest; 33 (all images) Image
Quest; 35t (panel) NHPA; 46–47 (all images) Image Quest.

Illustrations
Peter Bull 10b, 16b, 20t, 24b, 26b and 26t.
Anthony Duke 14–15, 50–51, 124–25, 154–55, 178–79; 214–215,
and all species maps appearing in the Directory of Freshwater Species
(pages 52–249).
Stuart Jackson-Carter 36–45.
Denys Ovenden 12b.

Jacket images: (front cover) main jacket artwork shows a brown trout
(*Salmo trutta*, see page 182); the photographs show (left to right) brook
trout (*Salvelinus fontinalis*), fog talking catfish (*Rhinodoras boehlkei*),
xingu cichlid (*Retroculus xinguensis*) and red-spotted green discus
(*Symphysodon aequifasciata*).
(Back cover) the photographs show (left to right) red piranha
(*Pygocentrus nattereri*), pig-nosed turtle (*Carettochelys insculpta*), giant
gourami (*Osphronemus goramy*) and American alligator (*Alligator
mississippiensis*).
All jacket photographs are copyright Image Quest Marine except for the
American alligator.

Frontispiece: A piraputanga (*Brycon hilarii*) swims over aquatic
vegetation in Brazil.

Endpaper: Image Quest Marine